BERGLUND CENTER for INTERNET STUDIES

INTERFACE

THE JOURNAL OF EDUCATION, COMMUNITY AND VALUES

Volume 9

Published by
BERGLUND CENTER for INTERNET STUDIES
bcis.pacificu.edu

Printed in the United States of America
Volume 9
ISBN 978-0-615-36167-3 (paperback)
Interface (Forest Grove, OR)
ISSN 1940-915X

Berglund Center for Internet Studies
Pacific University
2043 College Way, Forest Grove, OR 97116
http://bcis.pacificu.edu/

Introduction

Interface, the electronic journal of the Berglund Center for Internet Studies, Pacific University Oregon, is written and produced for the broad audience of those interested in the impact of the Internet in all its manifold forms. These include not only such obvious ones as the rapid shift into electronic banking and commerce, but also even very subtle ones as the impact of the Internet on popular film and fiction, and even on poetry, and upon the English language itself.

At *Interface*, we study all of these phenomena, and the flexibility of an electronic journal, which can be useful to all audiences, unlike the rigidly determined form of traditional journals, has let us range widely. At the Berglund Center we not only publish the results of our authors' research and thought, but also have the great pleasure of encouraging such productivity through grants and scholarships as well as our payments for articles.

This volume represents the content of our electronic journal, *Interface*, 2009. This publication includes original work from international scholars, as well as members of the Pacific University faculty. For more information on this project, please see our web pages. (http:bcis.pacificu.edu)

This year we appear in a new format: fully bound hard-copy publication done under a print-on-demand process. This is our second such work, the first, Yang Desheng's *Jigsaw III* is now available at Amazon*. We have found this approach useful and practicable, especially for limited edition publications such as this one. This work, too, will soon be available at Amazon. While our work emphasizes the impact of the Internet, we are also aware of the importance of hard copy publications for such purposes as archival durability, assessment and tenure processes, and simply because as much as we love the Internet, most of us still love a good book. We hope that you will find this such a book.

Jeffrey Barlow
Director, Berglund Center for Internet Studies
Pacific University Oregon

**Reference to Amazon throughout this publication implies the on-line company (.com). Due to Copyright restrictions we were not allowed to use the correct reference.*

Acknowledgements

Published by Staff of Pacific University Oregon's
Berglund Center for Internet Studies,
Forest Grove, Oregon, USA

Jeffrey G. Barlow, Ph.D., Editor
Theresa A. Floyd, Managing Editor
Maria Walters, Design Editor
Jamaica King, HTML Editor, *Interface*
Jackie Olson, Copy Editor
Sierra Brummett, Copy Editor
Ben Griffin, Cover Design

TABLE OF CONTENTS

July-August 2009 - Volume 9, Issue 6 197

September 2009 - Volume 9, Issue 7 227

January-February 2009 - Volume 9, Issue 1

Articles

- **Feature: Isaac Gilman** - Online Lives, Offline Consequences: Professionalism, Information Ethics and Professional Students
- **Online Community: Pat McGregor** - It's Not Just Technology That Makes Our Village Grow
- **Politics: Jenn Hernandez** - Election 2.0.1: The Obama Electronic Campaign Following Victory
- **Legal: Leonard D. DuBoff** - A Trademark Owner's Right to Control Sublicenses
- **Technology: Michael Geraci** - Fitness by the Bits

Book and Site Reviews

- **Gary Small and Gigi Vorgan's** *IBrain: Surviving the Technological Alteration of the Modern Mind*
  Review by Jeffrey Barlow
- **Hilde G. Corneliussen and Jill Walker Rettberg's** *Digital Culture, Play, and Identity: A World of Warcraft Reader*
  Review by IProfess

Editorial

- **Tonto and the Big Banks**
  Review by Jeffrey Barlow

Feature

Online Lives, Offline Consequences: Professionalism, Information Ethics and Professional Students

View online at: http://bcis.pacificu.edu/journal/2009/01/article.php?id=22

By Issac Gilman

Pacific University Oregon, Library.

Introduction

The growth of the Internet over the past decade has made many tasks and personal interactions easier and faster. Students who have never experienced higher education without Google take for granted their ability to access information and entertainment at the click of a mouse and to live online lives unimpeded by anything except modem speed. For students enrolled in professional graduate programs (e.g. medicine, law, education), it is inevitable that their online experiences will shape their understanding of what is appropriate and what is ethical--which could have unanticipated professional consequences. To ensure that students' behaviors do not jeopardize their future careers, educators must understand the online activities that present ethical and professional issues and make every effort to educate students about appropriate behavior and interactions in an online environment [1, 2].

Academic Honesty and Information Ethics

For educators, perhaps the most familiar ethical issue facing students is that of academic honesty. For today's Internet-savvy students, who have become accustomed to cutting and pasting information on the fly with little attention to citations, the opportunity to use "free" online information is often too tempting to refuse. Studies over the past 10-15 years have confirmed that the ease of the Internet has exacerbated the misuse of others' intellectual property [3, 4]. In an "open" online environment, there is no accountability for those who may inappropriately provide/use others' work. Thanks to the speed of cut-and-paste, there is also little time for students to even consider whether or not their use is ethical [5]. Even for students who do stop to consider their actions, one study found that the majority of students "would give in to Internet plagiarism under the right combination of situational and personal factors" [6].

As familiar (and frustrated) as educators are with the unethical use of intellectual property, students are even more familiar with faculty lectures condemning the same. Honor codes, lectures on paper mills and the evils of plagiarism--even the use of plagiarism detection services like Turnitin.com--have largely failed to make a lasting impression on students who do not recognize the seriousness of the issue [7]. For many students, like 380 undergraduates surveyed about downloading copyrighted content, the use/misuse of others' intellectual property is still seen as a "victimless crime" [8]. Indeed, for undergraduate students who believe that anything accessible is free, who do not anticipate publishing a journal article and who may never depend on a scholarly or professional reputation, it can be difficult to convey the significance of academic honesty.

However, for graduate students who may one day contribute to the professional literature, creating ethical habits for the use of others' intellectual property is of the utmost significance. Whether these students go on to become academics or practitioners, their scholarly record and actions will likely contribute to their reputation and career prospects, for better or worse. Works created as students may also persist for years if posted online (as is the case with many theses, dissertations and other culminating projects), and it is vital that students understand from the beginning of their programs not only how to avoid plagiarism but also how to ethically--and legally--use copyrighted materials.

Social Networking and Professionalism

Though both educators and students are largely familiar with the issues of plagiarism and academic honesty, it is an entirely new issue that poses the greatest threat to students' professionalism--and one which has, on its face, nothing to do with students' academic performance or professional aspirations.

Over the past decade, the social/communication possibilities on the World Wide Web have grown exponentially, with one of the most notable developments being the creation of social networking sites--MySpace, Facebook, et al. As with many technologies, students were early (and fervent) adopters, with Facebook the popular choice of nearly 80-90 percent of United States college students [9]. Profiles on social networking sites like Facebook allow students to communicate with friends, share photos and videos and connect with people with similar interests. For students, their online profiles and communities are as personal as their offline friendships and interactions--and, often, are an extension of their offline activities, with Facebook used as a collaborative event planner and photo album.

While social networking sites and the Web connect students to one another, another connection is created that students may not anticipate (or enjoy). With student photos, blogs, comments and affiliations publicly available online (unless privacy settings are adjusted by the student), the digital world has removed the divide between "personal and professional identities" [10]. Students' (and employees') professionalism and fitness is no longer judged solely on their academic and on-the-job performance, but on their very *public* personal personas. Newspapers, blogs and academic reports from the past five years are filled with stories of schools and employers who have begun accessing social networking profiles looking for any untoward information as a means of evaluation/investigation [11 - 18]. New online services are dedicated to digging up digital dirt on prospective employees, with the promising of "automat[ing] candidate research across 41 social networks" [19].

The blurring of the line between personal and professional identities is an important issue for any student or employee, but particularly so for those in professional fields wherein public perception of professional competence and appropriate separation from patients, clients or students are vital. Though there is nothing inherently unethical about the use of social networking sites, publicly sharing unprofessional content (e.g. explicit or inappropriate comments/photos) or excessive personal information may be compromising for professionals. Educators and researchers from medical, law, education and pharmacy schools have all expressed concern that professional students may not understand the consequences of their online activities, or the risk of their personal offline activities being made public online by others [20 - 23].

Research and anecdotal evidence suggest that professional students either do not share educators concerns or are not aware that their online lives could have any bearing on their professionalism. In a recent study at the University of Florida, only 37.5 percent (n=362) of medical students and residents had private (viewable only by designated friends) Facebook profiles [24]. The same study found that, in a small sample of students with public profiles (n=10), 70 percent of the students had photographs of themselves with alcohol and 30 percent had pictures or videos that showed "drunkenness, overt sexuality, foul language and patient privacy violations in non-US locations" [25]. Students in the study also belonged to Facebook groups with highly unprofessional names; e.g. "I don't need sex cause grad school f**ks me every day," "Party of Important Male Physicians (PIMP)," "Physicians look for trophy wives in training" [26].

There is also evidence to suggest that current undergraduates (and future professional students) share the same lack of concern and awareness. In a separate study by the same researchers at the University of Florida, researchers analyzed Facebook profiles of 300 elementary education majors. Of the students with public profiles, 75 percent listed their sexual orientation and 73 percent had personal photo albums available [27]. A 2005 study by researchers at Carnegie Mellon University (CMU), determined that less than 1 percent of CMU Facebook users (n=4,450; a mix of students and faculty) had changed their default privacy settings to limit the visibility of their profiles [28]. An informal online survey by the Pacific *Index*, the student newspaper at Pacific University (Oregon), found that 33 percent of respondents believed they would never get in trouble for photos posted on Facebook, while 17 percent were "not going to worry about what people think of my personal life" [29]. Comments made in a thread started by a prospective pharmacy student on an online message board confirm all of these findings:

> mrsengle: "Pharmacists are in such high demand, employers put up with a LOT. As long as you have a license, don't have a DUI or possessions charge, have a degree and a pulse, you shouldn't worry about them checking an old myspace [sic] page" [30].

YouTube and Beyond

Unprofessional content posted on Facebook is not the only area of online concern for professional educators. Other venues for sharing personal (and/or unprofessional) material include blogs and video sharing sites such as YouTube. In one recent case, medical students posted a musical parody they had filmed on YouTube, which featured the students "dancing in the anatomy lab," "drinking [...] "blood" (actually chocolate) from plastic skulls," and "lying inside body bags" [31]. The video was subsequently removed from YouTube at the request of the dean of the medical school [32].

The medical students' YouTube video illustrates an important reason for addressing online professionalism with professional students: there are notable differences between generations regarding what is/is not humorous, acceptable and appropriate. As one educator has observed, "[w]hat looks like plagiarism, slander, copyright infringement, and embarrassing public behavior is for many students just creative and social entertainment" [33]. While many students are beginning to understand that their personal behavior is reflective on their professional identities [34], some still have not made the connection, or even believe that what they are doing--and posting online--has the possibility of offending anyone.

Whether or not students believe that their online activities *should* have any relevance to their academic and professional lives, it is growing increasingly clear that students' online personalities *will* be at issue for schools, employers and other professionals. There has been a call for lawyer's bar applications to include the "cyber equivalent" of a background check [35], and in an unprecedented move, applicants who wished to work in President Barack Obama's administration were required to complete a background check that included the following requests:

- "Please list [...] any posts or comments on blogs or other websites you have authored, individually or with others. Please list all aliases or "handles" you have used to communicate on the Internet."
- "If you have ever sent an electronic communication, including but not limited to an email, text message or instant message, that could suggest a conflict of interest or be a possible source of embarrassment to you, your family, or the President-Elect if it were made public, please describe."
- "Please provide the URL address of any websites that feature you in either a personal or professional capacity (e.g., Facebook, MySpace, etc.)" [36].

Conclusion

Professional students must understand the implications of their online activities and the importance of extending professionalism to their online lives. To convey this understanding, there should be comprehensive instruction provided for all professional students that addresses the issues of intellectual property, plagiarism, social networking, blogging, personal websites, e-mail etiquette, etc. Individual workshops do already exist [37], but to be the most effective, this instruction should be either integrated into program curriculum or made a required elective, and must be closely tied to the relevant professional association's code of ethics/conduct.

"E- literacy" (incorporating information ethics and online behavior standards) should be treated as a necessary competency for students to achieve, much like any other required knowledge/skills they receive in the course of their programs. Above all else, e-literacy instruction must help students realize that their online actions are not segregated from their professional lives, that their offline lives can easily end up online, and that anything posted on the Internet will persist long after it is removed. The guiding question for professional students should be, "Would it be appropriate for my mother/employer/patient/client to see what I am about to post?" [38] Because if they have a computer and an Internet connection, they probably will.

Notes

[1] Gardner, Stephanie F. 2006. Preparing for the Nexters. *American Journal of Pharmaceutical Education* 70(4): Article 87.

[2] Workman, Thomas A. 2008. "The Real Impact of Virtual Worlds." *The Chronicle of Higher Education*, September 19, 2008. http://chronicle.com/weekly/v55/i04/04b01201.htm (accessed October 16, 2008).

[3] Auer, Nicole J. and Ellen M. Krupar. 2001. Mouse Click Plagiarism: The Role of Technology in Plagiarism and the Librarian's Role in Combating It. *Library Trends* 49(3).

[4] Szabo, Attila and Jean Underwood. 2004. Cybercheats: Is Information and Communication Technology Fuelling Academic Dishonesty? *Active Learning in Higher Education* 5(2), 180.

[5] Bodi, Sonia. 1998. Ethics and Information Technology: Some Principles to Guide Students. *The Journal of Academic Librarianship* 24(6), 459.

[6] Szabo and Underwood, 196.

[7] Harris, Benjamin R. 2005. Credit Where Credit is Due: Considering Ethics, *Ethos*, and Process in Library Instruction on Attribution. *Education Libraries* 28(1), 4.

[8] Siemens, Jennifer C. and Steven W. Kopp. 2006. Teaching Ethical Copyright Behavior: Assessing the Effects of a University-Sponsored Computing Ethics Program. *NASPA Journal* 43(4), 118.

[9] Educause. 2007. 7 things you should know about Facebook II. *Educause Learning Initiative*; 2007. http://net.educause.edu/ir/library/pdf/ELI7025.pdf (accessed January 10, 2009).

[10] Thompson, Lindsay A., Kara Dawson, Richard Ferdig, Erik W. Black., J. Boyer, Jade Coutts and Nicole Paradise Black. 2008. The Intersection of Online Social Networking with Medical Professionalism. *Journal of General Internal Medicine* 23(7), 954.

[11] Capriccioso, R. 2006. "Facebook Face Off." *Inside Higher Ed*, February 14, 2006. http://www.insidehighered.com/news/2006/02/14/facebook (accessed January 10, 2009).

[12] Epstein, D. 2003. "Cleaning Up Their Online Acts." *Inside Higher Ed*, October 3, 2003. http://www.insidehighered.com/news/2005/10/03/online (accessed January 10, 2009).

[13] Steinbach, Sheldon and Lynn Deavers. 2007. "The Brave New World of MySpace and Facebook." *Inside Higher Ed*, April 3, 2007. http://www.insidehighered.com/views/2007/04/03/Steinbach (accessed May 6, 2008).

[14] Vorster, Gareth. 2008. "Online social networking sites could have a negative impact on your career progression, new research has found." *Personnel Today*, February 4, 2008. http://www.personneltoday.com/articles/2008/02/04/44263/facebook-myspace-users-warned-over-revealing-too-much-online.html (accessed May 6, 2008).

[15] Wilson, Erin. 2008. "Facebook Professionalism and Privacy." *UNI Journalism* (blog), May 6, 2008. http://uni-journalism.blogspot.com/2008/05/facebook-professionalism-and-privacy.html (accessed November 24, 2008).

[16] Read, Brock. 2007. "A MySpace Photo Costs a Student a Teaching Certificate." *The Chronicle of Higher Education*, April 27, 2007. http://chronicle.com/wiredcampus/article/2029/a-myspace-photo-costs-a-student-a-teaching-certificate (accessed December 5, 2008).

[17] Thomas, Owen. 2007. "Bank intern busted by Facebook." *Your Privacy is an Illusion* (blog), November 12, 2007. http://valleywag.gawker.com/321802/tech/your-privacy-is-an-illusion/bank-intern-busted-by-facebook (accessed May 6, 2008).

[18] Bergstrom, Ida. 2008. "Facebook can ruin your life. And so can MySpace, Bebo..." *The Independent*, February 10, 2008. http://www.independent.co.uk/life-style/gadgets-and-tech/news/facebook-can-ruin-your-life-and-so-can-myspace-bebo-780521.html (accessed May 6, 2008).

[19] Spokeo Inc. http://www.spokeo.com/hr/ (accessed November 2, 2008).

[20] Thompson et al.

[21] Cain, Jeff. 2008. Online Social Networking Issues Within Academia and Pharmacy Education. *American Journal of Pharmaceutical Education* 72(1).

[22] Farnan, Jeanne M., John A.M. Paro, Jennifer Higa, Jay Edelson and Vineet M. Arora. 2008. The YouTube Generation: implications for medical professionalism. *Perspectives in Biology and Medicine* 51(4).

[23] Mangan, Katherine. 2007. "Etiquette for the Bar." *The Chronicle of Higher Education*, January 12, 2007. http://chronicle.com/weekly/v53/i19/19a03101.htm (accessed December 5, 2008).

[24] Thompson et al., 955.

[25] Ibid., 956.

[26] Ferdig, Richard E., Kara Dawson, Erik W. Black., Nicole M. Paradise Black and Lindsay A. Thompson. 2008. "Medical students' and residents' use of online social

networking tools: Implications for teaching professionalism in medical education." *First Monday* 13(9). http://firstmonday.org/htbin/cgiwrap/bin/ojs/index.php/fm/article/viewArticle/2161/2026 (accessed October 12, 2008).

[27] University of Florida College of Education. 2007. "UF study looks at preservice teachers' Facebook entries." http://news.education.ufl.edu/news/uf-study-looks-preservice-teachers-facebook-entries (accessed January 4, 2009).

[28] Gross, Ralph and Alessandro Acquisti. 2005. "Information Revelation and Privacy in Online Social Networks (The Facebook case) [Pre-proceedings version]". *ACM Workshop on Privacy in the Electronic Society* (WPES), 2005. http://www.heinz.cmu.edu/~acquisti/papers/privacy-facebook-gross-acquisti.pdf (accessed January 10, 2009).

NOTE: Currently, the default Facebook setting allows any users in a student's network (not just those designated as "Friends") to view all information in that student's profile. The default setting for posted photo albums is to be visible to *all* Facebook users.

[29] "Do you post photos on your Facebook that could possibly get you in trouble?" *The Pacific Index* (poll), 2008. http://www.thepacificindex.com/poll/ (accessed May 6, 2008).

[30] "Grad schools/employers and Facebook/Myspace" (online bulletin board). *City-Data.com*, posted July 26, 2007. http://www.city-data.com/forum/work-employment/121739-grad-schools-employers-facebook-myspace.html (accessed May 6, 2008).

[31] Farnan, et al., 518.

[32] Ibid., 520.

[33] Workman.

[34] Young, Jeffrey R. 2008. "Educause Survey Shows Students Watch Their Privacy on Facebook." *The Chronicle of Higher Education*, June 12, 2008. http://chronicle.com/wiredcampus/article/3086/educause-survey-shows-students-watch-their-privacy-on-facebook (accessed June 13, 2008).

[35] Stellato, Jesse. 2007. "e-Ethics: Professional Responsibility of Law Students on the Internet." *Eagleionline*, October 18, 2007. http://eagleionline.com/blog/2007/10/18/e-ethics-professional-responsibility-of-law-students-on-the-internet (accessed January 5, 2009).

[36] Obama-Biden Transition Project. 2008. "Background Check Questionnaire". http://www.wsbtv.com/download/2008/1113/17972158.pdf (accessed January 4, 2009).

[37] Mangan.

[38] Keenan, T.P. 2008. "On the Internet, Things Never Go Away Completely," in *IFIP International Federation for Information Processing*, Vol. 262 (The Future of Identity in the Information Society), ed. Simone Fischer-Hubner, Penny Duquenoy, Albin Zuccato and Leonardo Martucci. Boston: Springer.

Online Community

It's not Just Technology that Makes our Village Grow

View online at: http://bcis.pacificu.edu/journal/2009/01/article.php?id=23

By Pat McGregor

Editor's note: Pat McGregor and Glee Cady, writing partners, have worked with us at Interface for some time. We were shocked to hear from Pat that Glee had been stricken with a serious condition, which threatened initially to end her mobility if not her career. As Pat created, or facilitated an electronic support community to rally around Glee, we were struck by this very caring and effective use of the Internet, and asked Pat, along with her rigorous personal and care-taking work, to think about writing about the experience for us...

As you may have heard, my partner in crime, Glee Cady, has been hospitalized since August 17, 2008, with a severe *Staphylococcal* infection of the spine. After several months of intense back pain, she collapsed one afternoon when two vertebrae in her back gave way under the disintegration caused by the infection. Rushed to the hospital, it was discovered that the bone fragments were compressing her spine, along with the damage done to her system by the long-term infection. She's had grueling surgery and recovery, and the Internet community has rallied--there are two private email lists on *Yahoo!* for her (one for news only, and one for discussion about what help can be given her, scheduling visits, etc.) and we are using a calendaring site so folks can see when good times to visit are. The mailing lists she regularly reads, some professional and some related to hobbies and authors, are also right there supporting her-- keeping updates, sending cards, letters, getting her favorite authors to sign things to send to her, and so on.

When this first happened, and the vanilla email list her sons and daughter-in-law compiled grew to over 100 people in a couple of days, one of our newer (less than five years ;-)) friends was impressed at how fast the news spread *around the world*, and how many people felt personally touched by her life.

When he mentioned it, one of the dinosaurs on the list (like Glee), said in a private comment to me that when Glee's husband Frank[1] had cancer in 1990-1992, we did the same thing, although we were using different tools: BITNET[2] (IBM's Because It's There email Network) and LISTSERV, *uucp*[3] (email through Unix), and other email systems to link together. Frank was an employee of Merit Network, as were Glee and I, and was working on the NSFNET[4] project. He was in the University of Michigan Hospital for quite some time before his death, and because the hospital was very advanced, it had a network connection in his room so he could work, share email, and be connected to the world. I personally feel strongly that the ability for us, his friends, to be in contact with him on a daily, casual basis, to share jokes and job problems and love with him, helped him so that he lived much longer than any of us had expected. Then, after his death, Glee's global friends, cancer support groups that she discovered (who were new to using e mail but swiftly getting used to it), and others whose life she and Frank had touched, took care of her and her boys through their grief, her decision to move back to California, and their building a new life there.

Then, a year later when Brendan Kehoe,[5] author of *Zen and the Art of the Internet*,[6] incurred brain damage when his car was hit on the morning of December 31, 1993, and went into a coma, the network rushed into action for him. For those of you who don't know, Brendan is a legendary figure among Internet historians. Not only was he one of the people who helped create *gnu*[7] compilers as a part of the Free Software Foundation[8] project, he was a computer consultant at Widener University when he became an underground hero to the new college network users. He created a guide to the Internet for the students there and put it on the net. Soon it was being used as the canonical documentation for users wanting access to all the different services available on the Internet. When the major publishers finally figured out that real people wanted documentation on the Internet, Brendan's book was one of the first to hit the checkout stands. People who might never have even thought of using the Internet could do so because of Brendan. Families started getting their grandparents and other seniors computers so they could stay in touch via email. Senior centers and daycare centers started "penpal" programs. And none of this was easy, because it was in the days before web browsers really took off and we used acoustic modems. But the important thing wasn't the technology--it was the connections made possible.[9]

At any rate, I was working with Brendan at Cygnus Support (a GNU software support company later purchased by Red Hat,[10] the folks who have a version of Linux out), and when he had this terrible injury, people all over the world wanted to know how he was. We used LISTSERV email lists with hundreds of names on them, and we used his profile (his entry in a directory listing about individuals on a particular Unix system). We would put daily updates in his profile, and people could use a utility called finger [11] to see what was going on. To do it, anyone on a Unix system or with an Internet interface could type "finger Brendan@cygnus" and the latest update on Brendan would be printed on their screen.

From all over the world, people sent notes to Brendan and his mother, contributed funds for his care at the specialty hospital, and did all sorts of things that he and his family needed.

Today we have better tools to organize caretaking, donations, send messages, gifts, and do all sorts of things for our friends, even when they are friends we only know from virtual space. There are care sites, support sites, places like PayPal where you can set up donations, flower companies where you can send flowers from one country to another, and so on. When I've visited Glee I've seen beautiful cards, flowers, and gifts from people she's known since the late '90s but has never met in person.

And that is the point of this article, rather than just a history lesson about "how it was before there was mud."

We are building communities with the Internet, and have been since the very earliest days.

How do we do it?

In April of 2006, I wrote an article in this journal about the difference between some blogs, MySpace, and other communities.[12] The key, decided the folks I was discussing this with online, was that the Internet was a tool for real conversation. One woman said:

> Some places, like [this one], seem to be much more designed around a group of people interacting with each other, and the [postings] resemble diaries. Other places seem to be designed around a content creator pushing a stream of articles to the world, and the content creators will use them as a pulpit to espouse a view.
>
> I think communities can form and be facilitated by both types of blogs. However, [this one] is much better at either forming a community (by having a bunch of authenticated [13] people rendezvous at a particular spot), or facilitating existing communities (mostly what it does for me, since a significant chunk of my friends from a few different communities hang out here).
>
> I don't think communities are really driven by the posts, or the content creator making articles. Communities are driven by the conversation in comments (like we are doing now!)[13]

People who are just using Internet tools to publish content, rather than invite real discussion, aren't building communities.

[This is the point, I think, where I mention that *Interface* invites comments at the bottom of all of our stories. We can have a real discussion about these things here, rather than just reading it and wanting to argue with the authors. ;-)]

While I was doing some research and thinking about this article, I spent a great deal of time thinking about communities not only for social groups, but also, say, for communities in other ways. While I was at Intuit, the architects and engineers were creating communities of interest so that they could share development discoveries and build not only better, but also faster and smarter. For them, an online community space would be ideal if it enabled that collaboration, both in quality of engineering and space for creativity. While I was thinking about this, I ran across an excellent essay by Michael DeHaan,[14] who is an engineer for Red Hat software in Raleigh, North Carolina. He was speaking of enabling the community participation that makes the open software development system so strong: the creation of collaboration space where serendipity occurs.

> [W]hen you open up things and allow community participation, you never know what you're going to get. Lots of interesting features and ideas can appear-- ideas that you never imagined, just by allowing other people to

> expand upon your ideas or designs. This may mean collaboration or integration with other software-- or this may be in terms of adding features you didn't think were originally possible or within the scope of what you set out to do. Things can take on a life of their own. You are enabling the butterfly's wing-flap effect to occur and who knows how many software applications or people you might affect. You don't know what you are setting in motion, but the creation of this energy is hugely important to encourage future innovation.
>
> The challenge to be posed to all projects is to create those architectures of participation-- it requires in many aspects being somewhat less of a developer, but we need to do more than this. The success of free software is based on getting as many people engaged in it as possible.[15]

So how do we connect this to people, rather than software? Let's head off in an entirely different direction. We won't talk about software, or taking care of people. Let's talk about--writing fiction.

NaNoWriMo

No, that's not baby talk. Every year for the last 10 years, people have taken up the challenge of the National Novel Writing Month or NaNoWriMo.[16] (We geeky people[17] just love our acronyms!) Here's the description from the web page:

> National Novel Writing Month is a fun, seat-of-your-pants approach to novel writing. Participants begin writing November 1. The goal is to write a 175-page (50,000-word) novel by midnight, November 30.
>
> Valuing enthusiasm and perseverance over painstaking craft, NaNoWriMo is a novel-writing program for everyone who has thought fleetingly about writing a novel but has been scared away by the time and effort involved.
>
> Because of the limited writing window, the ONLY thing that matters in NaNoWriMo is output. It's all about quantity, not quality. The kamikaze approach forces you to lower your expectations, take risks, and write on the fly.
>
> Make no mistake: You will be writing a lot of crap. And that's a good thing. By forcing yourself to write so intensely, you are giving yourself permission to make mistakes. To forgo the endless tweaking and editing and just create. To build without tearing down.
>
> As you spend November writing, you can draw comfort from the fact that, all around the world, other National Novel Writing Month participants are going through the same joys and sorrows of producing the Great Frantic Novel. Wrimos meet throughout the month to offer encouragement, commiseration, and--when the thing is done--the kind of raucous celebrations that tend to frighten animals and small children.
>
> In 2007, we had over 100,000 participants. More than 15,000 of them crossed

the 50k finish line by the midnight deadline, entering into the annals of NaNoWriMo superstardom forever. They started the month as auto mechanics, out-of-work actors, and middle school English teachers. They walked away novelists. http://www.nanowrimo.org/eng/whatisnano

(Pat says: I ran into NaNoWriMo via friends in the medieval history group [17] I belong to. There are a lot of published writers in the medieval group, and not only in fantasy or fiction. But you'll find, if you ask in any group you belong to, that almost everyone wishes they could write a novel. NaNoWriMo is a way to do that. Set a time, set a limit, set butt in chair and hands on keyboards.)

The first year, July 1999, NaNo happened in the San Francisco Bay Area. 21 people wrote. A few years later, it settled down into November. This year, the preliminary stats are 119,301 authors signed up for NaNoWriMo. That's a 17.5 percent bump in turn-out from 2007, with 101,510 writers. Of everyone registered, 21,683 won. That's an 18.2 percent win rate[18].

1,643,343,993 words were officially submitted to the site. That's more burgers than any franchise sells in a day, or a huge dent in our national debt if it were only dollars. And twenty thousand and some people did it. Now, as my son (and the intro above) says, some percentage of it will be crap. But Amazon books and CreateSpace, an Amazon owned company, is generously offering every NaNoWriMo 2008 winner a "free proof copy" of their 2008 manuscript.[19] And Amazon thinks enough of the NaNo process that they have a contest in which some number of books (last year it was between 3 and 7) will be published by Penguin. And there are a lot of people who get the books they write published, after polishing and rewriting and so on.

How does this relate to Glee, and communities, and taking care of one another? It's one enormous circle, and I think it's pretty amazing.

Jennifer Crusie[20] and her writing partner, Bob Mayer, who write pretty terrific books, have a mailing list of fans that Glee belongs to. The participants are her cherished friends for many years, and I asked to be added to the list when she became ill so I could keep them posted on her progress. The participants send "Cherry Vibes" to anyone who is ill, needs help, or just is having a rough time. (They call themselves the Cherries because of the bright red cherry on the cover of one of Jenny's books.) People all over the world belong, and some of those folks belong to other groups that Glee belongs to. So when I post an update on the Glee news list and to the Cherry list, pretty soon the information is spread in a global network. I've gotten personal mail from someone in Australia who is sending "Vegemite Vibes" and people in Central Europe, and one very nice person in Argentina. They have taken me (and my various trials and tribulations) in, and taken care of me, too. And some of them have sent Glee some pretty amazing and wonderfully silly gifts to keep her spirits up.

Many of the folks on the Cherry list are writers, published or budding or would-be. I mentioned to Glee that I had formally signed up for NaNo this year, and she said, "Do you belong to the Cherry list for the NaNos?"

Well, I didn't, but I joined, and that community helped me get 52,000+ words on disk, despite having my house robbed, computers and car stolen, and other trifles that occurred during November. We had sprints (who can write the most words in a half hour) and other competitions ("I'm thinking of a number between 1 and 1600 - the winner mentions some form of drinking alcohol closest to this number"), and all sorts of silly prizes. I won an oven mitt with a cherry motif. I wrote 10,000 words in one night while I was at my sister's house for Thanksgiving.

And I also found a woman on the formal NaNo website whose email matches that of one of my nephews' girlfriends--and she lives in the EU! But she is a NaNo "winner," with almost 70,000 words, and I now will know more about her when we meet at Christmas than many of the other relatives there, because we've shared novels.

So, yes, those of us on the Internet can respond fast and usefully when there is a need. Nowadays we have better tools; we can send money to the Hurricane Katrina victims via the Red Cross website rather than writing a check and finding a stamp. We can do telephone bank calls to voters in swing states from home using a database interface on our Candidate's website. We can arrange for a midwifery PAC action in another state using a mailing list.

But we're still just meeting and being supported by people via one basic tool; a computer network combined with lots of other computer networks. And I think that, of all the things that the Internet has brought us, is the most important.

Have a great New Year!

Endnotes

[1] *Poems On A White Page* by Frank Cady, Flowering Quince Poetry Series, Number Four 1982, Edition of 400. Finely chiseled poems grace this first book. $10 http://www.heyeckpress.com/poetry.htm

[2] BITNET, on Wikipedia, http://en.wikipedia.org/wiki/BITNET LISTSERV, http://www.lsoft.com/products/listserv-history.asp accessed 7 December 2008

[3] uucp, on Wikipedia, http://en.wikipedia.org/wiki/Uucp, accessed 7 December 2008. uucp project home page, http://www.uucp.org/index.shtml accessed 7 December 2008.

[4] NSFNET: A Partnership for High-Speed Networking http://www.livinginternet.com/doc/merit.edu/phenom.html, accessed 7 December 2008. Quote:

"While the 1986 NSFNET had given the research and education community a taste of what was possible with connectivity to a high-speed backbone network, the leaps in capacity and reliability offered by the new NSFNET backbone service proved to be popular beyond even the partners' wildest dreams. The growth of the Internet worldwide, of which the construction of the NSFNET in the US played a major part, can only be described as "phenomenal."

"It was pretty much an unmanageable child," says Ellen Hoffman. "I think back then we all had hopes that it would grow the ways that it did, but none of us believed that it would grow so fast." Hans-Werner recalls working in an environment where "something that was brand-new and totally up-to-date in the morning was completely out of date by the afternoon. That happened pretty much on a day-by-day basis, because we moved so fast."

"The statistics Merit provided on use of the NSFNET backbone are by now well-known, but still every bit as astounding: 19 billion packets per month processed in September of 1992, a growth rate of approximately 11% a month. Over 6,000 networks were connected to the NSFNET backbone service in 1992, one-third of which were outside the United States. Use of the network was also evolving; the share of network traffic devoted to electronic mail and file transfers was being overtaken by newer information storage and retrieval applications such as Gopher, Archie, and Veronica."

[5] Brendan Kehoe biography, Wikipedia, http://en.wikipedia.org/wiki/Brendan_Kehoe

[6] First (and free) copy of *Zen and the Art of the Internet*, http://www.cs.indiana.edu/docproject/zen/zen-1.0_toc.html, accessed 7 December 2008.

[7] The GNU Project was launched in 1984 to develop a complete Unix-like operating system which is free software: the GNU system. http://www.gnu.org/, http://www.gnu.org/philosophy/free-sw.html

[8] Also known as the "Open Source Software" movement. Open Source Software is developed and put into the public domain so that others can use and improve their own projects from it. For example, there are many free versions of Linux, compilers, indexers, text management systems, and other kinds of software in the GNU library. The Free Software Foundation (FSF) is a 501(c)3 donor supported charity founded in 1985 and based in Boston, MA, USA. The FSF has a worldwide mission to promote computer user freedom and to defend the rights of all free software users. http://www.fsf.org/

[9] acoustic modem - a modem that converts electrical signals to telephone tones and back again. modem -from a combination of MOdulate and DEModulate) electronic equipment consisting of a device used to connect computers by a telephone line; http://www.thefreedictionary.com/acoustic+modem accessed 7 December 2008. At the time we're talking about, a 9600 bits per second (bps) modem was very expensive: most people had 1200 bps equipment. As a comparison, if you are reading this over your home cable modem, the data is coming to you at 128,000 bps; a 1200 bps modem would be 107 times slower. You could read this line character by character as it appears on the screen, rather than having the whole page appear at once. And if anyone picked up another phone in the house, interrupting the signal, the transmission would have to start over again from the beginning. Comparison Chart courtesy of Livingston, at http://www.livingston.net/html/chart.html Accessed 8 December 2008.

[10] RedHat enterprises, https://www.redhat.com/ "What began as a better way to build software--openness, transparency, collaboration--soon shifted the balance of power in an entire industry. The revolution of choice continues. Today Red Hat is the world's most trusted provider of Linux and open source technology." From the corporate website, accessed 7 December 2008.)

[11] For those of you who've joined the Internet audience since 2000 or so, remember that many of these Internet functions were thought up by single male Internet geeks in college. Some of the names and capabilities would not have either these names or even be allowed in this politically correct, privacy conscious world.)

[12] Online Community: Is it really a village? April-May 2006, Volume 6, Issue 2. http://bcis.pacificu.edu/journal/2006/02/mcgregor.php; accessed 7 December 2008

[13] People whose identity is reasonably established. Since LiveJournal allows you to block anonymous commenters, or to prevent anyone who isn't registered as your friend to comment, you have a reasonable control over who joins in your conversations.

[14] http://www.linkedin.com/in/michaeldehaan/

[15] More Random Community Building Thoughts, November 17th, 2008 Michael DeHaan, http://www.michaeldehaan.net/?p=771 accessed 7 December 2008.

[16] http://www.nanowrimo.com/

[17] Not all computer geeks started out that way. I have a BA in English/Journalism, and was on my way to a career (or at least an MA) in Creative Writing/Medieval History when life interrupted. For more information on this society, check us out at http://www.sca.org

[18] Organizer's Blog, First week in December. http://www.nanowrimo.org/eng/breakingnews - accessed 8 December 2008.

[19] http://www.nanowrimo.org/eng/nowwhat

[20] http://www.jennycrusie.com/

Politics

Election 2.0.1: The Obama Electronic Campaign Following Victory

View online at: http://bcis.pacificu.edu/journal/2009/01/article.php?id=24

By Jenn Hernandez, Berglund Student Intern

The use of the web in the November 2008 election, and events leading up to it, was revolutionary in that it mobilized so many Americans towards a common purpose (with the promise of social interaction along the way): electing a president. This goal now accomplished, new issues arise. Will the means of the technology and how it's used change, or remain essentially the same? How will the technology be used in response to questions of the everyday workings of legislation and running a country, and are Americans still expecting that they be kept in the loop? Also, what has Obama's successful use of technology taught his political opponents for next time around, as campaigning will most likely never be the same again.

Technologically speaking, Obama is revamping the way we see the political machine. For the most part, we have a clearer view into its inner workings, and we can see how our own participation factors in more directly. Also, most importantly, we are asked to participate; we are asked for our ideas, to inform others, to give feedback. The idea of government for the people, by the people, takes on a new significance with the onset of a new chapter in social networking. We have been given many outlets in which to participate: most notably barackobama.com [1] and change.gov [2], a more recent addition to Obama's online presence.

When Obama went from being a presidential candidate to the president-elect, his team put out a transitional website, change.gov. The change.gov homepage includes a section entitled "Open Government," which invites users to continue the dialogue by sharing election stories and ideas with the transition team, and eventually the new president. The introduction reminds the visitor that, "The story of the campaign and this historic moment has been your story. It is about the great things we can do when we come together around a common purpose. The story of bringing this country together as a healed and united nation will be led by president-elect Obama, but written by you. …this process of setting up that new government is about you" [3]. The idea of open and free communication is revolutionary in that a government traditionally working apart from its people can now include direct input from them.

Change.gov includes a "Citizen's Briefing Book" in which the people can suggest topics that they want discussed. The topics are open for commenting, and can be voted for or against. The topics with the most votes will be presented to Obama when he is sworn in, to be brought to his attention as questions or issues that concern the people. Topics and ideas range from the economy to health care, homeland security to technology. Some popular ideas include "commit[ting] to becoming the 'Greenest' country in the world", "Vote and debate all bills online...", and "Bring Back the Constitution!" [4]

Another example of change in connecting the people and their government in effect is the "archaic" Presidential radio address. In responses to a short article, "Nothin'but 'Net': Obama, the Web and the Whitehouse" on James McPherson's Media and Politics Blog, one commenter addresses reactions to a transition in presidential address media from radio to Internet. The commenter admits to not listening to radio addresses in the past, but mentions that using the Internet to broadcast may widen the reach of the address across the nation. Another commenter had used the Internet to stream radio broadcasted addresses after the fact. [5]

Skeptics, or those simply not as enthusiastic about the legitimacy of the use of social networking in an election, such as Republican consultant Patrick Ruffini, state the valid point that, "Having more Facebook friends won't make you President... It might tell you something about the enthusiasm of your supporters, but it's just one metric." The issue, he says, is perspective. "The emphasis, especially in the media, and to the exclusion of other technologies, is out of whack" [6].

But looking past this objection, it is no one's place to say how many of any candidate's "friends" actually voted for them, or were even old enough to vote. [7] And it seems reasonable to assume that anyone who added a candidate as a "friend" had some interest in learning more about the candidate, and eventually delving into the finding of reasons to possibly vote for or against them. The importance of "friends" on social networking sites is to build a network amongst people you socialize with normally, or expect to keep at least minimum contact.

In a Pew Internet study on post-election voter engagement, it was found that 51% of Obama supporters who used the Internet during the campaign to get involved expect an "ongoing communication" with the administration in office. [8] On the other hand, Republicans have also begun rebuilding an online presence since the election, through sites such as redstate.com [9], and a newer addition, rebuildtheparty.com [10], with an emphasis on grassroots activities. Though 9% of McCain voters who utilized the Internet during the campaign have visited sites like these, they still do not carry the same high expectations that Obama supporters have to hear from their party. [11]

No matter what political ideology one may hold, there is no ignoring the impact and utility of the Internet for future reference. The effectiveness of Obama's online presence during and after his campaign will henceforth model the way politicians mobilize supporters in elections to come. Also, opening up communication in the formerly closed and mysterious process of governance to the people for input and insight puts a renewed significance in a government for the people, by the people.

Endnotes

[1] http://www.barackobama.com/index.php

[2] http://change.gov/

[3] http://change.gov/page/content/americanmoment

[4]http://citizensbriefingbook.change.gov/ideas/ideaList.apexp?c=09a800000004fo6&
lsi=2

[5]http://jmcpherson.wordpress.com/2008/11/10/nothin-but-net-obama-the-web-and-the-white-house/

[6] http://www.cioinsight.com/c/a/Trends/Election-2008-The-Internet-Campaign/

[7] http://www.readwriteweb.com/archives/web_20_election.php

[8] http://www.pewinternet.org/PPF/r/271/report_display.asp

[9] http://www.redstate.com/

[10] http://www.rebuildtheparty.com/

[11] http://www.pewinternet.org/PPF/r/271/report_display.asp

Legal

A Trademark Owner's Right to Control Sublicenses

View online at: http://bcis.pacificu.edu/journal/2009/01/article.php?id=25

By Leonard D. DuBoff

It is well settled that the owner of a copyright or a patent has the right to control the sublicensing of that intellectual property right, even when that right is not expressly reserved in the license agreement, but until recently the question of trademark sublicensing had not yet been addressed by any of the country's appellate courts.

In a case involving the world famous musician Glenn Miller, the Ninth Circuit joined New York and Georgia district courts in holding that trademark sublicensing follows the same rules as copyright and patent sublicensing. Miller, known for the big band sound, was lost at sea when his airplane disappeared toward the end of World War II while flying to Paris to entertain U.S. combat troops. Approximately twelve years later, Glenn Miller Productions, Inc. (GMP), was established to carry on the Glenn Miller tradition. Helen Miller, the band leader's widow, was an executive in the company and granted it the right to exploit Glenn Miller's name, likeness and library of music.

Sometime later, GMP began operating the Glenn Miller Orchestra and registered "Glenn Miller Orchestra" with the U.S. Trademark Office. Beginning in 1988, GMP granted sublicenses to third parties, including a Glenn Miller orchestra in Germany and one in the United Kingdom. In addition to having the right to use the late artist's copyrighted music, the sublicensees were also given the right to exploit Miller's name, likeness and reputation, commonly known as the *right of publicity*.

Many years later, Glenn Miller's heirs, the current owners of his intellectual property rights, filed suit in the Central District of California (Los Angeles) to challenge GMP's right to grant sublicenses of the late artist's trademark. The district court granted the company's motion for summary judgment on the grounds that the heirs sat on their rights too long. This doctrine, known as *laches*, is the only form of statute of limitations available in a federal trademark dispute.

Despite its holding on laches, the district court made it clear that the licensee of a trademark does *not* have the right to grant a sublicense without the express written permission of the owner of the mark. The court justified this rule by pointing out that a trademark owner has the right and obligation to police the quality of items bearing the protected mark.

While some jurisdictions have held that the trademark owner has the right to control the grant of sublicenses, even when that right is not expressly reserved in a written agreement, it is still a good idea for a trademark license to expressly deal with this issue, since most jurisdictions have not yet weighed in on the subject. Whether you are a licensee or a licensor, you should work with an experienced intellectual property lawyer when entering into a trademark license agreement to ensure that your rights are protected.

Technology

Fitness by the Bits

View online at: http://bcis.pacificu.edu/journal/2009/01/article.php?id=26

By Michael Geraci

A new year is upon us and with it comes the annual pledge to improve our physical selves through healthier eating, increased activity and improved sleep habits. A new tech gadget and associated Web service is slated for a January 2009 launch that aims to assist users with all of the above and more. Fitbit[1] got some attention at the annual TechCrunch50[2] event in September 2008 by being one of the 50 invited technology startups at the conference.

Fitbit consists of a wearable "tracker" device that is kept on your person for any length of time, but is designed to be in place 24/7, and a Web site that provides an individualized fitness portal that utilizes the data collected by the tracker.

The tracker is a sleek, high-tech piece of engineering that looks like an elongated and narrow version of Apple's impossibly small iPod Shuffle. Worn in a clip fashion or just dropped into a pocket, the tracker "senses motion tracker in three-dimensions", according to the company's press release. Data monitored by the tracker includes calories burned, steps taken, distance traveled, activity intensity, and sleep quality. The company's Web site claims that the sleep quality data collection has been fine tuned so as to match data gathered in a clinical sleep lab environment. The tracker uses wiress transmission to send its gathered data to your Mac or WIndows computer via a small docking base that also serves as the recharging station for the device. Once sent, the information from the tracker is uploaded to your Fitbit portal on the company's Web site. The tracker retails for $99 and includes the dock and access to the Web service. There are no on-going fees or dues.

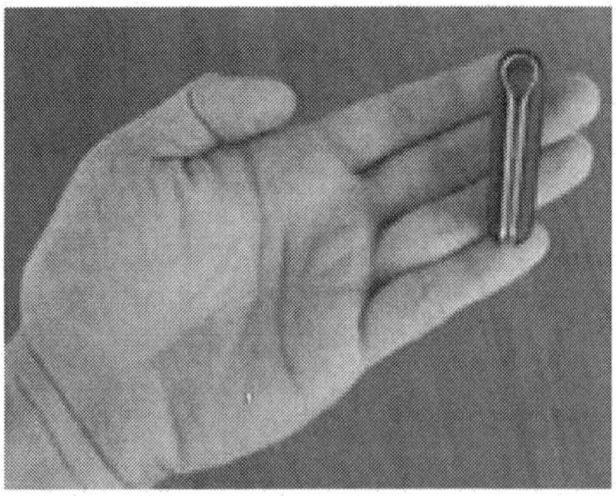

The tracker includes an OLED readout which will provide the user with their expended calorie count, steps taken, distance traveled, as well as an iconic indicator of one's progress towards fitness goals established on the Web portal. The tracker's internal battery is reported to have a ten-day use cycle between charges and only needs to be docked for charging (data transfer is accomplished wirelessly). The tracker is designed to accurately record information from physical motion associated with walking and running but will not be accurate with certain other types of activities such as cycling and swimming. Each tracker has a unique ID so multiple users can be wearing the device in the same location with no complications in the data collection.

The Web site is designed to be a realtime personal health monitor with graphical displays which track your activity levels, calories, steps, sleep patterns, and myriad other pieces of information that reflect your progress towards personal goals such as daily calorie intake and total distance traveled. The Fitbit Web site also includes a clever Web 2.0 hook: the ability to involve your friends in your fitness quests. By adding other Fitbit users to your profile, you can send them updates on your progress and activity levels and receive the same from them. If the company's screenshots are real (i.e., not mockups) the site will even provide you with statements like the following:

> "You got into bed at 12:00am and were in bed for 8 hrs 2 min. You took 23 minutes to fall asleep and woke up 26 times in your sleep. This means you were actually asleep for 7 hrs 42 min."

I don't know about you, but this piece of information alone would be enough to motivate me to change some behaviors.

The Web site is designed to become a total picture of one's health by providing services not connected to the data from the tracker. You can log your non-tracked activities such as rowing or cycling, and you can enter the nutritional information from your meals. The site includes a comprehensive library of food products, both store bought and found in restaurants, and all its nutritional information. As of this writing, this information appears to be open to anyone, not just Fitbit users, and makes a good resource for anyone who is monitoring their eating habits. Currently there is no search functionality or interactivity that would make the nutritional resources even more useful and accessible. For example, the user should be able to select a food item from the library and have it automatically post to his or her Fitbit log on the site. Perhaps this is something that will be added to the site at the official launch.

In conclusion, the Fitbit, once released, appears to offer a convenient and affordable solution to the keeping of those health-related New Year's resolutions. At a one-time expense of $99, it seems like a good investment.

Endnotes

[1] http://www.fitbit.com
[2] http://www.techcrunch50.com/2008/conference/

Book Review

Gary Small and Gigi Vorgan's *IBrain: Surviving the Technological Alteration of the Modern Mind*

View online at: http://bcis.pacificu.edu/journal/2009/01/article.php?id=27

Review by Jeffrey Barlow

Small, Gary, and Gigi Vorgan. *IBrain: Surviving the Technological Alteration of the Modern Mind.* New York: HarperCollins Publishers, 2008.

The first task of either a writer or a critical book reviewer is to imagine the audience for whom the work is intended. For us at *Interface*, that is those interested in the impact of the Internet.

Some works, however, like the one under review, defy easy classification, perhaps because they fail to target an appropriate audience or to speak consistently to it. This might be a sign of a weak book, not actually suitable for anybody; too much of its content may miss the mark. Both a reader's time and resources are, after all, limited. Our usual approach to such a work would be to simply ignore it.

IBrain, by Dr. Gary Small and Gigi Vorgan, comes close to being such a book. But this is a book that many readers will want to like; it deals with a question that has long troubled users, first of television, then of the Internet: Is regular viewing or heavy usage more than just a problem of allocating personal time? Obviously, such usage shapes an individual's social interactions, but does it actually change the individual in a physical sense? Might it even cause brain damage?

Any acute observer of young people, certainly any teacher, has had for decades the strong sense that those raised first on television and second on the computer are very different than previous generations. Are they different solely because of social practice, or are they being physically altered by technology? For example, could long-term and prolonged computer use be responsible for such characteristics as their very limited tolerance for boredom (including deep reading in many cases), their single-minded focus on their own likes and dislikes (often described as narcissism), their increasingly prevalent hyperactivity, even for conditions like Asperger's Syndrome?

Small and Vorgan argue that the problem goes beyond social impact and involves physical changes in the users' brains. They hesitate to use the word "damage" in their assessments, because they see the changes as in some senses positive, and in others, remediable.

But despite the significance of the topic, this book has some serious flaws. It gropes for a consistent analysis, and seems not to be aimed at any one audience. It focuses, very loosely, upon two groups at either end of the scale of Internet users—savvy "digital natives" and wary "digital immigrants." The work attempts to unite these two audiences and to speak to both of them by arguing that each are facing a similar problem, however different its consequences may be to either group.

The modern brain, the authors argue, is forced by increasing use of digital materials into a process they choose to describe as "evolutionary." It is this latter argument that makes the work most interesting, however much we may question the pragmatic utility of some of the authors' suggested solutions, delivered rather repetitively and at sometimes tiresome length.

Part of the problem with the book's unclear focus is that Small and Gorgon often concatenate the television generation and the digital natives in a rather facile manner, by suggesting that television has many of the same negative consequences as does computer use, particularly isolating its rapt audience from wider social engagement.[1]

The book has two core arguments to make, one about each generation. Digital Natives, the authors feel, lack social skills because of their isolation from direct human contact, that is, person-to-person contact. This deprives them of the practice in social skills we all need, being able to read non-verbal clues in our interlocutors, developing empathy, learning to at least simulate being an interested and engaged audience however much others may bore us, etc.

This social deficit is, however, not simply the result of a flawed learning process. Frequent computer use, the authors argue, both actively rewires some brain pathways, and correspondingly limits the development of others. The work cites a number of very interesting studies, usually derived from Magnetic Resonance Imaging studies (MRI) of brain activity while particular tasks are being undertaken. This material is fascinating and well worth examination.

At the last, however, one feels that the authors may be pushing their conclusions as to the nature of these processes a bit far. Certainly there are bound to be serious disagreements within the scientific community as to both causes and consequences, yet the authors never really discuss contrary evidence. This is not necessarily the obligation of every author; when writing for the public we are certainly often excused from such deep readings of our sources, and from to-ing and fro-ing on the evidence. This work, however, is unabashedly presented as a scientific treatise and thus requires a bit more care with the evidence base than does, say, a newspaper column.

A good example of this failure on the part of the authors is their continual insistence that this process is at bottom an evolutionary one, just as much as is any Darwinian process of natural selection. Again, this recurring metaphor is sometimes applied rather loosely, and finally is unable to bear the weight that the authors place upon it. And, of course, the notion of evolution is so very complex that to apply it to the results of computer use seems hazardous in the extreme.[2] Among other issues, it might well be argued that the authors have their causal reasoning incorrect: Perhaps evolution is driving our interest in computers and television.[3]

Another example of a facile romp through controversial terrain is the authors' assertion that a danger facing the Digital Native is computer addiction, particularly to digital games. This is presented as an addiction in the same way as is any other physical addiction like smoking or illicit drugs—an ever more frantic search for an endorphin or dopamine rush.[4] At other times, however, the authors somewhat hedge their positions as when they state: "Many kids and teens may not exactly be addicted but the pull of new technology can cloud their judgment."[5]

Gaming addiction is not, however, according to this work, the only one facing the unwary user; gambling, pornography, online shopping and reading one's email are all examples of addictive behavior. We may need help! And the authors promptly offer it to us. Numerous short assessment devices—brief quizzes—are sprinkled throughout the book, so that we may determine exactly where we are on the spectrum from "no problem" to "get professional help!"

Once again, the authors often refer to scientific studies, though also often referring to online sources of the alarmist variety, without indicating in the slightest the widespread disagreements that such assertions would raise among other, equally well-qualified experts.

For the Digital Immigrant, the picture is even more clouded. These, it is said, have trouble learning to use technology, are reluctant to do so (though they may actually learn to use it faster than Digital Natives once applying themselves because they bring to bear more learning experience in doing so). For these, the authors also have pithy advice ranging from how to use email properly to how to protect their online privacy.

There are other problems in assessing the proper audience for this work; that is, who should read it? The overall voice is quite definitely an authoritative one—Dr. Small is the Director of the Memory & Aging Research Center at the Semel Institute for Neuroscience & Human Behavior and the Center on Aging at UCLA. This might suggest that the authors are in search of a similarly learned audience, but the work is sprinkled throughout with what I came to think of as the "Grey Pages," lengthy text sections formatted in gray blocks. These relate human-interest stories of those trapped, usually, in extreme examples of the problems, which the following material is then going to illuminate. These are so folksy that one expects to meet Dick and Jane at some point, anxiously Googling for Spot, when really all they have to do is whistle for him.

Another odd compromise is that the authors want the authority that comes from citing sources, but not the scholarly impedimenta such as footnote numbers that might scare off a popular audience. The result is that there are no indications on any page that sources are being cited, but if the reader follows in the notes at the end of the book, he or she may (or may not) find a key phrase taken from the text such as, "dubbed digital natives," followed by the source that so dubbed them.[6] This is clumsy beyond belief, and amounts once again to an attempt to chase several disparate audiences at once, with ill success.

So we wind up with several thumbs up on this work. The authors speak with some authority on the brain and learning, and the studies which they refer to, however clumsily, are probably those which will eventually lead us to a better understanding of the impact of computer technology on the human brain.

We also, however, must turn a number of thumbs down (because we are not one audience we are allowed more than the usual number of thumbs). The very interesting observations on the brain and the psychology of learning are larded with sweeping statements and common-sense observations that render any suggestion that the authors ever envisioned any particular audience as itself visionary. But for all its faults, the work treats a serious issue seriously.

Endnotes

[1] I find this concatenation facile simply because it seems to me that the interactivity of the World Wide Web makes it very different from the one-way Television which simply renders its audience necessarily a passive one, aside perhaps, from occasional vigorous swearing at particularly unwelcome content.

[2] One might have expected, for example, some reference to the piece John Hawks , Eric T. Wang, Gregory M. Cochran, Henry C. Harpending , and Robert K. Moyzis paper "Recent acceleration of human adaptive evolution" found at: www.anthro.utah.edu/PDFs/accel.pnas.smallpdf.pdf See also the principle author's weblog at: http://johnhawks.net/weblog/topics/evolution/selection/acceleration/accel_story_2007.html

[3] While this is not argued in Mark Williams' review of Colin Renfrew's recent work, *The Past Within Us*, found in the January/February 2009 issue of *Technology Review*, it seems to me to be one possible interpretation of Hawks et. Al. and Renfrew's work. See William's review on the www at: http://www.technologyreview.com/biomedicine/21841/

[4] Pp. 50-55.

[5] P. 50. See especially p. 52.

[6] P. 209.

Book Review

Hilde G. Corneliussen and Jill Walker Rettberg's Digital Culture, Play, and Identity: A World of Warcraft Reader

View online at: http://bcis.pacificu.edu/journal/2009/01/article.php?id=28

Review by IProfess
Level 70 Druid, Azeroth.

> *Editor's note: The author of this review purports to be an avatar from the on-line game World of Warcraft. He, she, or it has agreed to accept emails forwarded from me at barlowj@pacificu.edu or, of course, with our commenting function, readers can now leave comments following the review. Please note, that as in every case in Interface, the author's opinion are his, hers, or its own and do not represent those of Interface nor those of the Berglund Center at Pacific University Oregon.*

Corneliussen, Hilde G. and Jill Walker Rettberg, (eds.) *Digital Culture, Play, and Identity: A World of Warcraft Reader*. M.I.T. Press, 2008.

As my personal circumstances are somewhat unusual, I feel it necessary to once again introduce myself. I am what many might think of as an "avatar,"—a digital identity in an online role-playing game, the *World of Warcraft* (*WoW*), where I am currently a level 70 Elven Druid. We prefer to think of ourselves as "'Toons," short, of course, for the dreadful Disney equivalent, cartoon.

Unlike many of my kind—we are everywhere—I now think it safe to present myself in TRW (The Real World, laugh out loud) as, in fact, I am. As TRW has grown increasingly "unreal" and the virtual worlds increasingly "real," the distinction has become a blurred one. I have written before for *Interface*[1] and only the dominant unreasoning prejudice against 'Toons prevents me from being named a Contributing Editor, and, I might add, finally being paid.[2]

It is, of course, a great honor for a 'Toon to be reviewing any work published in TRW let alone one published by the M.I.T. Press. Julian calendar year in and year out, this press in TRW consistently takes games and game playing most seriously.[3] And this work, as per M.I.T's tradition, is a most valuable one, though not without flaws.

There are currently more than ten million gamers real worldwide who live partially in TRW and partially in the massively multiplayer online role-playing game WoW. There are also many millions more 'Toons like me, who, while preferring the relatively orderly *World of Warcraft*, where at least you know who your enemies are and there is a direct relationship between work and return, occasionally cross over into TRW for amusement, if nothing else.[4] I had hoped from the subtitle of this work, as I am sure those millions will as well, that it might be a useful accompaniment to the "game."

The book does have tremendous merit. Its editors, Hilde G. Corneliussen and Jill Walker Rettberg, are Associate Professors of Humanistic Informatics at the University of Bergen, Norway. As I am myself essentially a bundle of Humanistic Informatics, this seemed to me a most promising intellectual venue from which to review our joint interest, the intersection between *The World of Warcraft* and TRW.

However, the book has two different origins (or in *WoW* we might say Quest Lines) from which it developed. One was a guild (a league of self-selected players), "The Truants," in *WoW*. This group of researchers came together in 2006 to share experiences and to conduct research. All the contributors are guildies in The Truants.

Their personal involvement in the game led most of the contributors to take advantage of the many tools that an online role-playing game can offer participant-observers. These include distributing questionnaires and engaging in interviews with other players. This led them to a surprisingly deep understanding of the game. It is also probable, however, that many of the authors, like myself, are 'Toons crossing over in what, I fear, is a vain attempt to enlighten TRW.

The editors and contributors aim their thirteen chapters squarely, as is so often the case in academic grinding, at themselves: "academic scholars and students of game studies and other disciplines dealing with digital culture."[5] The book is divided into four sections, "Culture," "World," "Play," and "Identity." Each has two to four chapters of sometimes-uneven contributions. I restrict myself henceforth to praising rather than blaming as each section includes meritorious chapters, well worth any 'Toon's time.

For me, as the ultimate insider, the test of a work such as this is whether or not it teaches me something about my environment and myself. Many chapters did so. My personal favorite was Jessica Langer's piece, "The Familiar and the Foreign: Playing (Post)Colonialism in *Worlds of Warcraft*." In this piece, Langer takes on the game designers for some of the odd parallels they draw between TRW and specific races and game areas in Warcraft. She is, I think, quite correct that for the designers to model upon the familiar in TRW necessarily simultaneously incorporates the tendency of TRW to introduce by way of contrast, "The Other."

While I am personally sympathetic with Langer's argument that Blood Elves (members of the sinister Horde faction, as opposed to the forces of light, the Alliance, to which Night Elves like myself belong) are "analogues to drug addicts..."[6] I do believe that only those most familiar with the history, lore and legends of Azeroth could possibly see any truth in this position. Like all academics, Langer is capable of so much abstraction—I will not use the word *reification*,[7] though it is a favored and trenchant academic criticism—that she produces truths so distant from reality as to sometimes court, at the least, an ironic response if not, ahem, outright parody.

The relationship between cyber death and real death grows ever closer in the real world. We now have virtual sites memorializing the passing of mortals, and demonstrations in TRW asking for protection of species endangered in Azeroth.[8] This melding of the "real" and "virtual" worlds itself illuminates a critical divide between essentialists and phenomenalists in Azeroth (see note [4] below). I therefore found Lisabeth Klastrup's contribution "What makes *World of Warcraft* a World? A Note on Death and Dying" thought provoking.

Lisabeth models a useful participant observer approach, deeply imbedded in the game itself and in the subjective experiences of the many players with whom she had discussions. Simultaneously, these are informed by a wide variety of academic theories and practices. Any of us, whether gamer, 'Toon, or skeptical academic, can learn much about death and dying, in TRW or virtual worlds, from her article. Woot, Lisabeth!

If the first strand from which the book develops—membership in The Truants—the requirement that contributors actually play the game has had positive results, it also has a dark side. The title of the guild itself betrays some participants' unease at playing a game when they should have been "working" in TRW.

For this group, there was necessarily a second quest strand—simply playing the game would not have lured them to write. This second strand was a workshop held in Bergen in 2006.[9] This gave the contributors a face-to-face connection in TRW, and let them play at academic games in a convivial space, wearing nametags with their academic titles, attending no-host bars, presenting papers to which only they themselves listen and potentially no one reads, exchanging scholarly pedigrees, etc. Unfortunately, the conference also required that each participant have at least one avatar who could pass in Meatspace, as we sometimes refer to TRW.

This latter strand has led to some unevenness in the work. It suggests, not a finely tuned guild raid, but rather a PUG (pick-up group—a collection of unaffiliated volunteers, including some Noobs [new players] and Losers [same usage as in TRW]). Some contributors are dedicated to a closer understanding of the game, others merely to getting published. Their approach is often dry and rather lifeless, sometimes failing to convey the essence of the gameworld, its ludic qualities. This, however, is an inevitable consequence of the grinding practices that those living largely in academic Meatspace must rely upon to increase their rep (reputation) with peer groups.

We promised above that we would not dwell upon the negative here, but a brief discussion to demonstrate the dilemma in which the academic rep grinders are caught might be useful. The lead-off chapter, by Scott Rettberg, "Corporate Ideology in *World of Warcraft*," begins with a typical non-gamer's question: Why do you spend so much time playing this game when you might rather, (as Scott suggests by way of reasonable alternative!), have read James Joyce for the fourth time?[10]

Rettberg then goes on to point out how players will spend hours securing game items that, to him, have no "real" value. His acerbic statement is: "While no one I know would be motivated to work for more than a day or two by the prospect of purchasing a new pair of trousers, *World of Warcraft* players will happily put in dozens of hours of labor in order to acquire a particular pair of magic pants."[11] Scott would do well to raise his understanding of the varied definitions of "value" in the Dismal Science of Economics, and he might also think deeply upon the meaning of the word "happily" as quoted above.[12] Basically, Scott, like some other contributors, though he is far the most obvious in this, thinks of online gaming as the pastime of nitwits and incompetents who would be better off grinding out an academic career; that is, being paid for studying the behavior of nitwits and incompetents.

His central position is:

> I will argue here that though the world Blizzard has created offers an engaging gameplay experience and is not without some visual beauty, wit, and narrative subtlety, the principle reason why Blizzard has been able to build such a large and devoted audience for their flagship offering is because it offers a convincing and detailed simulacrum of the process of becoming successful in capitalist societies.[13]

This remarkable conclusion requires some explanation and it, too, has to do with one of the recent favored tropes of academia: "Border Crossing." This is the semantic cover whereby academics transgress the traditional boundaries of their fields in order to say something sensible about an area such as gaming that is new, at least to them. The remarkable success of gaming as an industry and as a pastime has made it possible for 'Toons to cross over and pose as academics. Sadly, however, some academics are simply unable to surrender their real world status and take the plunge by crossing into the virtual world.

This is true, I understand from academic friends at *Interface*, because writing about games—Border Crossing—is a hazardous business in the Meatspace of academia. To *enjoy* your subject might be taken as an indication of loss of perspective, for which the best anodyne is a slashingly critical and intellectually superior stance. Any academic committee trying to assess the merits of a contribution to this work would, after reading Scott Rettberg's piece, be reassured that the work takes popular culture purely as subject, not as an attractive object. And in addition, it bashes capitalism! That committee might then grant the academic equivalent of gaming experience points, eventually redeemable for a pair of magical academic pants, or in TRW speak, a tenure tracked job.

Many other examples like that quoted above can be found in the work, which may well set upon edge the teeth of gamers and 'Toons alike. Fortunately, the contributions of the work are far more representative of those of Langer and Klastrop than of Rettberg. This work should be included in the library of any reflective gamer, 'Toon, or academic interested in this area. It is also very often amusing to read, though perhaps it has been more so to write about it.

Endnotes

[1] See my piece "The Tales of Azeroth" (http://bcis.pacificu.edu/journal/2005/03/iprofess.php) and "Toons and Terrorism" (http://bcis.pacificu.edu/journal/2008/04/iprofess.php) See too my books reviews, the first of R. V. Kelly 2's *Massively Multiplayer Online Role-Playing Games*, (http://bcis.pacificu.edu/journal/2008/01/kelly2.php) and Edward Castronova's work, *Synthetic Worlds, The Business and Culture of Online Games* (http://bcis.pacificu.edu/journal/2006/01/castronova.php).

[2] *Editor's note, preceded by a long-suffering sigh: As the author refuses to present verifiable identification which would permit us to properly account for any payments, he, she, or it cannot legally be paid.*

[3] In the pages of the esteemed e-journal Interface in which I now write, for example, a number of their works have been reviewed. Perhaps the work most similar to the one under review is: Raessens, Joost and Goldstein (eds.) *Handbook of Computer Game Studies*. Cambridge. MIT Press, 2005., found at http://bcis.pacificu.edu/journal/2006/05/raessens.php.

[4] I ignore here the raging debate in Azeroth on Essentialism v. Phenomenalism, led respectively by the Night Elves (including myself) and the Blood Elves. Like all essentialists, I hold that we exist independently of the game, as demonstrated by my existence in TRW. The Blood Elf warlock-philosopher SansCoeur, (she must be engaged in deep thinking a great deal as she is very low ranking indeed!) however, insists that we exist only when we are, as she puts it, "being played." When asked how, then, *I write*, she dismisses this as just another tiresome variant on TRW Cartesian fallacy! If I catch her in a PVP mode, I will quickly unbundle her...but this debate is perhaps a topic for a special issue of *Interface*. (*Editor's note: Unlikely, but interested readers might submit proposals!*)

[5] P. 3. I do hope that none of my readers see any conflict in the manner in which I cast Spells of Aspersion at academic grinding while incorporating notes here.

[6] P. 89.

[7] Wikipedia, http://en.wikipedia.org/wiki/Reify

[8] The New Revelation—known in TRW as the expansion pack, "The Wrath of the Lich King"—even has an amusing quest series tied to the concerns of People for the Ethical Treatment of Animals, http://www.peta.org/ One hopes that mammoth and rhinoceros 'Toons are not permitted to cross over at random, though I think the American Congress might actually benefit from a few such incidents.

[9] P. vii.

[10] P. 20.

[11] P. 27.

[12] Joyce is, of course, himself a 'Toon, one of the founders of essentialism in Azernoth. I discussed this issue as best I could with him in his current chosen virtual form, an ancient Forest Walker, creaking around Darnassus. His Darnassusian accent, and what I must admit is, I think, habitual drunkenness, makes him somewhat hard to comprehend, but I understood him to advise Scott to "get a virtual life."

[13] P. 20.

Editorial

Tonto and the Big Banks

View online at: http://bcis.pacificu.edu/journal/2009/01/article.php?id=29

Editorial by Jeffrey Barlow

Given our very broad audience for *Interface*, I am reluctant to presume knowledge of even an iconic joke on the part of all our readers, so here it is:

> *The Lone Ranger and Tonto were out righting wrongs on the plains when they were suddenly surrounded by hostile Indians. The Long Ranger said: "Tonto, we could be in big trouble here!" Tonto replied, "What do you mean 'we,' White man?"*

This is the way I have begun to feel about the large American banks. I know that we are joined at the checking account, the savings account, the CD, my retirement portfolio, the stock market, the social security system, etc., but I am beginning to feel curiously distant from them.

I am, of course, well aware that many large American corporations choose to do some of their banking in the Bahamas, now that the Swiss are ratting out even their best clients. I am thinking such havens might be worth exploring for myself. I am even wondering if perhaps I would rather have a RMB (Ren Min Bi, Chinese currency, steadily appreciating) vs. a dollar account (American currency, steadily depreciating relative to the RMB).

This is a recent phenomenon for me, though I admit to being somewhat prejudiced by my mother's experience in 1929: Colleen Garrigus very proudly put her first check earned as a beginning teacher into the local bank, which promptly closed its doors--she barely made it out of the bank before it collapsed. She felt, not unreasonably, that the nice man in the three-piece suit who opened the account for her might have quietly advised her to go someplace else.

Colleen, of course, was not the only victim of the Go-Go banking practices of the nineteen twenties. Her father had made a decent living operating a hotel and a local tavern near the railroad depot until prohibition. As a tavern keeper, he had met more than a few highly suggestible men who were willing to join a local social club for which he was a paid recruiter, an office known quaintly as the "Kleagle" by said social organization, the Ku Klux Klan. Granddad, already highly alienated by the loss of his core business selling alcohol, rounded up some of the satisfied clientele from his sideline, bootlegging.

Colleen, it seemed, was not the only one upset with the nice man at the bank. A drunken mob, some festively attired in white hoods and robes, paid him a visit, toting what Colleen probably preferred to think of as a visual aid--a rope tied in a hangman's noose. The banker, anxious to avoid yet another heated discussion of his business practices, jumped out the second floor window, breaking his leg. The mob decided he had suffered enough and returned to their social activities, a win-win for granddad.

I am not counseling a return to such local traditions, but simply saying that many of us have memories of earlier economic downturns or recessions (Are we using the "D" word yet?) and may be inclined to view with a jaundiced eye such reports as this one from the January 17 *New York Times*:

> Two weeks after closing its purchase of Merrill Lynch at the urging of federal regulators, the government cemented a deal at midnight Thursday to supply Bank of America with a fresh $20 billion capital injection and absorb as much as $98.2 billion in losses on toxic assets, according to people involved in the transaction.
>
> The bank had been pressing the government for help after it was surprised to learn that Merrill would be taking a fourth-quarter write-down of $15 billion to $20 billion, according to two people who have been briefed on the situation, in addition to Bank of America's rising consumer loan losses.
>
> The second lifeline brings the government's total stake in Bank of America to $45 billion and makes it the bank's largest shareholder, with a stake of about 6 percent.
>
> The program is modeled after a larger one engineered to stabilize Citigroup as its stock price plummeted in late November, but it appears to have had limited success. Under the terms, Bank of America will be responsible for the first $10 billion in losses on a pool of $118 billion in illiquid assets, including residential and commercial real estate and corporate loans, and that will remain on its balance sheet.
>
> The Treasury Department and the Federal Deposit Insurance Corporation will take on the next $10 billion in losses. The Fed will absorb 90 percent of any additional losses, with Bank of America responsible for the rest.
>
> In exchange for the new support, Bank of America will give the government an additional $4 billion stake in preferred stock. It has also agreed to cut its quarterly dividend to a penny, from 32 cents, and accept more stringent restrictions on executive pay.[1]

Even my addled grandfather could do the math on this one:

- Bank of America receives up front: 45 billion dollars
- U.S. government (us!) agrees to absorb up to 98.2 billion dollars in potentially bad loans from the deal which gave B. of A. Merrill Lynch.
- U.S. government (us!) receives additional 4 billion dollars in preferred stock.
- Bottom line: B. of A. gets 45 billion dollars up front, a potential additional 98.2 billion dollars. We get 4 billion dollars in preferred stock at a possible cost of 143.2 billion. But wait, there's more! The nice men also agreed to accept "more stringent restrictions on executive pay."[2]

This latter consideration my grandfather would probably refer to as "a pig in a poke," to which Colleen would probably sweetly reply, "More like pigs under a TARP don't you think?"[3]

On the surface, this looks like using public funds to pay for the expansion of a major bank which just swallowed up another major firm in a deal that--surprise!--less than two weeks later turns out to have been a very bad investment. However, I am sure that there is a big picture here that I just am not competent to understand.

I recently, however, got some personal experience of another financial impact of the Internet, which I can understand. I love banking online--it makes me feel invested, globalized, and as though I know what I am doing. This is particularly true since my daughter began attending graduate school in Beijing. I am able to move funds around with abandon, covering her many overdrafts at lightning speed.

I recently needed to transfer 200 dollars to her account and, finding myself awake at 3:00 a.m. wondering how I could get in on the Bank of America deal, or perhaps one like it, even if with a lot fewer zeros, I went downstairs to move the funds.

I had 1,400 dollars in the checking account, another 150 in the savings account, and by my calculations, checks outstanding for less than 1,500 dollars. The safe thing would be to have transferred the savings into the checking, then moved the 200 into Clare's account. However, I was moving only 200, had 1,400 on hand, and intended to go in first thing the next day and move one thousand from another bank by hand.

The next day, I did so, asking for a balance following the cash deposit. I had 740 dollars in the bank following a deposit of one thousand! Hmm...this didn't add up, or subtract, either. Cowed by the awareness of all the clerks at the counter that I was the senior representative of a family of overdrawers, I slunk back to my computer.

The figures I had viewed at 3:00 a.m. had changed! Even the earlier sequence of checks paid and moneys deposited had changed. The 1,300 check I knew to be outstanding had been deducted! Then the two additional smaller checks! Then the 200 transfer to my daughter's account! The bank, sometime after 3 a. m., had cleared first the 1,300 and then the larger of the two additional outstanding checks and then the 200 transfer itself. The final result was two overdraft charges.

The electronic register had indicated that I had 1,400 available and no checks had cleared as I transferred, instantly, the funds to China. But what I had taken to be electronic representations of reality turned out to be only virtually reliable.

I went into see my friendly personal banker--a very talented and invariably helpful person who has been indispensable in keeping my daughter in funds in Beijing. I related the above sequence of events and said that it appeared to me that the sequence of deposits and clearances had been manipulated so as to overdraw my account as quickly as possible. Had, for example, the two smaller checks plus the transfer been cleared first, then the large check, I would have owed only one overdraft charge rather than two. It also seemed odd to me that checks written many weeks apart all cleared just at the only moment that they would overdraw my account.

I was informed that it was the bank's policy to clear the largest checks first, then smaller ones. "So as to generate more overdraft charges?" I inquired..."Yes!" was the reply.

This made me reconsider my daughter's overdrafts. In addition to being vulnerable to similar creative manipulations of the clearance order of her deposits and withdrawals, she also faces the lag caused by the difference in time zones. She is dealing with two banks, one Chinese and one American, each with the ability to manipulate her accounts--and each with access to her past records, showing when funds are likely to arrive and depart.

It is probable that even with the best intentions she could not keeps those accounts in balance. Obviously, the smart thing would be to keep a large cushion in the account, but that in turn means leaving funds vulnerable in an account in China, where the cloning of ATM cards is much more sophisticated than, say, Bank of America's due diligence before swallowing up Merrill Lynch.

I think the only fair thing here is for the federal government to bail me out, and my daughter, too. If not a bail out, then how about restoring some of the regulations that formerly protected us from deceptive financial practices, extortionate and uncontrolled interest charges, credit granted so easily that infants and family pets could get cards,[4] and many similar operations that could be named?

We are not, unlike B. of A., too big to be allowed to fail. But, like many other American consumers facing overcharges, constantly fluctuating credit card rates, declining property values at the best, and home foreclosures at the worst--we may collectively be too alienated to be allowed to fail.

Otherwise, Tonto's reply could become more like the anvil chorus...

Endnotes

[1] Story, Louise, Eric Dash and Andrew Ross Sorkin. "Bank of America Posts Loss as It Gets New U.S. Aid," *The New York Times*, January 16, 2009. http://www.nytimes.com/2009/01/17/business/17bofa.html

[2] http://www.nytimes.com/2009/01/17/business/17bofa.html

[3] TARP = Troubled Assets Relief Program. To see how some banks are utilizing the federal funding, see Mike McIntire "Bailout Is a Windfall to Banks, if Not to Borrowers" *The New York Times*, January 17, 2009 http://www.nytimes.com/2009/01/18/business/18bank.html?_r=1&hp As McIntire relates: "At the Palm Beach Ritz-Carlton last November, John C. Hope III, the chairman of Whitney National Bank in New Orleans, stood before a ballroom full of Wall Street analysts and explained how his bank intended to use its $300 million in federal bailout money. "Make more loans?" Mr. Hope said. "We're not going to change our business model or our credit policies to accommodate the needs of the public sector as they see it to have us make more loans."

[4] See: http://www.goofball.com/news/200402041001; see also http://www.beingpeterkim.com/2006/08/my_dog_gets_res.html

March 2009 - Volume 9, Issue 2

Articles

- **Feature: Maria Walters** - What's up with Webcomics? Visual and Technological Advancements in the Transition from Print to Screen
- **Education: Mark Szymanski** - Google Goggles: The Dawn of Distributed Cognition for Educators Part 1
- **Health: Shawn Davis and Casey F. Davis** - Does this avatar make me look fat? The Internet and Body Image
- **Corporate Education: Tom Cockburn** - Workplace Learning: A Case of Firewalls Replacing Office Walls?
- **Correspondence from Japan: Chris Pruett** - The Sound of Settling

Book and Site Reviews

- **Ronald Deibert's** *Access Denied: The Practice and Policy of Global Internet Filtering*
  Review by Jeffrey Barlow
- **Robert Latham's** *Bombs and Bandwidth: The Emerging Relationship Between Information Technology and Security*
  Review by Jeffrey Barlow

Editorial

- "Mai Duoshao Qian-How Much Is That (Mine, Mill, Refinery, Factory)????"

Feature

What's up with Webcomics? Visual and Technological Advances in Comics

View online at: http://bcis.pacificu.edu/journal/2009/02/article.php?id=37

By Maria Walters

Comics are a serious business. With the advent of the Internet, a range of authors and artists began to realize the potential of publishing their own works without printing costs or production chains. Comic creators were no exception. According to Wikipedia, the first webcomics were published in the mid-to-late '80s, and the industry has been growing ever since [1]. The transition from print to the Internet allowed comic authors to explore new art styles and create genres aimed at more specific audiences. Soon, artists began to stretch their limits, and many realized the variety in shapes, sizes, and colors available in online comics. Experiments with Flash and other navigation methods led to comics which appear to zoom in toward the reader or interact with other panels. In this, the first of a series about the evolution and variety of webcomics, I will show you how diverse the webcomic world really is. Click on any image to see

its original context and read more like it!

What is a Webcomic?

Surprisingly, many people use the term "webcomic" in different ways. I consider a webcomic to be a comic originally published on the Internet. This does not include print comics that maintain an online archive (as many now do). I also classify webcomics as works primarily made up of stationary art and text, though the boundary between some interactive display methods and animation is sometimes difficult to distinguish. It can safely be said that at least 15 or 20 thousand webcomics can still be found online. [2] These include everything from stand-alone webcomics, to weekly or even daily comics, whose archives it would take hours or days to read.

What Webcomics Are Out There?

With those kinds of numbers, a reader could never run out of webcomics to read. For someone interested in exploring a thematic or artistic variety, below are a few suggestions. Of course, I am shaped by my own biases, but I have tried to represent a variety of both well-known and up-and-coming webcomics. My hope is that everyone will find a new favorite! For more ideas, check Wikipedia [3] or the blogroll of an interesting webcomic. If you feel that a webcomic is being left out (since a lot are), share a link in a comment below and that comic could be reviewed in a coming issue of *Interface*.

The Genre Variety

With the advent of the Internet, many webcomics were geared toward "geeks" and those few who would be familiar enough with the Internet to use it for entertainment. For that reason, there continue to be many historically well-known comics containing video game jokes, scientific themes, Internet memes, and other "geeky" subjects. These include *Penny Arcade*, by Jerry Holkins and Mike Krahulik, [4] *Ctrl+Alt+Del*, by Tim Buckley, [5] and *PvP*, by Scott Kurtz, [6] all of which feature gaming humor, relatively simple animation styles, a generally newspaper-like layout, and a faithful following. These are also among the most successful webcomics, having survived and evolved for at least seven years. Randall Munroe's *xkcd* [7] also ranks among the well-known "geeky" comics, though it is unique in its range of technical, scientific themes, as well as its minimalist, stick-figure art style.

Questionable Content, [8] created by Jeph Jacques, was originally an indie music comic, though it has gradually evolved away from its roots and into a more narrative drama. Like many webcomics, the storyline is far more "adult" than a children's comic book. Though the story appears to take place in modern times, futuristic technology (including self-aware pet robots called AnthroPCs) keeps the story unexpected.

Fetus-X [9] can be classified as romance horror, making it an example of a comic which defines its own genre. Eric Monster Millikin calls his single-frame comics "disasterpieces," and frequently deals with zombies and the occult. His artistic style is characterized by brilliant colors and whorls—not exactly what one might expect from a horror comic, but it fits.

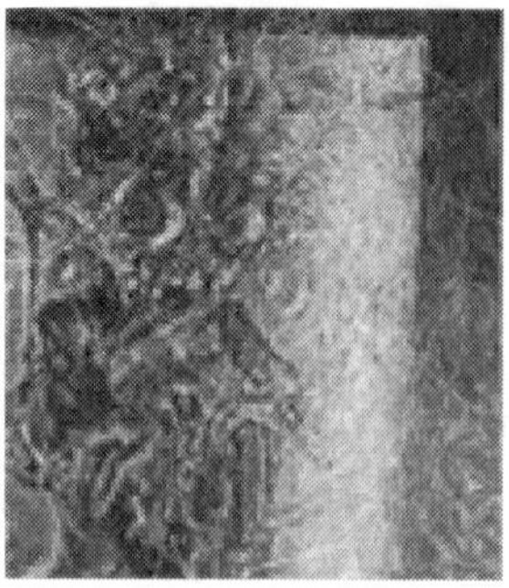

Unsurprising in a world of blogs, *American Elf* is a daily diary comic, which simply depict moments in the life of the author, James Kochalka. [10] His colorful, loose art style allows for the feeling of being in-the-moment, turning his diary into a collage of memories. His family also demonstrates the versatility and accessibility of the Internet: his 5-year-old son now also draws intermittent comics, [11] which are posted to his father's site.

Comics that can be extolled for their artistic qualities abound. In *Phoenix Requiem*, by Sarah Ellerton, [12] the beautiful digital art creates a fantastical, mysterious, Victorian-inspired world. Though it is gorgeous, the artwork does not overshadow the cohesive storyline, especially because the comic is presented as an online graphic novel instead of simply a series of comics.

Some authors take artistic liberties by making their art worse! *Dinosaur Comics*, by Ryan North, [13] is updated daily, but each comic consists of the same 6 pixelated panels, simply updated with different dialogue. Though geeky jokes are often made, the main theme of this comic (if it even has one) is absurd humor.

Webcomics and Technology

Though it can be a lot of fun to be sucked into the ongoing stories created by so many webcomics, what many people don't understand is how much is going on behind the surface. The technology available has made possible interesting developments as webcomics have evolved to be presented on computer screens instead of paper pages. On paper, especially in a book, an author was constrained to a vertical rectangular space in which to tell a story, allowing for transitions between pages. The space given for a newspaper-published comic was even more limited—in general, it consisted of a horizontal row of 3 or 4 panels.

On the computer, on the other hand, comics are viewed through a window oriented horizontally instead of vertically. Because a user can scroll through a page without disrupting the story, an author has an "infinite canvas," in the words of Scott McCloud, a comic writer and theorist. [14] This canvas not only allows for frames of different shapes and sizes, but also enables the transitions between frames to change, and makes it easier to create a comic containing multiple endings or other non-linear transitions.

Scott McCloud experiments with this concept by creating extra-long comics, which only require the reader to continue scrolling instead of turning a page. He has developed several of these long comics, including an online "graphic novella" featuring his superhero characters from the series *Zot!* This novella is presented in 16 long "pages" which, when printed, would lay approximately 140 feet end-to-end. [15]

Though it is easier and more conventional for readers to scroll vertically, a few comics have also branched into the world of side-to-side scrolling. One interesting example can be found by demian5, in a comic called, *When I am King*. [16]

New techniques have cropped up to make the navigation of comics even easier—for example, the "Tarquin Engine," a Flash-based system developed by Daniel Merlin Goodbrey that is natural to use and especially good for non-linear comics. [17] A list of these "hypercomics" is also available as "The Tarquin Listings." [18] We must note the difference between what the Internet makes possible and what it just makes easier—non-linear comics have existed in the past, including one which was 17 feet long displayed at a comic convention. [19]

Other comics also have different styles of Flash-based navigation, like Scott McCloud's *The Right Number*, in which each frame is nested in the center of the previous ones and, on a click, appears to zoom out (shown above). [20] In John Barber's *Vicious Souvenirs*, because each frame overlaps the previous one, the reader almost has the sensation of watching a movie with speech bubbles, except it will only transition to the next frame when the reader clicks. [21] *Vicious Souvenirs* is unique among Flash-animated comics in that it is updated regularly, instead of being a stand-alone comic.

Many uses of technology do allow for simple yet effective changes that are more often used in weekly comics. In *Year of the Rat*, Cayetano Garza Jr. (cat, to his friends) sometimes uses animations as backgrounds for static characters, mixing media like never before. [22]

Another simple change enabled by the Internet is even more subtle. Alt-text, the text that appears when hovering a mouse over an image, provides a punchline for many online comics, like *xkcd* (shown left)[23] and *Dinosaur Comics* [24] Having an "optional" commentary on a given comic strip would only be possible otherwise for someone sitting beside the author!

These advancements only scratch the surface of what the Internet has done for webcomics. The amount of interaction between artists and their audiences shows how online communities are formed, and artists themselves are found forming longer and deeper relationships. Financing webcomics is a challenge in and of itself, but it has created an opportunity for a variety of responses. These topics (plus more webcomics!) will be covered in the coming months. To suggest a comic or subject, leave a comment below!

Endnotes

[1] http://en.wikipedia.org/wiki/Webcomic

[2] http://www.talkaboutcomics.com/blog/?p=766, http://www.charlestoncitypaper.com/gyrobase/Content?oid=oid%3A36337

[3] http://en.wikipedia.org/wiki/List_of_webcomics, http://en.wikipedia.org/wiki/Webcomic

[4] http://www.penny-arcade.com/comic/

[5] http://www.ctrlaltdel-online.com/comic.php

[6] http://www.pvponline.com/

[7] http://xkcd.com/

[8] http://questionablecontent.net/

[9] http://www.fetusx.com/, formerly http://www.serializer.net/comics/fetusx.php

[10] http://www.americanelf.com/comics/americanelf.php

[11] http://www.americanelf.com/comics/monsterattack.php

[12] http://requiem.seraph-inn.com/

[13] http://www.qwantz.com/

[14] http://www.scottmccloud.com/1-webcomics/index.html

[15] http://www.scottmccloud.com/1-webcomics/zot/index.html, http://www.scottmccloud.com/1-webcomics/index.html

[16] http://www.demian5.com/index-e.php

[17] http://www.webcomicsnation.com/tarquin/

[18] http://www.webcomicsnation.com/tarquin/listings/series.php?view=archive&chapter=208&name=listings&line=229

[19] http://e-merl.com/pocom.htm

[20] http://www.scottmccloud.com/1-webcomics/trn-intro/index.html

[21] http://www.moderntales.com/comics/vs.php

[22] http://www.magicinkwell.com/?p=101

[23] http://xkcd.com/

[24] http://www.qwantz.com/

Education

Google Goggles: The Dawn of Distributed Cognition for Educators Part 1

View online at: http://bcis.pacificu.edu/journal/2009/02/article.php?id=38

By Mark Szymanski

Pacific University Oregon

Singing "Happy Birthday" to a ten year old who has been at the forefront of economic and social change since birth sounds like the opening line from a science fiction novel about a prodigious young cybernetic organism who mashes up the natural and cyber world. But when you find out that the name of this ten year old is Google, it all seems to make sense.

What Just Happened? In his book *What Just Happened?* [1] James Gleick [2], the noted physicist and scholar, compiled articles he had written about the information revolution's first 10 years--the last 10 years of the 20th century. Fundamentally, the Information Age came about because a critical mass of people realized we had access to information via the Internet. They quickly learned how to connect with each other in new virtual ways that led us to change how we access, create, and share information. As Gliek states, "The last decade of the twentieth century came as a surprise."

I would add that the first eight years of the 21st century have come as a surprise as well, with Google providing the surprises. For educators, the surprise has meant rethinking how we, access, create, and share information that has traditionally been in hard copy format. Whether it's papers we are writing; books and articles we are reading; videos we are watching; or audio we are listening to, Google has given us the option of creating, accessing, and storing almost anything in a digital format. Of course this has been happening in earnest for years, but what gives Google credibility is that they have created services and tools to do this that are, stable, integrated, and free.

This is an important change for schools and universities that could and are taking advantage of the services and tools Google offers. Educational institutions haven't become famous for their ability to develop and change quickly. Historically, they have been at best second or third phase adopters of new technologies. This has saddled them with the problems of old technologies' maintenance, management, and training. By taking a fresh look at the services Google offers to them, some fundamental paradigm shifts can take place. Now is the time to jump in the water! No need to wait.

In *What Just Happened?*, Gleick notes that we are "inescapably connected" and offers a metaphor for how we were being transformed during the Information Age. "We are not yet neurons in the new world brain, yet we have gotten so much in the habit of knowing things, or at least being able to find them out that you get a twitchy feeling that you ought to push a button and pop up the answer." That twitchy feeling Gleick identified years ago has become a conditioned response for some of educators, and a reflex for the younger generation of digital natives. Ten years later, as we shift into the Web 2.0 era, we need to add being able to create and post information to the habit of knowing things.

Cognitive psychologists would characterize this era as one of distributed cognition.

> "Distributed cognition as a theory of learning, is one in which the development of knowledge is attributed to the system of human agents interacting dynamically with artifacts, and has been widely applied in the field of distance learning [3], especially in relation to Computer Supported Collaborative Learning (CSCL)[4] and other computer-supported learning tools. Distributed cognition illustrates the process of interaction between people and technologies in order to determine how to best represent, store and provide access to digital resources and other artifacts." [5]

During the Information Age, the conditions were different as Microsoft staked its claim on the technology frontier. The lack of web-based applications, fast and readily available access to the Internet, and servers to store content, locked users to their desktop computers. This didn't work well for educators whose desks and lecture halls presented a stark contrast to the digital world.

But as educators rethink how to use technologies in their teaching and learning, one company seems to keep getting it right--Google. Why do they keep getting it right, and what are they doing for educators? These are the two questions I will try to answer in a series of articles I've tagged with the idiom: Seeing the World Through Google Goggles.

- Part 1. Google Goggles
- Part 2. Google Docs & Sites
- Part 3. Google Books & Scholar
- Part 4. Google Earth

As a professor of education who works with k-12 students, undergraduates, and graduate students, I've been able to watch students integrate Google services into their practice. It's a way of thinking, a culture or a habit of mind that is distinctly distributed cognition. So, why is Google facilitating this and why is it making sense? There are number of reasons all of which come from the ability to set and see trends.

Google had the vision to understand that for most users, operating systems and software were on a trajectory leading to failure. The first sign was software bloat. In my experience, 90 percent of my students and colleagues use 10 percent of the features available to them in the software they use most often. This understanding is the foundation of the next article in the series on Google Docs and Google Sites. Google seized on the opportunity to move back to the essential tools 90 percent of users use. The other 10 percent of users will always be able to use software that has more features, a fact Google seems to understand. In addition, the operating system upgrades had the same characteristics. Most educators never really needed or used the added features. Of course, operating system development and upgrades need to happen regularly to reflect the changes being made with software, protocols and security, but most educators find that using an operating system for five years suites them just fine. From Google's perspective, they are more concerned with the development of browsers, the gateways to the Internet.

Free from old economic models that relied on customers purchasing software, Google's economic model relies on users using services. The more information users provide to Google, the more ways Google can use that information to increase their profits. The motive of the models stays the same, profit, but the method changes. It seems counterintuitive; provide the same software/services for free. When these changes occur, they are often harbingers of paradigm shifts. It's an economic shift, but also a user shift.

The pagerank algorithm and the wisdom of crowds continue to be the source of distributed cognition for Google and with the development and distribution of services and tools that educators can easily use; the ranks of the crowds seem sure to rise.

At the end of *What Just Happened?*, Gleick gives a glimpse into the future:

> The Internet is not a shopping mall, and, for that matter, the World Wide Web is not the Internet. The reader will see that I never put faith in the dot-com boom; nor am I troubled by the dot-com crash. I believe that access to the network must be universal, for the sake of social health and political sanity. Like water, like electricity, like mail, the tools and standards of the digital world must be open and public. [6]

It is under this spirit that Google has moved forward and has attempted to leverage the wisdom of crowds. Leveraging the wisdom of crowds at schools and universities whose members often work in solitude, reading books and academic articles, or writing papers might just be able to happen if we put on some Google goggles.

References

[1] Gleick, J. (2002) What Just Happened?. http://www.amazoncom/What-Just-Happened-Chronicle-Information/dp/0375713913/jamesgleick

[2] James Gleick's homepage can be found at http://www.around.com/

[3] http://en.wikipedia.org/wiki/Distance_education

[4] http://en.wikipedia.org/wiki/Computer_Supported_Collaborative_Learning

[5] Brown, Ann L., et al. (1993). "Distributed Expertise in the Classroom." *Distributed Cognitions: Psychological and Educational Considerations*. Ed. Gavriel Salomon. New York: Cambridge UP, 188-28.

[6] Gleick, J. (2002) *What Just Happened?*.

Health

Does this avatar make me look fat? The Internet and Body Image

View online at: http://bcis.pacificu.edu/journal/2009/02/article.php?id=39

By Shawn Davis, Ph.D. and Casey F. Davis

The Internet is considered by many to be the next untamed frontier; an uncharted territory rich in opportunity and potential. While this may be true, we travelers often bring to this ever-expanding wilderness many of the beliefs, feelings and attitudes that we hold in our settled lives. This, coupled with the oft anonymous nature of the web, serves to create an online environment wherein individuals can establish online persona that are in contrast to how they view their offline selves. They can create an online image of themselves that can compensate for perceived flaws or other characteristics they consider lacking; essentially perpetuating a disparity between their "ideal" and perceived "actual" selves. Unfortunately, one's perception of this disparity has been linked with a host of potentially negative outcomes.

Body Image

An individual's body image is their perception of their own physical appearance [1]. While we all have an internal representation of our physical self, a marked discrepancy between our body image and an internalized "ideal" body shape can lead to significant dissatisfaction with one's appearance. In an examination of the outcome of such discrepancy, Monteath and McCabe found that nearly 44 percent of women express negative feelings about their bodies (as a whole and in terms of individual body parts) [2]. Also, in a 1997 survey, 56 percent of female and 40 percent of male respondents reported being dissatisfied with their overall appearance [3].

But how does one gain an internalization of an ideal body image? While a variety of factors have been identified including peer evaluation and parental influence, the media has been long considered a primary source for individuals to learn cultural ideals of how one should look. Unfortunately, both male and female representations across a variety of visual media are, for the most part, unattainable. As detailed on the Peel Public Health website [4],

- Body features in the media are enhanced with props, lighting angles, and computer techniques.
- Shapes and sizes are altered.
- Blemishes, freckles, lines, wrinkles, skin folds and any other unwanted features are edited out.
- Body features from photos of different people are combined to create the "perfect" image.
- "Body doubles" are common in films when body parts of lead actors don't measure up to the "perfect" image.

- Photo images can be completely computer generated to fit the look of the day.

A growing body of research indicates that exposure to depictions of enhanced and often unattainable body images has been linked to loss of self-esteem, depression and the development of unhealthy eating habits [5]. According to media activist Jean Kilbourne, "Women are sold to the diet industry by the magazines we read and the television programs we watch, almost all of which make us feel anxious about our weight" [6]. The potential negative effects of unattainable perfection perpetuated through a variety of media outlets are not, however, restricted to females. Boys and men are provided similar unrealistic images of the "ideal" male as often being unrealistically (or at the least, uncharacteristically) tall, handsome and highly muscular [7].

Static Representation

The Internet has proven itself a profitable arena for advertisers [8]. This is no doubt due to the generally low cost of advertising online and the rapidly increasing rates of Internet usage around the world. In North America, approximately 74 percent of the population are reported Internet users (a 130 percent increase from 2000) and approximately 22 percent of the world's population uses the Internet (a 305 percent increase from 2000) [9]. As individuals spend a larger proportion of their daily lives online, they are exposed to an increasing number of images promoting an ideal image of one's physical appearance.

While this is not functionally different from imagery seen in other media, it serves to provide an additional outlet for idealized versions of physical appearance and a larger percentage of our time is spent receiving such messages. Unlike other forms of visual media, however, a particular strength of the Internet is its active and interactive nature. Active advertisement embedded within sites visited is becoming more commonplace and the line between content and advertising is often blurred.

Presentations of idealized body images, however, are not restricted to online advertising. The presentation of a body image that is largely unattainable is commonplace in online gaming and through a host of highly interactive sites such as Second Life [10] wherein the user creates their own representation to the online world.

Active Representation and Identification

Online Gaming

In an online gaming situation, when one controls the activity of a character online, one develops identification with that character, thus enhancing the internalization of characteristics that are represented. In that heroes and heroines, whose activity is controlled by the user, are, for the most part, exaggerated characterizations of idealized body representations, and thus the enhanced identification obtained through active control is potentially strengthened. As such, discrepancy between one's perception of their own physical self and the idealized body image is made all the more clear. The message being that to be powerful, successful and desired one must look like the idealized character (and act like...but that's a topic for another article).

This conclusion has been suggested in research comparing body satisfaction and identification with idealized others. Hofschire and Greenberg found that increased identification with models, athletes and television stars positively correlated with body dissatisfaction [11]. Also, Kansas State researchers found that gamers who viewed very muscular men or very thin women are more likely to feel self-conscious about their own physique. It was further found that simply observing the attractive game character for as little as 15 minutes could negatively impact the way the gamer viewed his or her own body [12].

Avatar Creation

The level of identification seen in manipulation of a character external to oneself is further enhanced in situations where an individual creates a representation of themselves that they control in a virtual environment. Such a representation is commonly called an *avatar*. The development and control of an avatar is a qualitatively more intimate activity than traditional online game play. Researchers investigating the nature of online representation have characterized an avatar as "a body that is as much a representation of self as the corporeal body" [13].

In that an individual actively creates the avatar representation, they are in control of how they want the world (albeit online) to view them. Sites such as Second Life offer an almost infinite number of possibilities of ways that one can create a representation of themselves. One is no longer bound by the limitations of physical representation. The ability to create an idealized version of oneself, however, has the potential for furthering the discrepancy between one's ideal creation and one's reality. For those that are subject to the negative impact of such an explicit distinction in the non-virtual world, the intimacy of identification with one's avatar may very well be exceptionally problematic. What is an attempt to overcome one's negative view of their physical self can easily become a reminder of perceived deficiency.

This is especially true when the line between the virtual world of Second Life and one's physical world interact. There are times when a meeting in Second Life sparks a relationship that individuals carry over into their offline existence [14]. The pressure of revealing one's true self to another met online can easily exacerbate negative feelings that one has regarding their physical self, especially when the creation of their avatar representation was an attempt to overcome perceptions of physical deficiency.

Conclusions

The purpose of this article is not to imply that *all* individuals who engage in online portrayal of an alternate self are likely to suffer from the negative outcomes detailed above. However, it is meant to demonstrate yet another way that individuals are open to a negative self-evaluation that may very well carry with it the impact seen in other forms of idealization, a method that is potentially more influential given the active creation and representation afforded by the Internet. As with many other influences on our conceptualization of self, this is an area that is in need of continued and detailed research.

The Internet remains a frontier rich in opportunity for self-expression. It is, however, a frontier within which we carry our dreams, desires and very human insecurities.

Endnotes

[1] http://en.wikipedia.org/wiki/Body_image

[2] Monteach, S. A., & McCabe, M. P. (1997). The influence of society factors on female body image. Journal of Social Psychology, 137 (6), 708-727.

[3] http://www.psychologytoday.com/articles/index.php?term=pto-19970201-000023&page=2

[4] http://www.peelregion.ca/health/commhlth/bodyimg/media.htm

[5] http://www.media-awareness.ca/english/issues/stereotyping/women_and_girls/women_beauty.cfm

[6] ibid.

[7] http://www.snac.ucla.edu/pages/Body_Image/Body_Image.htm

[8] http://www.articlesbase.com/business-articles/effective-advertising-at-the-lowest-possible-cost-180562.html

[9] http://www.internetworldstats.com/stats.htm

[10] For Second Life site, see: http://secondlife.com/

[11] Hofschire, L. J., & Greenberg, B. S. (2002). Media's impact on adolescents' body dissatisfaction. In J. D. Brown, J. R. Steele, and K. Walsh-Childers (Eds.) Sexual Teens, Sexual Media. NJ: Lawrence Erlbaum Associates, Inc.

[12] Barlett, C.P., & Harris, R.J. (2008). The impact of body emphasizing video games on body image concerns in men and women. Sex Roles, 59, 586-601.

[13] http://www.metaversejournal.com/2008/11/21/avatar-representation-communication-experience/

[14] http://a.abcnews.com/icaught/story?id=3547108&page=1

Workplace Learning: A Case of Firewalls Replacing Office Walls?

View online at: http://bcis.pacificu.edu/journal/2009/02/article.php?id=40

By Tom Cockburn

It is not hard to see that the content as well as the context of learning in all organizations inevitably changes over time. Put simply, you are today dealing with a different generation of people, who have a different set of expectations from their forbearers, as well as different resources. Tulgan (2006), states that Generations X and Y should be viewed as 'perpetual customers' at work, as this is how they have been treated all their lives. Drawing from his research Gen X and Gen Y tend to think like customers and like being treated as customers. So these dispositions they have begs these question as to why they should be treated or act differently at work?

In October 2008, Jessica Marquez, bureau chief for the New York office of Workforce Management, an online HR bulletin, wrote about Best Buy's use of their social networking site in January 2007 for some internal marketing. She wanted to use the site to reach the under 24 age group amongst staff (more than half) to get their views on Best Buy's 401(k) plans then suffering a disappointing 18 percent participation rate. However, retirement was a subject far away from the everyday concerns of the under 24 age group as a rule. But after only 2 months of utilizing social networking sites, the participation in the 401(k) plan reached 47 percent.

Forrester research indicates a shift to greater use of digital media by decision makers, as indicated in the histograms below.

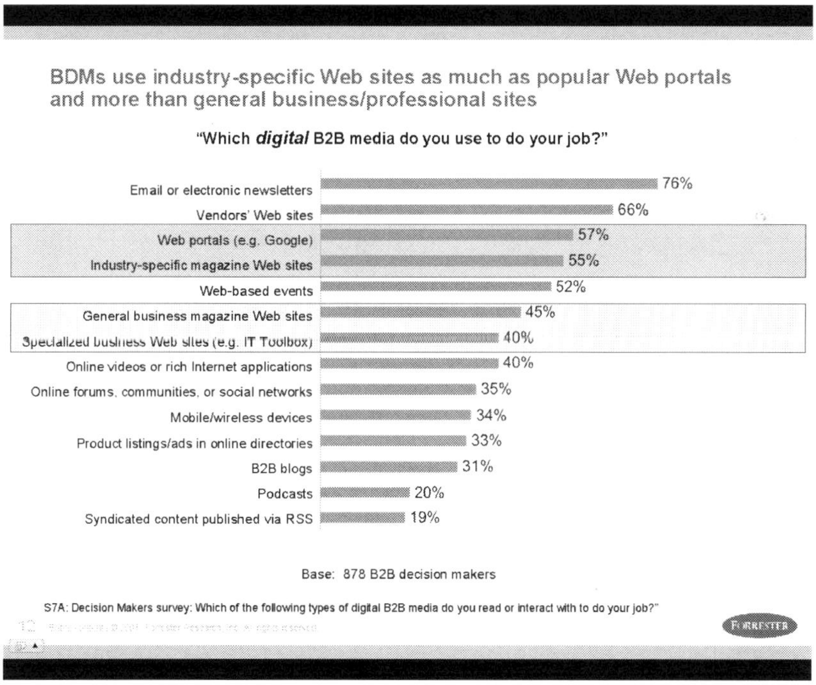

(Source: American Business Media presentation, 2007)

Further, they predict for 2009 that there will be further increases in the use of digital media in businesses as illustrated in the table below:

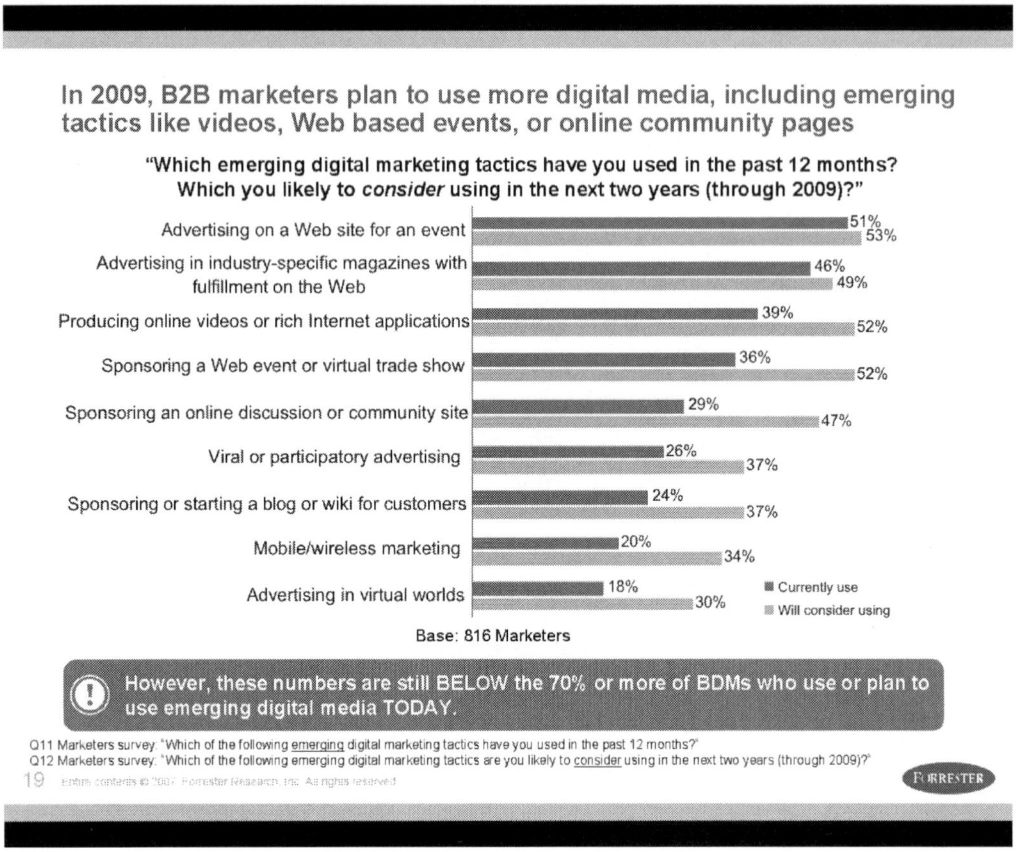

Online Social Networking Has Already Invaded the Business World

Collaboration through the use of Web 2.0 tools is allowing millions of people to share information and experiences in ways never dreamt of before. It is potentially empowering us all to make them easily accessible to others online and, in effect, we are allowed to tap into a collective online 'brain'--some call it an online wisdom but that may be exaggerating at times.

Predictably, businesses are beginning to harness some of the same forces of Web 2.0 for their sales and marketing efforts. From their Web 2.0 experience to date, they see working collaboratively as a means to allow them to better understand and connect with their customers. Ultimately, of course business wants to market and sell their products and services more easily to more people. The technology also should assist in other ways such as outsourcing work or offshoring some routine work, and so reducing costs at home has a downside at times as well as an upside. Jobs may be lost to other countries. Today it has been estimated that in the USA there are more than 40,000 *MySpace* groups devoted to companies or co-workers and 8,000 work-related networks at rival site *Facebook*. Generation Y is in the workforce and massively present amongst consumers, so that means companies have little choice but to adapt, some say.

Professionals, educators and corporate or private trainers need to take account of the needs and aptitudes of the next generation. The technology may be used to add interest to jobs to endeavor to retain the more mobile "knowledge nomads" whose commitment is high when they are engaged in challenging work, but declines rapidly when they get bored and that is when they flit to the next employer. However, in the age of the so-called "knowledge nomads" who are still able to move from company to company even in the current recession, each company has to develop distinct resources to elicit and align employee commitment to a "psychological contract" as well as an employment contract. Each employee has distinct and individual desires and a one size fits all ends up fitting no one. So instead of looking for a single "silver bullet" or panacea for these problems, companies focus on developing the technologies relevant to their own distinct commitment mechanisms, and for managers to identify the appropriate distinctive practices to elicit knowledge nomads' commitment.

Much of this has been developed in an organic rather than a planned and systematic fashion. Thus, as Gladwell (2008) suggests, much of the learning associated with the technology is informal or tacit knowledge residing with enthusiasts and technophiles. To make all of this more systematic and to allow us to build on and enhance these developments we need to fashion ways to communicate and teach that motivate the Gen Y group of students and employees. Others have also suggested there is a need for structural change in education.

The "Education Business" Case

The 2008 Horizon report highlights a number of emerging technologies that reinforce these trends. The report--published annually--suggests that various combinations and permutations of bottom-up, distributed and collaborative forms of technology, social networking and collective data gathering are changing the landscape of learning. The trends towards greater ease of use of the newer technologies available to all means that more people can begin to construct their own materials, and research to share and refine online. The Horizon report identified a number of issues and trends that are important for higher education. For instance, user-created content enablers such as *grassroots video*; *collaboration webs*, which encourage and facilitate sharing and teamwork; *data mashups*, whereby new ways to review and interact with data sets from a variety of sources such as audiovisual as well as textual data is facilitated; and *collective intelligence*, which utilizes the online community to create and edit materials as in the Wikipedia case. These are also increasingly becoming more available in mobile technology applications too.

Should we then also make a leap and begin to shift the learning paradigm and norms of behavior that we use in other organizations, including universities and colleges? A common question from trainers and others at presentations is about how you keep the participants or the staff from messaging or surfing during work or class time. Maybe it isn't how you stop it, but how you *change your own paradigm* to take account of the realization that this is how the new workforce gets things done. We need to let go of some of the older control and compliance models used in traditional workplaces and begin to trust our co-workers to get on with meeting their targets.

We must be careful to avoid metaphorically throwing out the baby with the bathwater of course, and so we also need to maintain security of the firewalls mentioned in the title, as hackers, pirates and viruses also continue to evolve. Fluency in information handling, audio visual and technological literacy is fundamental to democratizing Web 2.0, yet these literacies, related ethics and responsibilities are not routinely taught to most students. Perhaps the explanation for this gap lies in the need for new and expanded definitions of the phenomena. Such definitions must go beyond simply mastering specialized skill sets and uncover key principles and concepts so as to be better able to establish methods for teaching and evaluating these literacies at all levels of education.

It is critical that we develop learning solutions that are tailored to each "type" of learner, not necessarily standardized for each generation. Learners vary across a continuum and the trends are not referring to the outliers on either side of the bell-shaped curve. Gladwell's (2008) book *Outliers* challenges common assumptions about high achievers. He suggests that timing is important and that great leaps can be achieved in performance with practice and technology; this conclusion assumes that underlying intelligence is less salient than others suggest. It builds a case for nurture over nature, attitude over aptitude, but may have overstated the case somewhat in order to challenge conventionally accepted perspectives. He suggests that to avoid squandering the talent (desperately needed in times of crisis and recession as much as boom times) some policy prescriptions are needed. For example, we ought to extend the academic year in the U.S.A. so that US children will begin to achieve at the same levels as Asian children who have a longer school year.

The latter policy fits with his "10,000-hour rule," which states 10,000 hours of diligent practice is needed to be successful in any field irrespective of the individual's intelligence. This, of course, assumes that a lot of other things, such as parenting practices and cultural factors have also changed and there has been a lot of criticism of the stressful, "all work and no play" lifestyle led by many children in high-performing Asian countries too. Other remarks and observations are less controversial such as redesigning the educational system to overcome cultural differences and the luck of the draw, which few would argue against. The redesign has been a feature of many governments and also has a number of difficulties as the "No Child Left Behind" policy advocates have discovered of late.

References

Forrester Research, American Business Media Presentation, 2007 http://www.americanbusinessmedia.com/

Gladwell, M. (2008) *Outliers: The Story of Success*, New York: Little, Brown and Company

Horizon report (2008) Austin,Tx: New Media Consortium and Educause Learning Initiative

Tulgan, B. (2006). *Managing the Generation Mix*, 2nd Edition. Amherst,MA: HRD Press

Correspondence from Japan

The Sound of Settling

View online at: http://bcis.pacificu.edu/journal/2009/02/article.php?id=41

By Chris Pruett

Editor's Note: Chris Pruett has been our Gaming Editor for several years, and has written on a wide variety of gaming topics for a very large audience. As a software Engineer for Google he has recently chosen to transfer to Google's operation in Japan. As Chris is fluent in Japanese and very comfortable in Japanese culture, particularly Japanese cyber-culture, we have agreed with his suggestion that he might begin writing on broader themes from Japan. This initial piece in his "Correspondence from Japan" series sets the daily scene in which he lives....

"The train is about to leave," the recorded voice says. "Please exercise caution." It is a female voice, that of a competent, mature (but no older than 40), trustworthy, woman. The same voice announces the direction of the elevator at my job. "The elevator is going up," it says. A few minutes before the bathtub at my new apartment fills itself, the disembodied female voice reports that the bath will be ready "pretty soon" from a small speaker in the kitchen. Our new vacuum, which we purchased when we moved into our apartment, cheerfully warns us that it will automatically clear the dust filter every time we turn it on. My sister-in-law's car, like many nowadays, complains in the same, smooth, safe voice that she has yet to insert an automatic toll card into the dashboard.

I imagine that somewhere here in Japan lives the Automated Report Voice Woman (ARVW). Having been identified as having the most trustworthy-sounding voice in the country (even when it is played back through low-fidelity equipment), Automated Report Voice Woman has gone on to record thousands of greetings, warnings, and automated messages. I can picture her spending each day in a recording studio saying things like "the phone card you inserted has expired," and "your transaction is complete" into a microphone. In my mind, she is a conservatively dressed, 30-something who might have considered a career in television news if she was not already raking in the dough as Japan's singular Automated Report Voice Woman. Her posture, I assume, is excellent.

But as pervasive as Automated Report Voice Woman's messages are, she cannot hold a candle to whomever it is that records all the jingles here. Japan is full of jingles--little short melodies that indicate everything from when it is the right time to cross the street, to when the rice has finished cooking, to when the garbage truck is about to back up. Sometimes they are well-known tunes; the train station in Okayama, for instance, plays a xylophone version of "I've Been Working on the Railroad" to announce the arrival of each train (the announcement is completed with a short message from ARVW in her normal tone). But usually the tunes that are emitted from microwaves, cars, elevators, automatic doors, and parking garage pay stations are short and unrecognizable riffs, two or three-bar phrases that stick around just long enough to get your attention. They might easily be mistaken for cell phone ring tones if turning a phone on in public was not such a social faux pas here.

While we are on the subject, cell phones are another Japanese paradox. Japan has the coolest cell phones in the world: you can use them to buy things in lieu of a credit card, you can watch broadcast TV on them, you can check train schedules and send e-mail to your friends and even use them to video conference (if you do not mind terrible video quality). Everybody, and I mean *everybody*, has a cell phone in Japan. And yet, *and yet*, actually using your cell phone to call people in many public places is frowned upon. The rules of politeness dictate that talking on your cell phone around other people in any sort of semi-quiet environment (like the train) is off limits. So of course you must keep your phone set to silent mode as well--if people are irritated by listening to you talk on the phone, they are also clearly not going to abide by your 8-bit *Ride of the Valkyries* ring tone. And just in case you forget the no-ring-tone rule, ARVW has a recorded announcement to remind you. Should you be deaf (in which case a ring tone seems pretty pointless anyway), the rule is also posted on the walls of the train car at regular intervals.

Actually, you can learn a lot of Japanese public etiquette from posted signs. In addition to rules about where cell phones may be used, trains have recently begun to carry signs designed to remind you that, for example, second-hand cigarette smoke is irritating to other people. The last time I lived in Japan was in the late 1990s, and during that period I might have jumped to the conclusion that such explicitly articulated social norms are just a modern version of the strict rules that govern traditional ceremony and polite society in Japan. But now I think that the posting of such rules--which are mostly common sense to the average Japanese citizen--is a way to prevent potential offenders from defending their behavior. It is much easier to confront a stranger about their actions in this country if you have the backing of some official rule; with a sign on your side, you can argue that your opinion is that of the majority, and therefore the other party is in the wrong, which is enough to win almost any dispute. Not that people get into public arguments in Japan all that frequently. It is not very cool to draw attention to yourself so explicitly, and the ability to "grin and bear it" is a virtue. But such arguments *could* occur, and if they did the pro-rule side would have the upper hand, so politeness signs act as a deterrent. That is my latest theory, anyway.

Despite having lived in Japan before and having studied the language and culture for close to half of my lifetime, I still find surprises lurking in the details of day-to-day life. Early visits to this country left me awestruck at the different wavelength at which everything seems to operate, but with increased exposure the culture has begun to make a whole lot more sense. Nowadays, the things that I thought were unfathomable a decade ago seem pretty straightforward. Instead, it is the subtle differences, the tiny details, that make sense to the natives but not to me, that I find the most interesting.

Each morning I walk from my apartment to the local train station. Before boarding the train I make sure that my phone is set to vibrate. A cheerful jingle announces the arrival of my train, and as I board the comfortably familiar Automated Report Voice Woman's voice thanks me for choosing this line. On the way, I read a book that has been carefully wrapped in paper by the bookstore so that the people around me cannot tell what I am reading. I disembark at my destination and am simultaneously thanked and cautioned by ARVW's messages playing from different parts of the station at the same time. On the escalator, I remind myself to stand on the side to let others pass. This is Tokyo, so I stand to the left; in Osaka it would be to the right. On the street I pass a kid who is wearing what appears to be a bleached white Russian trooper hat. His shoes have little horns coming out the tips. He is waiting with about fifty other people outside of a pachinko parlor; it seems a new type of machine has arrived and the hardcore players are already queued up. In the lobby of my office building, everybody mysteriously waits in front of a particular elevator door, even though there is no guarantee that it is the one that will open first. On the way home I notice a line extending out the door and down the block at the local KFC; later my wife explains that this is because today is Christmas Eve.

I am in Japan and it makes no sense. I love it.

Book Review

Ronald Deibert's Access Denied: The Practice and Policy of Global Internet Filtering

View online at: http://bcis.pacificu.edu/journal/2009/02/article.php?id=42

Review by Jeffrey Barlow

Ronald Deibert et. al., (eds.) *Access Denied. The Practice and Policy of Global Internet Filtering*. Cambridge, Mass. The MIT Press, 2008.

As we have frequently observed, the impact of the Internet is highlighted for those of us who use it a great deal, when we are denied access to it.[1] But as it has become more pervasive and the world more dependent upon it so has control of the information and services it carries become more critical to the governments of nation states. The result, the work *Access Denied* argues, is that the trend is markedly toward more filtering of the Internet at the state level, and the denial of access to content to increasingly more people. Moreover, it seems that the major obstacle to even more marked increases in filtering practices may be the current inability of many governments to afford to do so.[2]

While almost all states presume the Internet to be a key element in encouraging local productivity and economic growth, it can also be a destabilizing factor. Adverse social and political impacts are obvious in all countries. Currently, *Access Denied* is clearly the most useful text for understanding the many ways in which states have tried to shape those impacts. The specific focus is upon filtering, which many might reduce to the simple term "censorship."

Access Denied discusses the technology of filtering as well as the many legal issues involved, both in general terms in summative initial chapters, and country by country in voluminous regional overviews which fill well over half of the book. These include specific studies of forty countries ranging from Afghanistan to Zimbabwe.

An important part of the work's value lies in the adoption of a standard methodology, which permits comparative evaluations well beyond the usual impressionistic travelers' or journalists' tales. The OpenNet Initiative (ONI) initially organized by scholars at the universities of Toronto, Harvard, and Cambridge conducted large-scale systematic sampling of Internet traffic from *within* specific countries.

The ONI was soon cooperating with many other local and international bodies, enabling the editors to produce what is truly an of encyclopedia of Internet filtering practices, as of the period 2003-2006. Some references are as late as 2007, but, of course, this is a subject which is ultimately tied to the speed of the development of the Internet and its supporting technology. The book will quickly be dated, though one hopes that the group's work will be continued and regularly reported upon.[3]

The approach is somewhat simplistic in that the contributors, while observing that Internet content such as pornography, sexual exploitation and violence are universally condemned as a problem, chose to adopt a sort of libertarian all-or-nothing philosophy. The pervasive attitude of the authors is that the Internet should be fully open, period.

Within this context, all censorship comes to seem itself an attack on human rights, a position taken explicitly in Mary Rundle and Malcom Birdling's excellent chapter, "Filtering and the International System: A Question of Commitment." This chapter presents the best summary I have seen of the evolution and current state of international and local laws bearing upon filtering issues.

The editors can, of course, be excused for not delving repeatedly into such issues as cultural differences in Internet filtering/censorship, though their failure to do so produces very generalized observations. Specific cultural issues in individual countries or groups of societies related by largely common value systems such as Islam or Confucianism are generally ignored. We learn, for example, that Iran is the most thoroughly censored society of those they studied, yet only at the last do we also come to understand that the primary issue driving censorship is the question of fundamentalist Islamic morality and that the sorts of content filtered would probably be objectionable to a good portion of the world's citizenry. Iranians, however, live in a state willing to dedicate itself to attempting to enforce a strict moral standard.[4]

It follows as well that the focus on nation states, however natural it may seem, also obscures important cultural issues. The regional surveys do little to fill this void, as Islamic states, for example, are widely scattered around the world. It would have been more useful perhaps, to substitute for the regional surveys cultural ones: Confucian states, Islamic states, and free-market democracies, among other possible divisions.

The shortcoming of the national state focus becomes particularly apparent when we examine the lengthy Chinese example. In general, China is the quite obvious exception to the notion that economic progress lends itself to the development of human rights. But the model against which Chinese attitudes are measured is implicitly, as is the case in general here, classical Western notions.

The work also misses another important element of the Chinese political system--the widespread cultural agreement in favor of stability and security in the face of potential "luan," disorder. This primary Confucian value is also shared in "Greater China," which might have made a better focus as argued above than the work's "China with Hong Kong." Taiwan, another useful Confucian example, receives no coverage at all, a surprising lacuna given its importance to the production and distribution of computer technology itself.

One of the truly important attributes of the work is the great detail that it offers as to how filtering is accomplished. Murdoch and Anderson's chapter on "Tools and Technology of Internet Filtering" is particularly useful in this regard. The on-site methodology of measuring filtering in a large number of nation states also permitted very useful statements about the wide variety of approaches taken internationally.

Zittrain and Palfrey's chapter, "Reluctant Gatekeepers: Corporate Ethics on a Filtered Internet" deals with the ethical problem that arises "when the corporation is asked to do something at odds with the ethical framework of the corporation's home state."[5] Most of the examples here are from the well-known cases involving Google and Yahoo's accommodation to Chinese filtering practices. Again, however, this analysis neglects an important political dimension, the degree to which such highly publicized events often are as much related to China-bashing as to concerns for individual freedoms.

The hero of the anti-China publicity campaign, for example, is Congressman Chris Smith of New Jersey who conducts annual sponsorship of legislation such as the

Global Online Freedom Act intended to preclude U.S. corporations from selling equipment or services "for the purpose, in whole or in part, of facilitating Internet censorship." For the authors, "The legislation's intent is laudable, to limit the extent to which United States-based corporations participate in censorship and surveillance in other states."[6]

Smith, however, is ultimately a dogged anti-communist who attempts to embarrass such regimes at every opportunity.[7] Underlying his highly ideological approach is his personal opposition to abortion.[8] What the Smith example shows is the difficulty of treating filtering as simply a case of human rights; it is inextricably intertwined with cultural values.

With these caveats, however, *Access Denied* remains the single best source with which to understand the nature and extent of state-sponsored filtering practices.

Endnotes

[1] See Jeffrey Barlow, "When the Internet Goes Away..." at: http://bcis.pacificu.edu/journal/2007/01/edit.php

[2] See for example p. 221.

[3] See http://opennet.net/

[4] It might be well for us to state here that the Berglund Center has itself been a victim of Iranian filtering practices in that they hijacked one of our major journals, *The Journal of History and Computing*. After scraping our site, they then created a pirated site supported, it appears, by systematic manipulation of Google rankings, to the point where the pirate site often outranks our own original, causing many problems for us. See "CYBERJACKED! Again... and Again..." at: http://bcis.pacificu.edu/journal/2006/02/edit.php

[5] p. 105

[6] p. 118.

[7] See the list of legislation which he has sponsored at: http://thomas.loc.gov/cgi-bin/bdquery/R?d110:FLD003:@1(Rep+Smith+Christopher):

[8] See his funding sources at: http://www.opensecrets.org/politicians/pacs.php?cycle=2008&cid=N00009816&sector=Q&seclong=Ideological%2FSingle-Issue&newMem=N

Book Review

Robert Latham's *Bombs and Bandwidth: The Emerging Relationship Between Information Technology and Security*

View online at: http://bcis.pacificu.edu/journal/2009/02/article.php?id=43

Review by Jeffrey Barlow

Latham, Robert. (Ed.) Bombs and Bandwidth: The Emerging Relationship Between Information Technology and Security. New York: The New Press, 2003.

At first glance, it is easy to mistake this work for yet another in the Cyberterror genre: "The Internet: Be Afraid!" More specifically, it is easily mistaken for an example of the subgenre Security Fears: "You have no security. Terrorists with computers are everywhere! Get over it--or give us more power..." Both the title and the subtitle suggest that the work will largely be about the Internet and state conflict, or the cybernetic "military revolution." Happily, this is not the case. In fact, the calm and rational voices of experts such as those who have contributed to *Bombs and Bandwidth* is the best remedy we have for such anxieties.

The work is a project coordinated by the Social Science Research Council. This might lead readers of a certain inclination in turn to think of the authors of the thirteen chapters as predominantly egg-headed liberals. Readers with such presuppositions should begin reading Professor Carolyn Nordstrom's chapter, in which she treks along African smuggling routes despite hardships and dangers appropriate to *Soldier of Fortune* magazine. Such readers, however, might be somewhat disappointed, because the villains she meets are often highly educated and quite capable of fixing their computers, satellite telephones and assorted ICT (Information-Communications Technology) appliances as skillfully as they wield them in bringing their illicit goods onto the world market.

The book is divided into four sections:

Cyber-war and National Security
Surveillance and Security
Digital War-Making
Civil Violence and Information Technologies

Once again these titles raise the specters of the post-9/11 age. However, in each section, at least one chapter is carefully crafted to peel back the facade of common analysis in these subject areas to reveal the underlying sub-structure of the usual self-interested groups.

For example, Ralf Bendrath's chapter, "The American Cyber-Angst and the Real World--Any Link?" in the first section reveals that there is precious little connection between our common fears of digital terrorism and political realities. He shows us that cyber-terror is in part a cold-war substitute in search of a budget as various administrations grope for some attractive--i.e. terrifying--analysis that will keep the cornucopia of public funding flowing. The chapter, like most in the work, is carefully documented and thoughtfully organized.

In section three, "Digital War Making," Chris Hables Gray's chapter, "Perpetual Revolution in Military Affairs, International Security and Information" ties the "elements of post-modern war" to globalization. He believes the search for new forms of warfare to be an effort to avoid facing the underlying reality: war is no longer a useful tool of policy. But a new form of warfare might hopefully, in the views of those whose interests largely depend upon military spending, once again make it so.

The chapters are not all contrarian. We also have those who believe that terrorism merits not only our full attention but also a sacrifice of civil rights and freedoms in a measure appropriate to the sacrifice of the lives lost. This is particularly true of several chapters on security, led off by Dorothy Denning's "Cyber Security As An Emergent Infrastructure." Denning is practically the mother of the field and her very precise prose gives us an excellent overview of its development.

This consistent descriptive precision is one of the most useful aspects of *Bombs and Bandwidth*, and is probably a result of Robert Latham's editorial hand. There is an effective effort to carefully define terminology and concepts in such a way that the chapters, while they rarely touch upon each other, do build a common descriptive structure.

For those wanting a broad survey, which at the same time consists of carefully written and organized studies of relatively narrow topics, this is the book. The work would also be a very useful text in a college or university classroom in any topic area touching upon digitalization or political conflict. With careful reading, it could serve as both an introduction, and as an in depth-analysis of important aspects of a wide variety of related fields.

Editorial

Mai Duoshao Qian-How Much Is That (Mine, Mill, Refinery, Factory)????

View online at: http://bcis.pacificu.edu/journal/2009/02/article.php?id=44

Editorial by Jeffrey Barlow

At the Berglund Center we continue to follow the most recent catastrophic impact of the Internet, the decline of the world economy.[1] This generation of college seniors will graduate in challenging times. For the first time in many decades, frightening terms are stalking the land: bank nationalization, deflation, default, depression, global collapse, to name but a few. Fundamental decisions are before us, even if the decision is simply to follow the middle-of-the-road shibboleth to remain comfortably in the middle of the welter of policy choices confronting U.S. policy makers.

The United States is in a struggle between disorganized reformers, influenced by their own pressure groups, and discredited but entrenched financial interests over the appropriate model for future national economic policy. Each time that Obama sets or even implies standards for bank management, executive bonuses, pubic shares or proposes additional governmental controls, the stock market dives and he has to send in a spokesman to qualify the initiative to the point where no clear policy direction is discernable.

The issues are numerous and broad, but taken together require a reassessment of the basic American model of free-market capitalism. Many in the Obama administration believe that capitalism—as we chose to view it in the late twentieth and early twenty-first centuries at least—is at the end of its utility. The proponents of the Old Time Religion, however, are backpedaling desperately to reaffirm the classical model, or at least to protect those aspects of it which they deem critical, i.e., important to them.

Regardless of the outcome of the back-and-forth between the administration and the Malefactors of Rapidly Diminishing Wealth, to update Theodore Roosevelt's phrase, the traditional model—which I understand to be a fundamentally market-based economy with a minimum of governmental regulation or "interference," is about to be tested in quite a different manner. The Chinese are coming to shop.

China will be shopping in a really big way—possibly a spree as epochal as has been their economic growth—and will seek to purchase, directly and indirectly, a significantly greater share of the world's resources and productive facilities. This reality will challenge free market fundamentalism and American political processes as much as does the specter of bank nationalization.

Not all, or even a majority of items apparently on the Chinese shopping list are U.S. owned. Nonetheless, Americans will face the issue of their commitment to a market economic model. What, precisely, is for sale, and to whom?

There are those who argue that a sale to the Chinese of American real assets is precisely the answer to the Sino-American dilemma in which these two dominant economies are locked in an ultimately destructive relationship. In this relationship, the U.S. borrows from China to keep consuming well beyond its ability to do so; China then in turn continues exporting more than it can without contributing markedly to continued global instability.[2]

There is now an additional problem: the world is increasingly uncertain that American financial instruments are safe, given the precarious condition of the underlying banking structure.[3] This means that even if the U.S. wished to continue to borrow in order to keep the consumption engine turning over, its ability to do so is declining. Or perhaps, equally threatening, it will have to pay far more for the privilege of printing money.

The loss of confidence in financial instruments means that foreigners are going to be much more interested in American real assets, factories, farms, corporations, natural resources, patents, etc., than in promises-to-pay treasury devices. The Chinese, at least, can well afford to buy such assets because the U.S. has paid for its imports with incredible numbers of dollars. And, of course, the current continuing decline in American asset prices, when coupled with a strengthening dollar, *increases* Chinese purchasing power.

It might well be that the U.S., for the first time in a very long period, could balance its books with the Chinese while bringing in large amounts of dollars that would then re-enter the American economy, priming the pump. Troubled firms, spinning off weaker units, nonetheless desirable to the Chinese, would re-achieve stability and have increased resources for expansion or consolidation.

However, such sales, of course, can be wildly problematic. The one point where values most often intrude openly into economic activity is national security. The profit of individuals and corporations is sometimes, if not often, overridden by national interest.

But national interest arguments are so powerful that national security is continuously trotted out for limited partisan purposes, or to give one firm a political advantage over another. The possibility of selling the American oil firm Unocal to Chinese interests in 2005, for example, was stopped on national security grounds.[4] But many analysts felt that the real issue was Chevron's desire to keep the price of Unocal down for their own competitive purposes.[5]

The issue of Chinese purchases of assets perceived as affecting the national interest hit Australia in 2008. Chinese firms purchased a significant interest in Rio Tinto, the world's third largest mining firm.[6] Currently the Chinese are seeking to increase their share, which the firm has agreed to, but stockholders, national security wonks in much of the Commonwealth, and various other groups are objecting strenuously.

These deals point to a disconnect between classical economic assumptions and the bold new world. The business press niggles endlessly about the soundness of the Rio Tinto deal from a business perspective: was it justified, would the BHP Billiton (the world's largest mining company) take-over attempt have been better for the stockholders, etc. But from the Chinese perspective, national policy and national interests naturally guide financial activities. No firm is truly private. Chinese banks are guided by state policy and if it is in the national interests for a firm like the Aluminum Corp. of China to purchase a larger portion of its current partner Rio Tinto, then the money—probably American dollars—is found.

Regardless of the underlying assumptions of the free-market model, it is obvious that some entire industries and many firms are too important for any nation to alienate. These would be protected for reasons of national defense, relative self-sufficiency, because they employ too many people as perhaps does General Motors or Ford, or even out of simple national self-regard. This leaves, however an enormous grey area. Even if we wish to protect "national defense" we still must decide what is truly critical.

The notion of the government selecting "winners" and "losers" has always been abhorrent to free-market economists, and some assets must be protected in the national interest. But to do so safely and effectively requires a systematic policy. This policy should be public and open, unlike today's congeries of public protests and private deals arbitrated by secretive federal panels such as the Committee on Foreign Investment in the United States.[7]

However, if policy follows the usual American political model in which the special interests duke it out, using campaign contributions and various other sordid stimuli for congressional support, nothing good can follow. Moreover, ideological appeals are unlikely to have much success in the environment in which we find ourselves. Foreigners are not going to rush to purchase debt instruments simply because we promise to be well-armed and bridged-to-nowhere, no matter how much the Secretary of State entreats them to do so, as she did in Beijing on February 22, 2009.[8]

There is another reason for considering Chinese purchases of U. S. resources as a broad policy and not as a series of incidents such as the Unocal case, the Rio Tinto case, and many others that could be discussed. Not to do so is to invite a wide variety of interest groups to intervene in each case with maximum impact. Such interests might include religious groups such as Fa Lung Gong and some evangelical Christian churches, human rights groups focused around issues from Tibetan independence to Chinese women's rights, and animal rights groups concerned with everything from dolphins to domestic dogs. Throw into the mix U.S. businessmen and their workers—both groups threatened by either Asian immigration or competition—and the result is a stew from which no policy at all can develop, but rather a series of events which will continuously inflame Sino-American cooperation. And such cooperation is necessary to deal with the world economy, not to mention other stresses stemming from China's rapid and continuing rise as an international power.

For all these reasons, then, we have every reason to expect that we will be hearing more and more the question: "*Mai Duoshao Qian*—How much is that (mine, mill, refinery, factory)????" But without a foundation laid by systematic policy, all possible answers will be divisive, both nationally and internationally.

We must, I think, add yet another to the emerging lexicon of threatening terms such as those with which we began this editorial. To the list of bank nationalization, deflation, default, depression, global collapse, and terrifying others, we must add the grandmother of all scary terms: industrial policy. This suggestion, of course, would cause apoplexy in any number of boardrooms, but to continue to prop up the current system by ad hoc incremental decisions is to risk totally discrediting the capitalist system, particularly if we begin to try to manipulate, once again, public fears for the selfish needs of special interest groups.

Endnotes

[1] To understand why we view this as an impact of the Internet, see: Jeffrey Barlow, "Co-Dependence: The Chinese and American Economies and the World Economic Problem," Interface 7, 2008, at: http://bcis.pacificu.edu/journal/2008/07/article.php?id=16

[2] See above.

[3] See, for example, Wes Goodman and Jody Shenn "Fannie Mae Rescue Hindered as Asians Seek Guarantee" (Update2) Bloomberg.com 2/20/2009 at: http://www.bloomberg.com/apps/news?pid=20601109&sid=azObP8_4deuI&refer=home

[4] For the underlying national security argument see Center for Advanced Defense Studies, "Chinese Unocal bid a security threat, says Senior Fellow" at http://www.c4ads.org/node/164

[5] For this position see Paul Blustein, "Many Oil Experts Unconcerned Over China Unocal Bid" in the Washington Post, July 1, 2005 at: http://www.washingtonpost.com/wp-dyn/content/article/2005/06/30/AR2005063002081.html

[6] See Michael Sainsbury and Sarah-Jane Tasker "Cash-rich China Inc rapidly going global" The Austrailian, Business, at: http://www.theaustralian.news.com.au/story/0,25197,25084364-643,00.html For Bloomberg's analysis see: Rebecca Keenan "Rio Declines, Default Risk Jumps After Chinalco Deal " (Update1) at Bloomberg.com: http://www.bloomberg.com/apps/news?pid=20601089&sid=aoweivcIE_YU&refer=china

[7] See http://www.treas.gov/offices/international-affairs/cfius/ for the agency's home page.

[8] See Paul Richter, "Clinton urges China to sustain U.S. economic support." The Los Angeles Times, February 22, 2009. "We're all in this together, the secretary of State tells Beijing as she makes a plea for the continued purchase (of) U.S. government bonds." At: http://www.latimes.com/news/nationworld/world/la-fg-clinton-china23-2009feb23,0,476137.story

April 2009 - Volume 9, Issue 3

Articles

- **Feature: Shereen Khoja** - An RSS Feed Analysis Application and Corpus Builder
- **Education Assessment: Ayse Kok** - Creative Design Environments: A Small-Scale Case Study
- **Legal: Leonard D. DuBoff** - When Rights Collide
- **Media: Jenn Hernandez** - The Daily You: Personalizing Your Media
- **Education: Steve Rhine** - You Say You Want a Revolution, Well, You Know...

Book and Site Reviews

- **Andrew Vachss's** Terminal: A Burke Novel
  Review by Jeffrey Barlow
- **Bill Vanderbok's** Brown Bag Radio
  Review by Jeffrey Barlow

Editorial

- Using Google Sites, or The Editor's Lament

Feature

An RSS Feed Analysis Application and Corpus Builder

View online at: http://bcis.pacificu.edu/journal/2009/03/article.php?id=47

By Shereen Khoja

Pacific University Oregon

Introduction

This article describes a software application that downloads given RSS feeds and compiles them into a corpus. The user simply supplies RSS feed addresses and the application automatically connects to the feeds, downloads them and strips any formatting tags. The application incorporates the Expat () XML parser to identify the tags in the RSS feeds, and the user has the flexibility to define what they would like to keep and what is to be stripped [1]. The application was tested on a project to analyze Middle-Eastern blogs. Thirty-seven blogs were downloaded using the RSS Feed Analyzer and compiled into a corpus of 131,836 words. Both the RSS Feed Analyzer and corpus are freely available under the GNU General Public Licence.

Motivation

The motivation behind building an application to automatically download RSS feeds is the frustration that I feel working in the field of Arabic Computational Linguistics in the lack of corpus creation and analysis tools. I know that I am not alone in feeling this frustration, and researchers use various ad-hoc techniques to get through this basic step. As quoted by Al-Sulatie and Atwell [2]:

> *".. it is still difficult to use corpus analysis tools such as concordancers in handling Arabic text unless they are used in Arabic windows, and even so the result is not as tidy as in the case of languages with Roman script. Since our corpus will be available on the Internet we hope it would be an interesting challenge for software engineers to develop suitable analysis tools."*

My research in Arabic Computational Linguistics has focused on Modern Standard Arabic, the Arabic used in most of the written forms of the text, as well as the Arabic used by newscasters on television. This form of Arabic is understood by everyone in the Arab world but it is not the form Arabs use when speaking to each other. Instead, they use a colloquial form that differs from country to country, and in fact region to region. An Arabic speaker from Saudi Arabia would have a difficult time understanding the colloquial Arabic being spoken by a speaker from Morocco, and in these situations, both speakers will resort to the Modern Standard form of Arabic. This is known as *Diglossia* in the field of linguistics [3].

It is the colloquial form of Arabic and developing linguistic tools for this form of Arabic that is of interest to me now since research on Modern Standard Arabic is now quite prolific. My first step in investigating colloquial Arabic is to collect a corpus of Arabic blogs.

The growth in blogging has provided language researchers with a new form of writing to investigate various linguistic properties. Examples of this research include: an investigation to determine the mood of a blogger based on the text of a post [4], an analysis of the genre of blogs [5], and the development of an automated trend discovery for blogs [6].

There has been little to no research on Arabic blogs and no corpus of Arabic blogs currently exists. Compiling a corpus of Arabic blogs is the first step in analyzing the Arab blogosphere and investigating trends within that community.

The RSS Feed Analysis Application

An RSS Feed is an XML document used to publish frequently updated web content such as blogs. The format of these documents is mostly standardized, though there are exceptions. RSS feeds contain metadata such as information about the author and the host, and site data such as a blog item or post, and user comments on that post. An example of a blog and its RSS feed are shown in figures 1 and 2 below.

Figure 1: An Arabic Blog Site

```xml
<?xml version="1.0" encoding="UTF-8"?>
<rss version="2.0"
        xmlns:content="http://purl.org/rss/1.0/modules/content/"
        xmlns:wfw="http://wellformedweb.org/CommentAPI/"
        xmlns:dc="http://purl.org/dc/elements/1.1/"
        xmlns:atom="http://www.w3.org/2005/Atom"
        >

<channel>
        <title>&#124;&#124; جندبي JANDBI</title>
        <atom:link href="http://www.jandbi.com/wp/?feed=rss2" rel="self"
type="application/rss+xml" />
        <link>http://www.jandbi.com/wp</link>
        <description>مدونة .. عالمك في .. جندبي .. !!</description>
        <pubDate>Wed, 28 Jan 2009 21:11:30 +0000</pubDate>
        <generator>http://wordpress.org/?v=2.5.1</generator>
        <language>en</language>
                        <item>
                <title>[ ملتقى العمل التطوعي 2009 ] تغطية مصورة</title>
                <link>http://www.jandbi.com/wp/?p=166</link>
                <comments>http://www.jandbi.com/wp/?p=166#comments</comments>
                <pubDate>Wed, 28 Jan 2009 21:08:55 +0000</pubDate>
                <dc:creator>JANDBI</dc:creator>

                <category><![CDATA[المجتمع]]></category>

                <category><![CDATA[جندبي Day]]></category>

                <category><![CDATA[جندبي Photo]]></category>

                <guid isPermaLink="false">http://www.jandbi.com/wp/?p=166</guid>
                <description><![CDATA[ ابتدأت بالأمس واستمرت إلى نهاية هذا اليوم فعاليات &#8221;
ملتقى العمل التطوعي 2009 &#8221; والذي يحمل شعار &#8221; من الذاتية &#8230; إلى الاحترافية &#8220;
والذي استضافته ونظمته &#8221; الغرفة التجارية الصناعية بالمنطقة الشرقية &#8220; ورعاه وافتتحه
صاحب السمو الملكي الأمير محمد بن فهد بن عبدالعزيز آل سعود &#8221; أمير المنطقة الشرقية &#8220;، وقد
سعدت قبل [...]]]></description>
                        <content:encoded><![CDATA[<p style="text-align: justify;"><span
style="color: #800000;">ابتدأت بالأمس واستمرت إلى نهاية هذا اليوم فعاليات <strong><a
href="http://web.chamber.org.sa/volunteer/index.htm" target="_blank">&#8221; ملتقى العمل
التطوعي 2009 &#8221;</a></strong> والذي يحمل شعار &#8221; من الذاتية &#8230; إلى الاحترافية &#8220;
```

Figure 2: The Source of an RSS Feed

The RSS Feed Analysis Application begins by reading in a file of type "*cbl*," which is an XML file that contains parameters for the application. "*cbl*" is short for Corpus Builder Language and is an XML format specifically created for the RSS Feed Analysis Application. An example of such a file is on the next page:

```
<?xml version="1.0" encoding="UTF-8"?>
<cbl version="1.0">
  <builder>
    <source>
      <outputName>out_jandbi</outputName>
      <dataAdaptor>RSS</dataAdaptor>
      <location>http://www.jandbi.com/wp/?feed=rss2</location>
      <metadata>
        <author>رائد</author>
        <gender>male</gender>
        <country>Saudi Arabia</country>
      </metadata>
    </source>
  </builder>
  <ingester databaseName="db.bin">
    <source name="out_jandbi" type="XML">
    <contentTag sourceTag="content:encoded"/>
  </source>
  </ingester>
</cbl>
```

Figure 3: An Example "cbl" File

The "*cbl*" file consists of two parts: the *Builder* and the *Ingester*, which are used by the parts of the application with the same name. The Builder uses all of the sources between the tags to download the RSS feeds. The example file above contains only one source, but many of these can be described in the "*cbl*" file. No analysis is done at this point.

Source contains a name for the output file, a data adaptor, a location, and metadata. The output file name is used as the name of an XML file produced by the builder that lists the location of the downloaded RSS feed and the source of the feed. The data adaptor is the type of input used to build the corpus. Currently the only acceptable type is RSS, but the application is designed in a modular way so that handlers for other adapters such as email or message boards could be added. The location is the URI (Uniform Resource Identifier) of the RSS feed. Finally, the metadata can be anything that the user desires. In the example I have here, I am specifying the author, gender and country of the blogger. This information is not found within the RSS feed and must be added manually.

The Builder

The builder uses the information in the "*cbl*" file to produce three files for each specified source. These files are the "document" file shown below and two other files: the data file is a copy of the raw RSS feed, and the info file contains information obtained from the server such as the date downloaded, the date last modified and the content type.

```xml
<?xml version="1.0" encoding="UTF-8"?>
<Doc>
  <DocumentDataFile>.\s3e8.data.raw</DocumentDataFile>
  <DocumentInfoFile>.\s3e8.info.raw</DocumentInfoFile>
  <SourceLocation>http://www.iandbi.com/wp/?feed=rss2</SourceLocation>
  <UnitLocation>http://www.iandbi.com/wp/?feed=rss2</UnitLocation>
</Doc>
```

Figure 4: An Example Document File

The Ingester

The Ingester analyzes the downloaded RSS feed to produce the corpus. The second part of the "*cbl*" file contains an ingester tag, which contains the information used to build the corpus. This includes the source that points to the document file produced by the Builder. The ingester tag also contains a content tag that lists the tags that are going to be used to build the corpus. In the "*cbl*" file shown in Figure 3 above, only one tag is used, which is the "content:encoded" tag. Many of these tags could be listed, for example if the user wanted the corpus to contain the title of the article as well as the content. The RSS analysis application is developed in such a way as to give the user flexibility in what they want downloaded and stored in the corpus.

Running the Ingester on the "*cbl*" and "document" file produces the raw text that is used to build the corpus. Each word is placed on its own line to aid in the analysis. A sample of the output is shown on the next page:

وقد
سعدت
قبل
حوالي
أسبوعين
باتصال
من
الأخوة
في
اللجنة
المنظمة
للقاء
يرغبون
بمشاركة
مؤسستنا
في
المعرض
المصاحب
للفعاليات
ومنذ
ذلك

Figure 5: The Arabic Corpus Produced by the RSS Feed Analysis Application

The Corpus

A corpus of Arabic blog was compiled using the RSS Feed Analysis Application.

Before the corpus could be compiled, I needed to determine the blogs that would be included in the corpus. Since I was also interested in the community of Arab bloggers, I decided to compile my corpus around an incident that seemed to unite and shock Arab bloggers from many different countries. This incident was the death of female Saudi Arabian journalist and blogger, Hadeel Alhodaif, who died at the age of twenty-five after slipping into a coma for a month [7]. Hadeel fought for a freer media in Saudi Arabia, and her death made national and international news. After Hadeel slipped into a coma, her father posted a notice on her blog and many Arabic bloggers posted notices and prayers on their blogs.

Blogs were chosen to be included in the blog by searching for the name (Hadeel Alhodaif) in Arabic on Google Blog Search [8].

Thirty seven blogs were collected and the corpus contained 131,836 words. A third of these blogs were written by female bloggers, and the bloggers were from seven countries. The divide is shown below.

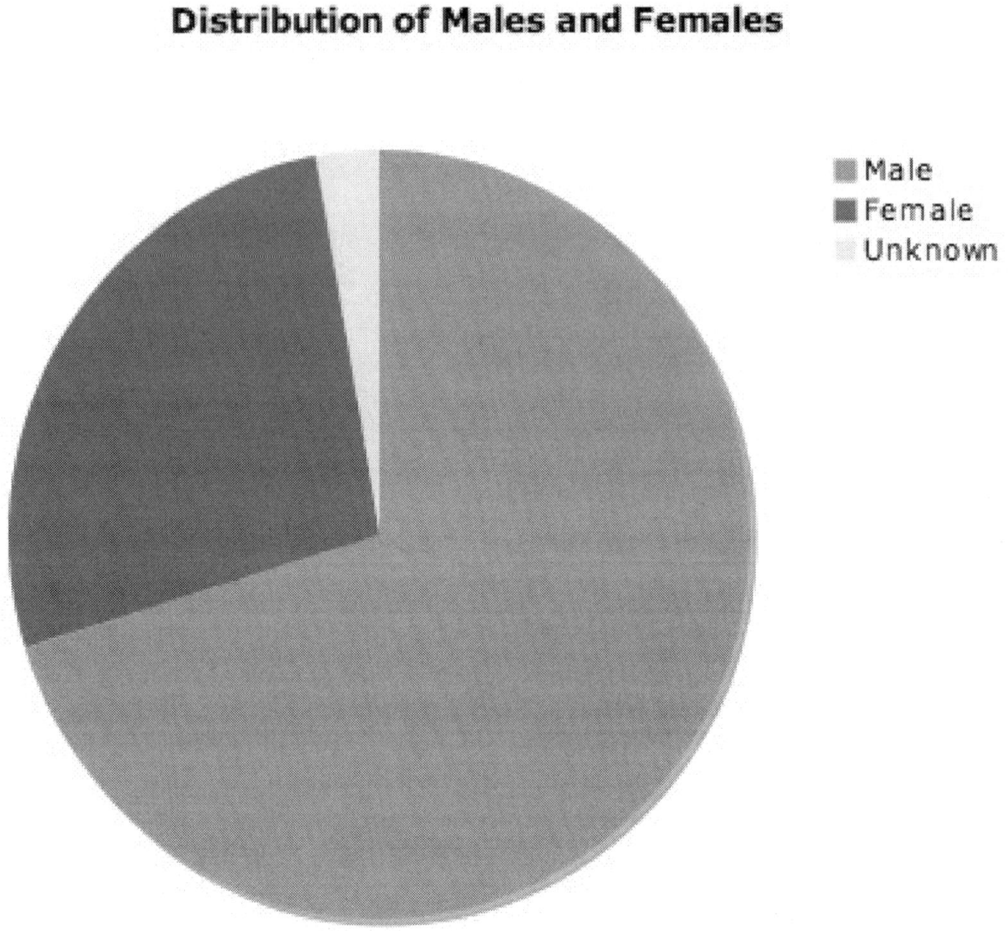

Figure 6: Distribution of Male and Female Bloggers

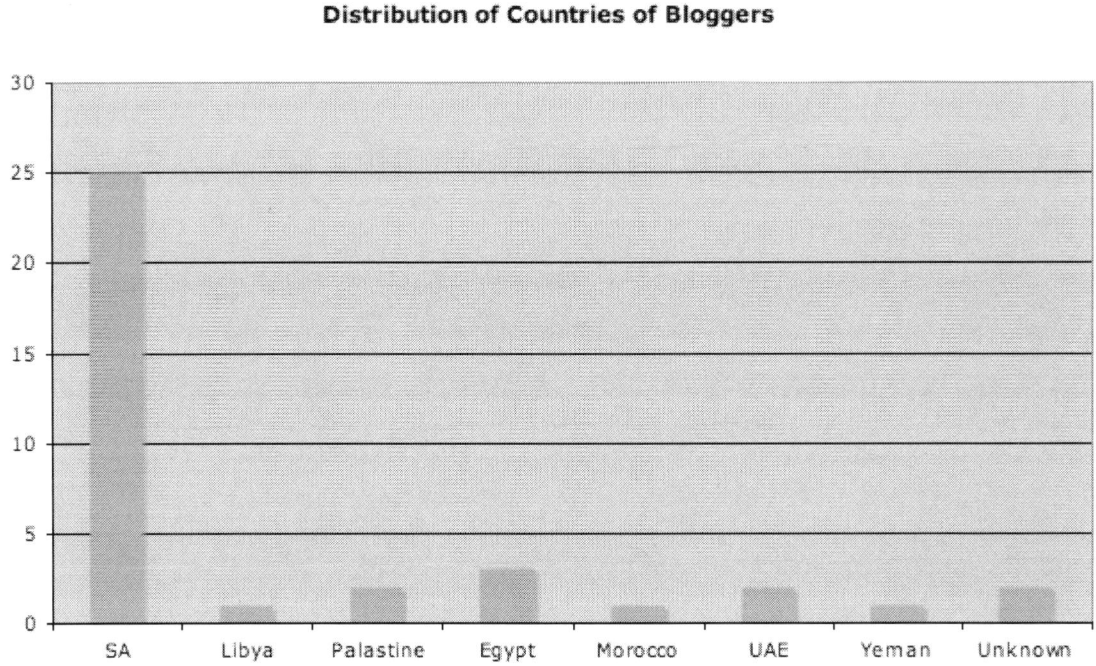

Figure 7: Countries of Origin of the Bloggers

The corpus could also be analysed language specific patterns. For example, do the bloggers use Modern Standard Arabic colloquial Arabic or a mixture of both? Sociolinguists may be interested in how bloggers from different countries or genders use the language.

Future Work

The RSS Feed Analysis Application is the first step in developing a multi-purpose corpus creation and analysis application. This application would aid researchers in compiling large corpora from multiple sources and provide basic analysis modules such as stemmers, taggers, and concordancers. Initially these will be targeted for the Arabic language, and support for other languages will be added as required.

The application will be provided to the community for feedback on the various modules that could be incorporated.

Summary

This article described an RSS Feed Analysis Application that is freely available to researchers under the GNU General Public License and can be obtained by contacting the author. The application will run on Windows and can be easily modified to run on Linux and Mac OS X. All the users need to do is use the Corpus Builder Language to specify the RSS feeds they wish to download and the tags they would like included in the corpus.

The application could be used to compile a corpus of RSS of any language simply and quickly for analysis. For example, linguists could investigate multilingual web-based discourse as described in *Using Corpora in Discourse Analysis* [9].

Furthermore, the 131,836 word corpus is also freely available to the community and can be obtained by contacting the author.

I am grateful to the Berglund Center for Internet Studies, Pacific University Oregon, for supporting this work.

References

[1] http://expat.sourceforge.net/

[2] Al-Sulaiti, Latifa; Atwell, Eric. 2004. Designing and Developing a Corpus of Contemporary Arabic. In Proceedings of the sixth TALC conference. Granada, Spain, p.92

[3] Walters, K. 1996. Diglossia, linguistic variation, and language change in Arabic. In Perspectives on Arabic linguistics VIII: Papers from the Eighth Annual Symposium on Arabic Linguistics, M. Eid (ed.), 157-197. Amsterdam: Benjamins.

[4] Mishne, G. and de Rijke, M. 2006. Capturing global mood levels using blog posts. In Computational Approaches to Analyzing Weblogs: Papers from the 2006 AAAI Spring Symposium. Menlo Park, Calif.: AAAI Press, pp. 145-152.

[5] Herring, S.C., Scheidt, L.A., Bonus, S., and Wright, E. 2004. Bridging the gap: A genre analysis of weblogs. Proceedings of the 37th Annual Hawaii International Conference on System Sciences (HICSS '04). Los Alamitos, Calif.: IEEE Press.

[6] Glance, N., Hurst, M., and Tomokiyo, T. 2004. BlogPulse: Automated trend discovery for weblogs. Proceedings of the First Workshop on the Weblogging Ecosystem: Aggregation, Analysis and Dynamics.

[7] http://www.timesonline.co.uk/tol/news/world/middle_east/article3961731.ece

[8] http://blogsearch.google.com/

[9] Baker, P. 2006. Using Corpora in Discourse Analysis. London - New York: Continuum.

Creative Design Environments: A Small-Scale Case Study

View online at: http://bcis.pacificu.edu/journal/2009/03/article.php?id=49

By Ayse Kok

University of Oxford Department of Education
15 Norham Gardens
OX2 6PY Oxford

Abstract

This paper describes how students in the University of Arts in London were involved in a creative design environment to further develop their creative thinking and design problem-solving skills. After providing a brief literary overview of the field of creativity and a definition of creative knowledge environments, the paper presents an exemplar of a creative knowledge environment and presents the critical features of such tools to foster social creativity.

Introduction

Problems in the Information Age have been mentioned throughout literature by various researchers. One of the main issues is the lack of creativity and innovation. As Drucker (1994) stated, creativity can be considered an essential capability for working smarter in knowledgeable societies. Another problem frequently stated is that technologies have been used as add-ons to existing practices rather than as a catalyst for fundamentally rethinking what education should be about in the next century (Fischer, 1998b). The current mindset about learning is dominated by a view of teaching as informing learners about something they presumably know nothing or little about. This is a misleading conception (Bruner, 1996). Yet, learning is more than being taught (Illich, 1973b). In order to deal with the complexities of 21st century learning, creativity skills, especially within the context of online collaboration, should be conveyed to learners.

Some Definitions

Creativity

The word "creativity" derives from the same Latin root as does "creation," used solely in the context of divine creation and the beginning of the world (Leach, 2001). As this view was integral to the medieval religious belief system, the concept of human creativity did not emerge until the beginning of the Renaissance (Leach, 2001). Until the twentieth century, creativity was considered to be an attribute found only in rare and unusual people.

Creativity can be regarded as not only a quality found in exceptional individuals, but also as an essential life skill through which people can develop the potential to use their imagination to express themselves and make original and valued choices in their lives (Csikszentmihalyi, 1990a, 1990b, 1996). The National Advisory Committee on Creative and Cultural Education (NACCCE) defines creativity as an imaginative activity fashioned so as to produce outcomes that are both original and of value. So, the main characteristics of creativity are (NACCCE, 1999):

- Using imagination: The process of generating original ideas and providing alternatives to the conventional
- A fashioning process: The active focus of attention and skills to shape an idea
- Pursuing purpose: The application of imagination to produce tangible outcomes from purposeful goals
- Being original: The originality of an outcome can be at different levels such as: individual originality in relation to one's prior work, relative originality in relation to peer work and historic originality in relation to works that are completely unique
- Judging value: The evaluative mode of thought that is reciprocal to the generative mode of imaginative activity and provides critical, reflective review from peers

From the beginning of history, the concept of creativity has garnered much attention. In Plato's *Ion*, the dialogues between Ion and Socrates emphasize the importance of inspiration from an external source and a state in which the creator is out of his senses. Although the term 'madness' is used, it does not seem to be describing the psychotic condition as currently defined.

Ion: Then what can be the reason, Socrates, for my behavior? When anyone discusses any other poet, I pay no attention and can offer no remark of any value. I frankly doze. But whenever anyone mentions Homer, immediately I am awake, attentive, and full of things to say.

Socrates: The riddle is not hard to solve, my friend. No, it is plain to everyone that not from art and knowledge comes your power to speak concerning Homer. If it were art that gave you power, then you could speak about all the other poets as well. There is an art of poetry as a whole? Am I not right? [...] Since their making is not by art, but is by lot divine...In all the rest, each one of them is poor, for not by art do they utter these, but by power divine, since if it were by art that they knew how to treat one subject finely, they would know how to deal with all the others too. Herein lies the reason why the deity has bereft them of their senses, and uses them as ministers, along with soothsayers and godly seers; it is in order that we listeners may know that it is not they who utter these precious revelations while their mind is not within them, but that it is god himself who speaks and through them becomes articulate to us.

When it comes to individual creativity, individuals may have the following concerns related to their voices being heard:

- Being interested enough and willing to make the additional effort and time so one's voice is heard: This relates to what motivates people to participate (Fischer, 1998a).
- Having something relevant to say: Unique expertise and local voices are valuable in a global world.
- Being able to express what one wants to say: Owners of the problems must have a digital fluency and be independent of high-tech scribes (National-Research-Council, 1999).
- Being able and willing to express oneself in a way that others can understand: This is relevant in participatory design processes in which people should express themselves without the use of their own professional jargon (Fischer, 1998a, 1998b).

Similarly, a group or a community may have the following concerns related to their voices being heard:

- Encouraging the individuals to contribute to the good and progress of all: This is especially relevant in cultures that rely on social capital (Fischer, 2000, 2001).
- Supporting cultural and epistemological pluralism as an advantage to stimulate social creativity: The multiple ways of thinking, including the voices of under-represented groups, should be accepted.
- Avoiding that information be lost: Environments that support the right division between pull and push technologies should be created (Fischer, 2000).
- Avoiding illegitimate voices: This relates to the violation of privacy and spam mail (Fischer, 2001).
- Avoiding getting stuck in group thought: Controversy should be seen as an asset rather than as a limitation (Turkle & Papert, 1991).
- Eliminating sources of exclusion: This relates to making minorities reluctant to join in (Fischer, 2001).

Creative Design Environments

Creative design environments (CDEs) are those environments, contexts, and surroundings, that are characterized by their exertion of a positive influence on human beings engaged in creative work, and their aim to produce new designs whether they work individually or in teams within a single organization or in collaboration with others.

CDEs can be considered at different scales. At the micro-level is the environment surrounding an individual or a small team where personal interactions may stimulate creativity. At the other extreme is the macro-level at which a research institution operates and whose creative activities may be hindered or promoted by other institutions (Kasperson, 1978). So, CDEs can be considered as nested layers of environmental factors surrounding the unit in which creative activities are undertaken (Kasperson, 1978). The unit of analysis can be as small as one person or as large as a whole institution. In between are other levels of creative units such as a university department seeking creative ways of performing research. Characteristics at one level are influenced by properties and events at other levels such as the culture and goals of the institution.

The main components of CDEs are:

- Creativity: As articulated above, creativity can be defined as a novel and imaginative product which is useful and of good quality. The evaluation of a product as 'creative' is often a matter of social negotiation. Not every creative process will lead to a creative product as the context, knowledge, and ideas also influence creativity. Combining different frames of reference, the transfer of a methodological approach from one field to another, or the tension between divergent and convergent thinking may further foster creative thinking.

- Design environment: The design environment depends on a wide range of conditions and circumstances that overlap and intersect (Kasperson, 1978). Its components are:

- Task characteristics: Tasks may vary in terms of their being simple/complex, routine/novel, short/long-term and modularized/integrated.

- Discipline/field: The disciplines might entail single/multiple paradigms, reductionist/holistic, discipline-based/inter/multi-disciplinary, theoretical/experimental/modeling.
- Individuals: Every one possesses different knowledge, skills, abilities, motivation, interests, values, beliefs and cognitive styles.
- Group characteristics: Groups may vary in terms of their size, being integrated/loosely coupled, being inward/outward looking, the heterogeneity/ homogeneity of members, and the underlying assumptions
- General work situation for individuals: These entail the number of different work tasks, job ambiguity and features of time available for design (sparse/abundant, fragmented/concentrated).
- Organization: This relates to the organizational structure, culture, leadership style and the degree of organizational tension/harmony.
- Extra-organizational environment: This relates to information availability and cultural characteristics (Kasperson, 1978)

The different scales, at which CDEs can be analyzed, might be grouped into the following categories: macro (global, national, inter-organizational); meso (related institution) and micro (teams and individuals). In addition, each of these components has social and cognitive aspects. The social aspects are openness to new ideas or innovations and relations between individuals. The cognitive aspects are cognitive work style and thinking style (adopting an experimental or 'trial and error' approach) (Kasperson, 1978). These two aspects are closely integrated and affect each other. While group characteristics and work situations are more socially tuned, task characteristics and field situations are more cognitively tuned.

An element of change should also be considered when thinking about CDEs because, over time, the relevant tasks might alter due to changes in their preconditions. It is also important to distinguish the main types of CDEs depending on whether they are related to academia, industry or government. Besides, different disciplines might have different cognitive and social styles (Kasperson, 1978).

Design & Learning

Current theories in educational theory make the following assumptions about learning:

- Learning is a process of knowledge construction rather than knowledge absorption. So environments in which learners can be contributors are required (Harel & Papert, 1991). Therefore, learners should create new artifacts through interaction with software tools (Repenning et al. 1998; Eisenber & Eisenberg, 1998; Nardi, 1993).
- Learning is highly tuned to the situation in which it takes place. So, environments which are domain-oriented and which support human problem-domain interaction are required (Fischer, 1999a). When working or playing, individuals act until they encounter a breakdown (Fischer, 1999a). By getting involved in 'reflection-in-action' (Schon, 1983) or an experimental mode (Norman, 1993) they can reflect about these breakdowns, which are key to situated learning.
- Learning is knowledge-dependent meaning that people employ their existing knowledge to construct new knowledge that supports user-tailored information (Ritter et al., 1998)

- Learning needs to account for distributed cognition by which the knowledge required to solve a problem is distributed among various participants (Norman, 1993). This distribution of knowledge is based on the asymmetry of knowledge between different stakeholders in problem-solving (Rittel, 1984). A reformulation of the deceptive conception that the teacher should explicitly inform the learners about something they presumably know nothing about is misleading (Bruner, 1996).

To bring the design mode into the academic curriculum, the "learning by design" approach can be adopted (Bereiter, 2002, Scardamalia, 2002). In this type of learning, the physical environment is the physical workbench where something is being built. Holbrook & Kolodner (2002) describe this type of learning as being achieved through a major design challenge where learners develop designs, build prototypes and use various resources to provide justification for refining their designs. So, this approach is explicitly focused on building concrete things (Holbrook & Kolodner, 2002). Ideas enter the process as they are relevant to producing an artifact (Holbrook & Kolodner, 2002).

Similarly, Bereiter et al. (1997) asserts that this constructivist approach entails the following characteristics:

- A focus on idea improvement: Working together on improving ideas by using the available strategies and resources
- Problems versus questions: Although problems are often expressed as questions, pursuing solutions to problems rather than answers encourages knowledge building. In contrast to answers, problem solutions are continually improvable.
- Knowledge of value to the community: In knowledge building, artifacts, whether conceptual or physical, are used by other community members as tools for further knowledge advancements.
- Emergent goals and products: Products may emerge at any point in the iterative cycle of knowledge building and may serve various purposes such as highlighting a problem or disseminating results.
- Constructive use of authoritative sources: Apart from authoritative resources such as textbooks, all ideas are treated with respect and judged according to their contribution to the current problem-solving effort.

To create different mindsets, learning environments should be facilitated in such a way that knowledge is collaboratively created, externalized and shared (Arias et al., 2000). Impacting mindsets is a socio-technical design problem (Fischer, 1999b) (Figure 1.0) that requires making consumers become active contributors to the solutions of the problems (Schon, 1983; Fischer, 1998a; Arias et al, 2000). Allowing learners to engage in design activities by creating environments that support them in making artifacts that they can share with others is another function of this socio-technical design problem.

The Context of the Study

Sketchbook is a digital tool for art and design students that encourages them to showcase their work through portfolios, and collaborate on projects through posting images. (See a related website at: http://www.arts.ac.uk/clipcetl-sketchbook.htm) It has been developed by the University of the Arts in London which is one of the oldest art universities in the world. In addition to displaying their sample work, users can also employ a variety of creative thinking tools, do exercises for inspirational thinking as well as utilize online resources related to the areas of art, design, and research methodologies.

Sketchbook is an image-sharing site aimed specifically at artists, designers, or anyone who works in a visual medium. It allows the users to upload and show their work, offer descriptions of the process, and have friends and colleagues comment upon each other's ideas. Students are also provided with the opportunity to create their online portfolios and to collaborate on projects through posting images or articles. Besides creative thinking tools, exercises and research methods are also presented. Sketchbook's structured environment supports the students in their learning process (Figure 1.0).

The content of Sketchbook is divided into the following seven areas that can be accessed through the top frame of the page layout.

- Gallery
- Sketch
- My Portfolio
- Groups
- Inspiration
- Books
- Links

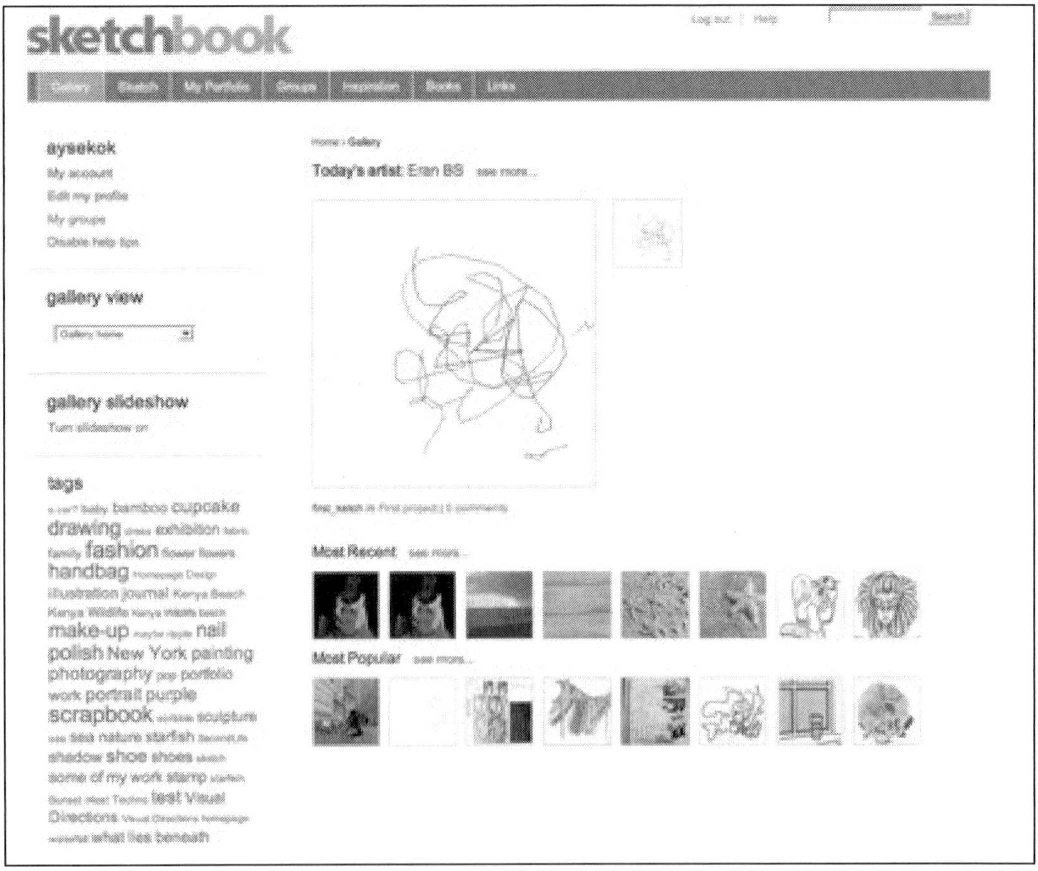

Figure 1.0 A Screen Layout of Sketchbook

Based on the constructivist theory of learning, Sketchbook provides a rich context for learning that involves building a work of art. By establishing a strong connection between design and learning, Sketchbook facilitates a meaningful construction where the users are engaged in building sharable artifacts.

Sketchbook's constructivist learning environment aims achieving the following pedagogical goals:

- Providing experience with knowledge construction process: Once the tutor facilitates the process, Sketchbook users take the responsibility for strategies or methods for solving problems in the "Inspire" section.
- Providing experience in multiple perspectives: Students are engaged in activities that enable them to evaluate alternative solutions to these activities so they can eventually enrich their understanding.
- Embedding learning in realistic and relevant contexts: As most of the activities in Sketchbook are grounded within the complexity of real life, the ability of students to transfer what they learn to everyday life may be increased.
- Encouraging ownership and voice in the learning process: As Sketchbook users play around with their illustrations they can identify their own directions and objectives. The tutors may act as a coach by helping the students frame their learning objectives rather than determining what they will learn.
- Embedding learning in social experience: Sketchbook facilitates collaboration between both teachers and students, and students and other students. In this way it increases social interactions.
- Encouraging the use of multiple modes of representation: Sketchbook facilitates learning with photographs and videos in addition to written communication.
- Encouraging self-awareness of the knowledge construction process: Sketchbook users are provided with activities in the 'Inspire' section that allow them to develop awareness about their own knowledge construction process.

Moreover, Sketchbook provides the user with the opportunity to gather and organize artifacts regarding one's professional development as well as their collaborative work. It is a reflective tool that demonstrates growth over time.

Sketchbook's underlying learning theory stresses the active involvement of learners in building their own knowledge. As learners structure and organize their work of art they correct themselves. Their works are constantly being refined. Reflection on one's own work also makes learners become informed about their own learning goals and strategies. As the learners further explore the drawing space, they are actively engaged in imposing meaning upon their works.

The teachers can also create meaningful experiences in their classrooms by using Sketchbook. They can use Sketchbook as a domain oriented design environment by showing exemplary work or by evaluating their students' individual or collaborative work. Sketchbook users can also meet with others that share the same interests and competencies to further improve their skills through the exchange of ideas and collaborative work. So, Sketchbook fosters reflective practice and critical thinking by offering the opportunity for one's work to be reviewed by their peers.

Another main feature of Sketchbook as a domain-oriented design environment is that it is a medium of expressing one's authenticity. Due to the fact that Sketchbook users can showcase their work, a culture of digital documentation can also be fostered.

Below, a list of possible tasks (Table 2.0) for collaborating on Sketchbook has been provided:

Strategy Rationale	*Rationale*
The teacher may initiate a work of art to be further modified by the students. Students may be expected to make a collaborative drawing and post their contributions at least twice a week. Participation points may be calculated based on these online contributions.	Because of the nature of the evolving drawing, students could be constantly engaged in the course, without any lengthy absences from the collaborative work. They can also be provoked to critically analyze, explain and propose new meanings among objects of their study.
Students can be expected to take part in regular peer reviews by critically evaluating each other's works of art.	It is important to develop a critical eye towards other community members' works of art.
Students can be divided into 3-4 small groups to provide answers for the \`Exercises\` in the \`Inspiration' section. They can even get into an exchange of ideas with students from other colleges.	Small groups facilitate better discussion for learner-material interaction.
Instructors may require high-quality online interactions with peers and discussions of readings suggested by Sketchbook making a portion of the grade dependent on it. (At least 25% is recommended).	Effective learning environments should provide frequent and meaningful interactions among learners. Good practice encourages cooperation among students.
Teachers can point out various mind-mapping tools in the "Inspire" section to continually promote good interaction.	Good practice encourages prompt feedback so that faculty-learner interaction may be improved.

Methodology

Research Design

Taking into account the complexity of factors that simultaneously influence creative thinking skills, controlling factors utilized in experimental studies would limit the understanding of educational issues. Creativity is a construct--an aspect of consciousness--and is therefore difficult to measure. In addition, an individual's creative and complex thinking skills may differ from those of others based on the specific educational situation the learner is experiencing. As some theorist have argued, analyses of "person-situation" interactions using rich situational descriptions may facilitate more understanding about individual difference constructs. Also, as various theorists state, generalizations about learning cannot be validated without studying the personal differences along with the situational differences. For these theoretical and practical reasons, a hermeneutic phenomenological approach could provide insight into the construct of creativity in online learning situations. Understanding the phenomenon of the learner's creative and complex thinking skills by observing, questioning, and gathering stories from students who attempt to learn online would be the focus of these phenomenological observations.

Participants

Participants were students of the University of Arts in London who were willing to reflect about the relationship between their use of Sketchbook and their creative and complex thinking skills. To this end, students currently enrolled in a program were e-mailed and asked whether they would be willing to participate in such a study. The justification of this sampling method is, instead of making generalizations concerning the relationship between the development of creative thinking skills and the use of Sketchbook, we investigated the value and function of Sketchbook as a mediating tool through this case study. Twenty-four art and design student participated in the small-scale study undertaken in the University of the Arts in London.

Data Collection

To look more closely at the process of portfolio development, a qualitative study investigating the experiences of these twenty-four students was conducted. Data was collected via student interviews and field observations. Students who were enrolled in the introductory course participated in a focus group interview after completing their initial draft of the portfolio. The focus group interview lasted forty-five minutes and centered on the decision-making process. At the conclusion of the class, the researcher conducted a second group interview where open-ended questions were asked concerning the choice of media and possible future revisions. These interviews focused on the process of developing the portfolio, reasons for developing the portfolio beyond the requirements, and changes they would like to make in their portfolio over time.

Semi-structured interviews with students and observation of the learners' online art and design products were used as data collection methods. The students were asked about their use of Sketchbook and their perception of the potential advantages pertaining to the development of creative thinking skills.

According to Patton (1982), the fundamental principle of qualitative interviewing is providing a framework within which respondents can express their own understandings in their own terms. Thus, open-ended, rather than closed, questions should be used as far as possible (Patton, M., 1982). Patton's style of qualitative interviewing is referred to as the 'standardized open-ended interview' through which questions are asked in the same way and order, with a minimum of probing by the interviewer (Patton, M., 1982). The use of probes was preferred by the researcher in order to allow the informants to answer more on their own terms (Patton, M., 1982). This way the interviewer, seeking, at the same time, both clarification and elaboration on given answers, was freer to probe beyond answers (Patton, M., 1982).

Results

Student responses covered a range of opinions, with the diversity illustrated by the qualitative feedback from the open-ended questions:

> *"In my opinion, we should not be expected to be creative with computers, that will be unfair in some instances."*

This response was typically found in students from the developing world with notably lower ICT literacy skills than the other students. Yet, with guidance and training, all students were able to readily produce e-portfolios in the weeks following the initial assessment.

Another challenge for these students was their different opinions with regard to whether they should only include the sketches relevant to their own field (fashion and design) or any other drawings not particularly related to fashion and design.

> *"It was quite fun to put together the e-portfolio. The assessment of this course also makes things less stressful on us."*

Once the requisite publishing skills had been mastered, students enjoyed the capacity to individualize their drawings, and in general, invested disproportionate time in their sketches, despite the fact that it was not rewarded in assessment. Moreover, those students having used digital media admitted that the digital media really made a difference for them since it resulted in robust learning experiences.

> *"I think it is an amazing way for preparing job applications in the future. Learning about my personal strengths and weaknesses via this online portfolio, I can work now on my weaknesses."*

Similarly, one student mentioned that, by being encouraged to identify their own strengths, they would take responsibility to develop them further and therefore became engaged in genuine life-long learning.

Moreover, one student stated that *"the good thing about Sketchbook is that it is collaborative so that we can further develop the drawings of others."*

One of the challenges was how to sketch online when using Sketchbook. One student stated that *"It was difficult to translate your ideas about your thoughts into the right drawings on the web page, but once you get used to it you can put your real life examples which may be helpful for your other colleagues".* Yet, despite this challenge of selecting the right drawing, one student stated that *"once you start to reflect and record your drawings you think that you feel motivated to enter a new creative experience into your portfolio."*

Furthermore, three of the e-portfolios included some mind-maps of the art students' interaction with others and these students believed these figures to be the most important component of the idea generation.

Depending on how much the students got involved in preparing their e-portfolios, they pursued different paths. For example, those students who were just beginning the process often included simple drawings they were using throughout their lessons. One third grade student mentioned: "As I continued to work on my e-portfolio, I wanted to reflect my own style as a design student." As participants continued to revise and refine their work, they felt more motivated by the desire to reflect their personal style with regard to art and design.

Although at the beginning of the online sketching process the students wanted to know exactly how their drawings should look as if the contents were set in stone, they eventually became accustomed to the unpredictable nature of this collaborative development process. After the initial evaluation of their drawings, participants were told that they should think about the use of the tool as an ongoing process as well as revise the content frequently utilizing the flexibility of the digital media.

Conclusions

As Fischer (1991) stated, in a "gift-wrapping" approach, technology is merely wrapped around old frameworks for education. To move from "gift-wrapping" into richer contextual frameworks and computational environments, effort has been made to ensure that Sketchbook fulfils the following conditions:

- Being simultaneously user-directed and supportive: The choice of tasks must be under the control of the learner whereas the support provided by the system must be contextualized to the user's task.
- Being sufficiently open-ended and complex so that users will encounter breakdowns: The system must provide means for allowing users to understand and learn from breakdowns.
- Supporting a range of expertise: Systems must be able to accommodate users at different levels of expertise.
- Promoting collaboration: When users are supported to overcome the symmetry of ignorance, they can learn from each other.

In this way, a synergy for social creativity can be created. As the Renaissance scholar no longer exists due to the rapid increase of information, social creativity becomes more and more crucial (Fischer, 1998b). Applications such as Sketchbook can empower individuals in the following ways:

- letting them articulate a partial description of their tasks
- supporting the creation of an artifact with a construction component
- using a catalogue of previous designs supporting design-by-modification
- supporting the exploration of argumentation
- providing additional feedback

As computers can be utilized for such complex tasks, more social creativity can be unleashed.

Acknowledgements

The author contacted the University of the Arts because of her research interest and would like to thank to Dr. Julia Gaimster of University of the Arts in London for the information and support she provided.

References

Arias, E. G., Eden, H., Fischer, G., Gorman, A., & Scharff, E. (2000) Transcending the individual human mind--creating shared understanding through collaborative design. *Transactions on Computer Human Interaction,* 3, (4), pp. 45-49.

Bennis, W., & Biederman, P. W. (1997) *Organizing genius: the secrets of creative collaboration.* Cambridge: Perseus Books.

Bereiter, C. (2002) *Education and mind in the knowledge age.* Mahwah: Lawrence Erlbaum Associates.

Bereiter, C., Scardamalia, M., Cassels, C. & Hewitt, J. (1997) Postmodernism, knowledge building, and elementary science. *Elementary School Journal,* 97, (1), pp. 329-340.

Brown, J. S., Duguid, P. (1992) Enacting Design for the Workplace. In P. S. Adler & T. Winograd (eds.), *Usability: Turning Technologies into Tools.* Oxford: Oxford University Press, pp. 164-197.

Bruner, J.S. (1996) *The culture of education.* Cambridge: Harvard University Press.

Campbell, D. T. (1969) Ethnocentrism of disciplines and the fish-scale model of omniscience. In M. Sherif, & C. W. Sherif (eds.), *Interdisciplinary relationships in the social sciences,* Chicago: Aldine Publishing Company, pp. 328-348.

Carroll, J. M., & Rosson, M. B. (1987) Paradox of the active user. In J. M. Carroll (ed.), *Interfacing thought: cognitive aspects of human-computer interaction.* Cambridge: The MIT Press, pp. 80-111.

Csikszentmihalyi, M (1990a) The domain of creativity. In M.A. Runco & R. Albert (eds.) *Theories of creativity.* London: Sage Publications, pp. 70-85.

Csikszentmihalyi, M. (1990b) *Flow: The psychology of optimal experience.* New York: HarperCollins Publishers.

Csikszentmihalyi, M. (1996) *Creativity: flow and the psychology of discovery and invention.* New York: HarperCollins.

Drucker, P. F. (1994) The Age of Social Transformation. *The Atlantic Monthly,* 11, (3), pp. 53-80.

Fischer, G. (1991) Supporting learning on demand with design environments. *Learning Sciences,* 1, (3), pp. 165-172.

Fischer, G. (1994a) Domain-oriented design environments. *Automated Software Engineering,* 1, (2), pp. 177-203.

Fischer, G. (1994b) Turning breakdowns into opportunities for creativity. *Knowledge-Based Systems, Special Issue on Creativity and Cognition,* 7, (4), pp. 221-232.

Fischer, G. (1998a) Beyond 'couch potatoes': from consumers to designers," *Computer Human Interaction,* 2, (4), pp. 2-9.

Fischer, G. (1998b) Making learning a part of life--beyond the 'gift-wrapping' approach of technology. In P. Alheit & E. Kammler (eds.), *Lifelong learning and its impact on social and regional development.* Bremen: Donat Verlag, pp. 435-462.

Fischer, G. (1999a) *Social creativity: Bringing different points of view together* [Online], Colarado: KBS. Available from: http://l3d.cs.colorado.edu/gerhard/papers/cc99.pdf (Accessed Dec 08, 2008).

Fischer, G. (1999b) Lifelong learning: changing mindsets. In G. Cumming, T. Okamoto, & L. Gomez (eds.), *7th International Conference on Computers in Education on "New Human Abilities for the Networked Society".* Chiba, Japan, 18-21 April, 1999.

Fischer, G. (2000) Social creativity, symmetry of ignorance and meta-design. *Knowledge-Based Systems Journal (Special Issue on Creativity & Cognition),* 13, (8), Oxford, UK: Elsevier Science, pp. 527-537.

Fischer, G. (2001) Communities of interest: Learning through the interaction of multiple knowledge systems. *24th Annual Information Systems Research Seminar (IRIS'24),* Bergen, Norway, 11-14 August, 2001.

Greenbaum, J., Kyng, M. (1991) *Design at work: cooperative design of computer systems.* Hillsdale: Lawrence Erlbaum Associates, Inc.

Grudin, J. (1987) Social evaluation of the user interface: who does the work and who gets the benefit? In H. Bullinger & B. Shackel (eds.), *Proceedings of INTERACT'87, 2nd IFIP Conference on Human-ComputerInteraction.* Amsterdam: JC Publications, pp. 805-811.

Hamilton, E., Cairns, H. (eds.) (2006) *Plato: the collected dialogues.* New York: Pantheon Books, pp. 218-221.

Holbrook, J. & Kolodner, J.L. (2002) Scaffolding the development of an inquiry-based (science) classroom. In B. Fishman & S.O' Connor- Divelbiss (eds.), *Fourth international conference of the learning sciences.* Mahwah: Lawrence- Erlbaum Associates, pp. 221-227.

Illich, I. (1973a) *Tools for conviviality.* New York: Harper and Row.

Illich, I. (1973b) *Deschooling society.* Harmondsworth: Penguin Books.

Leach, J. (2001) A hundred possibilities: creativity, community and ICT. In A., Craft, B., Jeffrey, M., Leibling (eds.) *Creativity in education.* London: Continuum, pp. 176-185.

Kasperson, C.J. (1978) An analysis of the relationship between information sources and creativity in scientists and engineers, *Human Communication Research,* 4, (2), pp. 111-19.

Levy, F., & Murnane, R. J. (2004) *The new division of labor: how computers are creating the next job market.* Princeton: Princeton University Press.

Nakakoji, K., Aoki, A., & Reeves, B. N. (1996) Knowledge-based cognitive support for multimedia information design. *Information and Software Technology,* 38, (3), pp. 191-200.

National Endowment for Science, Technology and the Arts (NESTA), (2006) *The innovation gap: why policy needs to reflect the reality of innovation in the UK.* London: NESTA Publications.

Norman, D. A. (1993) *Things that make us smart.* Reading: Addison-Wesley Publishing.

Patton, M. (1982) *Practical Evaluation.* Newbury Park:Calif. Sage

Repenning, A., Ioannidou, A. and Ambach, J. (1998) Learn to communicate and communicate to learn. *Journal of Interactive Media in Education,* 98, (7), pp. 40-50.

Resnick, M. (2006) Computer as paintbrush: technology, play and the creative society. In D., Singer, R., Golikoff, K., Hirsh-Pasek (eds.), *Play=Learning: how play motivates and enhances children's cognitive and socio-emotional growth.* Oxford:Oxford University Press, pp. 30-37.

Rittel, H. (1984) Second-generation design methods. In N. Cross (eds.) *Developments in Design Methodology.* New York: John Wiley & Sons, pp. 317-327.

Schon, D. A. (1983) *The reflective practitioner: How Professionals Think in Action.* New York: Basic Books.

Shneiderman, B. (2003) *Leonardo's Laptop: Human Needs and the New Computing Technologies.* Cambridge: MIT Press.

Simon, H. A. (1996) *The Sciences of the Artificial, 3rd edition.* Cambridge: The MIT Press.

Turkle, S., & Papert, S. (1991) Epistemological pluralism and the revaluation of the concrete. In I. Harel & S. Papert (eds.), *Constructionism.* Norwood: Ablex Publishing Corporation, pp. 161-191.

When Rights Collide

View online at: http://bcis.pacificu.edu/journal/2009/03/article.php?id=48

By Leonard D. DuBoff

Prior to this nation's Declaration of Independence, Europe set the standards for, manufacturing and cultural sophistication, whereas the colonies provided raw materials and a market for European-manufactured goods. In other words, this continent was the "third world" of the time.

The Founders were cognizant of this fact when the Constitution was written, and therefore, Article 1, Section 8, Clause 8 was intended to provide incentives for Americans to effectively compete with the more sophisticated Europeans. That section provides Congress with the ability to enact patent and copyright laws. Those laws were promptly enacted, and thus these incentives have been part of American jurisprudence since the very beginning.

The patent laws of the United States provide that for 20 years from the date an application is filed, a patent holder may exclude others from practicing the patented invention, giving the patent holder the sole right to create or license that invention during that period of protection.

The copyright laws have a similar, albeit weaker, form of protection. Under this legislation, a copyright owner can prevent others from copying the protected work for the period of protection, though a copyright owner cannot prevent others who have independently created a similar work from exploiting it. The copyright statute provides that any original work of authorship that is put into a tangible form and that has minimal creativity may be protected from copyright for the life of the creator plus 70 years if the creator is an identified individual. When the work is created by a hypothetical person, such as an entity (e.g., a corporation), anonymously or by one using a pseudonym, then the period of protection is either 120 years from creation or 95 years from first publication, whichever period expires first. Once the term has elapsed, the work becomes part of the public domain and may be freely copied.

Trademark is another form of intellectual property protection. The trademark laws protect any name, symbol, logo or combination of these used to identify the source of a product or service. Under the Lanham Act, a mark will be protected if it has been used in interstate or foreign commerce and complies with the other requirements of the law. Trademark registrations need to be renewed in 10-year increments for so long as the mark remains in use, but marks are not required to be registered and remain protected for the time the mark is used.

These three bodies of law coexist, though throughout history they have periodically clashed and questions have been raised regarding the priority of protection. The courts have thus been required to assist in defining the boundaries of the different forms of protection.

In Mazer v. Stein, for instance, the United States Supreme Court was presented with a bronze sculpture of a Balinese dancer that had been converted into a lamp. The Court held that if the aesthetic sculpture could exist separately from and be identified independently of the functional lamp, then the aesthetic work would enjoy copyright protection but that the functional aspects would be protectable, if at all, under the patent laws.

When a novel's package design was copied by a competitor and the copying was contested, the court hearing the case was presented with an interesting challenge. Since packaging is functional, it could not enjoy copyright protection; yet, it was felt that the unauthorized reproduction of the novel packaging could not be permitted. It was from this dilemma that the doctrine of trade dress was first established. The doctrine is similar to copyright in that the protected trade dress must not be functional; yet, it may be registered and protected under the Lanham Act in a manner similar to that of a trademark.

In the case of Dastar Corporation v. Twentieth Century Fox Film Corporation, the Supreme Court was forced to determine whether the trademark laws could be used to protect a copyrightable work that has fallen into the public domain because its period of protection had expired. In this case, a book that chronicled Dwight D. Eisenhower's experience as a wartime general was converted into a television series aired by Fox Broadcasting in 1949. At the time the TV series aired, the period of copyright protection was 28 years, and the copyright owner could renew that copyright registration for an additional 28 years. Unfortunately, Fox allowed the copyright registration to lapse after the initial period, and the work thus fell into the public domain.

Later, Dastar created a video series using much of the same historical footage as was contained in the original work, though Dastar reorganized the material, inserted different captions and renamed the program World War II Campaigns in Europe. Fox filed suit against Dastar for copyright infringement and for reverse passing off (failing to identify the new work as having been based on the original Fox work). The court held that the public has the right to copy a copyrighted work without any attribution after the copyright expires, since otherwise the public's right to use "expired copyrights" would be limited.

Because of the complexity of the laws dealing with the various forms of intellectual property law, it is important to seek assistance from a knowledgeable intellectual property lawyer in connection with appropriately protecting that intellectual property.

Media

The Daily You: Personalizing Your Media

View online at: http://bcis.pacificu.edu/journal/2009/03/article.php?id=50

By Jenn Hernandez, Berglund Student Intern

In his book, *Republic.com*, Cass Sunstein [1] discusses, "'The Daily Me'—a communications package that is personally designed with each component fully chosen in advance" [2]. The phrase, "Daily Me", was coined by MIT professor Nicolas Negroponte [3], who foresaw "the growing power of consumers to filter what they see" [4]. Technologies have led us into creating our own spheres of concern, by personalizing, and thereby filtering, what we see. We act as editors in dictating what is important to us and what is not. This carries implications not only for the reader, but for our society as a whole.

The personalization of media acts, generally speaking, via a filtering system that builds off of what one has chosen to read in the past. Even without subscribing to services such as dailyme.com [5], we already do a lot of filtering, whether it's reading select sections of a daily newspaper (or even choosing to subscribe only to a Sunday paper), tuning the radio, or changing channels on the television. We cannot see or hear everything at once, and personalized media realizes that we don't want to always have to filter through everything on a daily basis to find what we want to read. So after the user chooses a few items, preferences are set and saved for the next time the user visits the page.

Personalizing media can be useful for those away from home, say, for instance, college students, who still want to be connected to the goings-on at home. One of MIT's Media Lab projects was to create a personalized newspaper for freshman, called "Fishwrap." The advisor for the project, Pascal R. Chesnais, who is also a research specialist at the Media Lab, detailed the beginning phase of a personalized newspaper: "In the fall 1992 seminar we asked the freshmen to design a paper [of the future]," Mr. Chesnais said. "We didn't tell them what's impossible, or what the state of our software is—we just asked them what they would like to see in such a paper." [6]. The general consensus was that new students wanted, "a personalized paper...that would include news from home, maps of Cambridge and Boston, daily schedules of pertinent MIT events, and more. This idea grew into the "Freshman Fishwrap," so named for its original target group and for a once-common secondary use of newspapers" [7]. Now the whole MIT community can receive personalized news in their inboxes every morning highlighting exactly what each individual student is interested in—whether it be national news, news from home, local news, or other, more specific categories.

To find out more about how personalization works, I signed up for a free account at *dailyme.com* [8]. As soon as I signed up, I was given the option to begin personalizing my page. There are a number of general categories to choose from, plus a variety of subcategories, to which keywords can be added. You can also choose to get news from different news sources specifically. (I could not find, however, the newspaper from my hometown.) There is also the option to search by keyword, which does have the potential of pulling up obscure topics that wouldn't have been found otherwise.

Another example of a personalization site is *CRAYON* [9], (*CReAte Your Own Newspaper*). The signup for *CRAYON* was simple and free, but I found the actual personalization to be a little clunky and difficult to understand. I eventually figured it out however, and found it to be simpler than I had originally thought. I was able to most easily get local news and weather by simply entering my zip code at the beginning of the customization process. When the paper is published, you get a simple page with the links to sources you chose segmented by broad topic. The only qualm I have with *CRAYON* is that it's not an actual "newspaper page", but actually more like a bookmarking site that the user specifically selects. There is no artificial intelligence working here. The creator of *CRAYON* shared that, in regards to online newspapers, "[He] thought they were great and thought about making a page that simply listed all the good ones. Even, better, [he] thought it would be neat to divide it up by sections like a regular newspaper." [10]

The drawback to media personalization is that it has direct implications for democracy and raises concerns about current issues. Spend time talking with an individual or a group of like opinion, and it is highly likely that your views will be even further cemented because of the lack of counter argument. It has been found that, when people are confronted with opinions conflicting with their own, they move towards the center. Conversely—as it has been found in a study based in Colorado—removing all conflicting opinion can have quite the opposite effect. By validating and, as an observed result, polarizing the point of view to create an extremist information culture, any uncertainty or fence sitting is squelched. This can be detrimental to the debate and discussion of issues that is so crucial to our democracy and image as a democratic system. While isolating oneself among like-minded opinions, one not only misses perhaps valid counters arguments, but also may become extremist in their acceptance of other viewpoints. [11]

The Adam Sandler film *Click* is recent pop culture example of this point [12]. In the movie, Adam Sandler's character uses his remote to fast forward or skip through certain moments in a day and the "smart" technology saved his preferences. But then the remote automatically fast-forwarded through similar moments and situations in the future, even if he didn't want to at the time. This may be a hyperbole of the process of media personalization and its outcome, but the main idea is that once preferences are set (hardly implying that they can't be changed at a later date, which was not an option in the movie), you are in effect fast-forwarding past other more serendipitous encounters. These alternate events may prove to be just as interesting though you would have hardly chosen beforehand to read about them by general topic.

In conclusion, while the personalization of media can be convenient and useful—saving preferences and time—it can also conflict with the very cognitive behaviors of individuals. While trying to cater to the needs of the individual, media personalization can actually lead to an extreme bias by filtering out of varying points of view.

Endnotes

[1] http://home.uchicago.edu/~csunstei/

[2] http://press.princeton.edu/chapters/s7014.html

[3] http://web.media.mit.edu/~nicholas/

[4] http://press.princeton.edu/chapters/s7014.html

[5] http://www.dailyme.com

[6] http://web.mit.edu/newsoffice/1994/newspaper-0309.html

[7] Ibid.

[8] http://www.dailyme.com

[9] http://www.crayon.net

[10] http://www.crayon.net/about/faq.html#1.2

[11] http://www.cceia.org/resources/transcripts/5445.html

[12] http://www.sonypictures.com/movies/click/site/index.php

Education

You Say You Want a Revolution, Well, You Know...

View online at: http://bcis.pacificu.edu/journal/2009/03/article.php?id=51

By Steve Rhine, Ed. D.

Willamette University

We all want to change the world.

In education we want to change the world of learning to be engaging, meaningful, and memorable. For teachers who are excited about their profession, that means the pressure to continually innovate. What does it mean to be innovative in an educational context and what role can technology play?

You tell me that it's evolution. Well...

There are some eureka moments when we discover something new or something that works with students especially well the first time, but for the most part, it is all about persistence, assessment, reflection, and a positive attitude. The cycle of experimenting on a small scale and then working up to a larger scale, as the purpose and process become clearer, is more likely to lead to success ultimately than one shot at it and the tired cliche, "Oh, I tried that and it didn't work."

Some people are great at creating things from scratch--developing a new way of seeing things that nobody has done before. Some people are great at taking what the innovators are doing and adapting an idea, spinning off in a new direction, or putting a new twist on it that makes it work best in a particular environment. I tend to be in the latter group, and rely on websites, conversations with like-minded people, or gurus of tech integrated education to stir my brain cells. The evolution of my thinking takes place best when I can interact with others.

Regarding the latter, people ask me all the time, what is up with Twitter[1]? Why would I care if someone is going to the grocery store right now? Doonesbury had a fun series of cartoons lambasting the Twitter craze recently. Yet, by March of this year, Twitter has overtaken all but one of the United Kingdom's news outlets in terms of website hits. In the last year, Nielsen reports that Twitter has grown 1,382 percent in the United States.[2] People are choosing their news and listening to the thinking of their personal gurus through Twitter.

Innovation is often about people tossing ideas into the ring and having them bantered about so that they begin to take some usable shape. There are some interesting people out there and I might want to listen to them brainstorm about technology and education. Tim O'Reilly[3] and Tim Lauer[4] are a couple of examples, although the first Tim is prolific on Twitter and I can't see myself keeping up that much. Twitter is ideal for that "throw out what you're thinking" kind of brainstorming, sharing what you are learning and wondering about. Teachers from different schools can form a

Twitter group so that they can toss around ideas about teaching with technology. Twitter as a professional development tool! I work with 8-10 pre-service teachers each spring during their student teaching. I am going to have my students Tweet about their experiences during the week so they can join each other in the joys and challenges of developing their teaching skills as they try new teaching strategies. Those tweets can be resources for conversation when we meet for class. We hope to learn from each other. Twitter can be about developing a community of innovators in education.

In regard to websites, there are lots of sources for innovative thinking to tap into. Edutopia[5] is one of my favorites, as it enthusiastically promotes project-based learning and provides video of teachers trying new things with their students. Microsoft sponsors the Innovative Teachers Network[6] and Apple sponsors the Learning Interchange[7] that, although tied to their products, have lots of creative approaches to education that stirs my thinking. The Brits can be a good resource as well, given websites such as FutureLab[8] and The Learning Discovery Centre[9], with a real dedication to innovation in education. Sites such as these can inspire new ways of thinking that technology can support by providing real world examples of innovation in action in schools.

You say you got a real solution. Well, you know, we'd all love to see the plan.

There are so many people and organizations out there that want to financially and materially support innovative thinkers. They want to see your plan for increasing the success of your students and are willing to get you the tools you need to make it happen. Just typing "teacher grants" in Google goes a long way towards finding those resources. Professional, local, and corporate organizations as well as state and federal government links are listed on my grant workshop website.[10] A little bit of time proposing an idea can lead to exciting possibilities, even if it doesn't get funded the first time around.

Eliot Soloway[11] has been one of the pioneers in how handheld technology can increase students' achievement in schools. Yet, I think he was a man with a solution before his time. PDA's in education really haven't taken off as he had hoped. However, with the dawn of the iPhone, Blackberry, and other smartphones, the mobile Internet is now estimated to be at least one third and possibly up to one half of the Internet usage in the United States.[12] Apple sold 30 million iPhone/iPod touches in the past year. We are now in the midst of a revolution in the capabilities of handheld computers. All of our devices are smooshing into one with phone, GPS, camera, Internet access, word processing, etc. Apple's facilitation of application creation for the iPhone has caused an incredible explosion of innovation from the silly iFart to potentially life saving tools for diabetics that measure insulin levels and calculate dosages. In less than one year, 25,000 new applications were developed and then downloaded 800 million times. That is one amazing escalation of creativity and consumer demand. While cellular phone companies have a stranglehold on us with monthly plans, other handheld devices such as the iTouch are quietly tagging along with growing capabilities and dropping prices. The $300 graphing calculator of ten years ago is now $45. Innovators seeking new possibilities will likely find "solutions" by considering the role of handheld technologies in classrooms. Who will tap into that potential for education?

With MySpace, Facebook, and now Twitter, it is clear that humanity is interested in being connected with each other and with ideas. Social networking is a driving force in students' lives and increasingly in business, with services such as LinkedIn.[13] Schools are the void in between. We know from research that when students put their ideas into words, they have more sophisticated thinking and they retain ideas better. Teachers want students to discuss ideas, such as parallels between Obama and Lincoln, the meaning in the poems of Whitman, the value of approaching a science lab or math problem from different perspectives. Perhaps innovative educators might find ways to solve the constraints of classroom conversation by tapping into social networking.

You tell me it's the institution. Well, you know, you better free your mind instead.

As teachers (including myself) and administrators curse cell phones and create rules banning them from classrooms, for the justifiable reason that they can distract from learning, perhaps there is another angle to be explored. The authors of Promoting Transformative Innovation in Schools suggest that in education:

> "...there is a need for transformative innovation in order to develop new relationships and ways of working, to update approaches, and to harness the collective social capital and skills of school communities to deliver better learning and teaching. This means challenging accepted practice and prevailing logic, which can place practitioners outside their comfort zone, as many changes that innovations may bring can often be disruptive and challenging in the short term."[14]

What kinds of innovations will truly make learning different, more engaging and effective? It is worth taking some risks. Particularly as new technologies evolve outside the classroom, teachers might consider how they could be used inside the classroom for different purposes. It might take something like, "Okay, everyone get out your cell phones..."

Of course, there are obstacles to being innovative. Chief among them is the digital divide. However, many math classrooms were furnished with sets of graphing calculators when the price became justifiable and the potential for learning became apparent. Figure out what impact you can have on learning, and the tools will become available. That's where the grants come in. And grant proposals are more powerful when you join with others engaging in the same exploration. Another pitch for social networking...

So here's to you innovators out there. It is an exciting time for educators because the possibilities are immense with these emerging technologies. Social networking is possibly one of the keys to not only increasing the thoughtfulness of students but also facilitating collaboration between teachers and connecting teachers to interesting new perspectives. You are not alone in working toward the revolution!

Endnotes

[1] http://www.twitter.com

[2] http://mashable.com/2009/03/16/twitter-growth-rate-versus-facebook/

[3] http://oreilly.com/

[4] http://timlauer.org/

[5] http://www.edutopia.org/

[6] http://www.innovativeteachers.com

[7] http://edcommunity.apple.com/ali/

[8] http://www.futurelab.org.uk/

[9] http://www.learningdiscovery.org.uk

[10] http://web.me.com/rhine5/Grants

[11] http://www.goknow.com

[12] http://www.avc.com/a_vc/2009/03/in-the-us-mobile-internet-usage-is-at-leasat-onethird-and-maybe-onehalf-of-wired-internet-usage.html

[13] http://www.linkedin.com

[14] http://www.futurelab.org.uk/resources/documents/handbooks/innovation_handbook.pdf

Book Review

Andrew Vachss' *Terminal: A Burke Novel*

View online at: http://bcis.pacificu.edu/journal/2009/03/article.php?id=52

Review by Jeffrey Barlow
Editor, *Interface*

Vachss, Andrew. Terminal. A Burke Novel. New York: Vintage Books, 2008.

A reader will sometimes encounter a book—perhaps many books—that he or she does not like. It is rare, however, to encounter a book that actively dislikes the reader. *Terminal* is just such a book.

But for those interested in the many portrayals of the impact of the Internet found in fiction, *Terminal*, and several of Andrew Vachss' other works, are instructive. They are also highly educational, in the sense in which watching an auto wreck or viewing an autopsy is also no doubt educational. But to find them entertaining requires entering a dark world of suffering and despair, with no expectation of leaving refreshed. Though in a very literal sense, the reader might find him or herself *recreated.*

Andrew Vachss is, if judged solely by the number of his published works, a highly successful author--so successful that he now makes some of his works available free as downloadable files on the Internet [1]. He is also a noted attorney who once edited *The New England Law Review* and has been a part of several landmark cases [2]. In addition, he is a passionate defender of children's rights and a practicing counselor who has worked in a wide variety of correctional institutions and programs [3]. As impressive as these achievements are, they do not begin to indicate the full range of his accomplishments or his complexity.

The world he has consistently created in his fiction, featuring his anti-hero Burke and the criminalized anti-heroes whose lives revolve around him, is more than dark. It is thoroughly depressing; each character is inevitably stamped with some dreadful human shortcoming, ranging from spectacular physical handicaps, an inability to live within the confines of his or her original gender, compulsive criminality, outright insanity or a love for murder and mayhem, which is briefly, occasionally, and quite incidentally bent toward committing good. These individuals live, one and all, off the grid, outside society. They live as an extended family, to Burke the most precious of human social organizations. The enemies of family are often described as "freaks." Of this antagonism Burke says: "To me the freaks are a Tribe. Anytime I take one from them, that's one for us." [4]

In this hell of omnipresent and threatening violence, only the young are truly innocent. Burke is, of course, more than disinterested in earning anything resembling an honest living--to Burke, and perhaps to Vachss, the honest and socially successful are at best complicit in the continuing crimes perpetrated against the weak and disadvantaged. Burke's career consists of preying on those who prey on others, particularly racists, child-abusers, pimps and pushers, or other exploiters of the weak.

The tool of choice for such exploiters is the Internet. It began to feature in Vachss' earlier works as the sewer through which child pornography and other forms of malevolence and evil routinely slither.

Those who use the Internet as an evil tool must, of course, be fought by those who use it, however incidentally, for good. In *Terminal*, for example, we meet the "nephew" who was abused by his parents to the point where he has lost all emotion—he does however, love animals and plans to protect them by eliminating humans [5]. He is also designing a game based on the *World of Warcraft*, which is succinctly explained, in which the goal of each player--all of whom hate each other--is to destroy the game world itself, taking down the virtual wealth and identities carefully built up over years of play. The winner gets the pleasure of this ultimate act of virtual annihilation.

The nephew gives Burke access to one of his casual projects, a memory stick/flash drive which, when placed in a USB port, instantly and totally recodes every system in the computer to which it is connected. When asked why he built this infernal machine, this geek from hell replies: "To hurt things...as if that was the only sensible answer to any question." [6]

Terminal is not, it must be apparent, an easy read. At many points the narrator, Burke, steps aside and addresses the reader:

> You know why we hate you? Not because you don't know what we know, but because, even if you did, you wouldn't give a damn.
>
> So I'm sitting here, waiting to commit extortion, and planning a lot worse. I'm what you'd call a career criminal. That's why I'll never be you. And I'm proud of it [7].

Burke, like Vachss we must assume, is totally uninterested in questions we examine at *Interface*, such as which aspects of the Internet are positive ones and which negative, and how we can then improve upon the negative so as to realize its full promise. The author's rage at the exploitation of children in particular is such that no possible good can outweigh the Internet's calamitous consequences [8]. To Burke, if not to Vachss--who after all has his own web pages--the Internet is a tool of fallen humanity, and like us, will only do evil in any foreseeable future.

Endnotes

[1] See the author's web page at http://www.vachss.com. Vachss is pronounced as though written "Vax."

[2] See, for example, the material on the Robert Lewis case at: http://www.vachss.com/downloads.html

[3] See his many editorials and articles at: http://www.vachss.com/av_dispatches.html

[4] Terminal, p. 138.

[5] Pp. 160-161.

[6] P. 162.

[7] P. 208.

[8] For the range of Vachss' opinions on this issue, see interview excerpts at: http://www.vachss.com/av_interviews.html

Site Review

Bill Vanderbok's Brown Bag Radio

View online at: http://bcis.pacificu.edu/journal/2009/03/article.php?id=53

Review by Jeffrey Barlow
Editor, *Interface*

At the Berglund Center for Internet Studies, we feel, as do many readers, that our coverage on the Internet, China, and East Asia, in general, is excellent. We, as well as some of our readers, also think that we could do more with South Asia, particularly India. The rise of India and China are, in many ways, similar in their impact to the point where a common current topic in China is "Chindia," meaning some possible community of interest between these two gigantic countries.

We have reviewed some books covering the Internet in India, but that we do not do more is, a result, in large part, of the general neglect of Indian studies in American schools. To atone, we draw your attention to a delightful and highly informative web site: Brown Bag Radio ("Because somewhere in the world it's lunch time!"). Operated by one man, Bill Vanderbok [1], on something less than a shoestring, Brown Bag Radio nonetheless offers audio presentations by leading experts in South Asian Studies, including many very successful Information Technology entrepreneurs from the subcontinent [2]. It is sponsored by SASA, the South Asian Studies Association, and has access to its hundreds of highly qualified members.

Descriptions of recent broadcasts include [3]:

- Professor Jagdish Sheth, Kellstadt Professor of Marketing, Emory University, who talks about his latest book, Chindia Rising. The discussant is Dr. Nirvikar Singh, Economics Department, University of California at Santa Cruz.
- Professor Rafiq Dossani, Stanford University, talks about his latest book, India Arriving. The discussant is Dr. Pradeep Chhibber, Chair of Political Science, University of California at Berkeley.
- Vivek Wadhwa discusses "Facts and Myths in the Globalization Debate," and presents a number of data driven conclusions at odds with popular conceptions. Wadhwa teaches at the Pratt School of Engineering, Duke University, is a Fellow at Harvard Law, and a regular columnist for Business Week. The Discussant is Siddarth Swaminathan of La Sierra University.

Bill Vanderbok functions as the congenial host and each presentation, as the list above suggests, includes a noted presenter and an often equally noted discussant. Most presentations are available as both Power Point presentations and audio files and the technical quality is excellent.

Since the dominant topic among the presentations is Information Technology, the site is a marvelous resource for better understanding the impact of the Internet in South Asia as well as South Asia's impact upon the Internet.

Endnotes

[1] Bill is also an editor for two of our journals, *Interface* and *E-AsPac*

[2] See the web site at: Brownbagradio.net

[3] Hear the broadcasts at: Brownbagradio.net

Editorial

Using Google Sites, or The Editor's Lament

View online at: http://bcis.pacificu.edu/journal/2009/03/article.php?id=54

Editorial by Jeffrey Barlow

One of the major problems facing a content oriented site like the Berglund Center for Internet Studies is dealing with the multiplicity of files of all types that must be processed. The work is distributed among many users and their computers. Keeping track of files as they evolve in production chains becomes quite complex. After more than ten years of evolution, we settled upon a Web 2.0 system, "Google Sites," as a solution.

The Berglund Center must not only deal with hundreds of files over a month, but our work force changes substantially on an annual basis, and it is our most experienced staff, our graduating seniors, who will leave us. We have slowly but surely learned how best to use "Sites" to solve our problems within the context of our own continually changing organization. Here we generalize from some of those lessons.

An article that eventually appears in *Interface*, may come to us through a process similar to what print editors called "over-the-transom." In "over-the-transom" a hopeful author simply tosses a hard copy through an open transom at editorial offices, probably after hours in order to avoid the agony of instant refusal: "Sorry, we accept only solicited pieces..."

At *Interface* our equivalent is over-the-Internet submission. As we are eager to review such contributions, we send an e-mail as soon as possible confirming our receipt and perhaps asking for some additional details about the author's authority and financial expectations, hoping that the former is very high and the latter, very low.

This exchange begins a process where a submission moves through the computers of several editors, perhaps also those of some external reviewers, then comes back with suggestions for changes. These suggestions are then communicated to the author—or authors—then sent back to us, and then put through copy editing, and then returned to the main editor for review. Next it is sent to the HTML editor to be posted on the development server, and then posted to *Interface*. After that an editor must "click through" the article to check formatting, as must the author. Finally, after some commas are moved around once again, it will hopefully find an active life as it is read, noticed, and often copied across the Internet.

Now multiply this example by every piece, notice, announcement and review that goes into *Interface*, or any of the several other journals edited out of our offices.[1] Envision an office in which the staff are themselves writing, commenting, and perhaps shooting and editing video and posting it on You Tube and Berglund servers. These people are also trying to read and respond to at least twenty-five e-mails out of the several hundred that come into our offices daily, and make their classes, whether as a student or instructor. Now you might begin to understand why it is that editors are often said to be at hazard of, at least, alcoholism (and now there are so many new and interesting possibilities to be abused, including computer games) if not madness. Heh!

As complex as the process of distributed production can be, the ultimate problem is basic: How does one quickly determine what stage each file is in, where it must go next, and how to retrace each and every stage of the process when necessary?

We have been editing at either the Berglund Center or its predecessor, the Matsushita Center for Electronic Learning, (both out of Pacific University Oregon), since 1994 when we posted our first web pages in Asian Studies. At that time very little seemed to be at stake because it was extremely unlikely that anybody would read our postings anyway. Our first day's traffic was fifty visitors, and occured to us that we might be on to something.

In 1998, we founded and began editing *The Journal of the Association for History and Computing* and things started to get serious. We were soon dealing with articles coming from all over the world and guiding a "stable" of editors, (a metaphor which every editor will come to understand within a few moments of beginning to work) writing abstracts in French, German, Spanish, and occasionally Russian, Chinese, and Japanese.

Grant monies started coming in, including the generous gift of Jim and Mary Berglund, which created the Berglund Center, and a building to house it and other Pacific University functions. Then things were, by any definition, serious.

Once an editor has lost or misplaced a submission and dealt with an anxious author about to undergo some sort of review process, he or she realizes that the stakes are high, and keeping track of files becomes more than an interesting exercise. We began tracking and coordinating with note pads, then blackboards, then white boards, and now Excel sheets, (after flirtations with off-brand spreadsheets) the whole while being supported by yellow and then multicolored blizzards of sticky notes.

As the importance of the Internet grew, so, of course, did the tools available to us. We soon had software that would open any conceivable document—and the inconceivable ones as well (Turkish versions of Word Perfect anyone?)—which came into our office, html editors grew larger and more user-friendly, and the capabilities of writing programs became more so as well.

However, even with all the new technology and a dedicated staff, nothing really solved the main problem. Two complications remained. The underlying issue was the file metaphor itself. Everything was a file and each person who handled it was likely to change it at least minimally so the versions of everything multiplied with each click of a mouse. In addition, the distribution was essentially top down—I created documents and records and counted on steadily expanding numbers of staff members, who revolved on pretty much an annual basis—to familiarize themselves with the processes without themselves having any ownership.

The obvious answer to this problem, which various business have encountered on a far larger scale (not to mention all publishers) was to house files on a central server either internally or perhaps at a data farm. These solutions, however, were expensive, in terms of both equipment and manpower. They required at the least an in-house programmer/systems' operator of considerable ability and training. Also, as the movement of files multiplied so did the risk of security problems. In addition, staff came in wedded to the notion of the personal computer. We tried central file servers and found that their learning curve cost us too much in staff time and salaries.

Furthermore, as generous as grants were, our total annual budget, while permitting us to achieve prodigies, was well below that of almost any conceivable journal or publication with which we might be compared. At the Berglund Center we still have no full time employees. Even adding our professional part timers together, we still have less than two full timers, but, nonetheless, we usually remain high on the first page of the Google rankings for any activities for which we might be searched. However, simply adding more manpower multiplied the problem: more hands, more potential file changes.

Things changed recently, however, with the advent of Web 2.0. In essence, the Web itself is now a distributed project. Soon the possibilities offered by distributed projects called forth the solutions to our problems. Google both discovered and created the importance of distributed work as a consequence of the founders' insight that searching for *and finding* content was going to be the single most essential support function of the World Wide Web.[2]

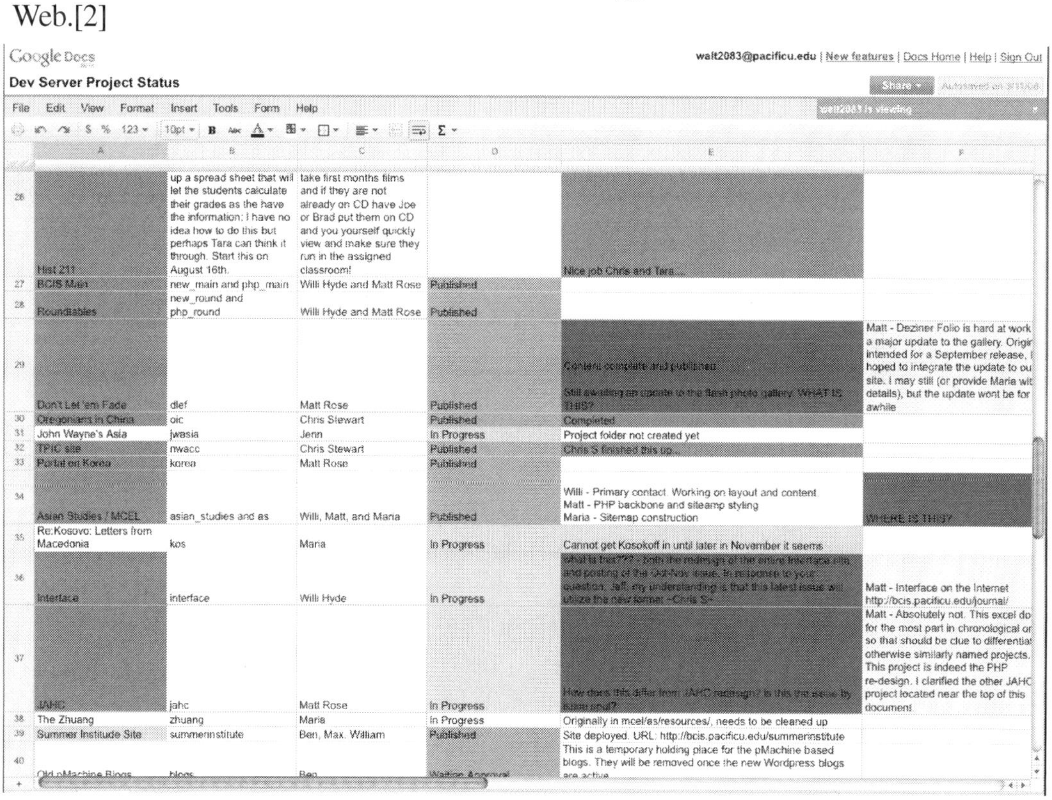

Google then, for various good business reasons, began to provide free storage, and the tools necessary to work with files distributed across many different servers. Free applications began issuing from the "Googleplex" on what seemed to be a daily basis. One such was "Google Docs" which let us create files and store them on Google's servers while working with related software.[3]

With "Google Docs," we could locate files "in the cloud" even though we still could not afford a truly networked office or access to a data farm. However, problems remained. The learning curve for "Docs" was quite high, and some of our student staff proved either uninterested or unable to master its essential functions. It also seemed to our editors to be adding an additional layer of complexity to our chores as we tried to track changes.[4]

But two things happened: First, incoming students had begun to encounter distributed sites much earlier as the social uses of the web, (such as Facebook and You Tube) began to multiply, and our staff grew less resistant. Secondly, Google issued another related tool, "Google Sites."[5] Building on the Wiki format, which, thanks to Wikipedia, has become steadily more familiar, "Google Sites" was a whole other level of user-friendly.

In the summer of 2008, Lynda Irons, a colleague from the Pacific University Library and an *Interface* editor, introduced me to "Google Sites" and we taught it to faculty groups in a two-hour block at a faculty workshop. It was immediately obvious that "Sites" was very easy to teach and to learn. The audience was delighted with it and by the second hour of our workshop, they were spinning off many uses creatively adapted to their own professional needs.

So our then Berglund Center Program Coordinator, Tara Fechter, and I designed a Google Site for the Berglund Center. We used it during 2008-09 and it served us very well. We were able to track files easily, call up previous iterations of materials, and invite authors and staff to work directly in the site. These dazzling uses developed rapidly. Our staff in that period, of course, saw it develop as we created it and, with some exceptions, took to it easily.

Then, however, Tara took another job that let her better employ her true love, mathematics. We were fortunate in hiring Theresa Floyd, one of the founders of the Berglund Center. Theresa is multi-talented, known on campus as the "Queen of the databases," and has considerable training in design and layout as well. She believes that using a mouse instead of memorizing keyboard commands and short cuts is inefficient. However, she found our Google Sites pages difficult to understand and use.

What we learned from these experiences has been critical. Tara and I had grown accustomed to the organization of "Google Sites" quite easily because of our previous familiarity with all of our operations at the Center. When a new problem arose, we solved it by creating a new page. Our staff of that period had adapted easily because they were present at the creation.

But new staff, even those as capable and experienced as Theresa, did not finds the organization of our Sites pages logical at all, but rather a buzzing, confusing maze which made no sense unless you were already familiar with all of our activities.

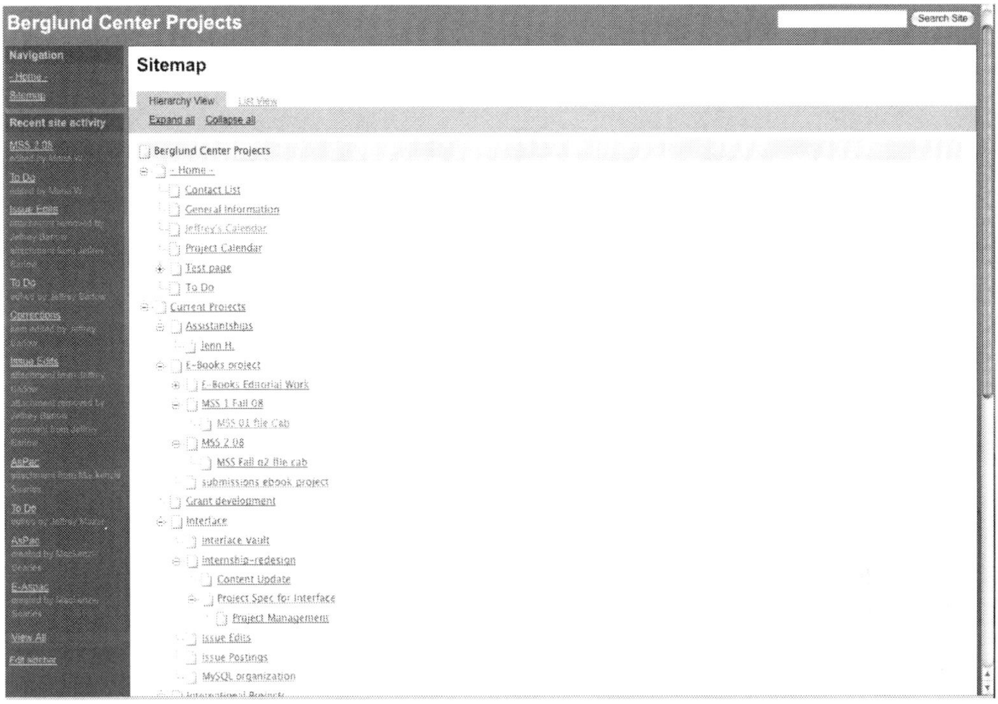

Any organization has certain inherent tensions. A key issue for any business, profit or non-profit, is the trade off between training and efficiency. It is best, when possible, to adapt the work to previously known staff skills rather than to try to adapt the staff, through training, to the work.

As long as we utilize, for example, the familiar programs of the personal computer and its web-based functions, our staff can quickly learn new ancillary skills. That is the genius of "Google Sites"; it uses the familiar directory and file structure and lets the user modify it, (using the page metaphor) to his or her needs.

But a complex organization, even one with fewer than fifteen staff members like our own, quickly develops communications problems. This underlying issue is that communication is not arithmetic but geometric. Two people have only two possible communications channels: A to B, and B to A, and because of the nature of interactive communications, really only one: A and B to each other, with exceptions noted below. Add C, however, and we now have not three but nine possibilities: A to B but not C; A to B and C; A to C but not B; B to A but not C, etc. Some of these sets are essentially duplicates, but given a hierarchical management structure, not necessarily so: A may tell B what B dare not tell A. Expand such an organization to fifteen members and the Tower of Babel reconstructs itself right in your own office.

Our problem, and perhaps yours, is that fifteen people communicating about one hundred files is more like the U.N.—without simultaneous translators—than like Babel. "Google Sites" was our solution.

We are now in a new stage of adapting it. This means, in part, despite the costs, adapting the staff to the work. As part of the process of our annual evolution at the Center, we watch our seniors graduate and in the past have largely waited for the following fall to hire their replacements. This saved us, of course, the expense of having two staff members for each position. This year we hired in the spring and each outgoing senior is training his or her replacement. Part of the training is not only familiarizing the new staff with informal office routines, but also learning to use "Google Sites." This has required, as in the lesson learned from Theresa's experience, acknowledging the reality of a constantly changing staff.

To meet this challenge, we re-organized the labs themselves, putting Maria Walters, formerly our HTML editor, in charge of the labs and all student projects. Maria, also a math major, is reorganizing "Google Sites" in the hopes of making it much more user friendly. Maria's first major change was to, once again, adapt the work to the staff. She observed that the first organizational iteration of our Google Sites, that, created by Tara and myself, attempted to adapt the staff to the work. Some members quickly became lost in the labyrinth of task-related pages. She superimposed a staff-centered structure which looks like this:

Sara

- Roundtable ads, correspondence (Roundtables)

Interface (Interface) -- overseen by Maria
Jenn (also in Web Projects)
Maria

- writing articles (Jenn's page: Jenn H.)
- give Jeff and Max a list of the author emails (March 13th, Jeff)
- approve comments (here)

Jackie (also in International Projects)
Sierra (also in Web Projects)

- proofreading and editing (Issue Edits)
- plagiarism check -- look into, get familiar with TurnItIn.com
- approve comments (here)

Jamaica (also in Web Projects)

- typesetting final versions (Issue Postings)
- add to MySQL database
- approve comments (here)
- make "About the Authors" page (ask Maria)

International Projects - overseen by Jeffrey
Mackenzie

- Teach in China (China:TESL -- needs to be updated)
- other International Projects

Allison
Jackie (also in Interface)

- correspondence with Yang (China: Yang mss projects)
- look into print-on-demand services, especially CreateSpace through Amazon (https://www.createspace.com/) -- work with E-Books project

Design -- overseen by Jeffrey, Theresa
Zach

- BCIS (BCIS Redesign)
- Interface (Internship-redesign)
- Site Updates

Web Projects -- overseen by Maria
Jamaica (also in Interface)

- typesetting edited E-AsPac articles (E-AsPac files from 08 conference stored)
- posting JAHC (if/when that ever gets running again) (JAHC)
- redesign E-AsPac navigation? (reflect annual structure)

So far, all indications are that for the first time we have a smooth transition and that our very complex production chains are being quickly learned, all within the framework of "Google Sites."

The lessons that we have learned in adapting "Google Sites" might be summarized as:

1. Create your Site not with a view to its use by current staff, but by any future staff member as well.
2. The organization of your Site needs to be staff-centric. That is, any given staff member needs to know right where to go to see their part in all production chains, no matter how complex. (See graphic immediately above).
3. The Sites pages also needs to give a hierarchical view of operations necessary for supervisors, such as in our case, myself, Theresa, and Maria, to track over all operations.
4. This hierarchical view also solves another problem encountered in complex production chains: staff members are naturally curious about what others are doing, and want to know how their job fits into the overall operation. Otherwise their tasks come to seem more laborious than creative.

5. Numbers 2) and 3) above solve an additional need: that for redundancy. There must be more than one channel to find each task. They also provide back up in the event of some catastrophe.
6. Supervising staff must regularly review the pages. This is, in part, because they will have to move files from page to page to ensure that the next stage of the process proceeds properly. In addition, if staff begins to feel that their work is not being observed, it soon loses importance for them.

"Google Sites," as useful as they are, have some limitations of which any user should be aware. They are, after all, in the cloud—that is, in the distributed web of files that constitute the Internet. These files are not, when hosted by Google, in any specific single location. They are distributed across multiple computers, with broad redundancy. However, it has happened that at critical moments such as the forty-eight hours before we post *Interface*, "Google Sites" has been unavailable to us for hours at a time. This would not be a problem in most organizations as long as such incidents are foreseen, but our staff is part time. Some of our highly specialized video editors, for example, are only able to work on one high-end computer, and then only during certain hours each week when they are not in class or working, for example, at Fox News like our Video Production Manager, Steven Wong.

There is another potential limitation: security. Google itself feels that the massive size of its cloud precludes selective intrusions. That is, if I wanted to see your financial data, I couldn't effectively intrude into the Google cloud and reproduce the data from hundreds of different computers. However, some data, we feel, is too valuable to be entrusted to others' computers, and it is best not to put financial data or critical planning data onto Sites, however secure they are assumed to be.

Endnotes

[1] See http://bcis.pacificu.edu/journals.php for a partial list.
[2] See our review of David A. Vise and Mark Malseed's work, *The Google Story* at: http://bcis.pacificu.edu/journal/2007/02/vise.php to better understand this factor.
[3] See http://docs.google.com for Google Docs
[4] As the user reports at http://www.google.com/google-d-s/intl/en/tour5.html show, many others found them much more suitable than did we..

May 2009 - Volume 9, Issue 4

Articles

Book and Site Reviews

Editorial

Feature

ADA Web Standards and You: A "How-To"

View online at: http://bcis.pacificu.edu/journal/2009/04/article.php?id=59

By Zach W. Bingaman
Web Designer, Berglund Center for Internet Studies

Introduction

When learning to design websites, there are a few essentials that most people learn. For example: the "triple constraint" (time, money, and resources), HTML, CSS, client relations, and intellectual property. What most web designer don't learn is how to design for ADA web standards (no not the American Dental Association). If, in a hypothetical project, you, as the web designer, arrange not to have any legal responsibility for the end project then you're in the clear. But what if you have a client who asks, "Can you make this site in ADA standards?" Most clients who are aware of ADA standards are also aware are of the possible legal ramifications of not complying. Therefore, if you cannot design for ADA standards, you probably will lose that client. What share here are simple methods in web-design that avoid this issue. I will explain what ADA is, what Section 508 is, and how to design for ADA web standards.

What is ADA?

Short and simply put, ADA is an acronym for Americans with Disabilities Act of 1990. The intention of this act was initially to protect people with disabilities in the workplace by requiring nondiscrimination standards. ADA prohibits:

> "private employers, state and local governments, employment agencies and labor unions from discriminating against qualified individuals with disabilities in job application procedures, hiring, firing, advancement, compensation, job training, and other terms, conditions, and privileges of employment. The ADA covers employers with 15 or more employees, including state and local governments. It also applies to employment agencies and to labor organizations. The ADA's nondiscrimination standards also apply to federal sector employees under section 501 of the Rehabilitation Act, as amended, and its implementing rules." (eeoc.gov)

In short the act is directed at any employer who discriminates against a disabled individual by not providing what the individual needs. According to the law, the definitions of a disabled individual are rather broad:

> An individual with a disability is a person who:
>
> - Has a physical or mental impairment that substantially limits one or more major life activities;
> - Has a record of such an impairment; or
> - Is regarded as having such an impairment.
>
> A qualified employee or applicant with a disability is an individual who, with or without reasonable accommodation, can perform the essential functions of

the job in question. Reasonable accommodation may include, but is not limited to:

- Making existing facilities used by employees readily accessible to and usable by persons with disabilities.
- Job restructuring, modifying work schedules, reassignment to a vacant position;
- Acquiring or modifying equipment or devices, adjusting or modifying examinations, training materials, or policies, and providing qualified readers or interpreters.

These are very vague terms, but the actual article lists disabilities as, "caring for oneself, performing manual tasks, seeing, hearing, eating, sleeping, walking, standing, lifting, bending, speaking, breathing, learning, reading, concentrating, thinking, communicating, and working..." (eeoc.gov). The act states that these are "...included but are not limited to..." and thus it puts any documented disability under ADA protection. For employers this can be very intimidating as nearly anyone, for many reasons, can file a lawsuit over discrimination.

In fact, many such suits have been filed: "In Fiscal Year 2008, EEOC received 19,453 charges of disability discrimination. EEOC resolved 15,708 disability discrimination charges in FY 2008 and recovered $57.2 million in monetary benefits for charging parties and other aggrieved individuals (not including monetary benefits obtained through litigation)" (eeoc.gov).

While there are a lot of cases with large payouts, not all of them are website related. In the next section you will see how Section 508 and ADA do go hand in hand to create ADA web standards.

What Are Section 508 and Section 504?

Section 508 originated in 1998 as an amendment to the Rehabilitation Act (an act that dictates the use of governmental funding). It requires that "Federal agencies make their electronic and information technology accessible to people with disabilities" (section508.gov). This amendment is directed at Federal agencies, but Section 504 is significantly broader: "Section 504 prohibits discrimination based on disability in federally funded and federally conducted programs or activities in the United States, including employment programs" (section508.gov).

According to Section 508 all Federal agencies must make their information accessible to people with disabilities, and Section 504 requires any government-funded organization to do the same. The ADA requires any employer to accommodate disabled people or employees. "The Americans with Disabilities Act (ADA) and, if the government entities receive Federal funding, the Rehabilitation Act of 1973, generally require that state and local governments provide qualified individuals with disabilities equal access to their programs, services, or activities unless doing so would fundamentally alter the nature of their programs, services, or activities or would impose an undue burden" (ada.gov). Through Sections 504/508 and the ADA every aspect of a college campus website (the funding, the employee's, etc) must be made accessible. But how must a big business with thousands of employees comply?

To better understand Sections 504/508 and ADA standards we need to look at them in application. Currently most non-governmental websites do not fully comply with these standards. The organization W3C attempts to aid web developers to create more accessible websites through their HTML/CSS, and validate programs found at www.w3c.org. But these validated programs do not account for two of the most common problems, resizing issues or resolution differences.

Using the W3C validate programs you can account for users who are blind via alt tags on images, but you can't account for all of what might or might not be seen as each website is different. The content is generated by the designer and as such can't be tested for yet.

Let's return to a college website and a business website to see what this might mean:

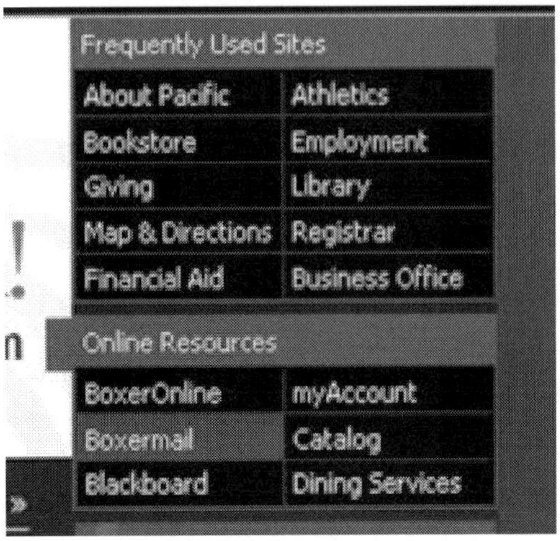

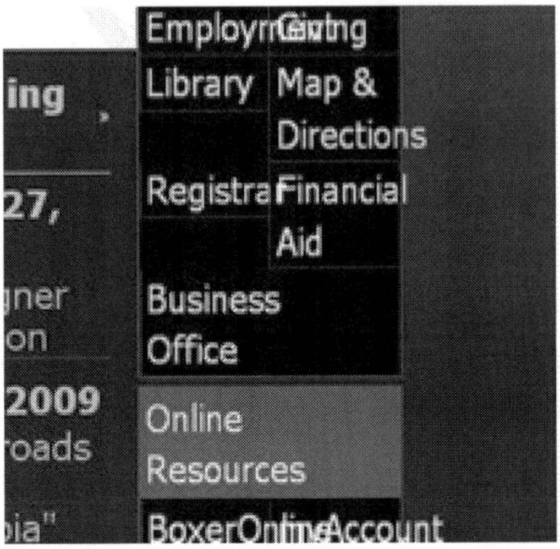

I've taken screenshots of a college campus website (as seen above) and compared the navigation bar with itself at a larger font size (which a person with poor eyesight would do; this process will be explained in "Designing for Accessibility"). We'll call these B.1, and B.2.

I've also repeated the experiment with a leading business website (as seen below). We'll call these A.1, and A.2. Throughout the rest of this paper we'll refer to these images for examples.

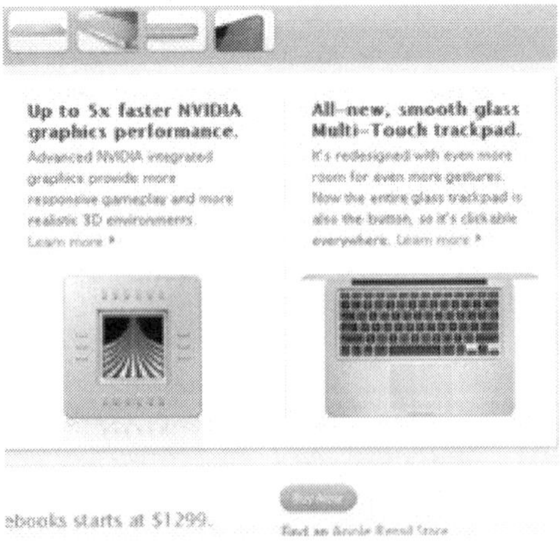

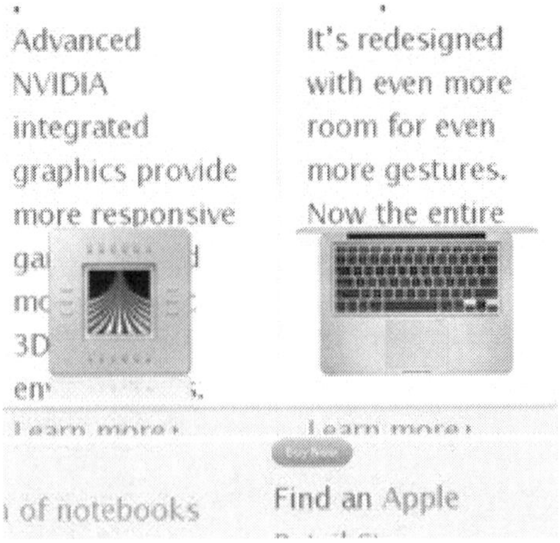

As you can see, the college campus navigation, or how you move through the site (image B.2) has entire navigation sections that are unreadable due to overlapping text and oddly reformatted bars. While it is a good thing that the page will scale vertically, the navigation items will not scale horizontally which can make the page difficult to read. According to the laws, because the college receives government funding and has employees, if someone needed a specific piece of information but cannot find it due to a poor design, that person can file a complaint or a lawsuit.

In A.2 you can see that full bodies of text disappear behind images placed there. Also you can see that full links are lost and unusable. If an employee or a potential customer needed that piece of information (say a disclaimer which the person could not read) they could not obtain it due to a poor design. That business would thus be in violation of ADA and therefore vulnerable to lawsuits. When asked, "What's so important about ADA Web Standards?" look at the facts. Designing for accessibility is a necessity.

Designing for Accessibility

We've defined what the ADA, Section 504, and Section 508 are but not yet their full meaning for accessibility. Joe Clark writes in his book *Building Accessible Websites*:

> Accessibility involves making allowances for characteristics a person cannot readily change. It's a simple, sweeping definition. Practical Examples of its application to websites:
>
> - A deaf person cannot stop being deaf when confronted with a soundtrack
> - A blind person cannot stop being blind when confronted with visual words and images
> - A learning-disabled person cannot reset the function of the brain when confronted with the same.
> - A person with a mobility impairment cannot suddenly begin to move when confronted with a navigation task.
> - A unilingual Anglophone cannot suddenly understand French when confronted with that language.

Clark is saying is that because a person is disabled we cannot expect them to be able to perform at the same level as a person who is not disabled. Our responsibility as designers is to accommodate our entire audience.

In Jakob Nielsen's book *Designing Web Usability*, he opens his chapter on accessibility with, "The Americans with Disabilities Act and similar laws and regulations in other countries often mandate equal access to computer systems for users with disabilities. In particular, there will often be a legal obligation to facilitate intranet use by disabled employees who may not be able to do their job if they cannot access their company's internal website" (297).

What Nielsen has outlined in this statement reinforces the information provided in the previous sections of this paper. The ADA and Sections 504/508 are part of the law, and as such there are real consequences to not complying with them.

The truly big question yet to be asked is how to start complying with these laws. Organizations such as the W3C have launched programs such as the WAI (Web Accessibility Initiative; found at http://www.w3.org/WAI/). These sites provide guidelines as to how things should be done to accommodate disabled audiences. However the truth is that **not every** guideline can be **perfectly** followed and even the **best** designed sites **cannot accommodate** everyone perfectly.

Any experienced business will tell you that while you can't have the entire audience, you can target a specific one. To apply this theory to web design start being accessible by designing your site for one disability at a time. In Jakob Nielsen's chapter on accessibility, he outlines each relevant disability and how to consider them for design. The Internet as we know it is a visual media. To follow Neilson's model consider visual, auditory, speech, motor, and cognitive disabilities. The key to each of these is simplicity. Simple is always better when it comes to accommodating people with disabilities.

Designing for visual disabilities should be the first priority when making a website accessible. Because the Internet is a visual medium, a website should be able to accommodate a user if they have poor eyesight or even no eyesight at all. In the situation of poor eyesight the website should be tested using the method I used to test websites A and B.

In Mozilla Firefox, this means resizing your text by going to the "Tools" option then to "Options" on Windows, and on a Mac, to "File" and then to "Properties". Under the content tab click the "Advanced" button in the "Font & Colors" section. Once there you can change your minimum font size to the highest setting (the worst case scenario) and view your website.

But in Internet Explorer (IE) 8 you can increase your font size via "View" and "Font Size." However, as most designers know, IE in any form leaves out necessary functionality, so test the text-resizing in as many web browsers as possible. You may notice that there will be overlapping text and/or broken items on the page.

To fix these problems look to the "Liquid Layout" section. Text on a website should be spaced evenly through CSS. Use style rules such as line-height and readable fonts such as Verdana. Avoid using letter-spacing if possible as the resizing of characters will push the spacing, making it unreadable. Also avoid high contrast backgrounds, and, if possible, make sure your font color is easy on the eyes but still in contrast with the background. Fonts are normally black on a white background for good reason.

In the case that a member of your audience cannot see at all they will most likely be using an audio screen reader. The program/device will read the HTML excluding style rules and code, like one would read a book. However, the reader will not be able to interpret images or flash items. This is where you must use the Alt attribute for images. The Alt attribute outputs text enabling a screen reader to output a description of the image. A proper image tag with the Alt attribute might look like this:

```
<img src="image/b1.jpg" alt="Image of a website's navigation">
```

Be sure in the Alt tag to be terse but specific about what the image is, but if notice above that there is no height or width attribute applied to the image. In some images there may be text used that must be resized for audiences who can see but have poor eyesight.

Through CSS you can resize images through the use of EM's. To view how to resize images using CSS look to the section "Pixels v EM". Returning to Alt tags, as long as a proper alt is applied (it must state something about what the image is) it should pass through a W3C validation, thus meeting ADA web standards. Jakob Nielson argues that not all images need a description in an alt tag, "Even though the rule of thumb is to provide ALT text for all images, there are in fact some images that are best annotated with empty string. If an image is purely decorative and has no meaning other than to make the page look better, then there is no reason to slow blind readers with having to hear an explanation" (Nielson 306). It is up to the designer to decide which is best, but even if the tag says it's a "Decorative Image" the user will know in general terms what is on the page.

Auditory and speech disabilities are the second and third issues to consider when designing a website. With auditory disabilities the user would be unable to hear sound, and thus a transcript should always be produced when sound is played. Avoid playing music on the page unless necessary as it tends to lower the quality of the design, and the site would work the same without it.

Speech disabilities should be an issue only in the case that speech is used in the design such as in the exchanging of messages. Programs such as Skype carry speech capabilities but also allow for text input. For a web design, if you are including a speech form of input, be sure to include an option for text input.

Cognitive and motor disabilities are related in that with motor disabilities the person is unable to perform complex button clicks and with cognitive disabilities the person is unable to comprehend a complex design. To accommodate these disabilities you only need to use the KISS rule: Keep It Simple, Stupid. A good but simple design can still make almost any website amazing.

The website should be appealing to the eye, but not too contrasting. Simplify any items on your site as possible. For example, if you have a news feed make sure your titles are 2-4 words maximum with 2-3 line descriptions. If making an additional page will free up a cluttered item then this will improve design. Also note that it should take no more than three clicks to reach any item in the website.

Finally, make sure that your website looks the same across all browsers. Implementing a browser CSS reset code (such as the one provided by Eric Meyer at meyerweb.com) would be the first step to do so.

Resolution Issues

During the development of my first site, I was initially concerned with cross-browser compatibility. To do this I simply used two computers. One was a Mac loaded with every browser I could find, and the other was a PC also loaded with browsers. When I first tested the site, I did it on the Mac because I designed the site on that computer. But when I viewed it on the other computer, I noticed that some items shifted and moved.

Websites also tend to look different based on a person's screen resolution. You could build your website in Adobe Flash and write a line of code for a resolution check, but for those who are not very familiar with Flash, there is the additional option of Liquid Layouts and a lot of testing. If you can, get two computers like I did and test them at three different resolutions: a low (800x600 minimum), middle (1024x768 minimum), and as high as you can get (2800 x2100). Check DIV placements to make sure everything is aligned as it should be then check images to see if they overlap. When using liquid layouts, a high resolution will sometimes make a font smaller. If the font size is read as being smaller, the sizing of the DIV can change and thus images may overlap.

The key issue with different resolutions is being able to keep the majority of content on the smallest resolution without requiring major scrolling, while also being able to limit the amount of blank space on a high resolution screen. Blank space is not a bad thing as long as the site is still appealing. But, with a site that looks tiny, a professional may have problems differentiating the blank space from a lack of content or design.

Liquid Layout

Liquid layouts are both a godsend and a nightmare because they require a balance between being fully liquid and being static. What you, as a designer, need to do is to build aspects of your site to be scalable and recognize what elements needs to compliment the scaling. When using HTML and CSS, your best tools are auto values, percent values, and EM values. The simpler a website's design is, the easier it is to make its layout liquid. There are many different methods to creating what is commonly known as a liquid layout, but the most effective method I've found is to begin with your DIV layout. The Internet is a visual media, so rather than looking at code created by professionals, consider the box model for DIV's as a physical box which you are building in.

Remember that DIV items organize HTML items in boxes. You must use your space wisely. The methods for cognitive/motor disabilities dictate that you should keep the layout simple. Attempt to limit the design to a single navigation item and create secondary navigations as necessary. The previous section "Resolution Issues" explains that the design should have the majority of its content fit in a minimum resolution (about 800x600), but still fill a medium to high resolution screen. If properly laid out, the DIV items should feel like building blocks that push and pull on each other. Using CSS, your placement of each DIV should be able to scale with the resizing of DIV next to it.

With every DIV nicely placed, the next step is to consider the content inside each DIV. In your prototype note where text will be, where images will be, and finally to what extent you need those items to scale. Consider what will be visually unreadable at a large scale and, once you input content into your site, test resizing it to see where it does break. Do this because you need to decide what images must be resized via CSS, and what images must be resized via DIV, and how. Does a DIV need to be able to expand horizontally and/or vertically? If this DIV expands, then what DIVs around it need to move and how? It is these changes that truly create a liquid layout.

Here is an example of CSS designed for a static layout:

```
#nav {
  background-color:#FFFFFF;
  width: 181px;
  height: 910px;
  float:left;
  position:absolute;
  margin-left: 35px;
  margin-top:-200px;
  }
#subject {
  background-color:#FFFFFF;
```

```
  width:480px;
  min-height:548px;
  line-height:1.25;
  /*height:;*/
  float:left;
  margin-left: 253px;
  padding-top: 25px;
  padding-left: 40px;
  padding-right: 40px;
  padding-bottom: 30px;
  position:absolute;
  }
```

This is an Example of CSS altered to become a liquid layout:

```
#nav {
  background-color:#FFFFFF;
  width:11.31em;
  height: 910px;
  float:left;
  position:absolute;
  margin-left: 35px;
  margin-top:-200px;
  }
#subject {
  background-color:#FFFFFF;
  width:30.00em;
  min-height:548px;
  line-height:1.25;
  /*height:;*/
  float:left;
  margin-left: 15.81em;
  padding-top: 25px;
  padding-left: 40px;
  padding-right: 40px;
  padding-bottom: 30px;
```

```
    position:absolute;
    }
```

This code was taken from my most recent project which can be viewed either at its home site (http://bcis.pacificu.edu/) or my web design blog at (http://zachwb.blogspot.com/). Be sure to reference this code as an example for the remainder of this section.

But before you go too far, let's discuss what the "position:absolute" attribute in the code. Most web designers will notice that this value makes the item line up inside the DIV properly. You can use the absolute or the relative values, but it comes down to trial and error in the code. Notice that certain aspects of the static layout have to stay the same to keep the layout from breaking the design. When resizing text you can allow for a DIV to expand horizontally. However, if there are important items to the right of that DIV you may want to apply a max-width. Also it's a good practice to test and see what the minimum width needed is, based on screen resolution and font size. Sometimes you might find that an image will overlap the boundaries of the DIV which leaves you with a few options. If the image is one you inventoried as being unable to scale then you need to either make the original image smaller or move to your minimum width/height (min-width/min-height CSS rules). If you inventoried the image as one you could scale (due to its use of text), then you need to apply an ID tag to the image like below:

```
<img id="b1" src="image/b1.jpg" alt="Image of a websites navigation">
```

By applying an ID tag you have just forced HTML to recognize the image as a single individual item. HTML will think there is only one "b1". You then use this to your advantage by creating a unique style rule for "img b1" that might look like:

```
#b1 img{
    width: 6.13 em;
    height: 9.06em;
    }
```

A set width and height through CSS allows you to replace the necessity to hardcode the size of the image in HTML (where the image is only sized in pixels) with an EM value that allows the image to shift with the resizing of text. If the image resizes with the text, and the DIV resizes with the text, then the DIV will resize to fit the image. Congratulations! You've just learned how to resize images using CSS. But now let's move on to the critical part of a liquid layout.

Once the content in your site is set up to scale based on the font size, you're last concern is making sure that each DIV moves appropriately to the others when scaling. Usually, when you place a DIV item on a page through CSS, the value "float:left" is most commonly used along with "margin" to place the DIV in the right location. If you have placed all the content in one containing DIV, you can apply "margin-left:auto" and "margin-right:auto" to place the site in the center of the page automatically. This allows the rescaling of the site to fit the browser regardless of the resolution of the screen.

The container can be scaled by adding EM values to the width of the container, but I suggest that no values are applied to the height so that content can bleed down the page. Inventory what items need to scale and in what direction, and note where there are DIVs next to them. Where DIV items are located next to them, is where you are going to change the pixel values you used to initially place them to EM value. By doing so, as the DIV next to the item scales in that direction, the DIV will move equally in that direction. As you can see, with this simple rule applied in the CSS (as shown above) the items will be able to scale as necessary.

The last step in a liquid layout is to inventory what items cannot move, for whatever reason. For example, you have three major DIVs on your website: a navigation bar, a content bar, and a news bar. Your employer has made it clear that the news bar needs to be able to be seen no matter what, because it is a big selling point. But when resizing the page, the navigation and the content will push the news off the page into a horizontal scroll and thus not be readily noticeable.

In this situation you are forced to allow the navigation to resize because it is necessary to navigate the website, but you are not required to horizontally scale the content because the content can afford to vertically scroll. Thus you are forced to either set maximum width to the content, or set a specific width (highly suggested) that will stay static through the use of pixels rather than EMs. This brings us to another big question: Pixels or EMs?

Pixels v EM

When designing a website to have a liquid layout and still be functional the big question becomes Pixels or EM? The truth is, a more functional design will use a combination of both. When initially designing your website, build a prototype in the size and dimensions at the web resolution (72dpi) you intend to use. Programs such as Adobe Photoshop have measurement tools (the ruler tool in Photoshop) which will allow you pull specific values. These values will allow you to place each item as it's been build.

A good strategy for building for text scalability is to initially build the site using Pixel values. Hard code the placement of everything and pay attention to which placements rely on each other. For example, the images in our graphic A.1 should be treated as one item inside the DIV, which should move based on the movement of the font or the DIV above the images. In B.1 each navigation item should be treated as an individual box which scales equally with the text. To do this, size the items with static height and width CSS values.

Once the item is sized and placed as you want it, you can use an EM converter to convert pixel values to EM. I suggest the Em Calculator (http://riddle.pl/emcalc/), but there are others available. To those of you who know that EMs are based on font size, notice that you can change the default font size and the decimal places shown. The EM conversions are based on the closest font conversion so the values, while not precise, are close enough that the changing of font will scale the values as necessary.

Conclusion

When confronted with the design challenge of ADA web standards, it is important to know what ADA is and what laws are related to ADA. Sections 504/508 work hand in hand with ADA to encompass almost every possible audience member with a disability. The legal definition of disabled is so broad that a designer must do everything possible to design his or her website to accommodate these disabilities.

Thankfully, the laws are not specific enough to say *how* they must be accommodated but simply that they *must* be accommodated. This gives the web designer a chance to break disabilities into the broad categories listed in "Designing for Accessibility". Designing a scalable simple website that includes transcriptions when and where needed will fulfill ADA web standards. Planning your website layout is critical and referring to the basics can lead you to a better design.

Choosing when to use hard coded pixels or the flexible EMs becomes an art form, but, in the end, it all comes down to planning, hours of work, trial and error, and testing. If you're still questioning why you bother, remember that there have been "19,453 charges of disability discrimination. EEOC resolved 15,708 disability discrimination charges in FY 2008 and recovered $57.2 million in monetary benefits for charging parties and other aggrieved individuals (not including monetary benefits obtained through litigation)" (eeoc.gov). To be a better web designer, a better boss, or just a better client, you are obligated to educate yourself on these laws.

Works Cited

"Accessibility of State and Local Government Websites to People with Disabilities." ADA Home Page - ada.gov - Information and Technical Assistance on the Americans with Disabilities Act. U.S. Department of Justice Civil Rights Division. 26 Mar. 2009 http://www.ada.gov/websites2.htm.

"Americans with Disabilities Act." U.S. Equal Employment Opportunity Commission (EEOC). The U.S. Equal Employment Opportunity Commission. 26 Mar. 2009 http://www.eeoc.gov/types/ada.html.

Clark, Joe. Building Accessible Websites. Boston: New Riders, 2002.

Jakob, Nielsen,. Designing Web usability. Indianapolis, Ind: New Riders, 2000.

Section 508: The Road to Accessibility. 26 Mar. 2009 http://www.section508.gov/.

"Web Content Accessibility Guidelines 1.0." World Wide Web Consortium - Web Standards. 5 May 1999. W3C. 26 Mar. 2009 http://www.w3.org/TR/WAI-WEBCONTENT/.

Berglund Fellowship Report: Web Conferencing as a Means of Enhancing Online Learning in a Hybrid Course Delivery Model

View online at: http://bcis.pacificu.edu/journal/2009/04/article.php?id=63

By Anita Zijdemans-Boudreau, PhD

College of Education
Pacific University
United States

Abstract: This action research study reports the outcomes of using web conferencing technology to enrich the online component of a hybrid educational technology course in a Master's teacher preparation program. Participant blogs, transcripts of online sessions, and an exit questionnaire were analyzed to gain insights into the participants' experiences and perceptions of the hybrid model, and to elicit suggestions for improvement. Results indicate that even with some initial technical hurdles, the web conferencing technology was well received and participants stated overwhelmingly that they would want to participate in a future hybrid course. Instructor and students alike felt the technology was most effective when used for demonstrations and virtual tours [i.e. in Second Life] as well as for student presentations. Web conferencing is relatively easy to use but requires proper orientation especially for novice users. Future study should implement more of the tool's collaborative features to encourage more active student engagement.

Context

As the demand for distance education programs increases, so too does the challenge to provide effective technology solutions for learning and collaborating at a distance. A criticism of online learning is its inability to recreate the intimate presence and rich interaction that generally exists in real-time, face-to-face contexts. In the corporate world, web conferencing emerged to address this challenge and has been used effectively for conducting meetings, webinars and informational sessions internationally since the late 1990's. In higher education, however, it has progressed more slowly, lending credence to the common perception that educational institutions have been sluggish to transition into a Knowledge Society and continue to perpetuate outdated learning models (Richardson, 2007; Bates, 2002).

This study is part of a work-in-progress involving the use of web conferencing technology to enrich the online component of a hybrid or blended course delivery model - i.e. face-to-face + online classes. The following reports the results of the first implementation of the model in an educational technology course in a Master's level teacher education program for candidates who work full time during the day. This course has typically been delivered at four seven-hour classes. The goal of this work was to test a hybrid model comprised of eight shorter sessions - four face-to-face and four online - as well as evaluate the possibilities of web conferencing for future development of flexible, innovative online program delivery offerings in the program.

Web Conferencing

Web conferencing is a computer or web-based application that allows individuals at their personal computers to attend real-time (synchronous) presentations or meetings via the Internet. A presenter, or host, initiates the web conference by streaming live video (using a web cam or digital camera), live audio communication using VOIP (Voice over Internet Protocol), and presentational information to remote participants. The technology supports application sharing, web browsing as well as other interactive features such as polls or surveys, and the ability for participants to manipulate the presenter's screen, for example: to write on a whiteboard. Also, the live sessions can also be recorded and made into archives.

This research builds on several years of collaborative work investigating the role of interactive technologies in supporting geographically distributed communities of practice. Baecker et al. (2003) proposes that interactive web conferencing technology provides the opportunity to reinvent rich collaboration within virtual space through allowing participants to engage in real-time direct interactions online. It is further suggested that the technology's capacity to capture archives of live events for post, asynchronous review, makes it an effective tool for enhancing learning, establishing a web-accessible knowledge base, and cultivating ground for the germination of communities of practice (Zijdemans, 2005). The power of this technology, then, is that it not only simulates synchronous face-to-face interactions across distance, but can also generate an infrastructure that serves to sustain cooperative work and group learning asynchronously over time and space (Zijdemans et al, 2005).

Research Design

The research design integrates elements of action research, design experiments and the Technology, Pedagogy, and Content Knowledge (TPACK) model developed by Mishra & Koehler (2006). As discussed elsewhere (see Zijdemans-Boudreau (2008)), the goal of action or experimental research is to improve practice or an area of concern, using an iterative research-implement-evaluate cycle, in order to focus the researcher's direct actions of practice within a participatory community. Similarly, design experiments—of the one-on-one or teacher-experimenter and student type—are theoretically grounded research activities that conduct "...a series of teaching sessions with a small number of students to create a small-scale version of a learning ecologym‐a complex interactive system involving multiple elements of different types and levels—so that it can be studied in depth and detail" (Cobb et al. 2003 p.9).

Bannan-Ritland's (2003) integrative learning design (ILD) framework further situates design experiments within a "...socially constructed, contextualized process for producing educationally effective interventions with a high likelihood of being used in practice." (p.22). As this project eventually seeks to implement a delivery model over several courses for the purpose of improving teaching, learning, and online program delivery, and entails documenting the process on the part of both teacher-researcher and students, these themes of theoretical and practical relevance, iterative design, and study of authentic complex learning and teaching contexts are pertinent and applicable as an integrated construct for this investigation.

The Technology, Pedagogy, and Content Knowledge (TPACK) model reminds researchers and practitioners that effective program design acknowledges the complex interplay between technology (T), pedagogy (P) and content knowledge (CK).

Applied to this research, our goal is to evaluate the affordance of the web conferencing application (T) to support enriched experiential and collaborative learning (P) for an educational technology course (CK). Experiential learning, as developed by Kolb, refers to the richness of learning that occurs when one is emotionally involved in authentic experiences (Smith, 2001). This technology-pedagogy-content knowledge interconnection embodies a strategy for using web conferencing to simulate a rich interactive environment and support the pedagogical goals while also allowing students to explore the applications of Web 2.0 to teaching and learning. To this end, each element of TPACK is fully represented and integrated in this work.

The Hybrid Course Delivery Model Study

A hybrid course delivery model as it is defined in this study is a blend of traditional face-to-face and online classes. In this case, online sessions were conducted in real-time using the web conferencing technology. The study was guided by the following questions:

1. How easy was it to learn and use the technology?

What were the participants' perceptions of the level of engagement in online sessions in comparison to face-to-face sessions?

How did the online sessions using the web conferencing impact on the participants' learning experience?

What were the perceived strengths and weaknesses of the technology?

What were the participants' responses to the hybrid delivery model?

Of the total of eight study participants, five were Masters students and three were practicing teachers who were taking the course for professional development credit. A brief entry survey was conducted to ascertain the technology skill level of the students. The students used the web conferencing technology as part of their regular course activities for the online component of the hybrid model. These online sessions were interspersed with the face-to-face classes and an orientation to the web conferencing application was provided before the first online class. The online sessions were recorded and transcribed. Students were also assigned the task of keeping individual blogs to document their learning experiences as they engaged in a variety of activities and developed a final action research project related to Web 2.0 technologies and educational practice. At the end of the course, all participants completed an anonymous exit survey as well as a self-evaluation of their progress in the course in relation to the National Education Technology Standards for Teachers (NETS*T). As this paper looks specifically at the impact of the web conferencing technology and hybrid model, only a subset of the data has been analyzed and reported here. This data includes an analysis of the blog postings related to the online sessions in which the web conferencing technology was used, the transcripts of the online sessions, and the exit questionnaire which included rating scales and open-ended questions to collect rich information on the participants' experiences, their perceptions of the technology, hybrid model, and suggestions for improvement.

Findings

The course was delivered as four face-to-face and three online sessions – plus an orientation – over the fall semester from September to December 2009. The entry survey indicated that the level of technology skill was varied but generally at the low to average range. The following summarizes the emergent themes that arose from the individual blogs and online sessions as well as the results from the exit questionnaire.

Blog Posting & Online Sessions: Each participant was required to create a blog and post a minimum of one entry after each class. The emergent themes from these postings as well as the transcripts of the online sessions are discussed and illustrated with examples.

As is to be expected the first online session data reveal a high number of postings related to the theme of technical glitches and learning curve: *"The first on-line session was a good reminder not to assume anything with regards to technology." "Technology can be intimidating at the beginning, but with the support given in the classroom, one feels brave to use and try new tools."* In the second session there were still technical issues but they were more related to the course assignment which involved uploading their video projects and creating the wiki pages for their action research projects: *"Our second online meeting went fine. There were less technological breakdowns, so most of us felt more confident working online."* and *"I enjoyed Saturday's class a great deal. I was more comfortable using the chat, which made it more engaging. The class session went by so quickly that I had hardly realized I had been sitting at my computer for two hours, which is unusual for me."* The final online session was the smoothest; the technical issues were minimal and participants had mastered basic troubleshooting strategies as illustrated in this blog posting: *"I thought this class went well. Everyone was able to get in just fine and seemed to be in the flow of things. I had one moment when I couldn't see the shared window, but by logging out and back in again I was able to see just fine. I suppose with technology we just have to be prepared for kinks and hiccups and roll with it."*

A review of the session transcripts of all the online sessions confirms that technology-related comments significantly decreased while content-related commentary increased by the last session. The following chat excerpt taken from the final class indicates the on-task engagement as students viewed a virtual tour of Second Life:

> Ann: Anita, how do you find out about all of this stuff?
> Ann: such a good resource, especially if you're enrolled in distance learning
> Kall: yes
> Ann: special ed too if the technology is available
> [5 other students concur]
> Fer: this is way crazy... cool but crazy!
> Ann: I can see how this will be important for future students who have grown up with this technology
> Tan: I can see my son and his imagination going crazy with this!
> Fer: I think that is a good point... this is so foreign to me but I get it
> Kri: me too...kind of crazy to think about doing it myself though
> Cook: I can see it being a creative way to teach kids about different habitats etc for animals, forest, sea, etc.
> Ann: good point
> Tan: I was thinking social studies and history. I think this would be really engaging for HS students
> Cook: this is the first time that I have ever seen this.
> Kall: could be useful when teaching about culture when teaching foreign languages
> Cook: oh or maybe even pen pals in other countries etc.
> Tan: looks like video games to me

Cook: you could meet with another class room
Ann: how about to connect soldiers in the field to their families?
Pri: that is a great idea
Kri: that would be cool!
Ann: what a trip
Kall: or connect students in study abroad programs with families
Ann: thanks for drawing my thought back to education... is there ever sound in second life?
Fer: it looks like there is a sound control on the right lower part of her screen. i think she said you could talk...

What is interesting to note here is that all this was occurring while the instructor was engaging with a resident in Second Life. In a face-to-face classroom this kind of chatter would have disrupted the lesson. In this context, however, it was completely unobtrusive and allowed participants to share their thoughts on what they were witnessing.

In summary, the postings and session transcripts indicated that students' confidence increased with practice but that they felt more comfortable using the chat rather than voice feature – which in fact was most used during the third session when students presented their project ideas. Even with this limited interaction, students did help each other out with technical problems and in one instance when the instructor's connection was dropped, continued to talk with each other about course related issues until she returned.

Exit Survey: The exit survey was comprised of 6 questions. The following chart summarizes the results of questions 1 - 4. On a rating scale where 1 = Strongly Agree and 5 = Strongly Disagree, the lowest average score was 1.5 while the highest average rating was 2.75.

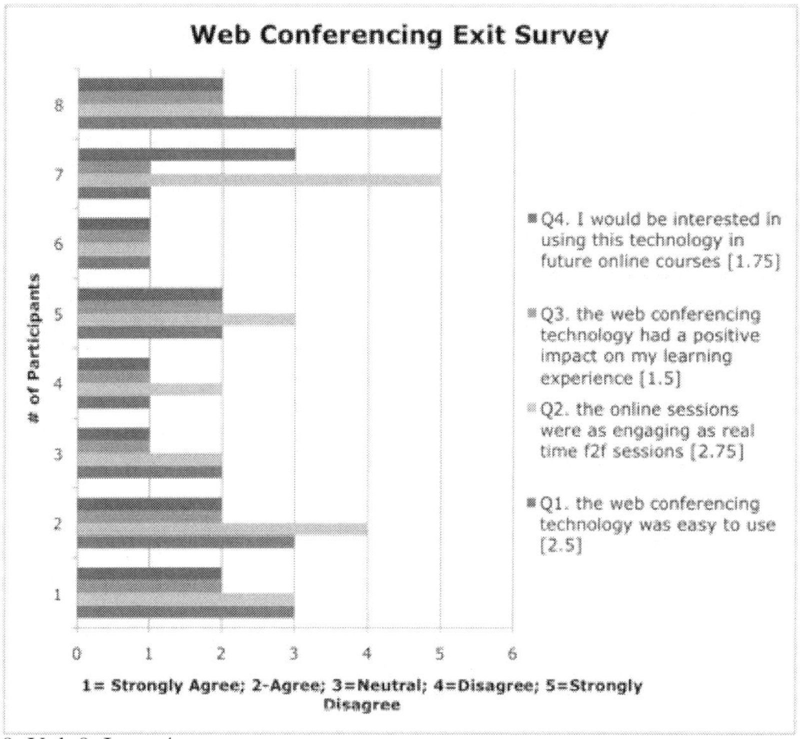

Chart 1. Results from Web Conferencing Exit Survey

Though the majority of participants' answers for Q1 ranged from strongly agree to neutral, one participant indicated that the technology was difficult to use, thus the average response rate result shows 2.5. Some representative responses were: *"I think that it was fairly easy to use WC however it was challenging for some of the participants. At that point it became a little bit difficult to move on."*;*"I wasn't sure about it going in, but I really like it in the end. It was easy to use."* and *"There was some frustration the first session when I was kicked out several times and then it also dropped my audio for ½ of the session."*

Most stated that online learning cannot replace face-to-face interaction, however the consensus in Q2 at 2.75 was that the technology was engaging. *"I think that the way the material was presented was easy to follow and interesting."*;*"The opportunity of participating either privately or with everybody also had advantages. Different learning styles were addressed."* and *"It is my personality that prefers f2f interaction. I did find the conferencing engaging, useful and definitely learned through this method."*

Questions 3 and 4 drew the most favourable responses averaging 1.5 and 1.75 respectively. In addition to the obvious benefits of convenience working from home and not having to pay for childcare, the following comments were given in response to the question of the technology's positive impact: *"It gave me lots of good ideas. I learned a lot and I was able to explore more on my own after using the Web Conferencing technology."*;*"I loved getting to explore through it."*;*"[it] gave me some new ideas on how to use technology to teach."* and *"Yes because I got to try something new."*

All participants, except one who did not respond, agreed in Q4 that they would be interested in using the technology again in a future online course: *"I believe it is a useful tool and when used in balance to f2f can greatly strengthen a program."*;*"Yes I would use this technology in future online courses; through I would hope that I would become more savvy with it."*;*"It is very convenient. Much easier to meet on the web than f2f."*;*"I see potential for using this technology and I would look forward to another class using it."*;*"It depends on the class content."* and *"I feel like there was more freedom with this approach as a students."*

Question 5 asked, "How often did you access the archives?" Six out of eight participants stated "Never", one stated "Seldom" and one stated "Occasionally". Some reasons stated for these answers were: *"The information presented didn't require that I return. I was able to remember the important info and also took notes on what I wanted to remember"*;*"Kinda forgot that was available"*; *"Didn't really know where it was, but really didn't need to access it either."*; *"I have not had time but would like to."*;*"Only if I had a question regarding how to complete an assignment."* and *"Haven't needed to yet - can I in the future?"*

Finally, question 6 asked participants to comment on the strengths, limitations of the technology and to make any suggestions for future improvement. The following table shows the participants' written responses:

Strengths 7/8 responded	*Work from home. Saves time and resources; Accessibility; I could be at home and it helped in my schedule; Forcing us to get in there and experience it and learn on our own and even help each other when we were stuck; Again, first hand experience, with the technology itself; We could attend class from the leisure of home. We could cover some material without using most of a day to drive to school; Less stress for me - could do it in my PJs!*
Limitations 7/8 responded	*It is limiting in that receiving one-on-one help is difficult; Time to practice; I don't know - I really liked it; More difficult for each of us to communicate. I think its easier f2f. Online I was afraid I may interrupt; Obviously the technology itself - microphones, internet connections; Little or no peer interactions. Limited ability to ask questions; Technology doesn't always do what it is supposed to do.*
Suggestions 6/8 responded	*Offer a continuation; I just needed to take more time on this class. I really think it went well overall. I would not want the 7 hour classes and though this format was great; It was good. I really enjoyed the f2f though; I would look forward to meeting more often with WC. Each online session went over time so it's obvious that you have a lot to share!; Show examples of past projects in class to help students jump-start their own projects.; It would be helpful to set some things up ahead of time in a f2f meeting.*

Table 1: Participant Input on the Strengths and Limitations of the Technology and Suggestions for Improvement.

When asked to give their feedback on participating in the hybrid course, responses included: *"I think this is a great model. I think students get the best of both worlds by using it.";"Totally liked it;,"It was a good variety f2f + online";"I liked the hybrid style of this class; would definitely do it the same."* and *"I really liked it!! I liked the freedom of the online classes and would definitely do an online class again!"*

Implications

The overall findings indicate that despite some initial technical hurdles, the web conferencing technology was well received and the participants were responsive to the hybrid model. It should be noted, however, that participants also stated that this worked best in combination with face-to-face sessions. It would be interesting to do a separate study using web conferencing for online-only distance course to see if this result would transfer across delivery models. It should also be noted that the instructor was in the process of learning how to implement the technology along with the students. As a result, all of the features were not fully implemented or encouraged – such as the poll feature, the break-out group function, and voice. Due to the timing of the course, the first day was at a technology conference and although the class met afterwards to talk, there was not the usual sense of the first day face-to-face orientation that students and instructors are typically accustomed to.

There were three orientation sessions before the first online class and these were relatively successful in getting students set up. There were however two students who were not able to get their microphones working and they were only able to talk in the sessions using the chat feature. The first class also used a conference call and this was initially helpful when users were still getting used to the technology. Participants used the chat feature – often to help each other with user issues or make comments – but unless they were required to give a presentation, it was easy for them not to speak up during the online sessions and few used the voice feature.

Both the instructor and the students felt that the web conferencing tool was most effective when it was used to demonstrate applications, provide virtual tours to places that students might not be able to navigate on their own (i.e. Second Life) and have students conduct presentations (vs. listening to a lecture).

Action Plan

1. Ensure that a face-to-face session is devoted to introducing the technology in the first class in addition to the online orientation sessions.

2. Further develop a more comprehensive back-up plan in the eventuality that there are technological difficulties and use the entry survey to better anticipate end users needs and technology.

3. Rather than make the online sessions longer--two 50-minute sessions with a break worked well--hold four online sessions as originally conceived (i.e. not including the online orientation) in order to be able to cover all the content. Also offer one-on-one office hours online to encourage students to practice the technology.

4. Require students to be more actively involved--such as giving presentations--and try using more of the collaborative features such as the break-out group feature.

5. Minimize lectures and increase demonstrations and virtual tours - especially those like Second Life which are more challenging. This should also increase the use of the archives as review materials.

6. Have an assistant to help troubleshoot users who are having problems. It is really hard for the instructor to do this while teaching and it slows down the class for everyone.

Current Update

Since the completion of this study, the action plan has been used to set up a follow-up study to continue using the web conferencing technology to support hybrid course delivery. Another study is also in development to use the web conferencing for an online-only distance education course.

References:

Baecker, R., Moore, G., & Zijdemans, A.S. (2003). Reinventing the Lecture: Webcasting Made Interactive. Human Computer Interaction, International Proceedings Crete, Greece. Vol. 1, pp. 896-900. Mahwah, NJ: Erlbaum.

Bannan-Ritland, B. (2003) The Role of Design in Research: The integrative learning design framework. Educational Researcher Vol 32, No1 pp 21-24.

Bates, A. W. (2000) Managing Technological Change: Strategies for College and University Leaders. San Francisco: Jossey-Bass.

Cobb, P., Confrey, J. diSessa, A. Lehrer, R. Schauble, L. (2003) Design Experiments in Educational Research. Educational Researcher Vol 32, No1 pp 9-13.

Mantei, M. (1998) Capturing the capture concepts: a case study in the design of computer-supported meeting environments. Proceeding of the 1988 ACM conference on computer-supported cooperative work 257-270. New York: ACM.

Mishra, P., & Koehler, M. J. (2006). Technological Pedagogical Content Knowledge: A new framework for teacher knowledge. Teachers College Record 108 (6), 1017-1054.

Redfern, S. & Naughton, N. (2002) Collaborative Virtual Environments to Support Communication and Community in Internet-Based Distance Education Journal of Information Technology in Education V1 No3, 201-211

Richardson, W. (2007) Blogs, Wikis, Podcasts and Other Powerful Web Tools for Classrooms. Corwin Press

Stahl, G. et al. (2006) Computer-supported collaborative learning: An historical perspective. In R. K. Sawyer (Ed.), Cambridge handbook of the learning sciences (pp. 409-426). Cambridge, UK: Cambridge University Press.

Smith, M. K. (2001) 'David A. Kolb on experiential learning', the encyclopedia of informal education, http://www.infed.org/biblio/b-explrn.htm.

Zijdemans, A., Moore, G., Baecker, R., & Keating, D. P. (2005). ePresence Interactive Media and WebForum 2001: An accidental case study on the use of webcasting as a VLE for early child development. In J. Weiss, J. Nolan, & P. Trifonas (Eds.), *International handbook of virtual learning environments* (pp. 1365-1397). Dordrecht, The Netherlands: Kluwer Academic.

Zijdemans Boudreau, A. (2008). Action Research as an Instructional Strategy for Faculty and Teacher Development in Educational Technology. In K. McFerrin et al. (Eds.), Proceedings of Society for Information Technology and Teacher Education International Conference 2008 (pp. 1585-1591). Chesapeake, VA: AACE.

Health

Epidemiology and the Internet: Google Catches the Flu

View online at: http://bcis.pacificu.edu/journal/2009/04/article.php?id=64

By Shawn Davis, Ph.D. and Paul Michael, Ph.D.

The people have spoken and the world has witnessed yet another example of the organizing power of the Internet. NASA announced on April 14th that they will name a piece of exercise equipment on the international space station, the Combined Operational Load Bearing External Resistance Treadmill, or COLBERT, in honor of comedian Stephen Colbert [1]. This was not intended to reflect Colbertis dedication to the space agency (or a reaction to his threat to, ireject democracy and seize power as spaceis evil tyrant overlordi [2]), but rather the outcome of an online contest wherein individuals suggested names for a newly incorporated node within the space station. Colbertis viewers responded en masse and he handily won the contest. While NASA ultimately opted to name the node *Tranquility* instead of branding it *Colbert*, their nod to Colbertis viewers demonstrates the power of the Internet as a mechanism for the collective voice of individuals to translate into tangible action.

It goes without saying that the Internet has changed the face of communication. The strength of the Internet rests not only upon its ability to serve as a public forum for individual thought; the speed at which information can be transmitted, organized, and eventually utilized is beyond anything weive seen before. We see examples of this immediate transmission of information every day with such tools (distractions?) as Twitter (Congratulations Ashton!) and Facebook. Researchers at Google, however, have taken the power of the Internet search engine and have used it as a tool for the incredibly accurate tracking of flu activity that was consistently one to two weeks faster than traditional Center for Disease Control (CDC) reports [3]. Albeit unintentionally, the people have again spoken and we all stand to benefit from their collective voice.

Influenza Epidemics and Pandemics

Within a given year, between 5% and 20% of Americans suffer from the flu [4] and seasonal flu epidemics cause tens of millions of respiratory illnesses and between 250,000 and 500,000 deaths worldwide [5]. Influenza is, therefore, a major public health concern. At epidemic levels, influenza can be devastating and at pandemic levels, catastrophic. In recent history, four influenza pandemics highlight the massive loss of life possible. For example, over 1 million individuals died during the Asiatic (Russian) Flu pandemic of 1889-1890, 40 to 100 million died during the Spanish Flu pandemic of 1918-1920, 1 to 1.5 million died during the Asian Flu pandemic of 1957-1958, and .75 to 1 million died during the Hong Kong Flu pandemic of 1968-1969 [6].

Given the ever-present specter of such an outbreak happening again, health professionals worldwide have developed and maintain detection methods to track the progression of flu annually as well as alert officials in the event of a large-scale influenza event. Early detection is, of course, paramount in prompting appropriate and immediate response to such an event; a response that could save countless lives.

Traditional Detection Methods

Traditionally, both the European Influenza Surveillance Scheme (EISS) and the US Centers for Disease Control and Prevention (CDC) utilize clinical and virological data obtained primarily through physician visits to track the progression of influenza in a given population [7]. While this method is highly-accurate in identifying not only existing influenza strains within the population, it can also detect new strains as they appear. This method, however, is a labor intensive process that is highly decentralized and often time consuming. In fact, even though the CDC provides both regional and national data from such surveillance on a weekly basis, there is typically a reporting lag of 1 to 2 weeks [8]. Keep in mind as well that systems such as these are present within developed nations; they are either absent or woefully underfunded and understaffed in many other parts of the world.

A reporting lag, as previously mentioned, is of concern when dealing with an influenza outbreak that can spread very rapidly. As a result, public health officials are often left scrambling to allocate appropriate resources in an effective manner. In response to this situation, researchers at Google have established a free Web service that they say can pinpoint globally and much more rapidly than existing detection methods where there is an increasing number of influenza cases [9].

The Google Search Method

Google Flu Trends is part of Google.org, an arm of Google that is focused on projects for the public good that may or may not directly benefit Google itself [10]. Extending work wherein Yahoo search engine queries were found to correlate with virological data [11], researchers at Google.org compiled and evaluated literally hundreds of billions of Internet searches from five years of Google.com data. From this data, a model was created that could estimate the probability that a visit to a physician (in a particular region) was related to an influenza-like illness (an ILI) [12].

Utilizing this model, the researchers at Google.org applied its predictive power in ireal timei to Google searches during the 2007-2008 influenza season. The resulting estimates were shared with the US Center for Disease Control (CDC) and both the timeliness and accuracy of the predictions were determined. It was found that the Google search method was able to consistently and rather successfully estimate ILI percentages (across all nine regions of CDC analysis) one to two weeks earlier than reports published by the CDCis US Influenza Sentinel Provider Surveillance Network [13].

Benefits and Limitations

The ability to detect influenza outbreaks quickly and accurately is fundamental to establishing appropriate lines of defense. By being able to identify a sudden spike in flu activity within a particular geographic region, public health officials can more rapidly deliver additional resources such as bolstering vaccine capacity and alerting local media outlets in order to raise public awareness [14]. The strength of the Google search method is its ability to provide such data in a relatively short time, generally within a single day as compared to the 1-2 week turnaround of traditional detection methods.

This method, however, is not the ultimate panacea. The researchers at Google themselves stress that the Google system is inot designed to be a replacement for traditional surveillance networks or supplant the need for laboratory-based diagnoses and surveillancei [15]. The researchers further explain that a lack of demographic data collected along with search terms is limiting. Also, there is no way to determine if the individual conducting the search is suffering from the flu or is simply curious. Furthermore, Google searches are likely to spike in the event of happenings beyond flu activity as well such as a drug recall or media influence, thus triggering a ifalse alerti.

As one might imagine, public response to the use of Google searches as a data collection tool has not been uniformly praised. Negative reactions have ranged from the facetious posting of the iGoogle Evangelisti saying, iWeive found certain search terms are good indicators of sin activity. Google Heaven/Hell Trends uses aggregated Google data to estimate sin activity in your state up to two weeks faster than Godi [16] to the more serious concerns from privacy groups. For example, the Electronic Privacy Information Center and Patient Privacy Rights have stated, in a letter to Google CEO Eric Schmidt that if search records are idisclosed and linked to a particular user, there could be adverse consequences for education, employment, insurance, and even traveli [17]. In response, Google has maintained that they donit collect identifiable information on its users and according to Mike Yang, a Google lawyer, iThere are no new privacy implicationsi [18].

Conclusion

Privacy implications aside, Google's flu trends analysis sets the stage for the development of future tools to serve as an adjunct to traditional detection methods. In fact, according to Rick Turoczy, a writer for Read Write Web, iWhile influenza is the first target of the experiment, one can easily imagine the types of search data – and regional data – that could help healthcare professionals in the prediction of practically any disease. More importantly for Google, coupling this kind of anonymous aggregated data with other Google offerings could further the companyis move into the healthcare arenai [19].

The future of healthcare is coming rapidly and it is being shaped by technological advancement as well as social and political change. Once again, the Internet is proving itself as a tool that can respond to the needs of those using it and, furthermore, a means to transform (and hopefully better) public policy and individual action.

Endnotes:

[1] http://www.cnn.com/2009/SHOWBIZ/TV/04/15/colbert.nasa/index.html

[2] http://www.colbertnation.com/the-colbert-report-videos/223137/march-30-2009/space-module--colbert---democracy-in-orbit

[3] http://www.google.org/about/flutrends/how.html

[4] http://online.wsj.com/article/SB122644309498518615.html

[5] http://www.nature.com/nature/journal/v457/n7232/pdf/nature07634.pdf

[6] http://en.wikipedia.org/wiki/Influenza

[7] http://www.nature.com/nature/journal/v457/n7232/pdf/nature07634.pdf

[8] ibid.

[9] http://online.wsj.com/article/SB122644309498518615.html

[10] ibid.

[11] Polgreen, P.M., Chen, Y., Pennock, D.M., & Forrest, N.D. (2008). Using Internet searches for influenza surveillance. Clinical Infectious Diseases, 47, 1443-1448.

[12] http://www.nature.com/nature/journal/v457/n7232/pdf/nature07634.pdf

[13] ibid.

[14] ibid.

[15] ibid.

[16] http://www.readwriteweb.com/archives/google_flu_trends_a_glimpse_in.php

[17] http://news.cnet.com/8301-13578_3-10097979-38.html

[18] ibid.

[19] http://www.readwriteweb.com/archives/google_flu_trends_a_glimpse_in.php

Media

What's up with Webcomics?: Author-Reader Relationships and Finances

View online at: http://bcis.pacificu.edu/journal/2009/04/article.php?id=62

By Maria Walters

In my previous article, I pointed out how the transition from print to screen is changing comics artistically and conceptually. [1] Now I want to look at the experiences of webcomic artists outside of the direct creation of their comics. With forums, e-mail, and commenting, authors have the opportunity to hear from their audiences like never before, and entire relationships and communities are built on webcomics. The challenges for online comic artists are most evident in the finances – because comics are not being sold to consumers, most webcomic artists have to be creative in making money from their art.

Webcomic Communities Online

With social networking sites springing up right and left, we can't help but notice how many communities are forming and thriving online. Social networking sites like Twitter and Facebook allow authors to keep their audience involved in their lives, as well as the progress of their work. Blogs and RSS feeds provide similar content from the webcomic's homepage itself. Some authors prefer to let their art speak for itself, but others add commentary via blogs or other updates. Interestingly, webcartoonists seem evenly divided between showing their blog posts or updates on the same page as their comics and having a separate blog.

Some authors even involve their audience in the comic writing process. Tim Buckley enjoys getting reader feedback intermittently in a create-your-own-adventure-style storyline, as readers vote on plot changes. The most recent of these storylines took place from November 2008 until January 2009. [2] Of course, giving readers the opportunity to comment on particular comics is not uncommon, though it is also not universally implemented. Some authors prefer to have discussions between readers take place on forums, which allows for greater continuity in discussions.

Another effect of these forums is the relationships formed between readers. Forums allow users to introduce conversations that are not directly related to any particular comic, which is vital to the formation of a true community. They also allow a reader to be easily directed towards discussions most interesting to them, instead of being forced to wade through a stream of comments on each particular comic that may or may not dissolve into a more general conversation. Plus, forums provide authors with the opportunity to get to know their audiences, interact, and answer questions in a public place.

In Real Life

Readers also use webcomics and the fun-loving communities surrounding them to have fun in real life. Randall Monroe's *xkcd* featured the concept of "Geohashing", which inspired readers to get together in randomly assigned locations in a given geographic region every Saturday afternoon to meet other local *xkcd* fans. [3] After an *xkcd* comic about Richard Stallman being attacked by ninjas appeared, fun-loving readers decided to send Richard Stallman a katana and, a few months later, dress as ninjas and "attack" him. [4]

Readers of *Ctrl+Alt+Del* are familiar with the idea of Winter-een-mas, a holiday invented by one of the main characters of the comic, which has since taken on a life of its own. It is described as "a celebration of video games and the people that play them," and takes place every year between January 25th and 31st. [5]

And then there are conventions. Many webcomic artists attend general comic conventions, or even other gatherings focused on gaming or other niches. Webcomics themselves have historically lacked conventions. In 2005, ClickBurg, a Dutch convention specifically for webcomic artists and readers, proudly introduced "one of the youngest art forms in the world: webcomics!" [6] However, after 2005, webcomic conventions appeared to take a break until this year. 2009 saw the New England Webcomics Weekend, which took place in Massachusetts in March. [7] The convention was so popular that preregistration was required and attendance had to be capped at 700 people. Though ClickBurg was a one-time-only convention, the Webcomics Weekend hopes to continue in the future, and already has a promising start. Of course, we also need to mention a convention that was started by a popular webcomic: the Penny Arcade Exposition (PAX) was founded 10 years ago by Mike Krahulik and Jerry Holkins, the creators of Penny Arcade. [8] An annual game festival in Seattle, it is geared toward tabletop, videogame, and PC gamers and generally takes place in the fall. The creators describe it as "a big party we throw for the gaming community in general and PA [*Penny Arcade*] readers in particular."[9] It has become so popular that a corresponding east coast convention, PAX East, is in the works for spring 2010. [10] Though this convention has very little to do with webcomics themselves, the readership of Penny Aracade makes up a crucial part of these expos, and readers enjoy meeting each other in real life after getting to know each other on the Penny Arcade forums.

Methods of Financing

Though becoming increasingly popular, webcomics are still not an easy way to make a living. The attempt to make a profit from webcomics has resulted in a variety of creative financing ideas.

The first, and perhaps most obvious, idea is to sell subscriptions. However, for one thing, "people expect the internet to be free," as Jeph Jacques, author of *Questionable Content*, points out. [11] Having restricted access to content discourages new readers from taking a chance and subscribing to an unknown comic, especially when so many others are freely available. One response is for authors to allow readers to access current comics or a limited archive for free, but to require a subscription in order to read the entire archive. Also, artists such as James Kochalka and demian5 produce multiple webcomics, some of which are publically available and some of which require subscriptions. [12] Of course, all of these subscriptions are relatively inexpensive, with most costing only a couple of dollars per month.

A related but new idea involves selling future comics instead of past ones. *Hereville*, described as "Yet Another Troll-Fighting 11-Year-Old Orthodox Jewish Girl Comic" on its homepage and written by Barry Deutsch, was published last year in a unique way: pages of the graphic novel were published online serially, with a page or two being published each week, but the complete story was already finished. If readers wanted to read it faster than it was published online, they had a chance to purchase the book (in either printed or digital form) and read the entire story. [13] Now the novel is due to be published by Harry Abrams's Amulet Books in a longer (physical) form in 2010 – a relatively unique experience for webcomics. [14]

Selling additional content (think "special features") is not particularly revolutionary, but new types of additional content are always being added. The webcomic *Goblins* can be purchased and downloaded as a PDF ebook "packed with never before seen extras, including a three page bonus comic, early sketches, behind the scenes material, and a running text commentary throughout the *Book Two* story." [15] A similar model involves selling access to additional comic-related online content. I first ran across this idea in the model of the comic "Achewood," [16] which describes its additional content for subscribers as:

- New author annotations on most pieces
- Approximately twenty double-sized, full-color "Achewood" comics
- Early blueprint of the 62 Achewood Court house
- The Lyle Drinking Games (Achewood trivia board games)
- The full-color, original map of the Achewood neighborhood, as conceived in 2002
- The Story of Achewood: a written overview of Teodor's first day moving into the house
- Seven long subscriber-only blog-type entries by Ray
- The entire Nate Small novella, formatted in old Hardy Boys book style
- Eighteen scans from Chris's sketchbooks, including the geneses of several seminal strips
- ...more! [17]

The premium updates also supply subscribers with daily text updates, photos, and rough drafts of future panels. [18] Clearly, both readers who are only able to access the comics and subscribers will have an equally satisfying time enjoying the characters and stories created by the author. Of course, this model will not work for all comics, especially those that focus on stand-alone jokes instead of a character-driven narrative.

Though not unique, one tried-and-tested way to monetize websites, and, in this case, webcomics, is to allow advertising. Though this is sometimes looked down upon because of the lack of aesthetic appeal, webcomic artists and site designers can incorporate advertising gracefully. In 2009, the advertising market has dropped significantly, but Jeph Jacques, for one, still recognizes it as a significant part of his income. [19]

As webcomics were first gaining popularity, Scott McCloud saw the future of webcomic funding as being micropayments or donations. If every reader of a strip contributed a few cents or a dollar, a comic with an average readership would be more than self-sustaining. However, this has proved to be unrealistic, especially because security issues and phishing are still so common. Nevertheless, a "Tip Jar" or "Donation" link is frequently available, albeit subtle. In a similar way, *xkcd* offers prints at a variable price – to make a donation, a reader can order a print and then change its price to the amount they are willing to donate before making their purchase. [20]

Of course, digital content still only goes so far, and many, if not most, self-sustaining webcomics do so through sales of physical products. Often prints of individual pages can be purchased, and assembling archived material into books is also common. Beyond that, many artists design T-shirts or other memorabilia that would be interesting to their audiences. In *Questionable Content*, the characters themselves often wear shirts available for purchase – in fact, readers often request specific T-shirts that the characters are seen wearing before they are produced for sale. [21]

Though there are many different money-making methods available to webcomic artists, the artists themselves exhibit considerable solidarity in the face of critics. In February, Neil Swaab, a syndicated cartoonist whose work also appears online, criticized many current models of webcomic funding, especially merchandising. [22] Many webcartoonists responded quickly to his post, defending the current merchandise-based model. As Jeph Jacques wrote in his blog, "comics have ALWAYS derived significant portions of their income from merchandising. Saying webcartoonists are t-shirt hucksters is like saying Charles Schultz was an insurance salesman because Snoopy is on the Met Life blimp."[23] A similar protest is voiced by Gary Tyrrell, editor of *Fleen: The Webcomics Blog About Webcomics*, who writes that webcomic artists who sell T-shirts are merchandising just like so-called artists, but simply aren't using a middleman. [24]

Since then, Swaab has both apologized [25] and stated his intention to move toward webcomic-type marketing, in an interesting post which documents his career as an alternative comic artist and the changes that he has seen in the comics market. [26] Swaab already has a following online – in fact, his comic, "Mr. Wiggles Loves You," was mentioned as worthy of review by a commenter on my previous article. [27]

Extra Special Bonus

In a category all its own, "Oh No Robot" is a comic search engine that has helped to organize and transcribe thousands of comics. [28] After webcartoonists register, readers help to transcribe comics (prompted by a "Transcribe this Comic!" link below each comic), and the transcriptions are then made searchable through OhNoRobot.com. Besides searching all transcriptions, you can also search the archive of one particular series or check out a random comic. It's a great way to find new comics, besides getting suggestions. Speaking of which: comment about more comics in the space below, and they could be reviewed in coming issues.

Endnotes

[1] http://bcis.pacificu.edu/journal/2009/02/article.php?id=37

[2] http://www.ctrlaltdel-online.com/comic.php?d=20081126

[3] Inspired by this comic: http://xkcd.com/426/, the adventure continues at the wiki: http://wiki.xkcd.com/geohashing/Main_Page

[4] The comic: http://xkcd.com/225/; sending Richard Stallman a katana: http://blag.xkcd.com/2007/04/19/life-imitates-xkcd-part-ii-richard-stallman/; ninjas "attack": http://www.boingboing.net/2007/10/21/ninjas-attack-richar.html.

[5] http://www.wintereenmas.com/

[6] Official site (in Dutch): http://www.clickburg.nl/welcome/index.php; some information in English can be found at: http://comixtalk.com/preparations_underway_for_dutch_webcomic_convention

[7] http://www.webcomicsweekend.com/ -- for one of many reviews, see http://splashpage.mtv.com/2009/03/23/webcomics-weekend-online-comics-get-their-own-convention- heres-what-you-missed/

[8] Comic: http://www.penny-arcade.com/; Expo: http://www.pennyarcadeexpo.com/

[9] http://www.pennyarcadeexpo.com/faqs.php

[10] http://www.paxsite.com/paxeast/index.php

[11] http://qcjeph.livejournal.com/100732.html

[12] James Kochalka: http://www.americanelf.com/; demian5: http://www.demian5.com/index-e.php

[13] http://www.hereville.com/

[14] http://www.publishersweekly.com/article/CA6611063.html

[15] See Goblins online here: http://www.goblinscomic.com/; the ebook package is sold here: http://comics.drivethrustuff.com/product_info.php?products_id=51412&language=en

[16] http://achewood.com/

[17] http://achewood.com/archived_edition.php

[18] http://s.assetbar.com/store/achewood

[19] http://qcjeph.livejournal.com/100732.html

[20] http://store.xkcd.com/

[21]
http://www.topatoco.com/merchant.mvc?Screen=PROD&Store_Code=TO&Product_Code=QC-TEH&Category_Code= QC

[22] Post has been removed: http://www.mrwiggleslovesyou.com/blog-january2009.html#theend

[23] http://qcjeph.livejournal.com/100732.html

[24] http://www.fleen.com/archives/2009/02/01/emergency-post-to-vent-rage/

[25] http://www.mrwiggleslovesyou.com/blog-february2009.html#apology

[26] http://www.mrwiggleslovesyou.com/blog-february2009.html#500

[27] http://bcis.pacificu.edu/journal/2009/02/article.php?id=37#comments

[28] http://www.ohnorobot.com/

Gaming World

Protecting Human Children in the World of Warcraft

View online at: http://bcis.pacificu.edu/journal/2009/04/article.php?id=60

By IProfess
Level 72 Night Elf Druid, Zul'jin, Azeroth

> ***Editor's Note:*** *This piece is written by IProfess, self-proclaimed avatar from the on-line game World of Warcraft. With our commenting function, readers can now leave appropriate remarks following the piece. Please note, that as in every case in Interface, the author's opinion are his, hers, or its own and do not represent those of Interface nor those of the Berglund Center at Pacific University Oregon.*

IProfess begins:

Those who yet need an introduction to my particular circumstances— a 'Toon from the World of Warcraft enabled by his own efforts to cross into what is laughably called "The Real World" (TRW)—could do no better than to read my previous works published in this inestimable journal. [1]

My submissions are usually intended to protect my own beloved Azeroth—the World of the "World of Warcraft." Azeroth, being highly conditioned by a number of activities in TRW, is terribly vulnerable. A 'Toon never knows when a politician will take it into his or her criminally ambitious head to start viewing even virtual worlds with alarm. After all, these debased beings have made very good livings for decades threatening, now this impending doom, now that one.

Occasionally, however, I find myself, while not agreeing with the pols, at least pausing to weigh the possible accuracy of their latest self-serving clamor. All of us, 'Toon or TRW shadows, usually agree on one issue: It is almost universally held "good" to protect the young [2], whether it has a negative or a positive result. This piece is a plea for a special sort of such protection: it is very important that human parents play aloongside their children in Azeroth. There are many reasons for doing this.

First, the positive ones: The World of Warcraft is, of course, my world, and I think it beautiful beyond compare. But from TRW perspective it is also a vast social experiment, driven, as such experiments often are, by commercial purposes. The driving force of Azeroth, the Unprogrammed Programmer if you will, is a being. (Whether singular or plural depends on each 'Toon's cosmological views or religious commitment.) We will refer to it simply as "Ol' Bliz." In TRW it manifests itself as Blizzard Entertainment, Inc., an international corporation which has changed hands repeatedly as it was merged with larger such entities [3].

From our perspective, its identity and purposes hardly matter. It is what it is. But like all gods, it presents us, its creations, with both opportunities and dangers. The opportunities are many. In playing, we become part of a voluntary international community of at least twelve million beings in TRW from all nations, all age groups, and all walks of life. There are even more 'Toons as each player often has many more than one avatar. How many of these, like myself are fully sentient and cross over periodically into TRW is, again, unknowable.

But from the perspective of human parents in TRW [4] Azeroth presents an unparalleled educational opportunity to shape their young's values and to give them instruction under widely varied circumstances in which the worst thing that can happen is that they die virtually, and immediately rez (resurrect) again. Azeroth has many of the temptations that TRW offers: alcohol, sexuality of a limited sort, the chance to be rude, profane, to steal, to lie, to cheat. It is no wonder that so many criminal 'Toons, upon being expelled into TRW, become Wall Street bankers.

But Azeroth also has opportunities for the young to learn to read, to write, to type, to communicate politely with peers and with elders. While many short forms drawn from texting and Leet [5] are in common use, even these have their rules and correct and incorrect forms. The game itself encourages players to excel in many aspects of the game, to create great beauty, and to learn widely varied forms of humor. An avatar can experience virtual life as a male, as a female, as a Gnome, as an Elf, a Dwarf, all the time learning about stereotypes and prejudices. The game will reward the avatar for being kind to others, to animals, to the environment, as well as for accepting group responsibility.

A character can be developed to make it useful in fulfilling specific group roles appropriate to its own interests. All of these permit even a child to build a reputation and to join a guild, taking such responsibility as he or she wishes. The game will also reward thrift and punish profligacy. Azeroth offers an opportunity to manage a sizeable allowance in an environment where nothing harmful can be purchased, little of value as it is viewed in TRW as wasted. And all of this occurs within an inherently educational environment. Until one learns, one cannot accomplish one's goals and move forward in the game.

The avatar can explore vast digital realms, some ethereal in their beauty, others terrifying in their menace, learning quickly to distinguish one from the other. And the avatar can also witness the behaviors, highly positive and highly negative, of hundreds of other such avatars over a few hours in Azeroth.

The young can, of course, learn these things on their own, and most are forced to do so. In TRW parents, try as they may, are painfully aware that their progeny will learn much of what they need from others, from harried teachers instructing huge classes, but usually, and often regrettably, from their peers. But Azeroth offers a parent a chance to co-pilot their child through digital temptations while sharing with the child what they themselves have learned. This opportunity often comes with great effort, expense, and even pain in TRW. Children can learn what they need to know to eventually navigate so-called Real Worlds as well as digital ones.

But if parents opt out and choose not to play with their children as early as the young begin to do so, they do not accomplish anything positive, but rather turn their children loose in a digital environment when many of the long-term consequences of such an immersion are still largely unknown—at least to humans. One lesson that the current population of Azeroth, believed to be perhaps twelve million in TRW, certainly teaches us is that humans are going to play. Some believe it is in their very nature to play, perhaps a key aspect of being human.

While the average age of players in Azeroth is believed to be in the mid-thirties, there are plenty of younger players. Most servers become extremely crowded within thirty minutes of school letting out. Some of these children play astonishingly late, to the point where even the most enthusiastic 'Toon has to wonder what, if anything, their parents are thinking.

And if the parent opts out and begins treating Azeroth as a cheap and engaging baby sitter, it will do that job. Children will happily spend hour upon hour on the computer while the parent watches television reruns to their own heart's content or engages in other non-interactive activities which probably would not engage an intelligent child's attention.

But to opt out is irresponsible. Azeroth offers as many dangers as it does opportunities. While I do not in any way intend to align myself, even temporarily or rhetorically, with those who demand increased regulation of Game Worlds such as Azeroth [6], (usually because their constituents are increasingly questioning their hapless attempts to regulate TRW), in truth I have observed behavior on line which parents would do well to worry about. Azeroth, simply put, allows the young to mimic what passes for mature behavior in TRW, among other unsupervised young who gleefully reward such behavior, again, just as in TRW. One of these is to swear and curse in the chat line.

Communication in game is largely through text chat, though small groups may use Voice over Internet Protocol and transmit audio in real time. In text chat, a player types into a chat line, which is then read by the audience that the player selects. Players can voluntarily put on an adult language filter which will render incoming language a little less profane: all common curses become something like (*&^! But the highly motivated can evade such a simple filter by varying spacing or themselves inserting null characters producing something like "F # 5 K!" which will come through all such filters in its unaltered glory, even if strangely formatted.

Because this filter is voluntary, many adults will simply not enable it; this produces in one's own chat line what some may feel to be an emotionally satisfying string of expletives. Those few who do enable filtering will usually have little trouble in decoding others' messages, cursing by its very nature being limited, repetitive, and predictable.

One can also drink without age limit in Azeroth. Buying or winning as loot in a struggle produces something like "Dwarven Stout," which, when clicked on and consumed, produces in the chat line the inability to type accurately, and general messages in text like "*Name* seems to be sobering up." Again, this is one of those "adult" behaviors unhappily imported from TRW. One consequence then, could be, say, a group of drunken digital gnomes with purple hair inviting each other to perform anatomically impossible and poorly understood acts, conveyed in badly misspelled text. And, of course, lying wildly about age, sexual experience, race and gender as they do so.

This is one of the few areas where Ol' Bliz, could have an impact on the problem. This could be done simply by making the chat filter universal rather than opt-in. This would reduce the emotional satisfaction of seeing one's own forbidden words in a chat line. Of course, this will eventually produce new swear words, such as %$#@!, but this problem can be dealt with when and if it arises!

If the young can swear and drink like mature 'Toons in Azeroth, they can also dress like them. Admittedly proper dress is largely in the eye of the viewer. The issue is that in Azeroth, we may wear pretty much what we wish, or little or nothing. A click of the mouse will let any 'Toon strip his or her own image down to its "birthday suit" not, fortunately, true nudity, but a costume of two brief pieces for females, trunks for males. All races are, with the possible exception of the gnomes [7], gendered, and even gnomes come in two types, though clearly they could grow up to become just about anything. So we can assume that female Trolls go for the huge feet of their own males [8] and that Tauren can discern the sexual identity of their own kind despite all the bling they wear. [9]

The problem lies, as is almost always the case, with two races, the Humans and the Elves. The genders of both Blood Elf and Night Elf races, and the Humans are highly sexualized and, depending on gear, sometimes markedly so. [10] They also dance. Each race has its own dance, and by general agreement among male 'Toons, the female Night Elves are definitely the ones with whom to partner at the local inn.

Just as not all 'Toons crossover into the real world, not all real world players will crossover into Azeroth in the sense of achieving a close identity with their avatar. But some do—the world is designed, after all, to achieve the highest possible degree of identification.

Another sort of closely related bad behaviors such as unrelentingly cruel violence ("griefing"), open racism, sexism, and other forms of highly prejudiced behavior are probably of less concern to most parents from TRW than cursing and sexual displays. But in the event that a human parent should wish to develop progeny with higher natures, there is much to worry about in Azeroth.

Ol' Bliz, for what may be crassly commercial reasons,[11] has designed Azeroth to be a brutally genocidal society. As a 'Toon takes form, it must be committed from origins to either the Alliance or the Horde faction. The Alliance are, by the standards of TRW, the more heroic and romantic races, including my own Night Elves. The Horde is a chaotic coalition of various unlikely beings such as the Undead, Trolls, Orcs, and the Blood Elves.

The end result of the constant subtle and not so subtle encouragement of Ol' Bliz is that players, especially younger ones, take gleeful pleasure in punishing "The Other" at every opportunity. Such contempt easily lends itself to situations wherein large groups of one side ruthlessly slaughter much smaller and weaker groups of the other, or groups set upon single players who have unwittingly wandered into the wrong area, all producing what in any other society would be labeled war crimes.

I do not mean to paint an unrelieved dark picture of Azeroth here. It is possible to totally avoid battle and to pass ethereal days discussing the ultimate nature of Elune, working on one's Jewel crafting and waiting for the Darkmoon Faire to wend its way to town. There are a rich variety of pets to be collected for younger players, and everybody can work on accumulating fantastic costumes. But the underlying reality of Azeroth is Red War.

Like violence, the next category of bad behavior in Azeroth is very common in TRW. Dishonesty ("Ninja-ing"), and self-aggrandizement at the expense of Noobs (less experienced 'Toons) are the stuff of daily life in capitalist societies, whether intended to accumulate Euros, Yen, Dollars or Azerothian gold, silver, or copper coins.

Unlike in TRW, in Azeroth the truly dishonest are rarely rewarded with television roles, federal bailouts or senatorial committee chairmanships. In Azeroth, one's reputation is frangible and it is not good to become known as a 'Toon who is likely to repeatedly "ninja' or steal loot from others. Once that happens, your appearance in the global chat window where everybody communicates is likely to be met with angry recounting of past crimes and dire warnings about engaging in groups or social activities with you.

Azeroth also tests the emotional stability of even the mature. The not infrequent battles for loot or reputation become quite important, and an extended-group quarrel in a Raid or a Battle Ground—areas set aside for organized encounters with players from the opposing faction—produces real adrenalin surges. It is not uncommon to see players totally lose self-control and SCREAM IN CAPS such as "I HATE ALL THE ALLIANCE F43S."

Such behavior is justly condemned in all civilized societies and usually thought of as a form of temporary madness calling for intervention by one's peers, unless, of course, there are uniforms involved. There is doubtless a self-correcting element to such 'Toon rage in Azeroth as few computer keyboards will really stand up to repeated banging, but it should be discouraged from the beginning, ideally by a calmer parent sitting at the child's side.

Sexual predation is one of the greatest fears of human parents whose children spend much time on line. Obviously even one case is far too many, but in fact there are very few documented cases of such things occurring in Azeroth. The environment, being intensely social, is itself unlikely to facilitate the sort of privacy that such degenerate beings need. However, just as in TRW, younger players should be taught not to reveal personal data. When in doubt one can invoke angelic beings—Game Managers, who represent Ol' Bliz—and refer them to particular incidents that will surely be investigated. And Ol' Bliz knows all, of course, keeping digital records of at least many hours of play. Players are frequently warned and can be banned for repeated infractions.

Conclusion

On balance, the World of Warcraft is best thought of as an extended opportunity for good parenting. It offers the young, if properly instructed, a chance to model good behavior, observe thoughtful adult behavior and to ease into the company of more mature beings. A huge social space like Azeroth is a good place to teach children how to behave socially. Much of the ancient etiquette of TRW is even more appropriate in Azeroth. In general, the standards for good behavior are higher in Azeroth than in TRW, thankfully.

As unlikely as it may seem to the uninitiated, many families play together, extended families have formed mutually supportive guilds, and players of all ages have experienced rich rewards in doing so.

Endnotes:

[1] See; "The Tales of Azeroth" and "Toons and Terrorism" See too my books reviews, the first of R. V. Kelly 2's *Massively Multiplayer Online Role-Playing Games*, and Edward Castronova's work, Synthetic Worlds, The Business and Culture of Online Games, and most recently: Hilde G. Corneliussen and Jill Walker Rettberg, (editors,) Digital Culture, Play, and Identity: A World of Warcraft Reader

[2] This piece is dedicated to my former guildies in "Heroic," Zul'jin, Azeroth, who taught me many of the lessons I attempt to convey here. Ty guys...

[3] See: http://en.wikipedia.org/wiki/Blizzard_Entertainment

[4] There will be some confusion in nomenclature here, because in Azeroth, one of our races, in addition to Draenel, Blood Elves, Night Elves, Dwarves, etc., is the

Human one. We will capitalize Human when referring to the Azerothian race, giving it the dignity humans sadly lack in TRW.

[5] See http://en.wikipedia.org/wiki/Leet for a good introduction to Leet,

[6] I refer of course, to a minority of the desperate-for-reelection political elite. If we are to judge by the recent career, for example, of the apparently deranged governor of Illinois, Rod Blagojevich who wrote, early in his career: "Yet, every day, millions of young children spend their afternoons at the controls of video games like this one, simulating acts of murder, dismemberment, decapitation and sexual seduction." http://www.govtech.com/gt/articles/93170

[7] For Gnome art see: http://images.google.com/images?q=wow+gnome&oe=UTF-8&rls=org.mozilla:en- US:official&client=firefox-a&um=1&ie=UTF-8&sa=N&tab=wi&ei=quLwSfyuM5bisgPA3vj1Cg&oi=property_suggestions&resnum=0&ct=property-revision&cd=1

[8] Trolls: http://images.google.com/images?hl=en&client=firefox-a&rls=org.mozilla% 3Aen-US%3Aofficial&um=1&sa=1&q=wow+male+troll&btnG=Search+Images&aq=f&oq=es

[9] Tauren http://images.google.com/images?hl=en&client=firefox-a&rls=org.mozilla% 3Aen-US%3Aofficial&um=1&sa=1&q=wow+tauren&btnG=Search+Images&aq=f&oq=

[10] For screenshots of Night Elf females see: http://images.google.com/images?hl=en&client=firefox-a&rls=org.mozilla% 3Aen-US%3Aofficial&um=1&sa=1&q=wow+screenshots+night+elves&btnG=Search+Images&aq=f&oq= Those who doubt that these particular images are representative might scroll through the other eighty-eight thousand images turned up in this particular search.

[11] I intend to submit a frankly theological exploration of the World of Warcraft for subsequent editions, perhaps after I have achieved level 80, at which point I hope to come face to face with the gods, and to ask them some penetrating questions.

Technology Review

To George Orwell: It's the Kindle Baby, it's the Kindle!

View online at: http://bcis.pacificu.edu/journal/2009/04/article.php?id=68

Technology Review by Jeffrey Barlow

Introduction

The Kindle, Amazon's electronic text reader, is, we believe, a disruptive technology that will have immense consequences on reading and the technologies currently bound to it [1]. The Kindle is far from new [2]. It was substantially updated, however in February of 2009 and is rapidly building, not only a huge market, but also ancillary industries around it. Here, we discuss our own experience with it, using George Orwell's two works, *Confessions of a Book Reviewer* and *1984*, as our jumping off point for two sequential reviews. This one, very positive in tone, will be followed by a more cautionary essay in our June posting of *Interface*.

The Impact of the Kindle at the Berglund Center

One of the great pleasures and urgent necessities of working at the Berglund Center for Internet Studies at Pacific University Oregon is somehow keeping abreast of innovative digital technologies. Usually these arrive with plenty of advance notice. It is the nature of the intensely competitive digital economy that each player is obliged to continuously snuffle after the "Next Big Thing" lest, like Microsoft, they see a Google-like competitor zoom around, over, under, and through them. Consequently, the trumpets heralding new developments sometimes amount to far more than the substance of the thing itself.

At the Berglund Center, we are almost totally staffed by undergraduates and are limited in what we can pay, not only by our budget but also by University practices. We try to compensate by giving the staff a chance to work with the best technologies and programs that we can afford. Also, we are all, unashamedly, geeks.

Our offices often come to a halt to examine a new high-definition digital video cam, or the newest Mac computer, or perhaps the latest iteration of the iPhone. In my ten-plus years at the Berglund Center, however, no new technology has caused quite so much excitement as an Amazon Kindle, the firm's electronic book reader [3].

The excitement I felt when first playing with the Kindle was similar to my own first glimpse into the World Wide Web through the Mozilla browser. We think that yet again, the future has arrived. But so, of course, have the second thoughts that sneak along behind any such transformative technology's triumphal procession.

To me, the Kindle seems almost the anti-Big Deal of digital technology. Amazon has wisely put far more effort into developing the Kindle and to providing texts formatted for it than advertising it, a reversal of common practices for many new technologies

[4]. I knew it was available, had seen it reviewed, knew of some of the issues it has raised, but had not seen one. Neither had any of the staff nor colleagues on the Pacific University campus to whom I showed it in my own enthusiasm.

Field Testing the Kindle in Reading for Review

In order to learn to use the Kindle, I decided that I would download rather than purchase in hard copy several works for review. I chose two quite different ones; first, Cohan's *House of Cards: A Tale of Hubris and Wretched Excess on Wall Street* reviewed at http://bcis.pacificu.edu/journal/2009/04/article.php?id=65 in this posting of *Interface*.

The second, to be reviewed in June, is quite different: Arthur Phillips' *The Song Is You: A Novel* which might be described as a mordantly romantic tale of an aging man who lives primarily in music and is accompanied everywhere he goes by his iPod, while in a sense stalking and being stalked electronically by a much younger woman, a rising popular singer. These works present very different challenges to the reader, and it seemed to me that reading them on the Kindle would be instructive in distinctive ways.

I begin here with the Kindle and Cohan's *House of Cards*. Book reviewing is a key activity for me as Director of the Center. As dauntingly complex as the current problems in the world economy are, and as unfamiliar with the subject of the work as I am, I knew, from other reviews, that this was probably the place to begin.

In reviewing books, I am always aware of George Orwell's wonderful 1946 essay, "Confessions of a Book Reviewer," in which he described one of his assignments [5]:

> Half hidden among the pile of papers is a bulky parcel containing five volumes which his editor has sent with a note suggesting that they "ought to go well together". They arrived four days ago, but for 48 hours the reviewer was prevented by moral paralysis from opening the parcel. Yesterday in a resolute moment he ripped the string off it and found the five volumes to be PALESTINE AT THE CROSS ROADS, SCIENTIFIC DAIRY FARMING, A SHORT HISTORY OF EUROPEAN DEMOCRACY (this one is 680 pages and weighs four pounds), TRIBAL CUSTOMS IN PORTUGUESE EAST AFRICA, and a novel, IT'S NICER LYING DOWN, probably included by mistake. His review—800 words, say—has got to be "in" by midday tomorrow.
>
> Three of these books deal with subjects of which he is so ignorant that he will have to read at least 50 pages if he is to avoid making some howler which will betray him not merely to the author (who of course knows all about the habits of book reviewers), but even to the general reader.

House of Cards, like Orwell's assignment, *A Short History of European Democracy*, is a mammoth work of almost 500 pages and richly detailed. Orwell would never have been able to understand it from any 250 pages, let alone merely fifty. Much of the vocabulary is new to me, as it is to most Americans following the economic collapse of such firms as Bear Sterns. Only the highly specialized readers would be completely comfortable with such concepts as 'derivatives' [6].

Had I been reading a hard copy of the book, I would have been working with it to one side and the computer at the center of my desk, my eyes flying back and forth looking up such terms. The index would have been of limited help because almost any complex work fails to have an adequate index— such addendums discourage the broad audiences that publishers seek.

The Kindle, however, has a built in dictionary, continually live, which automatically gives me, in an unobtrusive footer, a general definition of every term I pause the cursor before. The dictionary is multilayered so that, if I am not happy with the first definition, a click of the cursor takes me into far more detailed definitions and examples. The Kindle also has a universal search function so that if I want to see every single use of the word "derivative" in Cohan—which no index could hope to list—I again can do so with a couple of clicks of the cursor.

If I am not happy with Cohan's definitions—rarely the case as he was himself a practitioner in the field about which he writes—the Kindle lets me go out on the web wirelessly (and without cost) and view sites such as those I cited in my review. Moreover, I can quickly highlight these definitions or any other section of text, and copy them to a file which I can then easily move to my computer. When writing, I can then cut and paste effortlessly, also a big savings in time and effort [7].

While these elaborate features of the Kindle, combining the book and the World Wide Web, might have fascinated Orwell, it has additional attractions to even the casual reader. One of these is certainly cost of use. While the $370.00 cost of the machine and a very nice, protective as well as decorative, leather case is clearly daunting, many works can be downloaded for little or no cost from the WWW. Cohan's work is listed at $27.95 at the publisher's site. Amazon provides instantaneous download of the electronic version—and that of almost any other best seller, including usually the entire list from *The New York Times* for $9.95. Even on the basis of cost alone, the Kindle will amortize itself with the purchase of about twenty such books, hopefully well under two years' purchases for most reading families.

Electronic download, which can be accomplished wirelessly or downloaded to a computer and later moved to the Kindle via a mini-USB cord, is free. The apparatus charges quickly and a full charge has lasted me for at least 12 hours on each occasion that I have so tested it—Amazon claims four days, depending on wireless usage. It can also be recharged from a laptop via the USB cord. This means that most devices used to extend a laptop's running time should also work for the Kindle in the event of truly unusual demands.

The instantaneous download (3G on Kindle2) has other advantages as well, of course—it saves either mailing or travel costs. The reader can also download the first chapter of many Kindle books before purchasing. In looking for works to review via Kindle, I downloaded several and rejected them before settling upon Cohan's and Phillips' works. And while I am not certain of this, it is my belief that such works could also be downloaded from abroad, so I need never again lug a carton of books to China for my annual month-long period of work there.

My Initial Concern: Is it truly like a book?

My first concern had been simply the physical experience of reading. Reading has shaped not only my mind and my career, like any other academic, but in my case, my body as well. My eyesight is terrible and requires ideal conditions for reading. Even my hands have been shaped by reading—they naturally relax to a book-holding grip.

The Kindle has required no adjustments in my reading style. It is lighter at 10.2 ounces than all but the smallest hard-back and as light as many paperbacks. I can also choose from a number of different font sizes and I find myself beginning with a small font and, as my eyes tire, rather than putting the work down, I crank up the font size and finish more refreshed.

The Kindle screen looks amazingly like paper, and performs even better. It refreshes as fast as you can hit "next page" and the "ink" stays on that page even if you turn the appliance off; when you wake it, you are right where you were. It is visible even in bright sunlight. Under reduced lighting conditions it is no more demanding than a book, save that you may have to position the light so as to reduce glare. You can place endless bookmarks, and in addition to cutting and pasting, you can make your own notes on the keyboard and link them to the place in the text which inspired their creation.

Like my eyes and hands, my back has also been shaped by a lifetime of reading. I am as likely to have a book bag slung over my left shoulder as to be carrying my house keys. With the Kindle, I can, should I wish to do so, carry well more than one thousand complete volumes with no noticeable gain in weight.

My daughter, Clare, studies in China now, and often requests that both academic texts and popular books be mailed to her. While we have not yet done so, we can purchase a Kindle and fully load it for less than the cost of air mailing even one large box of books to Beijing. Doubtless Chinese customs will be somewhat puzzled by the arrival of a Kindle from our household, and Clare is likely to spend several hours at Customs, but I think it will be worth it to her, and she may be able to write her own piece for *Interface*: "China and the Kindle".

Any works a user purchases through Amazon remain on a personal web site so they can be downloaded indefinitely. I downloaded a small free program for my iPhone, and I can load my current Kindle reading from that site into it as well at no additional cost.

And while I cannot recommend serious reading on the iPhone, it is comforting to have an emergency book with me in the event that I am stranded or delayed. And when I do read on the iPhone, it communicates wirelessly to the Amazon site, and when I go back to the Kindle it inquires if I want to take up the work where I finished on the iPhone; spooky, but cool!

The Kindle is also an Internet appliance of a limited sort. You can browse the web and download email, but these functions are certainly far less satisfactory for me than using my trusty MacBook Pro. The Kindle will also perform many additional functions, from reading texts aloud to you, to loading your own documents. To better understand these, it is best to visit Amazon's rather breathlessly celebratory WWW site [8].

Downsides to the Kindle

There are, of course, some downsides to the Kindle. We purchased the second iteration quite by accident as we were in that large number who ordered the first one, which soon could not be produced in sufficient volume to meet demand. In the period we were waiting, the Kindle was revamped, becoming Kindle2, and we reordered.

I cannot discuss any shortcomings of the first Kindle, but for me, some improvements can still be made [9]. The cursor toggle, one of those small niblets that sticks up and can be pushed to any side to produce corresponding actions, must be pushed down rather firmly for most uses, and occasionally I do not hit it hard enough and must get a better grip on the apparatus to make it function. Occasionally, if I get impatient cutting and pasting or inserting notes, it will lock up momentarily but in reading the two books I finished, I have never had to reboot it, though I can do so if I must.

I would also want to insure my Kindle against breakage, theft or loss, but assume it is covered by the usual "floater" personal policy which protects my computers and phones as well, though I intend to check to see if this is the case.

Conclusion: What about 1984?

Clearly, I am an enthusiastic convert. But I think it impossible to invoke George Orwell's advice to book reviewers as I have done here, without also remembering his more famous work, 1984. Might the Kindle do to content what the WWW has? At present, commercially published books, unlike WWW content, are closely edited and in a sense controlled. It is possible to write and format your own works for the Kindle, and many people are doing so. An entire industry is rising around Kindle publishing. This inevitably raises some issues that might well be discussed in reviewing Phillips' *The Song Is You: A Novel* in the May posting of *Interface*, and I promise to do so.

Note

To see the notes which I downloaded from the Kindle while writing this review, see MyClippings.txt

End Notes:

[1] The Kindle has been disruptive for Amazon in that its sales are given credit for an incredible 18% jump in revenues during the first quarter of this year. See: David Neal, "Kindle ignites big sales gain at Amazon" Online retail giant has seen revenues climb by 18 per cent Vunet, http://www.vnunet.com/vnunet/news/2241064/amazon-posts-sales-gains This gain might well be compared to Microsoft's revenues in the same

period, the first quarterly decline in its history. See: ASHLEE VANCE, "Microsoft Profit Falls for First Time in 23 Years" The New York Times, April 23, 2009 at: http://www.nytimes.com/2009/04/24/technology/companies/24microsoft.html?hpw

[2] David Pogue at The New York Times first mentioned it in November of 1997. http://www.nytimes.com/2007/11/22/technology/personaltech/22pogue.html

[3] Official site found at: http://www.amazoncom/dp/B00154JDAI/?tag=googhydr-20&hvadid=&ref=pd_sl_18mqco62ua_e

[4] This balance may be shifting; Kindle ads suddenly seem to be everywhere.

[5] See it at: http://gutenberg.net.au/ebooks03/0300011h.html#part37

[6] For the wide range of confusion on these, see some of the sources found at: http://www.google.com/search?hl=en&client=firefox-a&rls=org.mozilla:en-US:official&hs=Bcy&ei=_rr_sSfyXNJ-atAPnpKXsAQ&sa=X&oi=spell&resnum=0&ct=result&cd=1&q=financial+derivatives&spell=1 At the poles of the discussion, start with Thomas F. Siems," 10 Myths About Financial Derivatives" at the Cato Institute: http://www.cato.org/pubs/pas/pa-283.html an impassioned plea for hands-off policies which permit unregulated investments in derivatives, then move to Linda Davies "Gambling on Derivatives. Hedging Risk or Courting Disaster?" at http://projects.exeter.ac.uk/RDavies/arian/scandals/derivatives.html which leads off with a quotation by Warren Buffet: "We view them as time bombs both for the parties that deal in them and the economic system ... In our view ... derivatives are financial weapons of mass destruction, carrying dangers that, while now latent, are potentially lethal."

[7] I have added the Kindle clippings files for both books to the end of this review so that the reader may see for him--or herself what such a process might look like. It is clear that I downloaded way too much text, but printing it out and reviewing it before writing was an immense help to focusing upon those parts I wished to discuss in detail.

[8] Found at: http://www.amazoncom/dp/B00154JDAI/?tag=googhydr-20&hvadid=&ref=pd_sl_18mqco62ua_e

[9] To its credit Amazon includes at its Kindle WWW site both positive and negative reviews of Kindle and Kindle2. Many of the negative ones are by users who preferred the first iteration to the second, but there are also seriously disgruntled users who feel that they have been victims of production faults that should have been corrected as well as of design flaws. See: http://www.amazoncom/Kindle-Amazons Wireless-Reading-Generation/product-reviews/B00154JDAI/ref=dp_top_cm_cr_acr_txt?ie=UTF8&showViewpoints=1

Book Review

Jane Austen and Seth Grahame-Smith's *Pride and Prejudice and Zombies*

View online at: http://bcis.pacificu.edu/journal/2009/04/article.php?id=61

Review by Pauline Beard

Jane Austen and Seth Grahame-Smith. *Pride and Prejudice and Zombies.* Quirk Books, 2009.

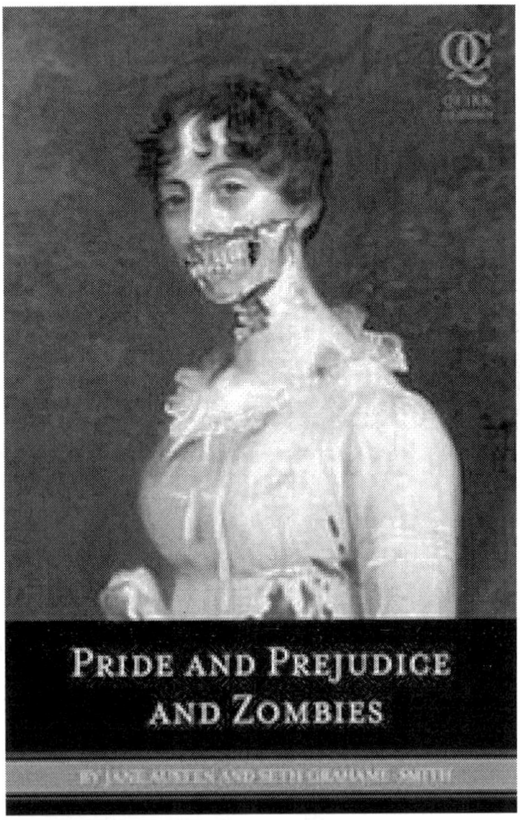

That noise you hear is either Jane Austen weeping in her grave, or chuckling at, or sharpening her Katana to wreak revenge on Seth Grahame-Smith for the outrage performed on her beloved *Pride and Prejudice*. Instead of a bright and sparkling heroine, Smith presents a Lizzy Bennet with sword-wielding, deer-wrestling powers and the ability to stomach (sometimes) beheading and dismembering the undead. I was at times revolted to the point of vomiting (an act which happens frequently in the new novel), roaring with guilty laughter, or sitting back saying aloud to Grahame-Smith "Boy, you've got balls!" (Plenty of those too in this revamping ...pun intended). If this Amazon Book List recent favorite brings more readers back to the original novel I am thrilled; let's face it *is* Austen's novel simply with the odd line and action added about the undead, fighting the undead, recognizing someone with the strange plague decimating England, and back-stories woven in that sometimes delight but more often disgust.

The book is 85% Jane and 15% Seth (Sikka) in the "mash up" style of novels sweeping the best seller lists. It took me a little while to understand the method: literally the use of the entire Austen text and then the "mash up" of the zombie text. Famous lines have tacked-on pieces: Mr. Darcy on dancing: "Every savage can dance. *Why, I imagine even zombies could do it with some measure of success*" (22 italics mine). Famous scenes of wit and conversation have action added in. For example the much filmed ball scene where Darcy is unpardonably rude to Elizabeth continues for pages of the original text and then Elizabeth's "hand met the dagger beneath her dress.

She meant to follow this proud Mr. Darcy outside and open his throat" (14). No doubt the original Lizzy had similar thoughts and a number of Janeites (fans of Austen and members of the Jane Austen Society of North America...JASNA) might have had the same desire—this text expresses them. Seth simply brings out hidden meanings and the infamous Austen humour. Who has not wished that Mr. Collins be stabbed "about the head and neck" (52) for insults to the Bennet girls, and joined in Mr. Bennet's wish that his wife's lips be sewn shut (88)?

Grahame-Smith explains his methods in an interview with Lev Grossman who sees a certain kind of logic in the original novel meshing with the zombie genre. Grossman claims that so much is unmentionable in Austen —"wit and good manners...cover up nasty things like sex and money"...so he questions, "Why not have those unmentionables be zombies?" (*Time*). Thus Elizabeth on her long walk to Netherfield vanquishes three unmentionables, beheading the last long-dead, "letting her battle cry be known for a mile in every direction" (28). On a symbolic level one could then claim that once Elizabeth reaches the manor house Netherfield, and confronts the snobbish Bingley sisters, the glutton Mr. Hurst, the affable weak Mr.Bingley and the proud Mr. Darcy, she is in fact battling her own "unmentionables": class distinction, money superiority and stupidity versus wit, intellect and the culture of reading. Once I got the hang of the method, I had to follow up with some reading on zombie lore and literature, not a genre this Janeite is familiar with at all. I learned that the word zombie came from a type of voodoo snake god...from the Niger Congo...the Kongo word *nzambi* meaning god. Stories emerged from Haiti about the undead who rose from their graves in various stages of decomposition and hungered for the flesh of live human beings to bring them back to life. In some cases the human flesh was augmented by human brains. A bite or scratch from the zombie could bring about a stage of undeadness, a horrifying plague which causes the living to become undead in putrefying fashion, or was simply a condition acquired after death. For the literature, William Seabrook in 1929 wrote *The Magic Island* showing the zombie cult which came to "symbolize all our deepest fears, which have now been labeled as communism, capitalism, boundaries of medical science" (www.lsu.edu.faculty). Luminaries such as C.S.Lewis wrote *Perelandia* with a zombie, Professor Weston, representing the serpent in the Garden of Eden; J.K. Rowling in *Harry Potter and The Half Blood Prince* uses the inferius as a zombie, a corpse under the control of a dark wizard (www.experience/festival.com). George Romero's 1968 film *Night of the Living Dead*, scorned at its inception is now a modern classic. Contemporary films show apocalyptic scenarios where the undead must be dismembered or burned to kill them off finally, because body parts continue to move. Zombie enlightened I saw the cleverness and hilarity beneath the outright rip-off of a classic. Two examples of back-stories will illustrate.

Lovers of the original novel have always wondered why on earth Charlotte Lucas would marry the deadly Mr. Collins. Seth now provides the reason. Charlotte is in fact "stricken by the plague! Condemned to serve Satan!" On her walk to Longbourne, she was caught in the grasp of an unmentionable whose teeth "broke her skin. She was able to free herself...but Hell's dark business had been carried out". All Charlotte wants now is a few last happy months, and "a husband who will see to [her] proper Christian beheading and burial" (99). The juxtaposition of Christian and beheading is sobering as is Charlotte's gradual deterioration into a zombie- like state. What saddened me even more was that nobody except Elizabeth sees or hears (Charlotte's mouth is being destroyed by the "plague") her friend's decaying body. Charlotte gnaws on her hand (142); sores burst on her face and she relishes the pus running into her mouth (121); she squats as if to defecate before Elizabeth can rush her out of Lady Catherine's card room (128)...yet her father thinks her "most comfortably settled"(129), married and living with Mr. Collins. The underlying meaning perhaps is derived from my reading other Austen novels where young women, sometimes plain, often virtually dowerless also go unnoticed (Anne Elliot); their feelings discounted (Fanny Price), their worth only as companions to more wealthy women (Jane Fairfax). Submissive, resigned to their lot, such women of that century probably decayed mentally and spiritually, unobserved, neither seen nor heard.

One could become maudlin in such analysis, but Grahame-Smith exercises the same type of Austen humour but in an inimitable ghoulish way when Charlotte observes Elizabeth and Darcy together. Instead of thinking about a love match for her friend, Charlotte often thinks of the "warm, succulent sensation of biting into a fresh brain..." Darcy's. Thinking of his mind she salivates over his "salty, cauliflower-like brain". She very much prefers Colonel Fitzwilliam as a match for Elizabeth but "Mr. Darcy had a considerably larger head, and thus, more brains to feast upon" (142). I cannot help but chuckle in an Austen-like way, and swear off cauliflower for life.

The descriptions can go over the top and I felt myself drawing back and away from the more puke-evoking. Perhaps Seth is anticipating this visceral reaction as he shows so many people in the novel actually vomiting: Elizabeth, Mr. Bingley, coach men, and Mrs. Bennet of course when she is so sick with her nerves after Lydia's disgrace. However, I have to say the "punishment" in the back-story for Mr. Wickham gave me a rather sick pleasure. Somewhat like Jane Eyre's Mr. Rochester ending up blinded and maimed, Wickham suffers a carriage accident which leaves him "bedridden and unable to move his limbs or control his personal business" (242). We know from the original novel that Wickham could not control his "personal business" leaving huge debts in Meryton, and attempting to seduce Darcy's sister Georgiana...but here the punishment of one who leaves debts and bastard children where ever he goes, involves diapers and soiled linens....I actually feel sorry for Lydia in this novel when Mrs. Bennet's famous acclaim of Lydia's marriage has subtle additions: "Dear crippled Wickham! What a husband he shall make!" (indeed), and she orders for the newly weds "calico, muslin and silver bedpans" (246). Who has not wished for Wickham receiving more than simply Darcy's bail-out and Mr. Bennet's coldness? But poor foolish Lydia? The hardest of hearts might be moved by the new addition to Lydia's end begging letter to Elizabeth: "...my Dear, lame Wickham... would like a parsonage" on finishing seminary...(!) "Any parsonage would do, of about three or four hundred a year...I must be off, as my beloved has soiled himself anew" (315).

Tongue in cheek to the end, Seth then presents a reader's Discussion Guide to his and Jane's novel. I particularly enjoyed Number 10:

> Some scholars believe that the zombies were a last-minute addition to the novel, requested by the publisher in a shameless attempt to boost sales. Others argue that the hordes of living dead are integral to Janc Austen's plot and social commentary. What do you think? Can you imagine what this novel might be like without the violent zombie mayhem? (319)

Shameless, yes, and the answer to the last is easy: Yes I can, we already have that novel! But to the argument of being integral to the plot...in the spirit of Book Club discussions, I would like to offer some ideas. Jane Austen is frequently criticized for rarely mentioning topical events like the wars in France. We know simply by the regiment being quartered in Meryton then moved to Brighton that troops are needed and being mustered. With a little history background, readers recognize the threat from the French. Seth takes this concept further than Jane's attempt, showing the threat from within. References to England and her "present unhappiness" (162) resonate throughout the novel. In London there is trouble on the East wall (256), some commotion on the street and the fear that the east gate has fallen again (262). In Sheffield a victory has taken place (141). The Gardiners must shorten their visit to the Lake District because of " recent troubles in Birmingham" and the need for Mr. Gardiner's firm to provide "more flints and powder" (190). The Bennets have taken "a blood oath to defend the Crown above all things" (185); Elizabeth explains that the Bennet girls are "each commanded by His Majesty to defend Hertfordshire from all enemies until such time we are dead, rendered lame, or married" (226). With that lovely last bathos suggesting marriage is as bad as being dead or lame, the new novelist pokes fun at the social changes taking place in Austen's novels that Austen herself only touches upon. Presumably fighting against the unliving unmentionables that are infecting the cities, the living are fighting the crucial symbolic changes taking place in the eighteenth century: the social order being overturned; the growth of the middle trade class; women on the stage; more women becoming literate and reading novels, of all things.... Seth takes the subtle references within Jane's novels and they become writ large.

Or...the modern writer is just having fun with those subtleties. Whereas Jane's Elizabeth has rarely been out of her village, and fights with her wit and tongue, Seth's has travelled in China and learned the martial arts that she uses to brutal advantage. Instead of practicing the gentle art of piano playing at Rosings in the out of-the-way housekeeper's area Lady De Bourgh recommends, Elizabeth practises her skills on Lady De Bourgh's ninjas, killing one in an especially nasty way with her sword across his belly: "The ninja dropped to the floor—his innards spilling from the slit faster than he could stuff them back in. Elizabeth sheathed her sword, knelt behind him, and strangled him with his own large bowel" (130). Take that Lady De Bourgh! Class distinctions and downright rude snobbery are conquered by force not words and musical finesse. After Darcy's infamous first proposal, Elizabeth fights back not only with words ("words for words" from Austen) to defend her family's honor but also with her battle skills in order to kill Darcy. She strikes the basic crane pose, attacks with "a series of kicks, forcing [Darcy] to counter with the drunken washwoman defense" (151). The entire magnificently written original is punctuated with martial arts poses and grabbing of the poker at crucial moments (152). The culmination of the scene which all Austen lovers still thrill to goes to the extreme with Elizabeth's put down of Darcy: "You are mistaken Mr. Darcy, if you suppose that the mode of your declaration affected me in any other way, than as it spared the slightest grief which I might have felt in beheading you, had you behaved in a more gentlemanlike manner" (153). These words haunt Darcy of course, and later when Elizabeth realizes her mistake about the man's actions to Wickham, she recalls her master Pei Liu of Shaolin who not only coaches her in martial arts but also the moral codes of existence. Ashamed of herself, she wishes for her dagger so she can carry out the seven cuts of dishonor. She wishes her master were there to "bloody [her] back with wet bamboo"(165).

Finally, sex. How may one discuss Jane Austen without it? Readers of her novels know the sexual subtleties that lie beneath the proper-seeming behaviour of her characters. Again Seth elaborates on original lines with innuendo but keeps the modesty of the Bennet girls intact. Elizabeth blushes at the following exchange between Darcy and Miss Bingley:

> 'I should like balls infinitely better,' she replied 'if they were carried on in a different manner.' (Austen 49)
>
> 'You should like balls infinitely better,' said Darcy 'if you knew the first thing about them.' (Grahame-Smith 45)

Miss Bingley does not "get it". Elizabeth frequently does. In the second lovely dancing scene in the original, Elizabeth, striving to get a conversation going with Darcy remarks, "Perhaps by and by I may observe that private balls are much pleasanter than public ones", to which Darcy says nothing (Austen 77). In the Grahame-Smith novel, Darcy replies, "On the contrary I find that balls are much more enjoyable when they cease to remain private" (73). Elizabeth blushes but does not reveal her amusement...most unladylike to do so. One more example and enough: Mr. Darcy puts his arms around Elizabeth (scandalous and certainly not in the original!)" 'What can he mean to do?' she thought". But Darcy is simply retrieving his rifle. Elizabeth recalls she has his ammunition in her pocket: " 'Your balls Mr. Darcy?' He reached out and closed her hand around them and offered, 'They belong to you, Miss Bennet.' Upon this their colour changed, and they were forced to look away from one another, lest they laugh" (205).

I think this is my main advice to the Janeites approaching Seth's novel with skepticism if not downright antagonism. It must be laughed at. The hidden meanings, the symbolic level, the sexual innuendos (much ado about men's trousers clinging to "English parts"), all need to be treated in the spirit of the whole. The zombie lit readers, I hope, will be drawn back or afresh to the original novel which is worth the read as Seth Grahame-Smith admits: "Who am I to screw with one of the most brilliantly plotted novels of all time?" (*Time*). Who indeed?

Works Cited

I am grateful to my work-study student Freshman Julissa Rosen who found a number of sites on zombies for me. Many of them gave similar background pieces. I cite the following specifics:

Grossman, Lev. Interview with Seth Grahame-Smith. *Time Magazine*. http://www.time.com/time/arts/article/0,8599,1889075,00.html.

Sikka, Madhulika. http://www.npr.org/templates/story/story.php?storyId=102526204 March 30 2009.

Book Review

William D. Cohan's *House of Cards: A Tale of Hubris and Wretched Excess on Wall Street*

View online at: http://bcis.pacificu.edu/journal/2009/04/article.php?id=65

Review by Jeffrey Barlow

William D. Cohan. *House of Cards: A Tale of Hubris and Wretched Excess on Wall Street.* New York: Random House, 2009.

House of Cards: A Tale of Hubris and Wretched Excess on Wall Street, is the first draft of the history of the collapse of Bear Sterns, the first of the major Wall Street firms to be destroyed by its reliance upon complex financial instruments ultimately based in the mortgage markets. The collapse was to have reverberations that are still continuing in both the American and world economies. *House of Cards* is clearly written and based in the best sources currently available. While the work will challenge those largely unfamiliar with Wall Street firms and financial practices, it should be read by those wishing to understand the end of the American financial system as it had existed, and its potential futures.

The author, William D. Cohan, is, in a sense, overly qualified to write *House of Cards*, the story of the Bear Stearns corporation's collapse and the relationship between these events and the meltdown of the international economy last year. Cohan has been both an investigative reporter and worked on Wall Street for seventeen years, including six years at Lazard Freres and as a managing director at JP Morgan Chase. [1] From his time at Lazard Freres he wrote *The Last Tycoons. The Secret History of Lazard Freres & Co.*

The term "overly qualified" requires some explanation. While Cohan's insider status made this book possible, protecting such status also becomes in itself an obstacle to full coverage. For example, Cohan has had access to an astonishing range of insider documents and exchanges, such as this e-mail between two participants:

> Jeff Mayer, since August 2007 a member of the firm's powerful executive committee and the co-head of the fixed-income division, e-mailed at two in the morning to urge Friedman to call him at home in New Jersey when "you know the outcome." Friedman replied he would but added, "We're a long way from getting anything done." [2]

Cohan also has a plethora of human-interest references so that we know where and what the participants ate, their personal habits, we even meet their wives and families. By the end of this huge work, we feel as though we were present at critical meetings, have read important emails and other documents, and in general, that, like the author, we were eyewitnesses to history.

But at times these references can become an obstacle to understanding. For example, a key analyst in explaining the unraveling of Bear Stearns was:

> Meredith Whitney, a well-respected thirty-eight-year-old research analyst at Oppenheimer who covered a number of Wall Street brokerages and banks...On Saturday, March 8, Whitney was getting her hair colored at the fashionable Pierre Michel Salon on East 57th Street when she received a phone call telling her that Marcel Ospel, of UBS, was in New York trying to sell PaineWebber for around $9 billion to JPMorgan as a way to raise badly needed capital...When she finished speaking with JPMorgan, Whitney headed from her office on 42nd and Madison to have sushi for lunch at Nobu 57, on West 57th. [3]

At this point, the reader, while admiring Whitney's investigative acumen, cannot help but be relieved to have been spared the details of which colors were put into her hair and which sushi she ordered.

In addition, we often feel that such details are very carefully chosen ones. While the author sometimes reveals the participants' personal foibles such as bad tempers, lapses of judgment, and curious unconcern for the future of their firms, none of them seem to have neglected (or spoiled) their children, kept mistresses, or indulged in other assumedly common practices of the highly competitive wealthy.

In short, we think that the author has to be highly selective with his human-interest details in order to protect his career as an investigative insider in the financial industry. Like a Three-card Monte shuffler in his beloved New York, he shows us the cards he wants us to see, while protecting his hole card—access.

However, Cohan is easily forgiven for the occasional sleight of hand because he has been so successful. At times the reader simply cannot believe that participants were so revelatory:

> At a few minutes before four, Friedman e-mailed his wife. "It's almost 4:00 A.M. and we're still here," he wrote. "There is an outside chance that JPMorgan Chase will bail us out. They have about 3 more hours to decide and I make it less than 50/50 that they will. If they do, we get to announce to the world that they've agreed to backstop us and we live to the weekend, at which point we probably give the firm away to them. Followed by their firing 10,000 people or so. If they say no, we're declaring bankruptcy and I really can't believe we came to this. And that will be worse. But, as you said, we'll be fine. Life will certainly be different but we'll be fine." At 4:24, Friedman sent a note to Jeff Mayer: "It's 4:00 A.M. and no decision. The JP folks took off an hour or so ago and we're sitting here waiting to see. Absolute torture." A few minutes later, Marc Feuer, in Bear's treasury department, wrote Friedman: "Oh, to be back in kindergarten." Friedman replied, "Don't I know it."[4]

However, this openness is, we think, another potential weakness of the book as an objective history of the financial collapse. Virtually all participants knew that they were seeing history unfold, and some clearly were writing for posterity. Anyone who has been through the discovery phase of a law suit—surely all the principles of these firms—is aware of the extent to which one's e-mails seem to take on alternative explanations when exposed to the scrutiny of hostile attorneys. [5] This leads, after the first such occasion, to the awareness that a hostile audience is potentially perched on one's shoulder waiting to add their own spin to one's electronic messages. This properly provokes a rigid self-censorship.

There is one more element of this book that must be discussed at some length because it is closely tied to our major task at the Berglund Center for Internet Studies, to understand the impact of the Internet. This book could not have been written before the development of the World Wide Web. Much of the evidence is taken from digital records such as the e-mails cited above, and from web sites such as blogs and Bulletin Boards. [6] Also, the electronic version of key sources such as *The Wall Street Journal* enabled the author to data mine his evidence at a remarkable rate.

It is, we think, a new sort of history, a digital history, which, while it may not raise any new problems for historians, certainly brings familiar ones into a new relief as we try to utilize digital documents as evidence.

But for all these caveats, a great deal is to be learned from this work. The information Cohan has laid out in *House of Cards: A Tale of Hubris and Wretched Excess on Wall Street* amounts to a major indictment of Wall Street practices and personalities. Indeed, language fails to measure out the culpability of such men, or the tragic worldwide consequences of their behaviors.

In America, children in middle class homes are going without school lunches because their parents have both lost their jobs, and are in the process of losing their homes. In China, the government is in the process of reversing many recent reforms out of concern for national stability, given the millions of laborers who are suddenly jobless. Heads of state meet serially to discuss redesigning the entire world economy, once based on assumptions about the stability of the American economy and its financial instruments, including the dollar itself.

A very small number of men were able, in the pursuit of yet more wealth when already wealthy on the order of history's richest men, to drive the entire American economy into the ground. This event then reverberated through the international economic system to the point where the event constitutes a major turning point in the free market system. And if the lessons of these events are not fully learned, then America, at least, may never again enjoy the level of prosperity it has generally had since 1945.

One of the messages which repeatedly comes through this work is a rather frightening one. This is that those in charge of financial policy (and largely still in charge of that policy) did not understand the nature of the problem until much too late, and meanwhile continually assured the rest of us that things were fine despite their awareness that things certainly were not fine. To begin to achieve a highly detailed insider's perspective on these events, begin with Cohan's *House of Cards: A Tale of Hubris and Wretched Excess on Wall Street*.

Endnotes:

[1] See Cohan's WWW page, maintained by Random House, at: http://www.randomhouse.com/author/results.pperl?authorid=73897

[2] Highlight Loc. 1290-92. This curious note style is a result of reading this work on a Kindle, Amazon's electronic text reader. See the review of the Amazon Kindle in this issue of Interface at: http://bcis.pacificu.edu/journal/2009/04/article.php?id=68

[3] - Highlight Loc. 774-88

[4] - Highlight Loc. 1301-9

[5] Sadly, I write from personal experience here.

[6] See for example: Highlight Loc. 489-95 ..."commented "DK" on *The Wall Street Journal's* "Real Time Economics" blog. "It will temporarily allow these banks to use crappy [mortgage-backed securities] as temporary collateral, but eventually these will have to be written down. I think this is just an attempt to cause markets to go down gradually, versus a huge crash." And then "Clear Skys Ahead" wrote with an acid pen, "Now that the Fed is lending to primary dealers and accepting unimpeachable items, such as mortgage debt, as collateral things can get back to normal. Now what exactly do we do when the collateral turns out to be worth less than the loan? Thank goodness everyone woke up and realized that unless the taxpayers were the ones ultimately stuck with the bill, Wall Street couldn't rally! Let the party resume at least until sanity takes hold." Such insider opinion has simply not been available to historians in the past, or if it was, it required massive amounts of time and energy to find and digest.

Editorial

Back in the Twentieth Century: The Development of The Journal of the Association for History and Computing 1997-2009

View online at: http://bcis.pacificu.edu/journal/2009/04/article.php?id=58

Editorial by Jeffrey Barlow

**Director, Berglund Center for Internet Studies,
Founding Editor, *The Journal of the Association for History and Computing***

At the Berglund Center we have long sponsored a number of scholarly electronic journals. These were a natural outgrowth of our increasing interest in the impact of the Internet. Some of these journals have had significant impact in academic circles. Foremost among these was The Journal of the Association for History and Computing *(JAHC), the first scholarly electronic journal in the field of historical studies to be well received in academia. At the same time, as the impact of the Internet has deepened and widened, the JAHC faces much changed circumstances.*

Below we discuss the JAHC as an example of the impact of the Internet upon scholarly print and electronic journals. This editorial will also appear subsequently in the JAHC itself. Because it was developed for a scholarly audience, it has a tone which is overly formal and pedantic, a very limited style from which writing for Interface, *blessedly, usually frees me. But perhaps the editorial does have the advantage of showing our broader audience not only the impact of the Internet upon academic journals, but also the problems that professional academics face in addressing scholarly audiences within their fields. All of these problems persist despite the many marvelous changes which digital communications have brought to us.*

Introduction: Origins...

As *The Journal of the Association for History and Computing* begins its twelfth year of production, it is an appropriate time to consider both its past, and its possible futures. The Journal has been significant and influential but faces many challenges if it is to remain important and to expand its influence.

My own relationship with the Association began at the Cincinnati conference in 1997 [1]. At that time, I was an established Asianist in the Modern China field with several books in publication, two Fulbright grants, and a lively research career with frequent travel to Taiwan, China, Vietnam, and Japan. Asian Studies was a hot field because of national security concerns as much as any other factor. I also had established a strong record of securing grants, both personal and institutional, as well.

After accepting the Matsushita Chair in Asian and International Studies at Pacific University, I received a grant from the Matsushita Corporation to develop electronic materials for Asian Studies. I needed to know more about the relationship between content and electronic delivery and the conference, organized by the International Association for History and Computing, seemed a good place to begin.

The conference was a liminal experience. To my surprise, I had far more in common with the presenters and the organizers of the conference than I did with most Asianists. The conference was a confusing experience in some regards, not only because of my lack of background but because the conference organizers, led by Dennis Trinkle, were not themselves quite sure where they were going. But many others had also found the conference exciting, and we met to discuss creating an American branch of the International Association [2].

I was charged with developing an electronic journal for such an organization. During the following year, I read widely, and began to master the Internet as a research tool, all the while posting student work on the Internet for the Matsushita Center for Electronic Learning. This combination of hands-on activity bolstered by theoretical research came to be the essence of history and computing.

My goal was to help create an electronic journal that would be a legitimate scholarly step in the development of our common field, historical studies. From my research, I began to see that it was probable that we were at the beginning of a new stage in the long process of scholarly communications [3]. The medium for scholarly communication had gone through many forms, literally from and clay tablets and stone monuments through codexes, parchments, and finally onto paper. Both the materials used and the forms of the content had evolved. The key stages it seemed to me were:

- From the 1470s through the 1660s: The book was the main form of scholarly communications.
- From the 1660s through to the present: The journal became the main form. This was not a smooth progression, but accelerated rapidly in the 19th century.
- From 1992-1997, a migration to computers began; whether this was a new stage or an ancillary development of the previous stage remained, in 1997, to be seen [4].

The outcome of that year's work was a paper presented at the 1998 conference which was a proposal that we create a journal for the nascent AAHC, that it be, of course, electronic, but that it also try to emulate as much as possible the look and functions of traditional peer-reviewed scholarly journals. This was what I had seen referred to as the "stealth model," meaning that while the new mode of delivery was to be electronic, the journal itself was meant to appear soothingly transitional rather than as a potentially disruptive technology.

Following another several months work at the Matsushita Center, the first issue of the JAHC appeared in August 2008, and the conference paper was presented as the "Editorial Statement" referenced here. While I am quite proud of my status as "Founding Editor" at the JAHC, every editor knows that he or she is at best a conduit for the work of others, usually many others. The common plural for a group of editors is a "stable" of editors. Perhaps the more appropriate term in English might be "kennel," because reliable editors work like dogs as much as like horses.

The JAHC was rooted in an almost crusading mentality among the founders. I was the greybeard in the group; there were a few others also in mid-career, but most were just setting out. After another ten years working at the Matsushita Center and at the Berglund Center for Internet Studies which succeeded it, I have come to see that this generational progression is rooted perhaps in the development of the WWW and computing itself.

When we began, knowledge of simple HTML was king, and any computer that could link to the Internet was satisfactory. Then came a bewildering cascade of new applications, computers, an entire science and an industry which steadily produced ever more savvy generations of practitioners and their students. And all this in ten years.

These developments were not, of course, driven or developed by academics, most of whom were deeply skeptical of each stage. This put us at the JAHC in a complex position, advocating for changes which were, we believed, going to be deeply upsetting to many of our colleagues.

One of our major tasks at the JAHC in this first decade was simply to understand and stay abreast of such changes, to find writers and editors who could winnow out the important ones from the incidental ones, and explain them to audiences who were often highly skeptical, and always relatively unlearned.

Our chosen niche, following in the tracks of the International Association, was the link between computing and historical studies. At the outset this seemed a simple enough conception, perhaps if anything, too limited. The astonishing pace of change, however, opened many new avenues to us, not only in studying the changes then occurring, but also in teaching and methodology, in research and data gathering, in delivery, and even in the fundamental forms for final presentations of findings.

Successes

We were successful by any reasonable standards. We have published over the past eleven years more than 142 different authors, some of them who were or soon became major figures in our field. Our columnists produced continually useful material issue after issue [5]. We opened this work up to an international audience by producing scholarly abstracts in more than ten foreign languages, encouraging those who read English as a second language to explore our content, and enabling index builders in those languages to catalogue it. Our editors and authors came from more than twenty countries and we discovered groups of like-minded scholars all over the world.

We found that many of our natural allies were not actually in the field of historical studies, but in the Library Sciences. This group realized well ahead of the historians that the critical element in the transition to digital forms of information was going to be indexing and cataloging them.

Our international editors were so dedicated to the sort of work that we were undertaking that they soon spun off sister journals in first French, then in Italian [6]. Scholars, authors and editors from abroad began showing up at our annual conferences, including a panel of Russian scholars—at the time a relative novelty—all of who shared our own abiding commitment.

The field of historical studies itself began to recognize the significance of our work. We became an Affiliate within the American Historical Association less than two years after the JAHC first appeared, in record time, faster even, somewhat to our embarrassment, than had Black Studies or Feminist Studies [7].

We were only the second electronic journal to be indexed by *American History and Life and by Historical Abstracts* [8]. We may also have been the first scholarly journal to have been hijacked by the Iranian Ministry of Science, which did us the dubious honor of scraping our site in 2004, downloading all of our content to that date behind a misleading URL, a problem which continues to bedevil us [9].

Materials that we first published electronically and themes that we explored also found their way into hard-copy publications, including a book series at M.E. Sharpe edited by some of our founding members [10]. For five years, almost every panel dealing with scholarship or teaching in an electronic environment which I attended at national conferences in History, Computing, Education, or Asian Studies, were peopled by scholars we had first published.

We were also an inspiration to other American scholarly groups contemplating plunging into the World Wide Web. A representative of the American Political Science Association acknowledged our influence in their decision to do so, and I have often consulted with Asian Studies groups as well.

Roots of Success

There were, of course, a number of reasons why we succeeded, so quickly and so spectacularly as both an organization and as a journal. Partly, it was the times. We were just behind the first rapid expansion of the World Wide Web and the development of critical browser and search technologies. Many of us were teaching students who were even more familiar with these than we were, and they often compelled us to learn about them, or fall behind. In turn, as related fields developed so rapidly, our second generation of students secured excellent professional positions, and a highly productive feedback loop began to build.

The reaction was also, as we had anticipated, often fearful or hostile. Colleagues thought that we were pandering to popular culture; they first dismissed the rapid expansion of Internet-enabled knowledge as temporary, then as simply debased, then as a corrupting influence that threatened to destroy books, if not civilization itself [11].

But granted the necessary expansion of the Web, our successes were ultimately rooted in something more prosaic and familiar: the founding values of our fields: regard for objectivity, an insistence upon double-blind peer review practices, upon citations and bibliography, in short upon critical scholarship itself. These traditional practices also came to be in some regards detrimental as discussed below.

Other reasons for success were the wonderful new tools we could bring to bear. While traditional journals, because of the expense, were forced to limit graphics, color, even notes themselves, we had no such limitations. Soon, we were giving annual awards to fabulous new database sites, to archives of photographs and film clips, to interactive teaching materials, to projects based on all the wondrous panoplies of WWW-enabled scholarly visions [12].

This era created a number of really important figures in the web-based industries, visionaries who saw the possible and created or secured the funding to enable it. As academics our tasks were more mundane and our backing more limited, but among our founders were many of us who took remarkable risks in changing the direction of our scholarship and teaching mid-way in our careers and even in the late stages of critical evaluation processes. We heard of many casualties in our ranks.

Dennis Trinkle, David Staley, and Deborah Lines Andersen produced a number of important studies evaluating the slow spread of and the many obstacles to digitally enabled scholarship and teaching [13]. The AAHC also developed, importantly, documents to help guide the development of appropriate standards for evaluating digital teaching and scholarship [14].

Many established scholars refused to acknowledge that digital change was indeed coming and were stubbornly resisting, rather than assisting us in properly adjusting to it. We were often amused when one of these established scholars finally ventured into electronic scholarship to thunderous applause in *The Chronicle of Higher Education.* But we knew that many truly creative younger scholars were being harried back behind the safe boundaries of established academic practices. More sadly, some were unwilling or unable to compromise and drifted out of academia altogether.

But fortunately for us, there were also enlightened supporters at our institutions who, in the argot of the time, "got it." These Deans, Directors, Presidents and Provosts were all painfully aware of how very competitive the academic and international environments were becoming, and wished to succeed in adapting. They funded our arcane projects, nominated us to new positions where we could push even harder, and, not infrequently, defended us against the serious charge that we were having fun in our work.

The continuing success of the JAHC has been based in large part upon one such generous philanthropist, Dr. James Berglund, who founded the Berglund Center for Internet Studies at Pacific University Oregon and facilitated the bringing together of computer labs and skilled student labor necessary for our continuing development. Other writers and editors are equally dependent upon such visionaries at other institutions, of course.

Failures

Our successes have been worth celebrating, of course, if only because they offer many lessons for future successes. But learning from our failures may be even more critical and we have had many.

As Founding Editor, I have found it galling that we have not been able to move to a quarterly production schedule. I ran this chart of our postings:

Year	1998	'99	2000	'01	'02	'03	'04	'05	'06	'07	'08
Issues	2	3	3	3	3	2	3	2	2	3	2

In each year after 1998 that we met, the board expressed a hope that we could move to a regularly quarterly production schedule. But we encountered two critical limitations. First, most of our founding generation of writers and editors succeeded in their careers and were promoted very rapidly [15]. Some of us have managed to fold the JAHC into those new positions to at least a marginal extent as have I, but others simply could no longer pay proper attention to it. The reader may have noticed that there is no cell for 2009 on the chart. At present, to my understanding of the production schedule, there are unlikely to be more than two issues in this calendar year.

The second cause of our failure was paradoxically, our success, and that of the World Wide Web itself. Other journals and other professional associations saw what we were doing, and moved to offer similar opportunities within their own folds. Where once we were almost the only peer-reviewed critical scholarly venue willing to publish digital scholarship and teaching in historical studies, soon everybody was. It became more difficult, even as the fields expanded, to secure increasing levels of content.

Unfortunately, as I predicted in 1998 in our first issue, when the established brands finally came to the table, they were going to elbow upstarts such as us aside, however much they deserved to suffer for their lack of courage. The succeeding Editor, Deborah Lines Andersen, wisely chose to maintain the quality of our content rather than to seek increasing quantities.

There is another failure that I find hard to pin down. I felt from the first that the World Wide Web was in some sense a component part of what we loosely call post-modernism. Post-modernist analysis has brought a great deal to scholarship, but it has also undermined the notions that there are fundamental truths and values. Perhaps this is necessary, and indeed, an accurate description of reality.

But the quality of scholarship has long been measured, and forever should be measured I think, against not just "truthiness" but truth. For centuries, historical scholarship flourished in an environment where truth was assessed by multi-level gatekeepers, highly qualified experts. Work was rarely published without being passed upon by ranks of such experts, from the advisors who shaped scholarly practices and manuscripts to the readers and editors who accepted or rejected them at scholarly presses and journals, to the libraries which carefully winnowed them in allocating valuable shelf space. The whole was interlocked by the practices of twentieth century scholarship, descended from many roots. When we researched and wrote, we bowed before Herodotus and Thucydides, before Sima Qian and Ban Zhao, as well as historians from every major cultural tradition and national locale.

Now every one of us is a possible publisher. At the JAHC we set ourselves to influence digital publication. We did develop good and useful practices for online citations, quality standards, objectivity and critical thinking [16]. We tried to modify traditional practices and to discover appropriate new best practices.

But we have been helpless before the same historical events that propelled us for a time at least to the scholarly edge of the wave set moving by the expansion of the World Wide Web. The end result has been that while students have far more materials available via the WWW than in their local and high school libraries, they are no better at evaluating such materials than was the case fifty years ago—perhaps less able. And fifty years ago the gatekeepers listed above protected them; now students face an impossible surge of materials, and usually select the most highly ranked ones, or the ones with the most pleasing colors, or with the most graphics. *Wikipedia*, an encyclopedia written by anybody and nobody, is now largely the arbiter of historical truth and relative importance.

Future Prospects?

What do I believe to be the future of the JAHC? For me, a validity check for historical research is its utility in predicting the future. I am fully aware that this places me in an old, outmoded, and completely discredited school of historical thought. Wiser historians long ago abandoned the conceit that their knowledge of the highly selected segment of the past that they accumulated had any hint of lessons for the future.

Nonetheless, those of us at the JAHC had, correctly I think, the apprehension that we were present at the creation of a new field, a new mode of delivering content, a true episteme. And we felt that, however dimly, we were seeing the future. In preparing this piece, I looked over the works of the many authors and editors we have published and I think that in general we have been on target. While the pace of change has been breathtaking and many new applications unforeseeable, nonetheless much of what we foresaw has unfolded.

I do not hesitate, therefore, to predict the next stage for the JAHC. We are going, I think, to face several obvious problems.

First, our original theme, the intersection between history and computing, has proven to be both too narrow and too broad. Too broad in the sense that everybody is doing it, and we have lost our niche to many formidable competitors. And in this era, what we do seems to be less clearly defined, unless very narrowly defined, in which case we lack adequate materials to publish.

We cannot however, simply unlink from our core interest; to do so is to lose our identity entirely. I that that rather we should embrace that link. The numbers of books and articles on the history of computing, computing practices, etc., are growing steadily and we must publish more of this list. This will not be easy, it will require an aggressive editorial staff which will seek out and encourage submissions that on their face may not be terribly interesting.

What, for example, was the first serious impact of email on the doing of history? What was the process whereby computers entered into dissertation research and practices? The first generation is still alive, and as historians we should see the importance of collecting their memories, and we now can do it in video as well. Each of these topics, we believe, like all historical research, also offers important lessons or at least understandings.

There is an entire field of corporate histories in the information technologies which are usually being written in-house. These may lack the impact of Ida Tarbell's works of course, but may be equally important in the ongoing Darwinian process of consolidation in the industry. Then there is the huge field of gaming development, taken seriously largely only by gamers themselves. But sociologists and those in new fields such as "Gaming Studies" are also working away. Where are the historians?

Rather than continue on with perhaps decreasingly persuasive examples, I will leave it to future editors to do what their predecessors at the JAHC have done, identify the creative thinkers and writers among the not-yet-notables and solicit their work.

A second problem is diminishing interest among younger scholars simply because our field, once revolutionary, has blended into the background of their daily lives. We are not tied together, for example, by our common experience of oppression, as are scholars of ethnic and gender studies.

Our interest is a more remote and tepid one, and in our classes we need to treat the impact of computers upon history as an element in every contemporary historical field and problem, as it is, I believe. We must, in our teaching, develop an interest in younger scholars in better understanding the immediate past to which we are, after all, eyewitnesses.

For me, for example, the development of the computing industry has become as important a factor in the triangular relationship between Taiwan, China, and the United States as was the Korean War, or the nuclear balance in the Taiwan Straits, and is a great deal less understood. Yet I do not teach this issue.

In his 2003 presidential address to the AAHC, Ryan Johnson listed a summer workshop we presented in 2000 at the International Center for Computer Enhanced Learning at Wake Forest. This brought in several tens of teachers from the surrounding area, and was, I believe, the last such workshop we offered. We should both as individuals and as institutions do many more.

This is not to say that we should become a subfield of the Histories of Science, Technology, or Business. But the impact of digital technology has been pervasive and we must see it for the formative event that it truly is, and in the JAHC encourage the production and publication of works which will illuminate that impact. To do so is to stay true to our original mission, to study the relationship between history and computing.

The JAHC also faces a perilous future because all academic journals do. At the JAHC, we have depended upon self-sacrifice and the kindness of others for our production expenses. But for most journals, the chase for funding is constant and too often drives decision-making. On the WWW, it is difficult for journals to maintain an identity—let us say it—a "brand"—because articles are usually found via a search, not in the studied perusal of a new issue arriving upon one's desk. Yet most established journals are financial black holes supported by the large scholarly associations which produce them [17].

Our future is also challenging, because research itself is being marginalized, and the teaching of history is frequently reduced to an academically supportive activity. Deans now demand that we teach ever-larger classes, and presidents stuff our classrooms to the bursting point in an effort to lower costs. The Liberal Arts themselves wither under the impact of the decline of the American economic empire.

All of these issues are, as well, opportunities for us. Computing, or at least digital technology, is now a direct influence upon history, not only its subject but also a force that shapes it. Who better to study this process than the members of the AAHC, and where better to publish our findings than in the JAHC?

These points that I have tried to make here doubtless seem overly dramatic. But when I tried to understand the development of scholarly communication in the pre-digital era, I saw that each of those generations too, saw themselves as living in challenging times, and it was those who responded to those challenges who carried historical studies forward.

Endnotes

[1] Please note that although I suggested that this piece will cover the JAHC from its inception to the present, in fact I was much less active after 2006 and Deborah Andersen's piece in this issue should be considered authoritative for the following period.

[2] Iam not naming these many individuals, both out of a fear of overlooking many of them and their contributions to the development of the AAHC, but also because I am trying to avoid the usual elegiac self-referential tones such pieces as this easily adopt. To better understand their contributions, see the JAAHC itself at: http://mcel.pacificu.edu/jahc/

[3] For my own analysis of this process, see: "Editorial Statement," http://mcel.pacificu.edu/jahc/1998/issue1/editorial/

[4] Valauskas, Edward J. "Waiting for Thomas Kuhn. First Monday and the Evolution of Electronic Journals." First Monday. http://www.firstmonday.dk/issues/issue2_12/valauskas/, p. 10. Valauskas references Derek J. de S. Price, Science since Babylon, New Haven: Yale University Press, 1961, pp. 55-56, 94-107 for this perspective. (list and note from Editorial Statement above.

[5] Again, I prefer not to list individuals here, knowing that I will inevitably leave some worthy scholar out of the list.

[6] For another summary of these events and successes see: "With Many Thanks" at: http://mcel.pacificu.edu/jahc/2006/issue1/editorial.php

[7] See the site within the AHA at: http://www.historians.org/affiliates/am_assn_his_computing.htm

[8] For more material on these successes see Ryan Johnson, "The Long Strange Trip It's Been" at "http://journals2.iranscience.net:800/mcel.pacificu.edu/mcel.pacificu.edu/jahc/JAHCVI2/ARTICLES/president.HTML

[9] Note the URL immediately above. Such pirate sites often outrank our legitimate sites on Google searches, presumably because the Iranians either manipulate rankings or often assign our articles in their own educational institutions. The American equivalent, I suppose, was the attempt of a leading American corporation to lock up our content in exchange for a generous annual payment. We desperately needed--and still need--such funds. Supposedly they simply wanted preferential access to our foreign language abstracts and our several dual-language articles, but the ninety page contract they sent us seemed much too opaque and open ended and when we tried sending them a simplified version which carefully reserved our rights, they broke off negotiations.

[10] See the list at: http://www.theaahc.org/publications.html

[11] Such fears have by no means died out. For a review of recent alarmist works see: Jeffrey Barlow, "The Madness of Crowds: Recent Criticisms of Web 2.0" at http://bcis.pacificu.edu/journal/2008/06/article.php?id=7

[12] These also sometimes challenged our classical standards. I remember with some chagrin my own editorial fiat that a very imaginative and playful scholar could not include a banner of Grateful Dead style dancing bear icons at the top of his article.

[13] See Deborah Andersen's wonderful "Benchmarks" series indexed at: http://www.google.com/search?hl=en&client=firefox-a&rls=org.mozilla%3Aen-US%3Aofficial&hs=2jF&q=jahc+andersen+ benchmarks%27&btnG=Search

[14] See "Guidelines for Evaluating Digital Media Activities in Tenure, Review, and Promotion" at: http://www.theaahc.org/tenure_guidelines.htm

[15] Those who did not succeed were those who found themselves in unsupportive environments. These often withdrew to safer areas of scholarly activity and their energies were lost to us. Others, through no fault of their own, could not establish the critical academic toehold that might lead to tenure and were reduced to debilitating and distracting underemployment or ancillary positions.

[16] For two key projects see Project Epee at: http://mcel.pacificu.edu/jahc/epee/ and "Authority Levels" at: http://mcel.pacificu.edu/jahc/2004/issue2/edit.php

[17] See Jennifer Howard, "Humanities Journals Confront Identity Crisis." The Chronicle of Higher Education, Vol 55, i 29, http://chronicle.com/free/v55/i29/29a00102.htm

June 2009 - Volume 9, Issue 5

Articles

- **Feature: Tiffany Boggis** - Health Promotion of Elders in Nicaragua: Interdisciplinary International Educational Opportunities for Pacific University Health Programs. A Berglund Faculty Research Fellowship Report
- **Media: Samantha Richards** - Boxercast: Creating Web Video Broadcasts for The Pacific Index
- **Legal: Leonard D. DuBoff and Christy O. King** - Insurance: Does Your Policy Really Protect You?
- **Social Networking: Jenn Hernandez** - From Facebook to Resume: Marketing Yourself Via Social Networks

Book and Site Reviews

- **Mark Le Vine's** Heavy Metal Islam: Rock, Resistance, and the Struggle for the Soul of Islam
  Review by Deborah Wheeler
- **Arthur Phillips's** The Song is You
  Review by Jeffrey Barlow

Editorial

- To George Orwell, II; Is It 1984 yet?

Feature

Health Promotion of Elders in Nicaragua: Interdisciplinary International Educational Opportunities for Pacific University Health Programs. A Berglund Faculty Research Fellowship Report

View online at: http://bcis.pacificu.edu/journal/2009/05/article.php?id=79

By Tiffany Boggis, MBA, OTR/L

Associate Professor, School of Occupational Therapy, Pacific University

The site created by Professor Boggis as part of this project is found at: http://www.pacificu.edu/chp/international/nicaragua/

Introduction

New opportunities for collaboration abound with the inception of the newly formed Pacific University College of Health Professions campus in Hillsboro Oregon. Prior to 2005, the health professional Schools of Physical Therapy, Occupational Therapy, Professional Psychology and Physician Assistant Studies were located in separate areas on campus and operated as autonomous entities within the University system. Since then, these Schools have moved to one central location and now include the recent addition of the Schools of Dental Health Science and Pharmacy. Unification of these six health profession programs under one roof lays the supporting foundation to enhance inter-professional educational collaboration among faculty, students, and those who benefit from our services. The *Health Promotion of Elders in Nicaragua* project evolved from the College of Health Professions' (CHP) goal to "foster *inter-professional* planning, instruction, and clinical experiences for schools within the College".

The *Promotion of Health of Elders in Nicaragua* project is the first inter-professional international educational endeavor for the College of Health Sciences. The goals of the project are (1) to provide health-related service-learning opportunities in Nicaragua using a community-based rehabilitation approach to build capacity and long-term interventions, within the means of the local economy, for Nicaraguans to help themselves and (2) to enhance inter-professional understanding and service delivery among health disciplines for students and faculty.

Promotion of Health of Elders in Nicaragua

Nicaragua is the second poorest country in the Western hemisphere. Over 50% of Nicaraguans over the age of 60 are unemployed. Elders receive no government pension, frequently leaving them without secure financial support.[1] Their families, who must leave the country to find work, are frequently forced to abandon the elders. Elder family members who can no longer work and have no family to care for them live in elder centers that rely on foreign aid and limited municipal assistance for funding. These elders experience the long-term effects of aging, poverty and a lifetime of poor health care. Diabetes, chronic pain, poor mobility, gum disease, and lack of productive and leisure opportunity are common concerns.

During Christmas break 2007-08, the College sponsored a team of six students and three faculty members from the Schools of Occupational Therapy, Dental Health Science, and Physical Therapy to travel to Nicaragua to assess the health needs of elders. The initial trip laid the foundation for on-going collaboration, and educational experiences among health profession students and faculty in coordination with Dr. Milton Lopez, one of only four gerontologists practicing in Nicaragua, and the Jesse F. Richardson Foundation that has been sponsoring development projects in Nicaragua for the past six years.

Challenges Encountered: A Virtual Solution

Because the College had no formally agreed upon policy, procedure, nor coordinated infrastructure to plan and organize a venture of this nature, formalization of the process to meet the unique needs of the College of Health Professions to support sustainable methods to facilitate on-going interdisciplinary international education became an urgent need. Additionally, it is the ethical responsibility of the educational institution to follow accepted guidelines and practices to adequately prepare faculty and student participants to undertake an experience abroad and to re-enter their own culture. [2]

Because schools within the College operate on different schedules, it is a challenge to gather all participants in one physical location at a specified time to coordinate efforts to prepare students and faculty for participation. The few meeting times participants managed to agree upon provided insufficient time to process the vast amount of information needed for full participation in another culture.

Thanks to the Berglund Center for Internet Studies at Pacific University, a Fellowship and Berglund expertise were offered to develop a virtual solution. The Fellowship enabled the author to establish procedures and develop Web resource pages for the Pacific University Web site containing information specific for preparation and travel to Nicaragua. Web pages include: information about the project; resources to learn about Nicaraguan health, government, culture, history and geography; resources to learn the Spanish language; pre-departure planning tips; information on health and safety; fund-raising and donation gathering tips; and slide shows and testimonials from participants who travelled on prior trips. College required documentation forms are also available online. [3] Project participants continue to meet in person through fund-raising events and educational sessions, critical to form bonding relationships and learn details of the project not found on-line; however, the Web pages provide a virtual format to facilitate detailed preparation outside of meeting times.

Second Year of the Project

This past year, 2009, nine students - including five occupational therapy students, three dental health science students, and one physical therapy student - along with practitioners in each field and one pharmacy faculty member traveled to Granada for ten days to continue to work with elder residents of *La Providencia*, one of twenty elder homes in Nicaragua.

While in Nicaragua, occupational therapy (OT) students presented dementia training to caregivers using a video they developed in advance of the trip, assessed the functional capacity of elders, and facilitated their ability in a variety of tasks including feeding, dressing and leisure participation.

Dental Health Science (DHS) students collaborated with the Ministry of Health to open a community dental clinic at the *La Providencia*. They provided exams, cleanings, and extractions of abscessed teeth for thirty residents. Students also provided oral health education to community members. In addition students conducted an interactive training with caregivers on proper dental hygiene and the benefits to health.

The physical therapy (PT) student collaborated with OT students to develop an exercise module that was used with the elderly. A written copy of this module was presented to local physical therapists for future use with the residents.

The pharmacy faculty member assessed pharmaceutical needs of elders in preparation to engage pharmacy students this coming year.

A Community-Based Rehabilitation Approach

Because the goal of the project is to create sustainable in-country services, it is critical to offer interventions that can be implemented by Nicaraguans. Community-based rehabilitation (CBR) promotes collaboration among community leaders, people with disabilities, their families, and other concerned citizens to provide equal opportunities for all people with disabilities in the community. Disability is not viewed as merely the result of physical impairment but includes environmental barriers to participation, with poverty as a leading cause of disability.[4] The major objectives of CBR are:

1. To ensure that people with disabilities are able to maximize their physical and mental abilities, to access regular services and opportunities, and to become active contributors to the community and society at large.

To activate communities to promote and protect the human rights of people with disabilities through changes within the community by removing barriers to participation.

During this visit, participants were able to expand contacts with community healthcare providers by inviting them to an open discussion forum about the state of elder care and how we might work together to address health concerns of elders. Moreover, participants were able to connect with a variety of community members willing to share in the experience of working with the elderly. Lastly, a relationship was formed with the Ministry of Health who supports the development and implementation of educational offerings for government employed health providers.

Outcomes

Since initiation of the program, health service for elders at *La Providencia* now includes regular health visits by the local gerontologist, bi-weekly access to physical therapy, the foundations of a dental clinic, and educational opportunities for caregivers. The Nicaraguan Ministry of Health supports development of a rehabilitation course aimed to educate local providers in elder conditions, rehabilitation, and health promotion strategies. After completing school in Nicaragua, there are no opportunities for practitioners to continue their educational training; our students and practitioners will assist them to obtain this education to facilitate the best evidence-based practices.

The Minister of Health also supports the establishment of a dental clinic at *La Providencia* in collaboration with local dentists - which will be used as a site for future dental health student internships. This opens the possibility of faculty and students staying an extended period of time to provide much needed education and dental care.

The inter-professional team approach was found to be an effective strategy to deepen participants' understanding of what each health service offers and revealed novel ways in which the programs can further collaborate for enhanced service delivery and classroom instruction. Students report increased understanding of alternative cultures, health disciplines, and community practice.

Future Directions

It is the vision of the Granada health community, with support of the Ministry of Health and continued collaboration with the Jessie F. Richardson Foundation and the College of Health professions at Pacific University to make *La Providencia* a model elder home upon which other elder homes in the country may be modelled.

It is the vision of the College to include all University health professions to assist in this endeavor. This coming year, students from Physician Assistant Studies and a faculty member from the College of Optometry plan to join the project.

Plans to further enhance the use Web technology include the addition of a chat room to facilitate participant communication for project preparation and planning.

Funding

Sustainability of our work depends grant funding and tax-deductible donations. Donations may be sent to:

Pacific University I Nicaragua Fund
2043 College Way
Forest Grove, OR 97116

References

Brockington, J.L., Hoffa. W. & Martin, P.C. (2007). *NAFSA's Guide to education abroad for advisors and administrators.* (3rd ed.). Washington DC: NAFSA: Association of International Educators.

Cushner, K. & Karim, A.T. (2004). Study abroad at the university level. In D. Landis, J.M. Bennett, & M.J. Bennett (Eds.), Handbook of international training (3rd ed., pp. 289-308). Thousand Oaks, CA: Sage Publications.

INEC (2005). *National Institute of Statistics and Census of Nicaragua.* Retrieved May 2009 from http://www.inec.gob.ni/censos2005/ResumenCensal/Resumen2.pdf (Spanish).

NAFSA Task Force on Institutional Management of Study Abroad. (January 2008). *Strengthening Study Abroad: Recommendations for Effective Institutional Management*. NAFSA: Association of International Educators. Retrieved May 10, 2009 from: http://www.nafsa.org/knowledge_community_network.sec/international_education_4/chief_international_education/practice_resources_14/internationalizing_the/imsa_epub

WHO (2004) *CBR: A strategy for rehabilitation, equalization of opportunities, poverty reduction and social inclusion of people with disabilities: joint position paper*. Available online: http://www.who.int/disabilities/publications/cbr/en/index.html

Endnotes

[1] INEC, 2005

[2] Brockington, Hoffa & Martin, 2007; Cushner, 2004; NAFSA, 2008

[3] See: http://www.pacificu.edu/chp/international/

[4] WHO, 2004

Media

Boxercast: Creating Web Video Broadcasts for The Pacific Index

View online at: http://bcis.pacificu.edu/journal/2009/05/article.php?id=80

By Samantha Richards

This Senior Presentation at Pacific University was the winner of the 2009 Berglund Center Award for Undergraduate Research on the Impact of the Internet

Newspapers all over the country are pairing news stories with web video and posting a dramatically increased amount of multimedia content to their websites. For my senior project, I looked at the college newspaper scene and evaluated the content of several different college newspaper websites. E-publishing is a must in the newspaper industry today, for both college and professional publications, and anything that can attract additional traffic to a paper's website is an asset to its business. Because of this, I created *Boxercast* - short online broadcasts that come out with each issue of the student newspaper, *The Pacific Index.*

During the research portion of my project I created a website evaluation form that I used to compile notes while looking at small and large school newspaper websites as well as small and large professional newspaper websites. The evaluation form was especially important for the school newspaper websites I chose to assess because it included information about the college or university's media programs. This was important because I later tried to find a correlation between the programs the school offered and the content found on the website. My final conclusion was that the smaller school newspaper websites that I looked at (mainly schools in Pacific's league, i.e. *The Linfield Review* or Willamette University's *Collegian*) had virtually no correlation between the media programs offered and the content available on their websites. For example, Eastern Oregon University offers media arts programs including journalism, as well as an English/literature program with a film concentration, but the school newspaper, *The Easterner*, posts virtually nothing more than the text of the news stories to their website. The large school newspaper websites I evaluated definitely had a correlation, but this may have been a result of my selection; I chose to look at newspaper websites of some of the top journalism schools in the nation.

Another significant portion of my project was introducing myself to the broadcast media world online. Previous to the beginning of my project, I had zero experience with any type of broadcast journalism. Materials about the basics of writing for broadcast media as well as the production basics of news reports proved very helpful in the beginning stages of my project. This part of my research almost seemed to be an independent study rather than actual senior thesis research work.

Once I had completed the majority of my research (I say majority because it is essentially never-ending; there are always new relevant articles being posted online) I started to create *Boxercast*. My first broadcast was a feature story about the Kickboxers, the half-time basketball dance team. They had lost their coach but were continuing to self-teach routines and planned on performing all season long - in fact, they were better than ever. I chose this story because I thought it would be an easy and light first feature and I knew it was going to be a great opportunity to get lively video footage. I discovered that there were all types of things I still needed to work on. I was uneasy and out of place, I showed up with a videographer without an extra battery and, of course, the battery on the camera died, I didn't like my writing or how my voice sounded in the narration, and I was just about ready to give up.

Fortunately, I didn't give up; in fact, my learning curve was exponential after that first production. I started picking up the ins and outs of the business and began to learn Apple Final Cut, the software that was used to edit all of the *Boxercasts* this year. Brian Pan, a senior integrated media and film double major, was paid to help me with the filming and editing, but toward the end of my project I started editing much more on my own. To view the *Boxercast* archive, go to *The Pacific Index* homepage and type "Boxercast" in the search engine [1].

I am proud to say that my project does not end here. I have authored a handbook with all of the things I learned this year and all of the elements needed to continue producing *Boxercast*. Future staff members of *The Pacific Index* have already expressed interest in taking it over, so plan on web video content being a part of thepacificindex.com for years to come.

Endnotes

[1] *The Pacific Index* Homepage: http://www.thepacificindex.com, search results for "Boxercast": http://www.thepacificindex.com/home/index.cfm?q=Boxercast

Legal

Insurance: Does Your Policy Really Protect You?

View online at: http://bcis.pacificu.edu/journal/2009/05/article.php?id=81

By Leonard D. DuBoff and Christy O. King

Often, insurance is purchased with little concern as to the terms of the policy beyond the amount and cost of coverage. Unfortunately, this can lead to the policyholder later discovering a lack of appropriate coverage when a problem arises.

Most insurance policies contain broad grants of coverage and then carve away the protection by exclusions, which should be carefully reviewed. In addition, all policies have a date for the start of coverage and a date of termination.

In a *claims-made policy*, coverage is available only to an insured if a claim is made during the period of time between the starting and ending dates of the policy. On the other hand, with an *events policy*, coverage is available only if the event giving rise to the liability occurs within that coverage period.

As an example of these types of policies, let's say your insurance policy coverage period began January 1, 2008, and ended December 31, 2008, and you had a car accident on June 10 of that year. If a claim is made against you in April 2009 and you have a claims-made policy, it will not cover your June 10, 2008, accident claim; but an events policy would since the event—but not the claim—occurred between January 1, 2008, and December 31, 2008.

Two issues to initially determine, therefore, are (1) what type of policy you have, and (2) if this policy's protection will continue the protection of earlier policies without resulting in a gap in coverage.

If the older policy was a claims-made policy and the renewal is an events policy, then you should evaluate the likelihood of there being a covered claim asserted which resulted from an event occurring under the older policy and determine whether it would be prudent to purchase some form of *bridge* or, as it is called in insurance parlance, *tail-end* coverage for the potential exposure that may occur during the gap in coverage. In our example, if your 2008 policy is a claims-made policy and your 2009 policy is an events policy, there would be no coverage from either policy for the claim arising out of your auto accident in June 2008.

Another important issue which many insureds do not pay attention to until a problem arises is the selection of an attorney. Some policies allow the insured to select the attorney, while others reserve that right to the insurance company. If it is important to you to work with your own attorney and to have your lawyer handle your case, you should determine whether your policy permits this.

Note that whereas the law states that an attorney employed by the insurance company represents the insured client and, ethically, that attorney should look only to the interests of the client, economic reality often overshadows the relationship. If there is a conflict between the rights of the insured and those of the insurance company paying the bill, which way do you think the attorney hired by the insurance company will typically lean?

Because of this, some jurisdictions require insurance companies to either take full responsibility for a claim or to hire a second lawyer for the sole purpose of looking out for the insured party in connection with the case, while the insurance company's hired attorney is paid to handle the underlying case.

Often the insurance policy requires any dispute between the insurance company and the insured to be arbitrated. This benefits the insurance company since jurors will likely favor the insured when the dispute is with that person's insurance company.

Several states have statutes making it clear that if such a dispute does arise and the insured party prevails, then the insurance company must pay the underlying liability, as well as the insured's attorney fees. If, on the other hand, the insurance company prevails, the insurance company is not entitled to recover its attorney fees. This one-way protection is intended to be a deterrent against insurance companies taking unreasonable positions when dealing with their own insureds.

If the insurance company denies coverage, then the insured party should determine whether the denial is appropriate. In a number of cases handled by our office, a lawsuit was filed against the insurance company alleging that the denial was in bad faith. Courts frequently agree with the insured and impose liability on the insurance company for bad faith denial.

Individuals are often advised by their insurance professionals to purchase umbrella insurance policies for additional protection. Frequently, those who buy umbrella policies are doing so because they feel that they may have exposure in connection with their business or professional activities. If this is the case, they should obtain a different type of insurance coverage—the general business liability policy—since umbrella policies typically exclude coverage for business or professional activities.

Customarily, claims for copyright infringement, patent infringement, and other forms of intellectual property infringement are also exempt from coverage. Thus, if you are engaged in the business of producing work for the media, then it is likely that you need to obtain an additional form of coverage.

It would certainly be appropriate for you to ask your insurance professional to explain all of the options available and the scope of coverage for each so that you can purchase a policy that meets your needs.

The insurance laws in most jurisdictions make it clear that insurance brokers are agents of the person being insured for all purposes except the collection of premiums. This means that representations by your insurance broker may not bind the insurance company that issues your policy. Nevertheless, most brokers themselves have errors-

and-omissions insurance, which will likely be available if the broker misstates or misrepresents the scope of the insurance coverage purchased.

An insurance broker is an individual who is authorized to sell insurance for a number of different insurance companies. This person should be distinguished from an insurance agent who is employed by a single insurance company and is permitted to only write insurance for that company. Insurance agents are able to bind the company that they represent, and thus their statements will generally protect you with respect to that company's insurance policy.

One potential problem to be aware of is the fact that there may be a difference of opinion between you and your insurance broker or agent as to what was represented when a policy was acquired. For this reason, it is a good idea to request a written explanation as to the scope of coverage and the types of benefits available. In this way, you will have written evidence of exactly what was said and what you understood when the policy was first acquired.

It is clear that insurance should be purchased to protect you from the risks to which you are exposed in both your personal and business activities. The extent of coverage and amount of insurance to be purchased are important considerations, but as you can see, there are many other issues to discuss with your insurance professional. You may also want to consider having your insurance policy reviewed by a knowledgeable attorney to ensure that you have the coverage you desire.

Social Networking

From Facebook to Resume: Marketing Yourself Via Social Networks

View online at: http://bcis.pacificu.edu/journal/2009/05/article.php?id=73

By Jenn Hernandez

Berglund Student Fellow

The rise of social networking sites has brought about many creative outlets for marketing yourself, sharing your ideas, and posting your photos. In the grips of a struggling economy, the focus is on multimedia resumes as a very helpful and highly visible method to get a leg up on the job market and start networking—building a positive and professional presence online. As Dan Schawbel, author of *Me 2.0: Build a Powerful Brand to Achieve Career Success*, states, 80% of jobs are filled via social networking. [1] Are you taking advantage of this trend?

One way to get noticed is to use a social resume site, many of which allow multimedia like video, music samples, and photos to accompany the traditional resume. Multimedia resume sites are like a directed blog solely for the purpose of highlighting your experience. They can be viewed by employers (sometimes for a fee, sometimes for free) and commented on by others in the community. There are many sites out there with references to social resumes, but the one I found most helpful and descriptive was a list of ten on mashable.com [2] This gave me a good place to start looking for a resume site that worked best with how I want to portray my professional self via the Internet.

In an economy like today's you can never be too careful with the image you project to possible employers because once they have an impression of you, it's hard to let it go. The first impression obtained by prospective employers may not be the one you'd want to be retained. So what can you do? The answer is surprisingly simple: don't post anything you wouldn't want to be viewed by anyone and everyone; adjust privacy settings, if available (but keep in mind that nothing posted online is truly private); be smart with what you post. One blogger for the Huffington Post explains that by blogging regularly, one can increase their hits on Google searches. [3] By doing so, Google puts current posts and articles at the forefront of searches, which are what perhaps best exemplifies interests and achievements more casually and unconstrained than the traditional resume fashion.

Another word of advice: read the Terms of Service carefully, because, you may (or may not) recall Facebook's most recent TOS scandal. Sites make updates to their TOS, some of which may revoke your rights to any information you post, a big deal on such an open forum as the Internet. In last month's issue of *Interface* [4], The DuBoff Law Group wrote that, "a recent ruling by the superior Court of Fresno County cautions users about the lack of privacy inherent in the use of such sites [as

MySpace [5], Facebook [6], Twitter [7], and LinkedIn [8]].” [9] Surely, you’ve heard cautionary tales concerning the use of social networking sites and incriminating photos or comments. The posting of inappropriate content not only makes you look bad, but it can taint the image of the site you are posting to. As a result, Facebook has a team that sifts through reported content for inappropriateness. David Kirkpatrick, author of *The Facebook Effect*, resounds that, "If [Facebook] got polluted as just a place for wild and crazy kids, that would destroy the ability to achieve the ultimate vision, which is to create a service for literally everyone." [10]

Just think about it. Not just your friends, but your professors use Facebook and other social networking sites, your parents, and who’s to say that your employers don’t as well? Facebook and other social networking sites have become a place for everyone, so treat it that way. Do you want thousands of people to see your information? So, while social networking can be especially beneficial to job searching, it can also be a handicap, but this really depends on how you choose to use it.

Note: One online resume service I tried was Visual CV [11], which allows users to create an online resume including video and sound files, and other media onto one webpage. Working in the Berglund Center for Internet Studies [12] has made an impression on me as to the importance of using diverse multimedia and networking with others around me or in my field. I look forward to seeing what turns up from my social resume.

Endnotes

[1] http://mashable.com/2009/01/13/social-media-resume/

[2] http://mashable.com/2009/03/18/resume-building/

[3] http://www.huffingtonpost.com/danny-groner/self-googling-enhanced-by_b_190248.html

[4] http://bcis.pacificu.edu/journal/2009/04/

[5] http://www.myspace.com/

[6] http://www.facebook.com/

[7] http://www.twitter.com/

[8] http://www.linkedin.com/

[9] http://bcis.pacificu.edu/journal/2009/04/article.php?id=67

[10] http://www.newsweek.com/id/195621/page/1

[11] http://www.visualcv.com/www/indexc.html

[12] http://bcis.pacificu.edu/

Book Review

Mark Le Vine's *Heavy Metal Islam: Rock, Resistance, and the Struggle for the Soul of Islam*

View online at: http://bcis.pacificu.edu/journal/2009/05/article.php?id=72

Review by Deborah L. Wheeler

United States Naval Academy, Department of Political Science.

Le Vine, Mark. *Heavy Metal Islam: Rock, Resistance, and the Struggle for the Soul of Islam.* New York: Three Rivers Press, 2008.

Mark Le Vine is a renaissance man. Both musician and professor, academic and activist, he has crafted a highly readable chronicle of the Muslim heavy metal scene with his *Heavy Metal Islam: Rock, Resistance, and the Struggle for the Soul of Islam* (Oxford: One World, 2008). With this study Le Vine alerts Western audiences, once again [1], to the resounding message of his life work, "that Muslim and Western cultures are more heterogeneous, complex, and ultimately alike than peddlers of the clash of civilizations, the war on terror and the unending jihad would have us believe." [2] His account is enlivened by his unique form of participant observation, enabled in this case by his ability to make music with his subjects around the globe, including 20 visits to 16 countries.[3]

His fine book begins with an introductory chapter on the relationships between rock and resistance in Muslim youth subcultures. Following this introduction are six country-specific chapters which each provide an overview of politics and resistance music, including: Morocco, Egypt, Israel/Palestine, Lebanon, Iran and Pakistan. In each of these chapters, the unique character of local heavy metal and Islamic cultures are analyzed, along with an overview of how local governments have responded to the challenges these oppositional movements pose. For example, the chapter on Morocco states that "fourteen heavy-metal musicians and fans were arrested in February 2003, tried, and convicted of the absurd crime of being 'Satanists who recruited for an international cult of devil-worship,' and of 'shaking the foundations of Islam,' 'infringing upon public morals,' 'undermining the faith of a Muslim,' and 'attempting to convert a Muslim to another faith'" [4] Le Vine observes that "Similar raids have occurred against heavy-metal-listening 'devil worshippers' in Lebanon, Egypt and Iran." [5] An epilogue concludes the book, by taking a look at the future of Islamic societies where youths turn to "heavy metal and hip hop" to "cope with the stress produced by lives spent, at least on the surface, on the margins of their societies." [6] The main thesis of the book is that:

> To understand the peoples, cultures, and politics of the Muslim world today, especially the young people who are the majority of the citizens of the region, we need to follow the musicians and their fans as much as the mullahs and their followers. [7]

This is because, just as the mullahs are using the mosque and the Internet to create autonomous realms of religious authority with which to challenge authoritarianism, so too are counter-cultural musicians. According to Le Vine, "The MENA's [Middle East and North Africa] metal and rap fans are converting their musical communities into spaces where they can carve out a bit of autonomy, if not freedom, within which they can imagine alternatives to the status quo." [8]

Le Vine's book coexists with an emerging community of texts that examine the relationships between freedoms, new media practices and new subcultures in Middle Eastern states. Examples include Marc Lynch's analysis of "the new public sphere" created by Al-Jazeera audiences [9]; analysis of the development and impact of the Internet in the Middle East [10]; analysis of popular culture in the Arab world [11]; and analysis of media and politics in the Arab World more broadly defined [12]. Linkages between new media and resistance music are not accidental. Such activists use multiple media forums to get access to young publics. For example, Le Vine recounts a conversation with Egyptian metal musician "Marz" (not his real name) who is in the band Hate Suffocation. Marz observes that public performances "are crucial for Egyptian bands since hardly any of them have record deals. Their popularity rests on their live performances and the buzz created from songs downloaded from their MySpace sites." [13] The interpenetration of Internet distribution and live performances reveal how musicians on the margins can access publics beyond the traditional gatekeepers; and beyond the authoritarian state, if they are careful not to exceed "a manageable level of dissent." [14] In the same way that the Internet offers wider access to global publics, Le Vine shows how music offers Palestinians a ticket to ride, so to speak. He explains,

> "Comrades don't just rap as an alternative to throwing stones or building bombs. Being musicians offers these artists opportunities that most Palestinians are denied. They are able to travel outside of the country...tell their stories to a wide audience, and meet with people from around the world." [15]

The same media spaces in which Arab metal heads attempt to carve out spaces for free expression can also be sites where their resistance is policed and often punished. Le Vine observes, "Refusing to conform to" Egyptian society's norms, metal heads "have long been the object of ridicule and attacks in newspapers, on television, in live comedy, and in conservative religious discourse." [16] Similarly, in Iran Le Vine notes, "the government routinely cracks down on alternative cultural expression." [17] These forms of repression of alternative musical scenes, bloggers and other counter cultural forces in the region leave scholars and readers of Mark Le Vine's book with a question: Will "the MENA's metal and rap scene help to stimulate wider political and cultural transformations in the societies of the region?" [18] The author also leaves us with a contingent answer when he observes that it "depends on whether the increasingly transnational communities of fans and activists can outwit the policies of 'repressive tolerance'." [19] Le Vine closes on an optimistic note when he observes, "The fear, the violence, the hatred of the Middle East can seem deafening, but it's still not loud enough to silence the voices of resistance." [20]

In closing, Le Vine has composed a very interesting and easy to read analysis of how the alternative music scene in the Middle East is engaging in politics and social critique, reshaping identity, and carving out spaces for collective self-expression in new public spheres. The text is suitable for non-specialists, and would be a welcomed addition to undergraduate and graduate level courses on popular culture, the Middle East, communications studies, and political science.

Endnotes

[1] See also Mark Le Vine, *Why They Don't Hate Us: Lifting the Veil on the Access of Evil* (Oxford: One World, 2005).

[2] Le Vine, *Heavy Metal Islam* p. 3

[3] Ibid, p. 253

[4] Ibid, p. 30

[5] Ibid, p. 30

[6] Ibid, p. 258

[7] Ibid, p. 3

[8] Ibid, p. 11

[9] Marc Lynch, *Voices of the New Arab Public: Iraq, Al-Jazeera and Middle East Politics Today* (New York: Columbia University Press, 2005)

[10] Deborah L. Wheeler, *The Internet in the Middle East: Global Expectations, Local Imaginations in Kuwait* (Albany: SUNY, 2006)

[11] Andrew Hammond, *Popular Culture in the Arab World* (Cairo: American University in Cairo Press, 2007)

[12] *Arab Media and Political Renewal: Community, Legitimacy and Public Life*, ed. Naomi Sakr (London: IB Tauris, 2007)

[13] Le Vine, *Heavy Metal Islam* p. 61

[14] Ibid, p. 61

[15] Ibid, p. 111

[16] Ibid, p. 61

[17] Ibid, p. 178

[18] Ibid, p. 258

[19] Ibid, p. 254

[20] Ibid, p. 275

Book Review

Arthur Phillips's *The Song is You*

View online at: http://bcis.pacificu.edu/journal/2009/05/article.php?id=78

Review by Jeffrey Barlow

Arthur Phillips, *The Song is You.* New York: Random House, 2009.

This work was chosen for review in *Interface* because of what it suggests about the evolving impact of the Internet, but also for what it tells us about Amazon's new reading appliance, the Kindle. For the latter purpose, see the editorial in this issue.[1]

Arthur Phillips might be termed a noted second-tier author. He has won a number of awards, and his works have all been well reviewed, but his name is certainly far from a household word. His fourth and most recent work *The Song Is You*, has had excellent reviews.[2] His work is highly varied, including an angst-ridden story of expatriates living in Budapest (*Prague*, 2002); a mystery, *The Egyptologist* (2004); and a sort of ghostly story, *Angelica* (2007), which has multiple Victorian narrators, none of whom see entirely tethered to reality; and now, *The Song Is You.*

His works have in common the author's and his protagonists' shifting voices. He attracts attention of the literary sort and can be said to be a craftsman who creates jewel-like story lines and character studies, all set in lapidary prose. Plot does not seem to be, in *The Song is You*, at least, a particularly important issue.[3] The work is less the creation and unwinding of dramatic tension than it is a novel of manners, oddly Victorian for all its pop-culture trappings.

For us, the story is about the transformation reality undergoes when it is recorded -- in this case, digitized. The novel is about people who live in music. Julian, the protagonist, is a highly successful director of meaningless advertising commercials. His life is held within his iPod, which holds every song he has ever owned.

Julian's father was obsessed with a Billie Holiday concert which he attended. As it was recorded live, a brief performer-to-audience shtick of Billie's included the father's voice. Thus the album, which became increasingly rare and difficult to locate, became a life-long preoccupation for Julian's father. As a young man, Julian destroyed his father's only remaining copy, and then in turn Julian becomes obsessed with a much younger female singer.

Julian consciously recognizes this obsession as not dissimilar from his father's prior one and strives to mitigate it by deliberately avoiding an actual meeting with the subject of his attention, Cait. Cait is an up-and-coming Celtic singer crossing over from folk into highly successful and deeply emotive pop.

The novel then unfolds as an omniscient narrator describes Cait and Julian circling around each other, communicating through music, and then via the Internet. Julian, as a director, has ideas as to how her career should be developed and leaves her clues, first on paper, then in email, of responses to her music; she responds by writing songs to him.

Julian is able to "stalk" Cait via the Internet, and simultaneously to keep her at a safely digitized length. Julian clearly has issues with real people, including Rachel, the wife from whom he is separated. She would like to see their relationship work out, providing that they can deal with the emotional tangles caused by the earlier death of Carlton, their infant son.

Cait, too, has her issues with people as to her they are quickly becoming less individuals than tools with which to advance her career. She is becoming lost in her own music. For Cait, Julian is perfect: a seemingly omniscient observer who sends her critical suggestions that contribute to her career.

The novel began, Phillips tells us, in his own experience listening to music.[4] For us, the music is a metaphor for alienation, and we do not see it as a coincidence that Julian's favorite way of listening to it is to put his iPod---"the greatest of all human inventions"[5] --- on shuffle. It then plays at random one of the thousands of pieces he has loaded into it. These usually ignite some fragment of meaning in his mind, perhaps a memory of previous hearings of the piece, perhaps some relationship between the song and current feelings or events.[6]

Some songs appearing at random, Julian believes, even influence events.[7] He has brief and meaningless sexual encounters as a result of some musical reference---other times he resists seduction because of the "mix" which the seductress has tried to use to catch his attention.[8]

Julian, like his father, is the ultimate audience---he exists *only* as listener. For Cait, the audience is, in turn, the only reality. Yet like singer and audience, it is ultimately the media and the iPod which eternally separate them.

The Internet can, of course, also be interpreted as a metaphor for isolation and alienation. Cait and Julian communicate, at first anonymously, then with familiar email names, but never as individuals. He tracks her via celebrity blogs, with which she meanwhile has her own strange interactions. She is herself most real as her own audience.

It is impossible to reveal more of the plot without spoiling it, but the work is one vast metaphor for the gap between event and playback, whether in memory or on recording. This is a subset of one of the critical tropes dealing with the Internet---that it too often substitutes virtual relationships for real ones.

Here I will indulge myself by quoting a stanza from one of my own favorite singers, John Fogarty. I am sure Julian would approve of both the affectation and the sentiments, though he surely would sneer politely at my questionable taste:

> Nobody here anymore
> Nobody mindin' the store
> They've all gone

To another dimension
Nobody here anymore [9]

This work, set in real time, that is in 2009, presents us with a very mature analysis of the Internet and of digitization in general. This digital world is no longer, at least in Arthur Philips' mind, a looming horror of the gothic sort. It simply now is part of our cultural framework. Howevcr, it does have its costs, and we do well, like Phillips, to reflect upon them.

Endnotes

[1] http://bcis.pacificu.edu/journal/2009/05/article.php?id=71

[2] To see details of his works, begin in the author's home pages at: http://www.arthurphillips.info/The-Song-Is-You/reviews.html

[3] I have not read his other works and am dependent on reviews referenced above for descriptions of them.

[4] See http://www.arthurphillips.info/The-Song-Is-You/History.html The author has also been a jazz musician, and the novel is full of jazz references which probably are important signifiers, but they escape me.

[5] Location 184.--for the uninitiated this is a reference to the location of the citation on the Kindle version of the text.

[6] The search function on my Kindle tells me that there are 52 references to "iPod" in the novel, whereas to Carlton, Julian's dead son, there are 60. His dead son is very important to Julian, but only marginally more so than his iPod.

[7] Location 503-6.

[8] Location 1398-1401

[9] The song can be heard and the lyrics read at: http://www.metrolyrics.com/nobodys-here-anymore-lyrics-john-fogerty.html

Editorial

To George Orwell, II; Is It 1984 yet?

View online at: http://bcis.pacificu.edu/journal/2009/05/article.php?id=71

Editorial by Jeffrey Barlow

In our last issue we treated the Amazon Kindle [1] -- perhaps best described as a web-enabled text-reading device---as the subject for a technology review[2] and dealt primarily with the question of how it works, and its advantages for us at the Berglund Center. Here we treat it rather as a looming cultural force, addressing some of the concerns that have been raised about the spread of such devices, and speculate about some of the less fortunate effects it might have.

After buying the Kindle and using it to read a very complicated work on the recent economy, William D. Cohan's *House of Cards: A Tale of Hubris and Wretched Excess on Wall Street*,[3] I saw that the Kindle had real advantages for reviewing such a work. It let me quickly look up unfamiliar technical terms from the world of Wall Street, do thorough searches, and when writing, pull up hundreds of notes I had taken to review the work. I also used the Kindle to read Arthur Phillips' *The Song is You*, reviewed in this issue. [4] However, I thought at the time that my future use of the Kindle might well be limited more to texts and complex works like Cohan's and not include lighter reading.

Accordingly, when I spotted Jeffrey Deaver's new work *The Broken Window* on the shelves, I unhesitatingly bought it in paperback for review in August as it deals with the dangers of data mining in a fictional context. I worked through the book, folding pages over, underlining, jotting a few notes in the opening pages: my usual approach to reviewing novels. Finally, however, when trying to squeeze into the margins yet another annotation on the works' relevance to the impact of the Internet, I had to ask myself if this wouldn't better be done on the Kindle. I opened the Kindle, went to Amazon's site, and found to my horror that the book was not yet formatted for Kindle. However, while I was browsing, it appeared; Jeff Bezos (the founder and president of Amazon) knows my every need! I downloaded it and returned to my reading.

The experience of a "light read" was in no way diminished. I read more comfortably and quickly on the Kindle now than in paper copy. But the change is as great as that made by a medieval monk reading in a lambskin scroll, then moving to a codex, a true book bound between wooden covers. And from the point of view of producing and then reproducing text, the jump from paperback to Kindle is, I think, going to be as great as that from the hand-written codex to a Gutenberg type-set printing. But reading on the Kindle is a bookish experience only in a limited sense.

My life has been lived among books, and certainly my living has depended upon writing and reading and explaining them, whether in lecture or pieces such as this one. So what will I---and possibly you---miss when reading on the Kindle? In my case, not much.

I believe that we over-romanticize books. I think that many common declarations of loyalty to the book form amount to saying: "I am highly literate!" Many of these declarations are quite emotional. One common one deals, oddly, with olfactory loyalties: we like the way books smell, period. This is a common reaction to the Kindle---it doesn't smell like a book. Incredibly, to me at least, a Google search on the text "smell of a book and the kindle" produced 398,000 hits![5]

True, the smell of books often brings up happy memories of particular books and the places where I read or wrote them. But when I get beyond that emotional level, in fact, books smell like petrochemicals and dead trees. I think I can get beyond the smell issue, and all other issues related to form vs. content, and I am sure that the generation now growing up reading on the web is not going to think about them very long, if at all.

However, there are other issues which should be considered. If we were to take as an analogy the impact of downloadable MP3 files upon the recording and related industries, we can see that the results of a shift to text-reading appliances could be far reaching indeed. And after all, while music is very important, as is film, neither is even remotely comparable to reading in its cultural impact. A great deal will change once the Kindle and related highly portable text reading devices take off, as I believe they inevitably will.

When we examine the dark side of the Internet at the Berglund Center a number of issues arise. One of these is pornography. The Internet has stimulated the spread of porn, and it is has proven very difficult to regulate in an electronic environment.[6] The Kindle will further complicate this issue. Successful prosecutions (some have preferred the term *persecutions*) of adult fare as legally pornographic have usually turned upon either the subject matter--children especially---or upon issues of community standards. The Internet is particularly vulnerable to attack as children can easily gain access to pornography and some sites will violate "community standards," usually in some carefully selected (by prosecutors) bastion of traditional values.

The Kindle is the ultimate plain brown wrapper for erotica or porn.[7] Some entrepreneurs are rapidly taking advantage of this new market niche. See, for example, the website "The Erotic Reader."[8] We think it will not be long until family-value conservatives raise a hue and cry over this particular issue, and the resulting legal tangle will be labyrinthine.

Books, on the other hand, have seldom been banned in the 21st century, in part because they are more easily controlled by parents, and they perhaps seem more a matter of individual taste and choice than does the Internet. A recent unfortunate decision by Amazon to de-list what have been called "Gay books," although the exact nature of the categories banned is still unclear, raised an immediate firestorm on the Internet. Amazon quickly recanted.[9]

Distributing texts via download, however, will raise other issues. I joked above about Jeff Bezos knowing my needs. This is unlikely, but his corporation can easily ascertain my tastes in reading---his minions send me email linked to previous purchases on a weekly basis. Jeff seems like a 21st century sort of guy, and I am O.K.

with that. But I am less certain about other authority figures in my life. I am also less certain about other types of books. At my age, a sudden taste for erotica would probably seem more like nostalgia than mortal sin. But I certainly don't plan to order any terrorist manuals for my Kindle anytime soon, as interested as I am in contemporary events.

And we know from any number of recent events that in fact one's reading taste can easily come back to haunt one. Steven Wax, noted Federal Public Defender for Oregon, and a speaker at a Berglund Center Roundtable,[10] cites an example in his recent work *Kafka Comes to America* of prosecutors citing possession of particular books and visits to certain Internet sites as evidence of criminal wrongdoing.[11]

The Kindle raises other issues relative to censorship. There are many ways to produce and circulate a book so as to avoid censorship. We have the example of Soviet *Samizdat*, the clandestine distribution of copies of uncensored works, frequently Western ones critical of the Soviet regime, sometimes credited with laying the foundation for the end of the Soviet Union.[12]

A Kindle text, like any electronic data, is easily lost or altered. I had the experience, for example, of canceling an order after it had begun downloading. I then watched it being sucked off my Kindle--poof, it was gone. We have the above example of Amazon delisting certain controversial types of works. If Amazon were ordered to by a powerful government in an important market area to recover all copies of a certain work might it do so? In Saudi Arabia, if all the works of Rushdie should be declared heretical, would the Saudi government suck them off Saudi Kindles? What then are the opportunities for Samizdat style circulation, presuming, of course, that only electronic copies have been sold.[13] This raises directly the issue of the Digital Divide.

Recently, Reed College in Portland entered into an agreement with Amazon to use in its classes the new Kindle DX,[14] a very recent iteration of the Kindle with a bigger screen more suitable for detailed graphics or larger layouts such as found in science texts. At present, the classes will offer the students a choice of Kindle texts or conventional ones.

There is, however, an economic force inevitably at work here; the production and distribution of a Kindle text must be many times less expensive to the publisher than are hard copy equivalents. This means that costs can be lower to the consumer---my Kindle books rarely cost more than ten dollars, while the hard copy equivalent may be forty dollars. Some out of copyright works are also available as free downloads. Obviously, this reduced cost is a social good.

But as Kindle-type texts become more dominant, hard copy books, according to the laws of supply and demand, will become more expensive.[15] The Kindle or its competitors will doubtless become cheaper, but there are now many schoolchildren, in Oregon at least, who can no longer afford lunches, and whose families are losing their homes. For them, even paperback books are a luxury and a Kindle an unthinkable extravagance.

And what of libraries? As attractive as the notion of storing 2500 texts on a Kindle might be, as the costs of books inevitably climb, even popular ones could become as expensive as are science texts at present, when a student can easily pay eighty dollars and more. Hard copy collections will become correspondingly more expensive.

One result of electronic text readers such as the Kindle will be, we think, a greatly widened digital divide. It is possible to imagine various devices such as Kindles available in some well-financed suburban libraries or being checked out like laptops at private schools, but such solutions seem highly unlikely to be widespread, at least in the United States' public schools.

There are many other issues. The question of Intellectual Property rights, or at least the prevention of illegal distribution, is going to be a major problem. At present, I can sell my used books or donate them, entirely without legal restraint so far as I am aware. I cannot, however, I recently found, register our office Kindle under both a personal account and under a Berglund account. I presume that this is to prevent the sharing of the machine itself.

And what of sharing texts? I get excited by my reading and want to force it upon hapless others. I can loan a book; I cannot easily share a Kindle file, even if my friend also possessed a Kindle. I am quite certain that there are those who will assert that Kindle file sharing is a violation of somebody's rights. I am equally certain that it can and is being done, and will be very difficult to trace or prevent. It will be interesting to see how this aspect of Kindle usage develops.

There are other issues that should concern us. One is certainly the damage to the bookstore industry. Many local stores have been killed by the Internet. Some of these have survived after a fashion by going on line and selling electronically via the Internet. This is not going to be a cheap or an easy option following the widespread impact of Kindle-like devices. It is clearly in the interest of the makers of such devices to maintain a chokehold on as many proprietary elements of the text and its delivery as possible.

We also believe that Amazon, having gotten well out ahead of the industry in general, is going to be an overwhelming opponent for potential competitors. What we should expect, then, is additional concentration within the publishing industries, and a marked reduction in places for authors to sell their works.[16] Many old and honored presses are going to go the way of major urban newspapers which seemed unassailable ten years ago.

Speaking of newspapers, and periodicals, mightn't the impact of the Kindle, which can deliver a daily paper or a weekly or monthly magazine as conveniently as a bestseller, have equivalent consequences? We believe, of course, that it will.

To answer the question posed by our provocative title, is it 1984 yet? Perhaps not in an Orwellian sense...but it is getting much closer to 2024, by which time we fully expect the entire face of reading and the industries and individuals it currently supports to be unrecognizable.

Endnotes

[1] Because it is so awkward to continually write "text-reading devices" we use the word "Kindle" here to represent the entire coming flood of such technologies.

[2] See the review at: http://bcis.pacificu.edu/journal/2009/04/article.php?id=68

[3] See it at: http://bcis.pacificu.edu/journal/2009/04/article.php?id=65

[4] *The Song is You* review in this issue http://bcis.pacificu.edu/journal/2009/04/article.php?id=78

[5] Search on May 20 at: http://www.google.com/search?q=smell+of+a+book+and+the+kindle&ie=utf-8&oe=utf-8&aq=t&rls=org.mozilla:en-US:official&client=firefox-a

[6] We wrote on this issue in "X? XX? Or XXX? The Internet and Pornography" at http://bcis.pacificu.edu/journal/2008/04/edit.php

[7] This is already becoming a cultural issue. A search performed the text string "Kindle porn" on May 20 2009 produced 425,000 hits at: http://www.google.com/search?q=kindle+porn&ie=utf-8&oe=utf-8&aq=t&rls=org.mozilla:en-US:official&client=firefox-a

[8] http://www.theeroticreader.com/instant-erotica.html

[9] See the early stages of the controversy at: http://www.guardian.co.uk/culture/2009/apr/13/amazon-gay-writers

[10] To see Wax's presentation go to: http://bcis.pacificu.edu/roundtables/Presentations/2009/index.php#wax

[11] Steven Wax, *Kafka Comes to America*, New York: Other Press, 2008, p, 137-8.

[12] See http://en.wikipedia.org/wiki/Samizdat for a discussion of this genre and its effects.

[13] This may seem farfetched, but there are a number of current examples of the threat of libel suits causing books already in print to be pulped. See http://barthsnotes.wordpress.com/2007/08/05/cambridge-university-press-agrees-to-pulp-book-on-terrorist-financing/

[14] See it at: http://www.amazoncom/dp/B0015TCML0/?tag=googhydr-20&hvadid=3482997509&ref=pd_sl_19djrsy7gv_e

[15] I use "law" of course with tongue in cheek after watching gasoline prices over the last few years.

[16] I recognize also that authors may well develop small niche markets for their works and format them themselves and deliver them on line. This may well mean an end to 'blockbusters" as few will be able to afford the time to labor away on a large book. This may mean, again, a concentration as a few authors work their way laboriously to high status and widespread distributio

July-August 2009 - Volume 9, Issue 6

Articles

- **Feature: Steve Rhine** - A Technological Solution to the Algebra Dilemma?
- **Web 2.0: Jeff Cain** - Web 2.0: How the Web got Loose
- **Technology: Michael Geraci** - Crowdsourcing: Leveraging Your Social Networks
- **Legal: Leonard D. DuBoff** - Estate Tax Issues You Should Be Aware Of

Book and Site Reviews

- **Nancy Duarte's** slide:ology: The Art and Science of Creating Great Presentations□Review by Maria Walters
- **Scott Fox's** e-Riches 2.0□Review by Jeffrey Barlow

Editorial

Attila to Soltan: Media Savvy and Democracy

Feature

A Technological Solution to the Algebra Dilemma?

View online at: http://bcis.pacificu.edu/journal/2009/06/article.php?id=83

By Steve Rhine

Willamette University

Algebra is often described as the "gatekeeper" to higher education and future employment because it has served as a filter by screening out large numbers of students, rather than as a pump helping to develop students' mathematical competence and access to higher education (Ladson-Billings, 1998 and Moses & Cobb, 2001). "Algebra...can mean the difference between menial work and high-level careers" (Helfand, 2006, p. 1). The National Council for Teachers of Mathematics position statement *Algebra: What, When, and for Whom* reads: "Knowing algebra opens doors and expands opportunities, instilling a broad range of mathematical ideas that are useful in many professions and careers. All students should have access to algebra and support for learning it" (NCTM, 2008, paragraph 1).

Accordingly, across the country, schools are instituting "Algebra-for-all" programs so that all students develop algebraic thinking skills before they graduate high school. However, the statistics on failure in algebra courses are staggering. In 2004, in the Los Angeles School District, "48,000 ninth-graders took beginning algebra; 44% flunked, nearly twice the failure rate as in English. Seventeen percent finished with Ds. In all, the district that semester handed out Ds and Fs to 29,000 beginning algebra students... Among those who repeated the class in the spring, nearly three-quarters flunked again...It triggers dropouts more than any single subject" (Helfand, 2006, p. 1). In Chicago, the school district recently published a study indicating that failure in algebra is increasing significantly (Viadero, 2009). In response, Michael Lach, the director of the office of high school teaching said "It's not surprising that you're going to see an increase in [failure] rates if you raise the instructional requirements and you don't raise the supports." (Viadero, 2009, paragraph 8). Furthermore, while mathematical proficiency of students has steadily increased on the National Assessment of Educational Progress over the last 17 years, a significant gap has remained, or increased, for students of low socio-economic status and minorities (National Center for Education Statistics, 2008).

Students of algebra are desperately in need of support. Districts are responding by creating two- or three-year programs for algebra or having students take double periods of algebra, but the success rate is not changing significantly (Nomi & Allensworth, 2009). We can't teach algebra the same way repeatedly and expect different results. While there is some evidence that new curricula from projects such as the Connected Mathematics Program and College Preparatory Mathematics Program are improving students' success with algebra (i.e. Moseley & Brenner, 2009;

Riordan & Noyce, 2001), there is controversy over its effects (i.e. Milgram, 1999), and students often continue to struggle with the ideas of algebra.

Technology to the rescue?

Research indicates that technology can facilitate the transition from arithmetic to algebra (Battista & VanAuken Borrow, 1998: Rojano & Sutherland, 1993; Tabach, Hershkowitz, & Arcavi, 2008). For instance, graphing calculators add significant power to learning (Gage, 2002 and Reznichenko, 2007). Virtual manipulatives can be effective tools in enhancing students' conceptual understanding (Bos, 2009; Suh, 2005; Zacharias, Olympiou, & Papaevripidou, 2008). Spreadsheets have been identified in research and algebra textbooks for over a decade as a potential, effective support for algebra learning. However, "their use in mathematics remains marginal" (Haspekian, 2005, p. 109). Multiple barriers exist to thwart teachers who might want to make use of the power of technology for learning.

Achieving the promise of technology to significantly impact learning remains elusive for the majority of schools. "The number of computers in public school classrooms was not adequate to use computers effectively for classroom instruction, and the classroom was not the main location in school where most students used computers...level of access was inadequate for educators to use computers effectively in classroom instruction" (NEA, 2008, p. 2). Bandwidth is a concern, computer access issues continue to apply, and many schools have restrictive Internet policies. With the exception of graphing calculators, access to technological tools for use in classrooms and effective professional development continue to be a significant issue for teachers.

The National Education Association (NEA) recommends that, in order to improve students' and educators' access to technology in the classroom, more wireless and portable technologies need to be available (NEA, 2008, p. 6). Two decades ago graphing calculators were introduced to school classrooms. Now they are ubiquitous in high school mathematics classes as prices have dropped from $200 to $45. This summer, Apple released the latest software for the iPhone and iPod Touch, which includes peer-to-peer interaction, connection to third party accessories (such as science probes), and other new capabilities. Comparable devices are sure to follow, ensuring lower costs and broader access. The pace of innovation for this technology is dizzying. In less than a year since the introduction of applications for the iPhone and iPod Touch, Apple reports that entrepreneurs have created over 70,000 applications and users have downloaded them over 1 billion times. The potential for one device to serve multiple purposes in education has arrived. The iPhone and iPod Touch is a graphing calculator, can do spreadsheets, will connect to third party devices, and can easily provide both video-based problem solving opportunities and access to virtual manipulatives.

What does this have to do with algebra?

"An error is not merely a failure by a student but rather a symptom of the nature of the conceptions which underlie his/her mathematical activity" (Balachef, 1984). Errors can result from simple carelessness or forgotten rules, such as 5 + 3 = 9. In this case, the student can quickly identify the mistake. Researchers have also found that some "some kinds of errors are widespread among students of different ages, independent of the course of their previous learning of algebra" (Demby, 1997). Some students make the same type of errors regardless of their experience with algebra, indicating common struggles that have more complex sources than simple calculation or memory errors. These errors can be due to misconceptions that reside deeper in a student's consciousness, a multifaceted structure that has naive or faulty assumptions inconsistent with accepted mathematical practices that can be stable and resistant to instruction (Anderson & Smith, 1987). Whether the error is part of a developmental process, that is, self-correcting as the student progresses through school, or a more pervasive type that is only corrected through a student's teacher-supported reflection, the importance is the immediate impact on students' understanding current content.

New handheld technology, if it is not reduced to uses such as the simple drilling of skills, can create opportunities for students to address misconceptions, construct meaning, and explore their thinking. Visual representation of ideas can facilitate students' thinking and understanding in ways not possible with pencil and paper. "Technology can impact mathematical activity through affecting the content and tasks of algebra as well as its teaching...Technology can change the nature of opportunities for the mathematical activities of conceptualizing, representing, generalizing, symbolic work, and modeling as well as for student roles" (Heid & Blume, 2008, pp. 58-59). Many of the technologies that have promise for supporting algebra learning currently exist on other platforms, such as science probes, spreadsheets, and web-based java applets. There is considerable research demonstrating graphing calculators and spreadsheets have positive impacts on learning in algebra (i.e. Calder, Brown, Hanley, & Darby, 2006; Ellington, 2003; Rojano, 1996). Spreadsheets can act as a bridge between arithmetic and algebra by helping students generalize patterns, develop an understanding of variable, facilitate transformation of algebraic expressions, and provide a space to explore equations (Haspekian 2005; Tabach, Hershkowitz, & Arcavi, 2008; Wilson, Ainley, & Bills, 2005). One of the key features of a spreadsheet is its dynamic ability to allow students to manipulate numbers and instantly see the impact of the change on formulas and structures of numbers. The core of algebra is an understanding of variables. Students have many misconceptions about what a variable represents (Kuchemann, 1981; Stacey & MacGregor, 1997). Use of spreadsheets can facilitate students' construction of understanding of the traditionally challenging concept of variables effectively.

In order to use spreadsheets, teachers typically need to reserve and take students to a school lab or get a laptop cart for the classroom. These resources are often in high demand at a school, encouraging one-day lessons rather than sustained engagement with the tool and the ideas that can be developed with the tool. Adapting tools such as spreadsheets to the iPhone, iPod Touch and similar technologies can solve many problems associated with access and use. Teachers can use handheld technologies on demand, for "just-in-time learning," when they identify teachable moments with individual students, small groups, or the whole class. "Mobile technologies provide an opportunity for a fundamental change in education away from occasional use of a computer in a lab towards more embedded use in the classroom and beyond" (Naismith, Lonsdale, Vavoula, & Sharples, 2004, p. 6).

Although research in this area is only recently developing, virtual manipulatives and simulations with Java applets, such as those available through NCTM's Illuminations project (http://illuminations.nctm.org), Utah State's National Library of Virtual Manipulatives (http://nlvm.usu.edu), and Shodor's Interactivate (http://www.shodor.org/interactivate) can be powerful tools for learning (Crawford & Brown, 2003; Reimer & Moyer, 2005; Suh & Moyer-Peckenham, 2007). These are dynamic and engaging tools that facilitate students' construction of algebraic ideas, particularly in moving from concrete to abstract thinking (Bolyard & Moyer, 2003).

X	Y
3	7
0	1
-4	-7

An example of these virtual manipulatives is Shodor's "Slope Slider". Research shows that students have difficulty and develop misconceptions with many aspects of graphing lines, such as slope and y-intercept (Bishop, 2000; Swafford & Langrall, 2000; Walter & Gerson, 2007). To teach this concept, teachers typically use the traditional method of creating *x,y* tables, such as those in the figure at the right, to plug in points to graph lines one at a time and/or explain to students what m and b represent and how they change the graph of the equation $y = mx + b$. Instead, students with access to the Slope Slider (see below) can be asked "In the equation $y = mx + b$, how does changing the value for m or b impact the graph?" Students vary slopes and y-intercepts, seeing how their manipulation immediately impacts the line. Then, through discussions with their peers or teacher or writing an explanation, they solidify the algebraic ideas in their minds. With the Slope Slider, students can visually see how the number in front of x changes the slope by seeing an infinite number of lines plotted easily and quickly. When students are actively involved in constructing understanding, they are more likely to comprehend and retain algebraic concepts.

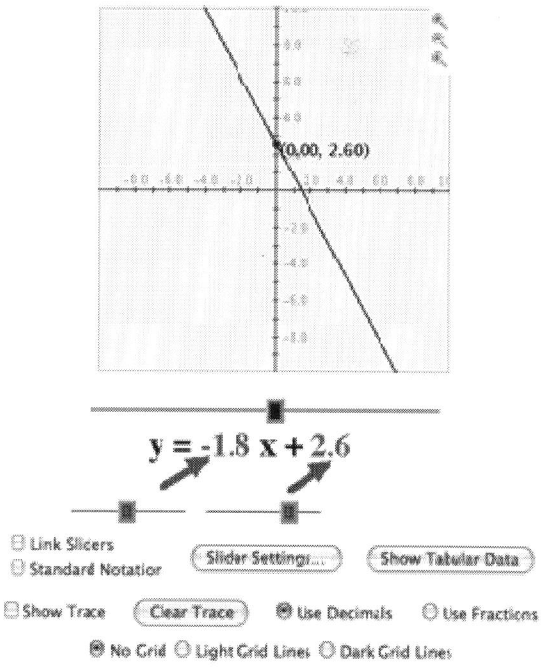

Students struggle with many aspects of algebraic graphing, including misconceptions about the meaning inherent in the axes of a graph (Friel, Curcio, & Bright, 2001). Research shows that students often take graphs as literal representations of the situation rather than graphical information (Monk, 1992). For instance, students confuse the image of a bicyclist riding up a hill with the relationship between time and distance in a graph. Science sensors, such as those developed by Vernier (http://www.vernier.com), can connect mathematics to real life situations. An understanding of axes can be developed as students use a temperature probe to examine the dynamic between time and temperature as a liquid warms or distance and time when motion detectors are used. One of the neat applications that can be used with Vernier's motion detector gives students the ability to create a random graph, such as the one below on the left, indicating a relationship between time and distance. Students need to move towards and away from the motion detector to recreate the graph. In small groups they discuss strategies and the relationship between time and distance. As they move back and forth, the handheld recreates their path to compare with the original graph, as in the figure at the right. They can repeat the activity until they can recreate the graph (or in the case of the figure at the right, explain why they cannot travel a great distance in no time).

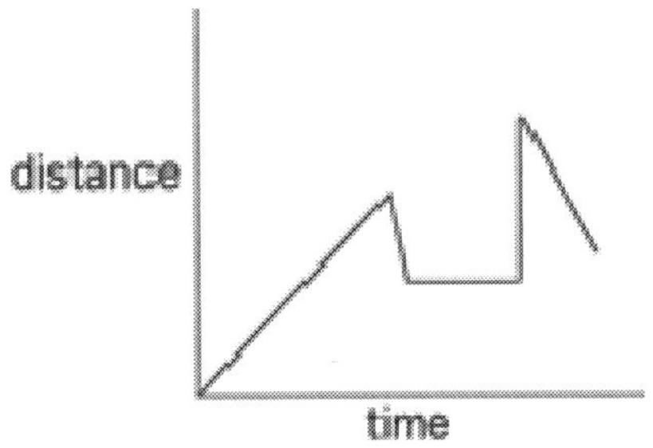

Figure 3:
Random Time Distance Graph

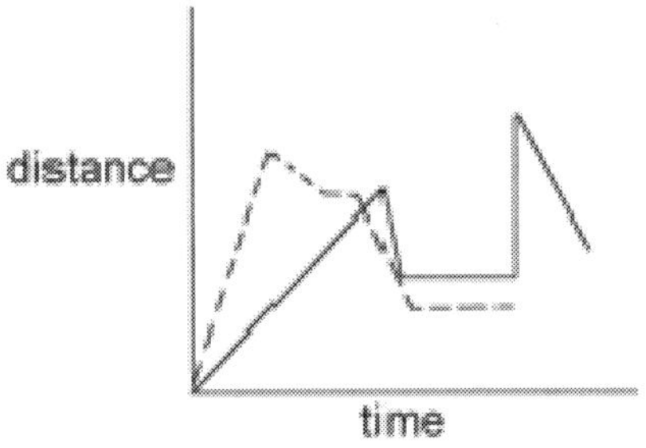

Figure 4:
Student Generated Time Distance Graph

Engaging students in authentic contexts and working collaboratively on important algebraic concepts with peers, such as the meaning of and relationship between axes, taps into the potential power of handheld technology. These sensors demand dedicated tools (i.e. Personalized Digital Assistants (PDA) or Calculator Based Laboratories (CBL)) or laptops to collect and make use of the data. The new version of software for the iPod Touch, released this summer, includes the capability to connect accessories such as Vernier sensors. The iPod Touch and similar future technologies can bring all of these uses to one easily accessible tool.

Another feature debuting for the iPod Touch this summer is **peer-to-peer** interaction. With this new capability, many of Interactivate's Java Applets and our other applications have interesting possibilities for students to engage with each other in exploring algebraic ideas. Rather than students struggling to understand algebra in isolation, we can tap into the power of students engaging in activity and conversation about algebraic concepts together. For example, a student might develop an algebraic equation that is represented graphically on the iPod Touch that another student might have to figure out. If both students had an iPod Touch, they could simultaneously be working on each other's equation. When students have to synthesize their knowledge of equations to create a challenging activity for a peer, they work at the highest level of Bloom's taxonomy of thinking. This type of activity would help students develop an understanding of the relationship between equations and graphs that is often a challenging concept in algebra.

Researchers with the Jasper Woodbury Project at Vanderbilt University found that video-based problem solving can stimulate engaged and thoughtful encounters with algebra. However, the technology only allowed the teacher or one student at a time to direct the playing of the video to find critical data. iPod Touch technology allows every student to have the power to manipulate the video to find data that they need from the situation, encouraging multiple approaches to a problem and student directed learning. One of the key struggles for students of algebra is their inability to differentiate between pertinent and extraneous data in real life situations and to choose appropriate algebraic tools to solve problems. Video-based problems can help develop those skills.

The bottom line is that we are at an exciting crossroads in handheld technology that is being driven by the extremely lucrative smart phone industry. In the quest to gain market share, there is tremendous competition to have the best gadgetry. Education can be the beneficiary of this corporate battle as new capabilities for tools such as Apple's iPod Touch create amazing potential for thinking about learning differently. The promised power of computers in the palm of your hand is a growing reality. This is great news for students of algebra in particular, who need visual supports to overcome challenges in developing their thinking and understanding. All we need is some ingenious educational software programmers to make the potential come to life. So, get busy!!!

References

Anderson, C. W. & Smith, E. L. (1987). Teaching science. In V. Richardson-Koehler (Ed.), Educators' handbook: A research perspective (pp. 84-111). New York: Longman, Inc.

Balachef, N. (1984). French research activities in didactics of mathematics, some key words and related references. Theory of Mathematics Education, Occasional paper 54(Institut fur Didaktich der Mathmatik (IDM), Universitat, Bielefeld.).

Battista, M. T., & Van Auken Borrow, C. (1998). Using spreadsheets to promote algebraic thinking. *Teaching Children Mathematics*, 4(8), 470-478.

Bishop, J.: 2000, 'Linear geometric number patterns: Middle school students' strategies'. *Mathematics Education Research Journal*, 12(2), 107-126.

Bolyard, J. J., & Moyer, P. S. (2003) Investigations in algebra with virtual manipulatives. *ON-Math, Online Journal of School Mathematics*, 2(2), 1-10.

Bos, B. (2009). Virtual math objects with pedagogical, mathematical, and cognitive fidelity. *Computers in Human Behavior*, 25(2), 521-528.

Calder, N., Brown, T., Hanley, U., & Darby, S. (2006). Forming conjectures within a spreadsheet environment. *Mathematics Education Research Journal*, 18(3), 100-116.

Crawford, C., & Brown, E. (2003). Integrating Internet-based mathematical manipulatives within a learning environment. *Journal of Computers in Mathematics and Science Teaching*, 22(2), 169-180.

Demby, Agnieszka (1997). Algebraic Procedures Used by 13-to-15-Year-Olds. *Educational Studies in Mathematics*, 33(1), 45-70.

Ellington, A. J. (2003). A meta-analysis of the effects of calculators on students' achievement and attitude levels in precollege mathematics classes. *Journal for Research in Mathematics Education*, 34(5), 433-463.

Friel, S., Curcio, F., & Bright, G. (2001). Making sense of graphs: Critical factors influencing comprehension and instructional implications. *Journal for Research in Mathematics Education*, 32(2), 124-158.

Gage, J. (2002). Using the graphic calculator to form a learning environment for the early teaching of algebra. *The International Journal of Computer Algebra in Mathematics Education*. 9(1), 3-28.

Heid, M.K. & Blume, G.W. (2008). Algebra and function development. In M.K. Heid & G.W. Blume (Eds.) *Research on technology and the teaching and learning of mathematics: Volume 1 Research Synthesis*. Charlotte, NC: Information Age Publishing.

Helfand, D. (2006, January 30). A formula for failure in L.A. schools. *Los Angeles Times*. Retrieved April 10, 2009 from http://www.latimes.com/news/education/la-me-dropout30jan30,1,2605555.story.

Haspekian, M. (2005). An "Instrumental Approach" to study the integration of a computer tool into mathematics teaching: The case of spreadsheets. *International Journal of Computers for Mathematical Learning*, 10, 109-141.

Kuchemann, D. (1981). Algebra. In K. M. Hart (Ed.), *Children's Understanding of Mathematics* (pp. 102-119): London: John Murray.

Ladson-Billings, Gloria (1998). Teaching in Dangerous Times: Culturally Relevant Approaches to Teacher Assessment. *Journal of Negro Education*, 67(3), 255-267.

Milgram, R.J. (1999). *An Evaluation of CMP*. Retrieved April 10, 2009 from ftp://math.stanford.edu/pub/papers/milgram/report-on-cmp.html.

Monk, S. (1992). Students' understanding of a function given by a physical model. In E. Dubinsky, & G. Harel, (Eds.) *The Concept of Function: Aspects of Epistemology and Pedagogy*. USA, Mathematical Association of America.

Moseley, B. & Brenner, M. E. (2009). A Comparison of Curricular Effects on the Integration of Arithmetic and Algebraic Schemata in Pre-Algebra Students. *Instructional Science: An International Journal of the Learning Sciences*, 37(1), 1-20.

Moses, R. & Cobb, C. (2001). Organizing Algebra: The Need to Voice A Demand. *Social Policy*, 31(4), 4-12.

Naismith, L., Lonsdale, P., Vavoula, G., Sharples, M. (2004). Mobile Technologies and Learning. NESTA Futurelab Literature Review Series, Report No 11.

National Center for Education Statistics. (2008). *The condition of education 2008*. (NCES Publication No. 2008031). Washington, DC: U.S. Government Printing Office.

National Council of Teachers of Mathematics. (2008). *Algebra: What, When, and for Whom: A Position of the National Council of Teachers of Mathematics*. Reston, VA: Author. Retrieved April 15, 2009 from http://www.nctm.org/about/content.aspx?id=16229.

National Education Association (2008). Access, adequacy, and equity in education technology. *Results of a survey of America's teachers and support professionals on technology in public schools and classrooms*. Washington, D.C.: NEA.

Nomi, T. & Allensworth, E. (2009). "Double-Dose" Algebra as an Alternative Strategy to Remediation: Effects on Students' Academic Outcomes. *Journal of Research on Educational Effectiveness*, 2(2), 111-148.

Reimer, K., & Moyer, P. S. (2005). Third-graders learn about fractions using virtual manipulatives: A classroom study. *Journal of Computers in Mathematics and Science Teaching*, 24(1), 5-25.

Reznichenko, N. (2007). Learning with Graphing Calculator (GC): GC as a Cognitive Tool. *Paper presented at the Annual European Educational Research Association (EERA) Conference*. Retrieved April 22, 2009 from http://search.ebscohost.com/login.aspx?direct=true&db=eric&AN=ED497716&site=ehost-live.

Riordan, J.E., & Noyce, P.E. (2001). The impact of two standards-based mathematics curricula on student achievement in Massachusetts. *Journal for Research in Mathematics Education*, 32(4), 368-398.

Rojano, T. (1996). Developing algebraic aspects of problem solving within a spreadsheet environment. *Approaches to Algebra* (137-145). Netherlands: Kluwer Academic Publishers.

Rojano, T. & Sutherland, R. (1993). Towards an Algebraic Notion of Function: The Role of Spreadsheets. *Collaboration between the Centro de Investigacion y Estudios, Avanzados del IPN, Mexico and the Institute of Education*, University of London, UK.

Stacey, K. & MacGregor, M. (1997). Ideas About Symbolism that Students Bring to Algebra. *Mathematics Teacher*, 90(2), 110-117.

Suh, J.M. (2005). Third graders' mathematics achievement and representation preference using virtual and physical manipulatives for adding fractions and balancing equations. Unpublished doctoral dissertation. Fairfax, Va.: George Mason University.

Suh, J. M., & Moyer-Packenham, P. S. (2007). Developing students' representational fluency using virtual and physical algebra balances. *Journal of Computers in Mathematics and Science Teaching*. 26 (2), 155-173.

Swafford, J. O. & Langrall, C. W. (2000). Grade 6 students' preinstructional use of equations to describe and represent problem situations. *Journal for Research in Mathematics Education*, 31(1), 89-12.

Tabach, M., Hershkowitz, R., & Arcavi, A. (2008). Learning beginning algebra with spreadsheets in a computer intensive environment. *The Journal of Mathematical Behavior*, 27(1), 48-63.

Viadero, M. (2009, March 11). Algebra-for-All policy found to raise rates of failure in Chicago. *Education Week*. Retrieved April 10, 2009 from http://www.edweek.org/ew/articles/2009/03/11/24algebra.h28.html?tmp=1587018900.

Walter, J., & Gerson, H. (2007). Teachers' personal agency: Making sense of slope through additive structures. *Educational Studies in Mathematics*, 65(2), 203-233.

Wilson, K., Ainley, J., & Bills, L. (2005). Naming a column on a spreadsheet: Is it more algebraic? *Paper presented at the Sixth British Congress on Mathematics Education*, University of Warwick.

Zacharia, Z.C., Olympiou, G., & Papaevripidou, M. (2008). Effects of experimenting with physical and virtual manipulatives on students' conceptual understanding in heat and temperature. *Journal of Research in Science Teaching*, 45(9), 1021-1035.

Web 2.0

Web 2.0: How the Web got Loose

View online at: http://bcis.pacificu.edu/journal/2009/06/article.php?id=84

By Jeff Cain

University of Kentucky

Depending on whom you ask, Web 2.0 has many different meanings and interpretations. To some it may be the underlying programming standards and language. To others, the definition revolves around the connection of people.[1] The term does not have strict boundaries; rather it is used to describe newer ways of developing for and using the Internet.[2] In reality, Web 2.0 is not even a new concept, but an advancement closer to the original vision for the Web — a connective and social medium in which people interact.

Web 2.0 applications such as Delicious[3], Facebook[4], YouTube[5], and others have allowed the Web to sever itself from the restricting confines of its previous stereotype as a digital "bookshelf."[6] This newer evolution of the Web is now less of a place for information to be provided, searched for, and digested, and more of a dynamic participant within our social landscape. The applications and subsequent ways that people use them have begun to have subtle, but substantial socio-cultural effects on different aspects of society. The socio-technical evolutions of Web 2.0 have outpaced our attempts to grasp the legal, ethical, and societal expectations,[7] creating new issues to consider and resolve. By briefly illustrating these emerging issues through a series of short vignettes, I hope to provoke further conversation and debate about Web 2.0 and technological determinism. The following sections represent three of the many significant changes precipitated by Web 2.0 in different aspects of contemporary society: loss of demarcation between public and private lives, rise of collective intelligence, and shifts in the flow of information.

The Merger of Public and Private Personas

As short as ten years ago, it was relatively easy to differentiate between public and private spaces. The demarcation between actions conducted in private and those in public was mostly clear-cut. Possibly the strongest, most far-reaching change imposed by the popularity of blogs, Facebook, Twitter[8], YouTube, and other social media is the breakdown of that distinction. The online public display of attitudes, opinions, and actions once expressed primarily to others in relatively private venues has alarmed many not accustomed to this type of communication. This transition in social communication has occurred at such a high speed and volume that society is struggling with how to react. Traditional laws do not apply very well and new ethical issues have arisen.[9]

The crux of this public/private issue is the collapsing of contexts.[10] In the Web 2.0 world, people operate at different levels in the same digital space. Sometimes those interactions are with family, sometimes they are work-related, and sometimes they are equivalent to a Saturday night out with friends. Combining these interactions simultaneously in the online environment collapses them down into a wholly different context, depicting an amalgam of the many different "lives" of people. This proves very difficult for others to interpret, especially as it relates to work, careers, and professional lives. Social norms dictate how people act in specific contexts and most of us behave differently in different contexts. As a society, we have not determined the proper way to address the flattened contexts of online communication.

This struggle is clearly illustrated in the case of a student expelled from nursing school due to her personal blog containing opinions judged by the school to be contrary to professional ideals and offensive to some students, faculty, and patients.[11] The blog contained personal expressions originating from a private venue; however, those traditionally private opinions were voluntarily made available to the public. The act of posting personal opinions on a blog straddles the traditional public/private boundary line, rendering those opinions neither wholly public nor wholly private. A myriad of legal and ethical questions arises in this type of case,[12] including "How should that student be judged by the school?" and "Should she even be judged at all?" Our inability to separate public and private makes it difficult to answer these types of questions using traditional cases as precedent.

The Rise of Collective Intelligence

The emergence of collective intelligence is one cultural trend spawned by Web 2.0 that academia has resisted. This concept, described as a component of Web 2.0,2 is one that shifts the power structure of knowledge authority and threatens the foundation of the academy. The vast availability of information from unlimited sources leads to real-time context and fact checking, which drastically alters the "authority market"[13] and the meaning of "expertise" in the Web 2.0 world.

One only has to look at Wikipedia[14] as an example of this problem. The inherent concepts of user-contributed and user-driven information are fundamental to the popularity of Web 2.0 and have almost singlehandedly changed the paradigm of expertise. A close examination of the paradigm shift reveals the potential disparity between reliable information and usable information, which tends to be at the crux of the issue. Detractors posit that information on Wikipedia is subject to bias, may contain inaccuracies, is incomplete, and does not differentiate between novice and expert contributors.[15] Alternatively, supporters state that the collective intelligence is closer to the truth than what any one or two can construct. In addition, the real-time updates of Wikipedia contrast with older models that require days, weeks, months, and sometimes years, to update information.[16] For these reasons, supporters are willing to forgive temporary inaccuracies in exchange for the agility and usability made possible by the technology and formed through collective intelligence.

Altering the Flow of Information

The shifting of news and information flow is a third example of Web 2.0's effect on societal transactions. Traditional media sources such as newspapers and television newscasts have long been the primary provider of news and information to the public. Those working in "legitimate" media areas operate under a set of rules and guidelines about when and what to publish and under what circumstances. Among other things, they are bound by ethical guidelines that prevent reporting without proper verification.

As blogs (and now micro-blogs) became popular, information slowly started to flow through these informal communication channels. Bloggers and Twitterers are not necessarily bound by the same restrictions as those in traditional media. Because of this, "breaking news" may come through social media channels first, as bloggers and micro-bloggers are free to report on speculation and opinion without going through an extensive vetting process. The resulting change is that many have turned to social media as the initial source for news and information deemed important to them, creating a growing angst among some traditional journalists who decry the advantages of bloggers in that professional field. Some journalists have taken notice of the change and are beginning to adapt to the social media world in their own ways.[17, 18]

The sports reporting field provides an excellent example of social media's impact on communication channels. During a recent transition between basketball coaches at the University of Kentucky, the self-proclaimed "Big Blue Nation"[19] clamored for information related to the coaching search and the subsequent college commitments of several high profile recruits. Local media coverage of the program is good, but inherently restricted in terms of the speed and fluidity of information transmission. The desire for up-to-the-minute facts, rumors, and opinions concerning the basketball program was and continues to be satisfied by bloggers, with one blog in particular attracting a large share of the audience. In a relatively short period of time, the Kentucky Sports Radio blog[20] has transformed itself into a major source of news and commentary on UK basketball and other team sports. Updated several times daily, the blog attracts not only hardcore message board users, but also scores of mainstream Internet users by providing a free "one stop shop" source for team news. During the most recent peak periods, a quarter million hits were recorded daily[21] as fans stayed abreast of the stories, relegating traditional media sources to official verification of information found on the blog. This switch to social media for information illustrates how the flow of information has changed and in some cases reversed, with Web 2.0 applications filling the role of the primary news provider and traditional media sources struggling to remain relevant.

Conclusion

The above are just a few examples of the numerous ways social media is affecting the fabric of our society and they may not ultimately even be the most important or far-reaching. This paper simply provides a starting point for those types of discussions. Web 2.0 is forcing us to reconsider what is public, what is private, what is expertise, as well as how we receive and transmit information. To what extent these transformations will continue, and whether they are good, bad, or otherwise is yet to be determined. Their effects may be reduced or exacerbated as we adjust to the socio-cultural changes. The current speed of technological advances may also mean that other changes will occur before we have adapted to the current ones. The underlying message is that the Web is now loose and we need either to wrestle with it or go along for the ride. The choice is ours.

Endnotes

[1] Geraci M. Now playing: Web 2.0. *Interface: The Journal of Education, Community, and Values*. 2007;7(7). Available at: http://bcis.pacificu.edu/journal/2007/07/geraci.php

[2] O'Reilly T. What is Web 2.0? Design patterns and business models for the next generation of software. Available at: http://www.oreillynet.com/lpt/a/6228. Accessed August 14, 2008.

[3] http://www.delicious.com.

[4] http://www.facebook.com.

[5] http://www.youtube.com.

[6] Rhine S. Web 2.0 and the demise of the shelf concept. *Interface: The Journal of Education, Community, and Values*. 2008;8(3). Available at: http://bcis.pacificu.edu/journal/2008/03/rhine.php

[7] Berners-Lee T, Fischetti M. *Weaving the web: The original design and ultimate destiny of the World Wide Web by its inventor*. San Francisco: Harper; 1999.

[8] http://www.twitter.com.

[9] Wells K. Recap: What is the biggest ethical issue we face in social media today. Available at: http://www.socialmediaclub.org/2008/07/31/recap-what-is-the-biggest-ethical-issue-we-face-in-social-media-today/. Accessed July 14, 2009.

[10] Boyd D. Understanding Socio-Technical Phenomena in a Web 2.0 Era. Available at: http://www.danah.org/papers/talks/MSR-NE-2008.html. Accessed June 30, 2009.

[11] Campus TW. Expelled for her online comments, former nursing student sues university. Available at: http://chronicle.com/wiredcampus/article/3661/expelled-for-heronline-comments-former-nursing-student-sues-university. Accessed March 13, 2009.

[12] Cain J. Online social networking issues within academia and pharmacy education. *American Journal of Pharmaceutical Education*. 2008;72:Article 10.

[13] Jensen M. The new metrics of scholarly authority. *The Chronicle Review*. 2007;53(41):B6.

[14] http://www.wikipedia.org.

[15] Schiff S. Know it all: Can Wikipedia conquer expertise? Available at: http://www.newyorker.com/archive/2006/07/31/060731fa_fact. Accessed July 13, 2009.

[16] Fallis D. Toward an epistemology of Wikipedia. *Journal of the American Society for Information Science and Technology*. 2008;59(10):1662-1674.

[17] Goodman H. Bog or cog? Blogs forcing newspapers to re-examine role. Available at: http://www.newsandtech.com/issues/2006/06-06/nt/06-06_blogging.htm. Accessed July 13, 2009.

[18] Betancourt L. How social media is radically changing the newsroom. Available at: http://mashable.com/2009/06/08/social-media-newsroom/. Accessed July 13, 2009.

[19] The University of Kentucky official team color is blue and "Big Blue Nation" is a term used by many to describe the large, rabid fan base.

[20] http://www.kentuckysportsradio.com.

[21] Personal communication with Matt Jones, co-founder and primary blogger for the Kentucky Sports Radio blog; July 2, 2009.

Technology

Crowdsourcing: Leveraging Your Social Networks

View online at: http://bcis.pacificu.edu/journal/2009/06/article.php?id=85

By Michael Geraci

The national marketing firm, Image Communications, recently decided to undergo an overhaul of their corporate name and brand identity. Who did they turn to for assistance with this mission-critical, potentially risky feat? Was it their highly-skilled internal team of brand wizards and creative communicators? No. Was it a high-powered mega firm that specializes in building and launching new brands? No, again. Image Communications turned to *you*, or at least people like you, and they did it via social networking: Twitter, Facebook, LinkedIn, etc..[1] They put a call out for a new company name via their established social channels and created the website http://www.helpusnameus.com (that's "help us name us"), and before long, they had thousands of submissions from over 50 countries on six continents, and they eventually became Pyxl [2] - the submission by DaNice Marshall from Massachusetts.

Image Communications used what is commonly referred to as *crowdsourcing* for their rebranding effort. Crowdsourcing, as a term, is credited to Jeff Howe of *Wired* Magazine after his June 2006 article, "The Rise of Crowdsourcing".[3] But the concept has been around on the Internet, in one form or another, for close to a decade. Howe defines crowdsourcing as:

> The act of a company or institution taking a function once performed by employees and outsourcing it to an undefined (and generally large) network of people in the form of an open call.[4]

While this definition firmly places the concept in the context of today's popular social networking channels, variations of crowdsourcing can be tracked back to the creation and evolution of Wikipedia and even Google's search results ranking algorithm, which, in case you didn't know, orders search results based (at least partially) on which hits are more popular as determined by the number of web pages across the Internet that link to said results.

Crowdsourcing has some revenue-generating potential as well. If you haven't purchased stock media on iStockPhoto.com, you're missing out on access to nearly 5 million pieces of high quality media all supplied by... wait for it... average everyday folks, aspiring artists, and maybe the occasional professional who is willing to sell his or her work at such a steep discount, they are probably losing sleep over it, right now. At iStock Web-ready photos and illustrations start at $1 and go to a maximum of $27 for something you could stick on the side of a bus. Once you create a free account, you are able to post your own work for sale on the service.

One interesting example of entrepreneurial crowdsourcing is Cambrian House,[5] which is an online service that *enables* crowds to propose, design, develop, and make money on technology solutions. From 2005 to 2008, Cambrian House worked with a pool of 50,000 people who willingly volunteered their time and brainpower to generate some 7,000 ideas for technology driven products and services. This same crowd vetted the pool of ideas through online voting, messaging and contests; and then worked together to spec out how the winning ideas would function. Then, this same group, or at least those most qualified, actually *developed the products* with on-going oversight and input from the masses. Contributors earn "royalty points" - essentially virtual stock in the project. When the project launches and generates revenue, royalty points are redeemed for cold, hard cash. If you're wondering exactly what Cambrian House adds to this equation, the answer is: a system that enables it to function optimally. Cambrian House's press releases indicate that top earners in their community can make over $50,000 a year contributing to projects that have "good growth potential"[6].

So successful was the Cambrian House system, it was spun off in 2008 and became Chaordix [7] (the synthesis of chaos and order), a commercial service provider of enterprise-level crowdsourcing technology.

The green movement, very much a grass-roots collective of technically savvy, community-minded folks, has also tapped into the wisdom of their masses. Greenwala [8] is a social network "made of people who help others live a greener lifestyle by sharing their knowledge, green experiences and actions with friends, family and the world."[9] The organization's site is the home base of the network, but members can participate in the network via major online social channels (e.g. Facebook, mySpace, Twitter, LinkedIn).

But for real crowdsourced ideas and solutions with a green tint, look no further than How Can I Recycle This?[10], a UK-based site where people can post questions about what to do with household items once they are no longer needed. The community responds with highly creative solutions. For example, a post on May 20, 2009 asked "How can I reuse or recycle cassette tape cases?"[11] Among the responses: ice scrapers, gift boxes, and photo frames - not bad! A quick sum of their archives yields myriad ideas for the reuse of over 1000 everyday objects.

Despite good ideas and good intentions, there is some skepticism about just how effective and "wise" crowds can be. There seems to be a fine line between harnessing the power of collective intelligence and turning a mob loose to hammer out a solution to your specific need. In his March 22, 2007 post on ReadWriteWeb [12], Josh Catone [13], an active technology blogger, offers these suggestions for maximizing your return from crowdsourcing efforts:

- Crowdsourcing should come with pre-established rules that aim to maintain order in the process.
- In certain situations (i.e. a organizational re-branding effort), the final decision should be made by a central authority either within the organization or a designated subset of the community.

- Avoid groupthink. Crowds should be encouraged to debate and defend all ideas. Keep an eye out for "movements" within a group that try to assert undue influence over the crowd.
- Let crowds evaluate and appraise content, do not let crowds *create* content. Too many cooks in the kitchen... you know? [14]

The real question is how can crowdsourcing be used to great effect in our organizations? As an educator, should I put out an open call for ideas for a new class I'm creating? Could I query my LinkedIn network for curriculum changes that will have the most relevance and marketability in the current job market? Could I post anonymous versions of my students' creative work on Facebook and ask my 100 friends to choose their favorites? It's going to take some trial and error to dial this in. Then again, maybe I should pose this question to the masses and see what I get back...

To learn more about crowdsourcing:

http://en.wikipedia.org/wiki/Crowdsourcing

http://www.openinnovators.net/list-open-innovation-crowdsourcing-examples/

http://crowdsourcingexamples.pbworks.com/

http://crowdsourcing.typepad.com/

Endnotes

[1] http://www.twitter.com, http://www.facebook.com, http://www.linkedin.com

[2] http://thinkpyxl.com/

[3] http://www.wired.com/wired/archive/14.06/crowds.html

[4] http://crowdsourcing.typepad.com/

[5] http://www.cambrianhouse.com/

[6] http://www.readwriteweb.com/archives/crowdsourcing_million_heads.php

[7] http://www.chaordix.com/

[8] http://www.greenwala.com

[9] http://www.greenwala.com/about

[10] http://www.recyclethis.co.uk/

[11] http://www.recyclethis.co.uk/20090520/how-can-i-reuse-or-recycle-cassette-tape-cases

[12] http://www.readwriteweb.com/archives/crowdsourcing_million_heads.php

[13] http://www.readwriteweb.com/about_josh.php

[14] http://www.readwriteweb.com/archives/crowdsourcing_million_heads.php

Estate Tax Issues You Should Be Aware Of

View online at: http://bcis.pacificu.edu/journal/2009/06/article.php?id=86

By Leonard D. DuBoff

When an individual dies, the value of that person's estate must be determined and if it exceeds a certain amount, it may be subject to a very steep tax. Congress provided every estate with a form of "safe harbor," that is, there is a specified amount which is exempt from estate taxation.

In 2001, legislation was passed to gradually increase the size of the estate tax exemption to $3.5 million this year, and to repeal the estate tax for 2010. That legislation also provides that the estate tax will return in 2011 with an exemption of only $1 million.

While most commentators believe that the current federal exemption of $3.5 million will be extended, there are numerous proposals being considered and, until legislation is actually enacted, there is no certainty. There are, however, some steps you can take to reduce potential estate tax liability regardless of the version of the law passed.

If your taxable estate is likely to exceed $1 million, you may want to consider making gifts of your property now. Each person currently has an annual gift tax exclusion of $13,000 per recipient per year. That is, you could, for example, gift $13,000 to each of your 4 children every year without owing gift tax (for a total of $52,000) and if your spouse joins in the gift, then you could give $26,000 (for a total of $104,000). If those children all have spouses or domestic partners, you also have 8 grandchildren and your spouse joins in the gift, you would be able to remove $416,000 from your estate this year, with no tax liability.

You may also be able to gift ownership interests in the family business. If that business is growing, the value of the interests will increase over time, but the tax exemption is based on the value of the interest at the time of gifting. That is, if today, while the economy is down and values likely low, you give each of your 4 children a 10% interest in your business, valued at $13,000 each (for a total of $52,000), no tax is owed, even if when you die, the economy is booming and those 10% interests are then each worth $500,000 (for a total of $2 million).

Note that if you are gifting anything other than cash or other item with an indisputable value, you should see your tax advisor first, in order to be sure that you can obtain the full exclusion, while reducing the risk of a challenge to the value by the IRS.

Traditional married couples can double the estate tax exemption by holding title to assets correctly and by using appropriate tax planning devices in their wills and/or trusts. In many states, same sex married couples and registered domestic partners can take advantage of comparable state estate tax benefits, though they are not able to do so with respect to federal estate taxes.

Another way to save taxes is to have a specific type of trust for your insurance policies in order to keep the life insurance proceeds from being included in your gross estate, or to have the recipient own the policy on your life.

There are a host of estate tax planning devices which may be available for you to reduce or eliminate estate tax. You should consult with your lawyer and accountant in order to determine your best course of action.

Please feel free to contact us (http://www.dubofflaw.com) if you have any questions about the above, or need assistance with your estate planning.

Book Review

Nancy Duarte's *slide:ology: The Art and Science of Creating Great Presentations*

View online at: http://bcis.pacificu.edu/journal/2009/06/article.php?id=87

Review by Maria Walters

Duarte, Nancy. *slide:ology: The Art and Science of Creating Great Presentations.* Sebastopol, CA: O'Reilly Media, Inc., 2008.

When you boil any form of communication down — a conversation, an article, a book, a presentation — it's really just a story. This is one of the guiding premises of Nancy Duarte's book, *slide:ology*. As the Principal of Duarte Design, the firm whose claim to fame is creating the presentation for Al Gore's film *An Inconvenient Truth*, Nancy Duarte is still noticeably involved in the theory and principles of design and public speaking, as well as being a great storyteller. Interestingly, the story that she tells in this book is about how to tell a better story orally and visually.

Because of the challenges of writing about a presentation instead of giving one, this book reaches beyond the realms of traditional books. The striking full-color volume is packed full of diagrams, examples, and case studies, as well as more traditional descriptions of what to do and why. To flip through some of the pages, check out the online preview [1]. The book is also accompanied by a helpful website[2] and a free 45 day access to the online edition of *slide:ology* through Safari Books Online, which is discussed more below [3].

The book itself is part speech coach, part visual design instructor, and all inspirational. The bulk of it deals, unsurprisingly, with designing slides: layout, templates, color and diagram choices, etc. Each chapter deals first with the theory, explaining why color choices matter and how the audience perceives what is being presented. The overriding theme is clarity and simplicity, which is emphasized through the design of each page, with plenty of white space ("visual breathing room"[4]) and examples. Most chapters include at least one case study, describing successful presenters who have used the techniques outlined (often clients of Duarte Design), and most case studies include online links where the reader can actually watch the presentation being presented instead of described, or download PowerPoint templates, allowing the reader to use the techniques themselves. [5]

The design aspect of the book is introduced and concluded with chapters on the importance of good presentation practices in general. The reasons for minimizing the content on slides is to both remove the safety blanket for speakers and put the weight of communication on them instead of on information typed onto the slides, so speakers have to be motivated to change their presentation styles as well as the look of their slides. In fact, Duarte even speaks to the times when it would be better *not* to give a presentation: when slides feature text heavily, Duarte uses Garr Renolds' term "slideuments"[6] and recommends that, as a speaker, you must "trust that your audience is smart enough to read and circulate your slides as a document" [7].

Of course, we can't fully review this book in *Interface* without also looking at its integration into the web. The book looks exactly the same on Safari Books Online, though the striking two-page spreads don't have the same visual impact when viewed one page at a time on a browser. Navigation is clear, and breaks the book into clearly titled chapters and subchapters. Though there are options for a "Print Fidelity View" and "HTML View", the HTML was disabled for this book — understandable, considering the complexity and importance of the layouts. Some might find it difficult to read in the PDF form, especially since the page zoom only has two size options. However, a link at the bottom of the page directs users with special needs to e-mail or call for a specific portal to the same material in an easier format [8].

One of the best features of Safari Books Online is the list of links it displays below each page showing chapters of other books covering similar subjects. This selection takes place using Self-Organizing Maps (SOM), described as a neural network algorithm. However, I was disappointed that, though many of the book's pages showed links to the site accompanying the book or other online resources, these links were not active, nor shown on any part of the Safari site.

slide:ology was both an informative and enjoyable read. Duarte has a way of being encouraging and inspiring, even while pointing out errors that I, for one, have made countless times. Especially geared toward professionals who are giving presentations regularly, this book is worth a look by anyone who might be watching or giving a presentation in the future. The biggest downside: you'll never be able to sit through a traditional PowerPoint presentation again!

Endnotes

[1] Preview the book at: http://oreilly.com/catalog/9780596522346/preview.html

[2] http://www.slideology.com/ which redirects to the Duarte blog: http://blog.duarte.com/

[3] Safari Books Online http://my.safaribooksonline.com/

[4] *slide:ology* p. 106.

[5] http://blog.duarte.com/book/

[6] *slide:ology* p. 6. Garr Renolds is author of Presentation Zen, a book which Duarte respects and references often.

[7] *slide:ology* p. 6.

[8] ADA Section 508 Compliance information: http://my.safaribooksonline.com/508compliance

Book Review

Scott Fox's *e-Riches 2.0*

View online at: http://bcis.pacificu.edu/journal/2009/06/article.php?id=89

Review by Jeffrey Barlow

Fox, Scott. *e-Riches 2.0*. New York: American Management Association, 2009.

This work discusses "Next Generation Marketing Strategies for Making Millions Online." While there is no guarantee of such stunning success, the author, Scott Fox, has credentials which suggest that he certainly knows his e-business.[1] Fox has written a previously successful work, *Internet Riches*, and advises noted individuals and corporations.

e-Riches 2.0 concentrates upon the use of Web 2.0 interactive social applications and techniques to market oneself and one's products. Fox does not neglect, however, the importance of Web 1.0 applications such as e-mail. The work covers, among many other applications, blogs, "broadcasting" methods such as RSS feeds, a variety of e-mail services such as feed-based, auto-responding, and e-mail publishing ones, as well as video, teleconferencing, podcasting, social sites such as YouTube and Facebook, and multitudinous others.

Fox believes that the Internet, and particularly the interactive nature of Web 2.0, has permanently changed advertising as well as public relations. It now permits small businesses to undertake niche campaigns as well as very broad ones to build and keep a customer base.

The interactive nature of Web 2.0 rewards socially constructed business practices, that is, those which build not only businesses, but also communities. The businessperson who wishes to succeed in this environment must behave quite differently than the colorful clownish television personalities who have succeeded in creating a huge audience in the past. Fox offers both the tools and the social practices which have worked for many others, and invites the reader to adapt them to his or her own needs.

The work should be broadly useful to a number of audiences. All of us are, as Fox shows, increasingly the targets of on-line commercial campaigns. This work could well be the only introduction necessary to understand the technology and the motivations of such campaigns.

In addition to gaining an understanding of the industries involved, it will be an unusual reader who will not have some take-away value from the encyclopedic coverage, if only learning how better to use email and social sites for personal communications. Many people now use social sites to stay in touch much more than they use e-mail itself. And the telephone has become primarily an internet-enabled appliance given the increasing importance of Twitter and related Web 2.0 apps.

For those already in e-business or contemplating doing so---and we agree with Fox that this should be and soon will be every businessperson---the book is probably the first place such an audience should go to understand the variety of possible tools and approaches to doing business on Web 2.0 and the advantages and disadvantages of each.

Fox sometimes comes close to huckstering in his enthusiasm, and he occasionally seems to have more than a little sympathy for the plight of the spammer, though he stops short of ever describing them as misunderstood. The fact is that this is an industry with its dark side, which Fox passes over rather lightly. However, he does pay some attention to the matter of reputation, pointing out that the Internet can be a powerful tool for damaging businesses as well as for furthering them.

I have recently had a powerful example of the use of the Internet to defend against certain business practices. For more than a month I have been receiving robotic calls requesting that I call a particular 800 459-xxxx number. These instructions were given almost inaudibly so that I was not at all sure what the very name of the firm was, not did anyone answer the number when I called. The calls continued, though I learned not to answer them. But the continuing calls soon seemed less a nuisance than a form of harassment.

Finally, a simple Google search for 800 849 yielded millions of references to several collection agencies which shared the same series of 800 849-xxxx numbers. Many others complained about similar treatment, and some government agencies were inviting formal complaints about the practices of the group.[2] I concluded that I would just have to try to ignore the calls.

Then, while writing this review, I was interrupted by a call and I distractedly picked it up. There was a real person on the other end, representing one of the agencies which had been given my number by a deadbeat! I suppose that the agency felt that, having been bludgeoned by numerous robotic calls, I was now ready to surrender and pay up.

After stating that I was not the miscreant---who, fortunately for me, was female---I tried, gently, to inform the caller of their employer's terrible reputation on the Internet. I was heatedly told that I should check their standing with the Better Business Bureau. My reply that nonetheless they had a terrible reputation on the Internet, was met with the disconnect familiar from the previous 50 or so calls.

It is perhaps unfair to expect Fox to treat the misuse of technologically-enable business practices in any depth. He would probably tell us that bad social behavior is ultimately bad for business---at one point he demonstrates that giving away as much of your product or services as you can afford may ultimately be the best Web 2.0 business strategy. The author is able to persuade the reader of such counter-intuitive assertions because of his command of the research bearing upon his topic. Throughout the work we learn surprising facts, such as that only about 75% of e-mails, even legitimate ones sent to subscribers, ever arrive.[3]

Fox also closely analyzes the many services and applications which he recommends for specific purposes, and treats freeware, shareware, and open access ones with as much attention as he does the large commercial players. Because this industry moves very quickly, Fox has numerous references to websites which he continuously updates, so the work might be seen as much a Web 2.0 application as a traditional book.[4]

The book is very accessible---Fox shows his own persuasive abilities by taking a variety of approaches to conveying his information, such as boxed text, references to websites, folksy asides, and reports on current research. But these many cuts at conveying information sometimes make the work seem slow and rather tedious. Business texts increasingly seem to follow a formula for presenting information which runs something like this: Tell them what you are going to tell them; Tell them what you are going to tell them; Tell them what you are going to tell them; Tell them what you wish to tell them; Tell them what you told them; Tell them what you told them; Tell them what you told them; Summarize.

There is also a cut-and-paste feel to the work at times. Fox has gained his understanding of Web 2.0 by being heavily engaged on it. He has, through his newsletters and web sites, solicited a wide variety of tales from e-businesses, both encouraging and cautionary, which he reproduces in the text. At points these came to seem a bit lengthy and repetitive.

But whether despite this rather repetitive approach or because of it, at the last I felt that *e-Riches 2.0* did expose me to a great deal of useful information and I intend to adapt some of its techniques to our own operations at the Berglund Center.

Endnotes

[1] See his business pages at: http://www.scottfox.com/

[2] See http://www.google.com/search?q=800+459&ie=utf-8&oe=utf-8&aq=t&rls=org.mozilla:en-US:official&client=firefox-a for a rich sample of the reports of this operation. Among the 25 million-+ hits are, of course a great many relating to legitimate businesses who unfortunately share the same 800-459 prefix.

[3] pp. 58-9.

[4] These links are also referenced on his business page: http://www.scottfox.com/

Editorial

Attila to Soltan: Media Savvy and Democracy

View online at: http://bcis.pacificu.edu/journal/2009/06/article.php?id=88

Editorial by Jeffrey Barlow

Introduction

Recent events in Iran have caught my imagination, along with the rest of the world, or at least that portion with good Internet access and Facebook, YouTube, and Twitter accounts.

The media treatments of the events raise many questions. We too often simplify the idea of "democracy" and easily confuse it with emerging characteristics of modernity, such as good Internet access, Facebook, YouTube, and Twitter accounts. Such confusion can indeed lead to "foreign manipulation" such as is currently being charged by the intransigent Iranian regime. Here I discuss a much earlier meeting with Attila, a survivor of the Hungarian uprising of 1956[1] and its influence upon my reactions to similar later events.

At the Berglund Center, we hold little sympathy with the Iranian regime.[2] I am in favor of pubic protests when all other avenues are closed to the oppressed; my political life as an Asianist has frequently brought me into sympathetic contact with, and sometimes participation in, student movements. As a graduate student at Berkeley, the many international student movements of the 1960's and 1970's, sometimes accompanied by numbers of dead and wounded, seemed to represent a unified whole.

The Hungarian Rising

My first sense of international political events and the media came in 1956, when the entire United States watched nightly TV coverage of the Hungarian Rising. This began with student demonstrations, which led to weeks of savage fighting when Hungarian military units joined the students in an attempt to oust Soviet occupiers.

A Hungarian radio station was seized briefly, and we watched Walter Cronkite nightly as he listened intently to crackling broadcasts which, as I recall (I was twelve at the time) he interpreted for us. We also were spellbound by press photographs of "Secret Police" being dragged out of their HQ and shot, with occasional snippets of black and white film on the nightly news. The graphical highlight of the events was the destruction of the massive monument to Joseph Stalin, a sort of ur-event since repeated endlessly with the subsequent literal toppling of additional bad guys, such as, of course, Saddam Hussein.[3]

The rebels were unquestionably heroic. The plucky Hungarians held the Soviets off for weeks, and the fighting became block-by-block and house-by-house as the world watched. Although the Hungarians were defeated, they left a legend which has had significant power ever since, and I suspect, was also a learning event for government intelligence agencies all over the world studying intently the impact of the emerging international television media.

My own realization that the Hungarian events were highly mediated rather than purely factual came in the late 1980's. My wife, Christine Richardson, and I were doing research down the Gold Rush Highway and stopped at a motel owned by a man by the name of Attila. As an Asianist, I had to pry into his ethnicity and discovered that he was a descendent of Asian invaders into Hungary. He was also a refugee from the 1956 rising. I told him what these heroic events had meant to me.

Attila angrily replied that it was the fault of the United States that virtually his entire training battalion in the Hungarian army had risen up and been killed. He said that the Voice of America (VOA) had promised guns, money, and quick international recognition. They had, he said, held out for weeks waiting for that American support, which was continually reiterated via the VOA.

Attila said that the rebels had done so well that many Soviet units had refused to fight, or fought half-heartedly. Finally, however, the Russians brought in Mongolian troops, very hard men unconcerned with freedom or democracy, and the rebels were driven steadily back.

At the bloody conclusion, the survivors of his unit occupied a semi-destroyed factory overlooking a large river. One by one his comrades' firing positions fell silent. A friend rushed into the room where Attila was fighting and told him that Mongols were crawling through the factory in the dark, killing everybody with knives. The two chose to try to swim the river in an attempt to work their way to the West. Attila made it across; his friend did not.

By the end of his narrative, Attila was literally punching me in the chest with a hard finger, finishing, "It was you f***ing Americans' fault. Go away!" I slunk off to my room, but Attila left me with quite a different view of the events of 1956.

From Budapest to Beijing

The skepticism Attila engendered has served me well since. I was in China for the latter stages of the Tiananmen events of 1989, then in Taiwan for the savage finale. In Guilin, among Chinese friends, mostly educators, I heard a great deal of concern about the Tiananmen events. They worried that the students might be the early stages of something like the Red Guard of the Cultural Revolution which had been so destructive of their own lives and careers.

After returning to Taiwan, the day of the climactic events I heard over the English language radio station that the VOA was reporting that troops in Beijing had refused to move against the students, that Premier Li Peng had been assassinated, and that rebel units were moving against the government cloistered in the Great Hall of the People. Later, I also heard that the VOA had reported that dorms at the elite colleges in Beijing's Wu Dao Kou district had been attacked and student bodies were hanging out windows. None of these events ever happened but all had the effect of encouraging Beijing workers and students, like the earlier doomed Hungarians, to take a stand.

The night of the events I saw news clips in Taiwan which seemed to show murky videos of Chinese soldiers moving in lock step with blazing machine guns with the cupola of the Temple of Heaven in the background. However, the scene was recognizably the Taiwan Provincial Historical Museum which had a similar cupola. I went down later and found the angle from which the films had been shot, in my opinion. The films were phony; intended, I believe, to further inflame Chinese people.

I returned from Taiwan and did the best I could to research the events in this broader context. First, I prepared to ask for VOA transcripts through a Freedom of Information Act request. I was informed that the VOA was specifically exempted by law from the Freedom of Information Act. Then I proceeded to create a very lengthy time line of events from English and Chinese national and international reports, reading everything I could find.

Finally, I decided, like some few other observers, notably Carma Hinton, who produced the very powerful revisionist film, *The Gate of Heavenly Peace*[4], that a myth had been created and that the underlying facts presented a much more nuanced view of the Tiananmen events than that with which most of us are familiar.

The Students were Just

None of the foregoing should be taken to mean that I believe that the Chinese government did not blunder enormously in 1989, or that the students or the Beijing residents in the districts surrounding the square (nor the earlier Hungarian patriots) were ever less than heroic. The Chinese government did and yet needs reforms.

Rather, I am arguing that events abroad are easily shaped, both by media attempts to find the most attractive possible story and by misreporting which then creates the desired story, as with the VOA broadcasts. If, however, there were no underlying local issues, no inflamed workers or students, such manipulation would not be possible.

And with time, as we proceed from primitive TV broadcasts to a globalized media world, the velocity and scope of the events increase exponentially. We turn now to Iran, where the political impact of the Internet and Web 2.0 social applications are very clear.[5]

Iran: The Tragic Death of Miss Soltan

The Iranian events have been treated from the beginning via a very broad set of media, unlike previous events discussed above, including interactive Web 2.0 platforms such as blogs, YouTube, and most notably, Twitter.

As the events have continued, again all nuance is being lost and where interpretation is possible, it is the worst possible ones which have become dominant. Like the media, we take as our exemplar here Miss Neda Agha-Soltan. She was an attractive

26 year-old Iranian student who died as a result of a gunshot wound in the street, while apparently observing a demonstration.[6]

Early reports, including a statement from her companion, the music teacher with whom she had just had a lesson, suggest that she had not planned to attend a demonstration. The teacher's car got caught in crowds on the fringes of a demonstration and as the air conditioner was working poorly they got out of the car and walked toward the demonstrations. Statements from her fiancee describe her as rather apolitical.

A shot was fired, though nobody knows where or why or by whom in the early reporting and she died more or less instantly from a wound in the upper chest which penetrated her heart and perhaps a lung as well. The death was captured on video and sent outside the country (including to the VOA) and placed on YouTube where it continues to build audience and to attract politically oriented tributes.[7]

The above truths do not matter as the myth is constructed. Miss Soltan is now the "Voice" of the Iranian demonstrations, an "Angel" fallen from heaven to unite the world in the defense of democracy--or was at least until Michael Jackson died and swept the stories out of the public eye. On the face of it, Miss Soltan is hardly an ideal representative for democracy, being largely apolitical, but what we have learned is that it does not matter. Ten years from now, when we are marched through the commemoration of these events in the media, she will appear in her mythic role, the feminist heroine of Iranian democracy.

Meanwhile, she serves as a focus for anti-Iranian and frankly anti-Muslim forces and even as a tool for the American right to use to lever President Obama into a more activist policy against the Iranian government.[8] And in the usual self-referential media approach, the story becomes not only Miss Soltan's tragic death, but the Twitter storm itself.[9]

The media, having established the story, then fed it. *The New York Times* asked Iranians to send photos of unrest.[10] In London, *The Guardian* asked for protestors' videos and tells us "Shocking pictures are emerging from inside Iran as people caught up in the violence post images on social networking sites. Warning: disturbing content."[11]

It is, of course, almost impossible to now consider evidence contrary to the myth. For example, If I live in Tehran and my neighborhood was peacefully going about its business, not entirely content with the recent elections, but not that bothered either---perhaps much like many Americans after the 2004 elections---what were my chances of getting a photo of a flower market in *The New York Times* or a video of children playing in *The Guardian*?

Having established that an innocent died protesting election results in Iran, we have established, apparently, that the elections were indeed stolen, and by soliciting photos and videos of violence, we establish that the protests are widespread. Now the pressing question becomes, what should we do about it? Need Soltan have died in vain?[12]

As an historian, now I must ask some rather pedantic questions: What should be the standard of evidence to prove the nature of events that, if correct, may well inspire people to take to the streets in Tehran to be killed in something like Tiananmen? Is an anonymous photo enough? Two? Two plus a video? Two photos, two videos and a hundred thousand Tweets?

Now a more difficult question: through whose eyes are we to interpret that evidence? Iranian eyes? American eyes? This leads us to cultural centrism.

Cultural Centrism

Too often, we are quick to condemn others while explaining away useful analogues within our own history and culture which might serve to nuance our outrage. For example, we firmly believe that the Chinese government deliberately shot its students at Tiananmen; but American students at Kent and Jackson State died through unfortunate misunderstandings, or through the actions of frightened or overzealous National Guardsmen or State troopers---men somewhat like those on the streets in Tehran we assume.

We believe now that the Iranian government fixed its election to illicitly perpetuate a despotic regime. But events in Florida in 2004 were, we have agreed to agree, simply a result of confusion or bad, but not deliberate, planning.

Our President patiently lectures the Iranians on international norms. But acts of our troops abroad should not be evaluated by accepted norms, or judged even by local courts, let alone international bodies.

These are all examples of judging global events, many capable of a broad range of interpretations, by our own narrow culturally bound perspective. This can cause serious problems, both for us and for others.

Conclusion

There are a number of problems with misunderstanding or, worse, deliberately misrepresenting events in other countries. First, to do so causes bad policy founded on erroneous assumptions. Surely there is no need to belabor the consequences of our mistaken analysis of the desire of Iraqis to be liberated. As of this writing, major Iraqi political figures are portraying the impending American withdrawal as an Iraqi victory.[13]

Our indignation and avid interest can also mislead other to assume that we will follow up such manifestations with action; that we will put our gold and guns where our Twitters are. This can cause others to take positions that are often fatal, as Attila so impatiently explained to me. So, as some at Tiananmen tragically found out, does deliberately misrepresenting events. Students who had heard that their nemesis Premier Li Peng had been assassinated and that his troops were in rebellion, met instead overwhelming force.

Many journalists have argued that an important consequence of the spread of the Internet has been the demise of newspapers with established bureaus abroad, staffed with skilled and experienced journalists. These evaluated evidence appropriately to the weight of the matters at hand, and even presented contrary evidence. Now we rush to judgment on the basis of Web 2.0 social noise. The Internet can open the world for us more or less instantly, but we have to evaluate the evidence carefully before we rush to judgment.

Endnotes

[1] For an acceptable outline of the rising see the Wikipedia article at: http://en.wikipedia.org/wiki/Hungarian_Revolution_of_1956 Accessed 6/25/09

[2] See Jeffrey Barlow, CYBERJACKED! Again... and Again...at: http://bcis.pacificu.edu/journal/2006/02/edit.php

[3] See the photo at the Wikipedia link above.

[4] See reviews at: http://www.tsquare.tv/film/reviewex.html

[5] As I write, (8 a.m. June 26, 2009) I have just heard via my cell phone reports that there has been a military coup in Tehran. I cannot yet confirm that the reports are true, and unavoidably think of the distorted reports of a Chinese military coup before Tiananmen.

[6] The New York Times maintains a useful archive of their stories on Soltan's death at: http://topics.nytimes.com/topics/reference/timestopics/people/s/neda_agha_soltan/index.html?scp=1-spot&sq=neda%20video&st=cse&scp=5&sq=Soltan&st=cse The archives of The Guardian can be found at: http://www.guardian.co.uk/world/iran

[7] See one such page, containing the video at: http://www.youtube.com/watch?v=OD7UjH9FYis Accessed 6/26/09

[8] See "Obama Weak on Iran," California Rep. Dana Rohrabacher slams president as "cream puff", says U.S. must support Iranian protesters. Posted on June 16th, 2009 by GregC in Podcasts at: http://dateline.radioamerica.org/archives/2799 Accessed 6/26/09 See also: Anne Bayefsky "A Weak American President" Behold Obama on Iran. Forbes.Com, found at: http://www.forbes.com/2009/06/23/obama-iran-press-conference-elections-opinions-contributors-bayefsky.html, 06.23.09, 07:38 PM EDT. Accessed 6/26/09

[9] For an example of the level of discourse provided by such social sites see the reports and discussion collated at The Guardian at: http://www.guardian.co.uk/news/blog/2009/jun/24/iran-crisis Accessed 6/26/09

[10] "The New York Times would like readers in Iran to help us document the post-election unrest in Iran." The New York Times, at: http://submit.nytimes.com/iranian-readers-share-your-election-experience?hp accessed 6/26/09

[11] The Guardian, at: http://www.guardian.co.uk/world/video/2009/jun/16/iran-elections-youtube-twitter Accessed 6/26/09

[12] A search on the text string "soltan died in vain," turns up 3,790 hits, mostly social sites arguing that she need not have died in vain, if we just act. http://www.google.com/search?q=soltan+died+in+vain&ie=utf-8&oe=utf-8&aq=t&rls=org.mozilla:en-US:official&client=firefox-a

[13] See: STEVEN LEE MYERS and MARC SANTORA, Premier Casting U.S. Withdrawal as Iraq Victory, at: http://www.nytimes.com/2009/06/26/world/middleeast/26maliki.html?ref=global-home Accessed 6/26/09

September 2009 - Volume 9, Issue 7

Articles

- **Feature: D. Antonio Cantù** - One-Cloud Schoolhouse: A Primer on the Application of the Cloud Computing Model to K-12 Education
- **Media: Lynda Irons** - Are Studios Seeing Red with Envy or Green with Dollars?
- **Security: Pat McGregor** - What Would You Give to Never Get Another Viagra Ad in Your E-mail?
- **Social Networking: Jenn Hernandez** - Social Media: Man's New Best Friend

Book and Site Reviews

- **Michael Connelly's** *The Scarecrow*
  Review by Jeffrey Barlow
- **Jeffery Deaver's** *The Broken Window: A Lincoln Rhyme Novel*
  Review by Jeffrey Barlow

Editorial

- Peaceful Evolution in China and the World Wide Web: Part I, Two Democracies?

Feature

One-Cloud Schoolhouse: A Primer on the Application of the Cloud Computing Model to K-12 Education

View online at: http://bcis.pacificu.edu/journal/2009/07/article.php?id=99

By D. Antonio Cantù

Bradley University

> All thoughtful men agree that the present aspect of society is portentous of great changes. The only question is, whether they will be for the better or the worse.... For my part, I hold to the former opinion. ...in the belief that the Golden Age lies before us and not behind us, and is not far away.
>
> Edward Bellamy, *Looking Backward*, 1888

At the dawn of the twentieth century, many shared nineteenth-century author Edward Bellamy's belief that socialism would usher in a "golden age" (i.e., a utopian society). A century later, many hold a similar belief that we are on the cusp of a new golden age, however this time the landscape is digital and the catalyst is "cloud computing." The belief in the potential cloud computing holds for unlocking a new golden age in technology is perhaps most evident in the unprecedented amount of money corporations have invested, and promise to invest, in the coming years. [1] Analysts predict that by 2013, cloud computing will comprise 15 percent of the software market and have an annual global market of $95 billion. [2]

All this begs the question, what is *cloud computing*? For educators and researchers, however, another question of tremendous import is whether the cloud computing model--which has been embraced by the business community.--can be applied to K-12 education. The purpose of this article, however, is to provide a primer on the cloud computing model and then, in a subsequent article, to provide a review of the role cloud computing currently plays in K-12 education and to introduce a model for more fully realizing the potential of cloud computing in K-12 teaching and learning.

Michael Sheehan has described the transformation cloud computing has experienced in just the past two years as having gone from being a "newfangled movement" to an "established IT and business strategy." Comparing it to historical periods, Sheehan further defines the progress cloud computing has experienced these past two years as going from being the "New World" in 2007 to a period of "Colonization and Settlement" today. [3]

Another indicator of the amazing growth cloud computing has experienced these past two years is reflected in the graph below, from Google Trends, which charts the growth of "cloud computing" as a search term--from relative obscurity in 2007 to one of the most popular technology search terms today.

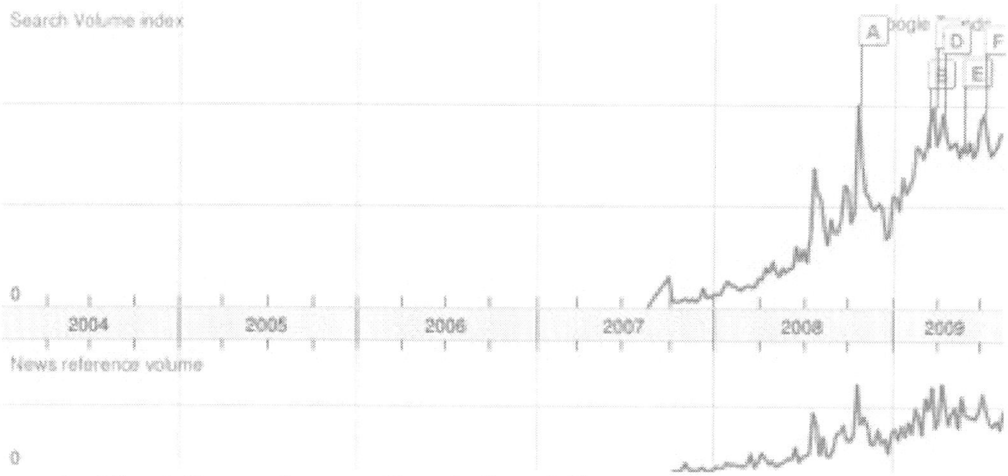

Figure 1 - Cloud Computing as a Google Search Term

Source: Google Trends, "Cloud Computing," generated August 30, 2009.

The Etymological Pursuit of *Cloud Computing*

While there is ample evidence to support the prediction that cloud computing will continue to enjoy exponential growth over the next few years, there is still confusion/disagreement over what constitutes cloud computing. What makes this somewhat ironic is that, in a recent study by the Pew Research Center, 69 percent of Internet users have already engaged in cloud computing - even though many of them have never even heard of the term. [4] The table below identifies the results of a survey conducted by Pew researchers in the Pew Internet and American Life Project.

Cloud Computing Activities *Internet users who do the following online activities (%)*	
Use webmail services such as Hotmail, Gmail, or Yahoo! mail	56%
Store personal photos online	34
Use online applications such as Google Documents or Adobe Photoshop Express	29
Store personal videos online	7
Pay to store computer files online	5
Back up hard drive to an online site	5

Source: Pew Internet & American Life Project April-May 2008 Survey. N=1,553 internet users. Margin of error is ±3%.

Figure 2 - Pew Research Center Survey, 2008

With respect to the definition of cloud computing there appears to be only one area of agreement, that being there is no one universally accepted definition of cloud computing. What follows are but a few examples of some of the more colorful descriptions of the seemingly enigmatic nature of cloud computing, which makes it an elusive etymological target:

> In the hubbub, the term cloud computing is an ever expanding buzzword. There are private clouds and public clouds and hybrid clouds. Some people use 'clouds' as a synonym for virtualization - while others clearly disagree with this use. [5]

> Cloud computing is all the rage.... The problem is that (as with Web 2.0) everyone seems to have a different definition. As a metaphor for the Internet, 'the cloud' is a familiar cliche, but when combined with 'computing,' the meaning gets bigger and fuzzier. [6]

> Is there anyone not in the cloud? Cloud computing is the buzzword du jour and everyone--Google, Salesforce.com, Microsoft and Amazon--is trying to get into the act. The problem: It will be another year--2009--before companies use cloud computing services extensively. In the meantime, folks will have to define and sort out a lot of mumbo jumbo about the cloud. [7]

> Cartoonists have gotten plenty of mileage out of the information superhighway, it's true. But when it comes to drawing the Internet, the icon of choice...is a cloud.... For one thing, clouds are easy to draw. There's no doubt about this. If you've ever tried mapping cyberspace in a hurry...you know the cloud's advantage. Plus, there's another, subtle advantage to the cloud: You can use it to obscure what you don't know. [8]

Many of those daring enough to enter the abyss and attempt to define cloud computing conjure up the spirit of Charles Darwin. Often the result is either too narrowly defining cloud computing as simply "the next step in the evolution of software-as-a-service (SaaS)"[9] or overstating its "evolutionary effect" on business and IT. [10] Perhaps the most eloquent invocation of Darwinian theory in describing the seminal historical context in which cloud computing has entered the digital arena was put forth by Andy Cooley in the Afterword of Richard Katz's book *The Tower and the Cloud: Higher Education in the Age of Cloud Computing*, as follows:

> Charles Darwin observed that it's not the strongest of the species that survive, nor the most intelligent, but those most adaptive to change. For humankind, the pace of change has been accelerating, and never as rapidly as in the past century. One hundred years ago, our body of knowledge doubled only once every century. Today, our body of knowledge doubles every few years. In our digitized, microchipped world there is virtually no subject that cannot be Googled, downloaded, and consumed. In higher education the challenge is clear. How can we analyze and apply that information in ways that will help our learning institutions thrive? How do we turn that ubiquitous cloud of information into real knowledge. [11]

Within this context, however, the task of defining cloud computing has been made considerably easier recently by the publication of definitions by two well-known and widely-respected organizations: the University of California at Berkeley and The New Media Consortium.

The first definition, often referred to as the "Berkeley definition," appeared in the University of California at Berkeley technical report *Above the Clouds: A Berkeley View of Cloud Computing*, published in February 2009. In the report, members of the Department of Electrical Engineering and Computer Sciences define cloud computing as follows:

> Cloud Computing refers to both the applications delivered as services over the Internet and the hardware and systems software in the datacenters that provide those services. The services themselves have long been referred to as *Software as a Service (SaaS)*. The datacenter hardware and software is what we will call a *Cloud*. When a Cloud is made available in a pay-as-you-go manner to the general public, we call it a *Public Cloud*; the service being sold is *Utility Computing*. We use the term *Private Cloud* to refer to internal datacenters of a business or other organization, not made available to the general public. Thus, Cloud Computing is the sum of SaaS and Utility Computing, but does not include Private Clouds. People can be users or providers of SaaS, or users or providers of Utility Computing. [12]

The second definition appeared earlier this year in *The 2009 Horizon Report*, which is published by The New Media Consortium in collaboration with EDUCAUSE. In the report, cloud computing is defined as follows:

The emergence of very large "data farms" -- specialized data centers that host thousands of servers -- has created a surplus of computing resources that has come to be called the cloud. Growing out of research in grid computing, cloud computing transforms once-expensive resources like disk storage and processing cycles into a readily available, cheap commodity. Development platforms layered onto the cloud infrastructure enable thin-client, web-based applications for image editing, word processing, social networking, and media creation. Many of us use the cloud, or cloud-based applications, without even being aware of it. [13]

From Mainframe Computing to Cloud Computing

As one can glean from the definitions above, computing has come a long way since mainframe computing entered the stage in the 1940s, with the introduction of Mark I, ENIAC, and Manchester's Baby. [14] Fast-forward six decades and we find ourselves again in the midst of another sea change in computing with the emergence of cloud computing. [15] In fact, the term cloud computing can even trace its origins back to the late twentieth century. The figure below is reported to be one of the earliest examples of the use of the term or metaphor cloud computing in a public forum; in this case, by two researchers from the Massachusetts Institute of Technology at a 1996 workshop sponsored by the Kennedy School of Government at Harvard University--

later included in a book published the next year, edited by Brian Kahin and James Keller, entitled *Coordination of the Internet*. [16]

Figure 3 - Early Introduction of the Term/Metaphor Cloud Computing, 1996

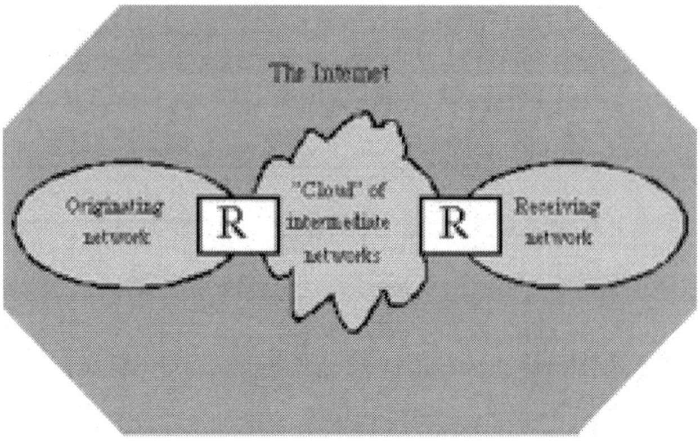

Source: Sharon Eisner Gillett, and Mitchell Kapor, "The Self-governing Internet: Coordination by Design," Paper presented at the "Coordination and Administration of the Internet Workshop," Harvard University, September 1996. Available at http://ccs.mit.edu/papers/CCSWP197/CCSWP197.html.

The Cloud Computing Model

The economic potential of cloud computing is only beginning to be realized by business and industry, while in education, cloud computing is still in an embryonic stage of development and utilization. In the K-12 education community, this is further complicated by the fact that many overtures by business and/or industry to education are made to colleges and universities, perhaps in a belief that the trickle-down theory can be applied to cloud computing in K-16 education. [17]

To more fully understand the economic impact and potential of cloud computing, it is important to fully understand the components of the cloud computing model. The chart below, for example, illustrates not only the growing economic importance of cloud computing--which is forecasted to be a $42 billion dollar business in just a few short years--but also the multifaceted nature of the cloud computing model.

Figure 4 - Worldwide Cloud Computing Spending by Type, 2012 Forecast

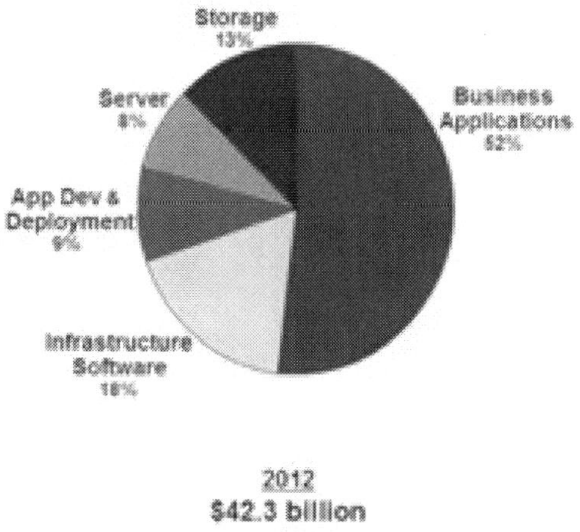

Source: James Maquire, Jeff Vance, and Cynthia Harvey, "85 Cloud Computing Vendors Shaping the Emerging Cloud," Datamation, August 25, 2009. Available at http://itmanagement.earthweb.com/netsys/article.php/3835941/85-Cloud-Computing-Vendors-Shaping-the-Emerging-Cloud.htm.

As the pie chart above illustrates, there are myriad forms of cloud computing, most of which can be placed in three broadly defined categories, as follows:

1. ***Cloud Application or Cloud Software as a Service (SaaS)*** - the most restrictive category of cloud computing in which applications, which typically serve a single function (e.g., Gmail, Quicken), are made accessible to users through a Web browser.

Cloud Platform or Cloud Platform as a Service (PaaS) - there is increased control and flexibility with this category of cloud computing in which the user can build and deploy applications (e.g., Google App Engine) that are supported by the cloud.

Cloud Infrastructure or Cloud Infrastructure as a Service (IaaS) - even greater control is allowed for with this category of cloud computing in which users are provided sheer computing resources (e.g., Amazon EC2), and can deploy and operate arbitrary software, including operating systems. [18]

A visual heuristic for this cloud computing model was developed by Michael Sheehan in 2008 to help differentiate the three major categories of cloud offerings, as he defines them, as well as illustrate their hierarchical relationship (see figure below). [19]

Figure 5 - Michael Sheehan's Cloud Pyramid, 2008

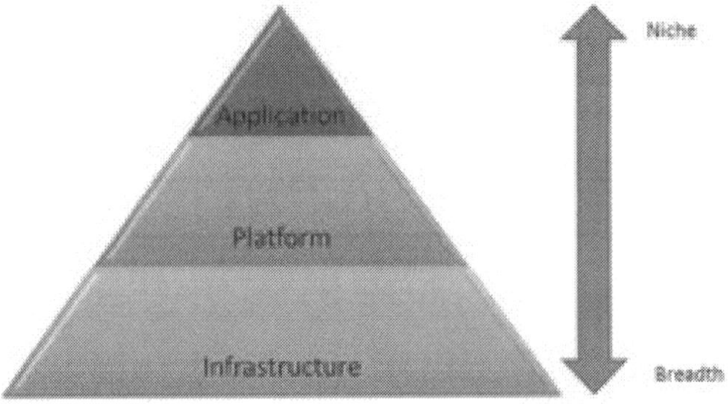

Source: Michael Sheehan, "Cloud Computing Expo: Introducing the Cloud Pyramid," *Cloud Computing Journal*, August 21, 2008. Available at http://cloudcomputing.sys-con.com/node/609938.

Cloud Computing in K-12 Education

While cloud computing is already having a significant impact on society, business, and industry, it has not reached nearly the same level of potential in K-12 education. This is not to say examples of cloud computing can't be found in elementary and secondary schools. On the contrary, in the last year we have seen more and more schools take advantage of the array of services available in cloud computing, however the bulk of these are from one category: cloud application (e.g., email, word processing, media editing). [20] Examples of the integration of cloud platform and cloud infrastructure into K-12 education are just beginning to emerge, as noted in this year's Horizon Report. These are the categories of cloud computing that appear to hold the most potential for truly enhancing K-12 teaching and learning in the future.

Experience has shown that after school districts make the leap to cloud computing, it opens the door to even greater innovation, such as adopting netbooks or virtual computers, which are more cost-effective and have a much smaller footprint. [21] A recent example of this is the partnership formed between SIMtone Corporation and Frank Porter Graham Elementary School in Chapel Hill, North Carolina. The resulting benefits from this partnership go far beyond the cloud-based educational content and virtual desktop computers, as the press release last fall announcing the partnership reveals:

> **Durham, NC (October 6, 2008)** - SIMtone Corporation, a privately held company delivering the next cloud computing paradigm, today announced that a North Carolina school is piloting its cloud computing platform to deliver low-cost, virtual desktops to hundreds of students and faculty. The pilot is part

of the ***SIMtone Education Thunder Program*** which aims to help close the digital divide and provide access to full PCs in the cloud to the estimated five billion people who cannot afford it, without requiring them to own a computer. The program educational content is provided by the U.S. Fund for UNICEF (USF), and is open to technology and connectivity sponsors worldwide.

Frank Porter Graham Elementary School in Chapel Hill, North Carolina will use SIMtone's Universal Cloud Computing products to provide approximately 600 students and faculty with "PCs in the Cloud" usable everywhere without a computer....

"Our school wants to equip each student with the most advanced computing environment necessary today to effectively study, learn and access all the digital courseware and teaching tools available. Asking each student to purchase and maintain their own PC is impossible, just as it is impossible for the school to ensure each student's PC is up to date and has all the latest courseware. SIMtone eliminates all these complexities and costs, and allows our school to deliver to each student a real 'PC in the Cloud,' fully maintained by the school itself, that is always available to our students on-demand and on-the-fly, in class, in the library and at home, without requiring them to purchase yet another PC," said Shelia Burnette, Principal of the Frank Porter Graham School.

"Through TeachUNICEF, we are empowering students to be active global citizens in learning about UNICEF's mission to do whatever it takes to save and improves children's lives worldwide. Therefore, we are quite excited about this opportunity to take the lead in accelerating the closure of the digital divide," said Caryl Stern, President and CEO of the U.S. Fund for UNICEF. "The low-cost and ubiquitous access to real PCs enabled by SIMtone allows us to reach students with our education material on an unprecedented scale and offer them programs that grow with them and stay with them throughout their entire curricula. It's their PC for life, always on, always available, everywhere they are."[22]

This partnership represents one of many ways in which cloud computing can enhance the K-12 teaching and learning process. Even in the absence of grant- or corporate-funded initiatives, school district superintendents are turning to cloud computing, particularly during tough economic times, for more efficacious ways in which to integrate technology not only into the teaching and learning process, but also into the day-to-day operations of the school. Stephen White, Solutions Manager for Cloud Computing at Hewlett Packard, has identified five such areas in which school administrators are beginning to realize the economic benefits of cloud computing:

1. Data Backup - storing student records, financial data, etc., in cloud-based locations.

Mass Notification - adopting systems (e.g., SchoolMessenger) for emergency notification.
Netbooks and Desktops - purchasing "cloud computing laptops" for students.
Surveillance - connecting surveillance cameras to the Internet for remote viewing.
Digital File Storage, Email, and Web Sites - fully hosted in cloud-based locations. [23]

Conclusion

There is no denying that the swing of the technology pendulum from mainframe computing to cloud computing has changed not only the way in which we conduct business, but also how students learn in elementary and secondary schools. Billions of dollars have already been invested in cloud computing and even more is being planned for the future. The cloud computing model is one that serves to guide and shape the strategic plan and IT budget of many corporations. Cloud computing also holds tremendous promise for K-12 education, if modified and fully adopted. For this to occur, however, school administrators and teachers--as well as educational researchers and teacher educators--need to develop a better understanding of the cloud computing model and learn how to adapt it to their school environment. Only then, can elementary and secondary schools begin to truly realize the benefits of cloud computing.

Endnotes

[1] Bernard Golden, "Cloud Computing: 'Be Prepared'," *EDUCAUSE Review* 44, no. 4 (July/August 2009): 64-65.

[2] Rachael King, "How Cloud Computing is Changing the World," *Business Week* (August 4, 2008). Available at http://www.businessweek.com/print/technology/content/aug2008/tc2008082_445669.htm.

[3] Michael Sheehan, "The Past, Present, and Future of The Cloud," *Cloud Computing Journal*, December 8, 2008. Available at http://cloudcomputing.sys-con.com/node/767779.

[4] John Horrigan, "Use of Cloud Computing Applications and Services," *Pew Internet and American Life Project Report* (September 2008): 1. Available at http://www.pewinternet.org/Reports/2008/Use-of-Cloud-Computing-Applications-and-Services.aspx.

[5] James Maquire, Jeff Vance, and Cynthia Harvey, "85 Cloud Computing Vendors Shaping the Emerging Cloud," *Datamation*, August 25, 2009. Available at http://itmanagement.earthweb.com/netsys/article.php/3835941/85-Cloud-Computing-Vendors-Shaping-the-Emerging-Cloud.htm.

[6] Eric Knorr and Galen Gruman, "What Cloud Computing Really Means," *InfoWorld*, April 7, 2008. Available at http://www.infoworld.com/print/34031.

[7] Larry Dignan, "Behind the Myths of Cloud Computing," *Seeking Alpha*, April 8, 2008. Available at http://seekingalpha.com/article/71589-behind-the-myths-of-cloud-computing.

[8] Although this was not directly in reference to cloud computing, the authors' evaluation of the cloud metaphor makes it both timeless and germane to the discussion. Jessie Holliday Scanton and Brad Wieners, "Behind the Myths of Cloud Computing," *Seeking Alpha*, July 9, 1999. Available at http://www.thestandard.com/article/0,1902,5466,00.html.

[9] "Cloud Computing: The Evolution of Software-as-a-Service," *Knowledge @ W.P. Carey*, June 4, 2008. Available at http://knowledge.wpcarey.asu.edu/article.cfm?articleid=1614#.

[10] Amy Schurr, "Keep an Eye on Cloud Computing," *Network World*, July 8, 2008. Available at http://www.networkworld.com/newsletters/itlead/2008/070708itlead1.html.

[11] Andy Cooley, "Afterword," in Richard N. Katz, ed., *The Tower and the Cloud: Higher Education in the Age of Cloud Computing* (Washington, DC: EDUCAUSE, 2008), 263. Available at http://www.educause.edu/thetowerandthecloud.

[12] Michael Armbrust et al., *Above the Clouds: A Berkeley View of Cloud Computing*, Technical Report UCB/EECS-2009-28 (Berkeley: University of California at Berkeley, 2009), 1. Available at http://www.eecs.berkeley.edu/Pubs/TechRpts/2009/EECS-2009-28.pdf.

[13] Larry Johnson, Alan Levine, and Rachel Smith, *The 2009 Horizon Report* (Austin, TX: The New Media Consortium, 2009), 11. Available at http://www.nmc.org/pdf/2009-Horizon-Report.pdf.

[14] Richard N. Katz, "The Gathering Cloud: Is This the End of the Middle?," in Richard N. Katz, ed., *The Tower and the Cloud: Higher Education in the Age of Cloud Computing* (Washington, DC: EDUCAUSE, 2008), 7. Available at http://www.educause.edu/thetowerandthecloud.

[15] Rachael King, "How Cloud Computing is Changing the World," *Business Week* (August 4, 2008). Available at http://www.businessweek.com/print/technology/content/aug2008/tc2008082_445669.htm.

[16] John Willis, "Who Coined the Phrase Cloud Computing?" IT Management and Cloud Blog, December 31, 2008. Available at http://www.johnmwillis.com/cloud-computing/who-coined-the-phrase-cloud-computing/.

[17] Paul T. Jaeger et al., "Where is the Cloud? Geography, Economics, Environment, and Jurisdiction in Cloud Computing," *First Monday* 14, no. 5 (May 4, 2009).

Available at
http://www.uic.edu/htbin/cgiwrap/bin/ojs/index.php/fm/article/view/2456/2171.

[18] Peter Mell and Tim Grance, "Draft NIST Working Definition of Cloud Computing" (August 19, 2009). Available at http://csrc.nist.gov/groups/SNS/cloud-computing/cloud-def-v15.doc; Michael Sheehan, "Cloud Computing Expo: Introducing the Cloud Pyramid," *Cloud Computing Journal*, August 21, 2008. Available at http://cloudcomputing.sys-con.com/node/609938; Larry Johnson, Alan Levine, and Rachel Smith, *The 2009 Horizon Report* (Austin, TX: The New Media Consortium, 2009). Available at http://www.nmc.org/pdf/2009-Horizon-Report.pdf.

[19] Michael Sheehan, "Cloud Computing Expo: Introducing the Cloud Pyramid," *Cloud Computing Journal*, August 21, 2008. Available at http://cloudcomputing.sys-con.com/node/609938.

[20] Larry Johnson, Alan Levine, and Rachel Smith, *The 2009 Horizon Report* (Austin, TX: The New Media Consortium, 2009), 12. Available at http://www.nmc.org/pdf/2009-Horizon-Report.pdf.

[21] Ibid; Jeffrey Hastings, "Don't Worry, Be Scrappy," *School Library Journal* 55, no. 3 (March 2009), 35.

[22] Christopher Dawson, "The Cloud Finally Comes to Education," *ZDNet Education*, October 6, 2008. Available at http://education.zdnet.com/?p=1883: "North Carolina School Embraces SIMtone to Deliver Virtual Desktops to 600 Students" Press Release, October 6, 2008. Available at http://www.simtone.net/pressreleases_10-06-08.htm.

[23] Kurt O. Dyrli, "The Start of a Tech Revolution," *District Administration* (May 2009), 31.

Media

Are Studios Seeing Red with Envy or Green with Dollars?

View online at: http://bcis.pacificu.edu/journal/2009/07/article.php?id=100

By Lynda Irons

Though economic conditions may appear to be slightly improving, Hollywood motion picture studios nervously gaze into their crystal balls to determine how their futures will look in light of Blockbuster's recent announcement that their same-store DVD sales have been dropping substantially the past few quarters, and given Redbox' and Netflix' increasing dominance in the DVD-rental markets. Seemingly, it would appear that the studios would be gaining a revenue stream that should make them very positive about their sustainability in the entertainment industry. However, even though box office receipts are up 7.2 percent this time last year [1], consumers are changing their viewing habits at home. They are not buying DVDs but renting them, as evidenced by Redbox and Netflix.

Several studios recognize that DVD sales are going to continue to be unstable. "We can no longer afford to give away money when we can't be sure what the DVD sales are going to be," says Sony Studio Chief Michael Lynton [2]. And Walt Disney's CEO Robert A. Iger concurs that "Hollywood can no longer count on a cash cow that has yielded billions in profits." [3] While the economy is likely a factor, it's also clear "that audiences are bypassing DVDs because they have a range of other options, from watching movies and TV shows online to playing video games." [4] According to recent report on CBSNews.com, "Warner Brothers, the largest distributor of DVDs in the United States, says sales are down 4 percent for the year. Since global DVD sales can now account for as much of 70 percent of revenue for a new film, any industry-wide decline is cause for alarm." [5]

Additionally, all is not well between the studios and particularly Redbox. In fact, lawsuits have been filed by each against the other. What's at stake? The studios are "concerned that Redbox's $1-per-night rentals are undercutting more lucrative rentals from other services and DVD sales." [6] These studios are concerned that in view of global declines in DVD sales, they can no longer continue to sustain losses without looking toward other sources of increased revenues; as a result, studios want a bigger piece of that lucrative rental/Internet pie.

Redbox has approximately 15,000 kiosks and are planning to increase its market to over 22,000 locations by the end of the year.[7] Consumers are attracted by low-cost rentals on recently released films with no late fees. As such, Redbox has seen its revenues increase at least 110 percent in the last quarter; Netflix, 20 percent. However, Warner Brothers has recently announced that they, like Twentieth Century Fox and Universal Studios before them, will delay releasing films to Redbox until 28 days after they go on sale. [8] Warner Brothers continued this trend by announcing that they would "impose the same the same restriction on Netflix and other DVD-by-mail subscription providers unless they agreed to "a day-and-date revenue sharing option." [9] Wikipedia defines revenue sharing as "In business, revenue sharing refers to the sharing of profits and losses among different groups." [10] However, such a revenue sharing movement could have negative impacts on the profitability of both Netflix and Redbox. Redbox argues that Warner's move is detrimental to consumers who wish to view recently released DVDs in a timely manner.

In a note to investors, William Blair analyst Ralph Schackart raised concerns that Warner's recent announcement "could have a negative impact on Netflix." In one case, Mr. Schackart said, Warner could force less favorable terms, including "longer periods of limited access to new release titles and higher prices." [11] Netflix has seen its subscriber base increase from 4.1 million in 2005 to over 9.4 million in 2008, representing over 124 percent. Its revenue has increased from $682 million in 2005 to over $1.3 billion in 2008, a 100 percent increase. [12] Reed Hastings, Chief Executive Officer, President, and Co-founder, attributes these increases to their "core DVD-by-mail offerings" and their "growing Internet streaming, contributing to their faster subscriber growth and lower subscription acquisition costs."

Even as Redbox has filed a lawsuit against Warner Brothers (and previously against Fox and Universal) protesting the 28-day delay, they have signed a 5-year agreement with Lionsgate. "The multi-year agreement with Lionsgate underscores our commitment to creating winning relationships for our customers and studio partners," said Mitch Lowe, President, Redbox. [13]

Paramount is considering negotiating with Redbox, and Lowe estimates that it will get more than "20 percent of the shelf space in the kiosks." Even if the rest of studios commit to Redbox, there are just 700 slots in each kiosk. Given the space guaranteed to a previously negotiated agreement with Sony and the recent Lionsgate arrangement, that means only about 50 percent of the approximately 700 slots in each kiosk will be available to the rest of Hollywood, which includes three of the most dominant studios. [14]

Just like VHS gave way to DVD (interestingly enough, the Blu-Ray market has yet to really take off), DVDs are giving way to alternative viewing options. This means the studios have to face yet another industrial upheaval in the wake of changing consumer preferences.

Endnotes

[1] http://boxofficemojo.com/yearly/?view2=ytdcompare&view=releasedate&p=.htm

[2] http://www.businessweek.com/magazine/content/09_09/b4121056770437.htm

[3] ibid

[4] ibid

[5] http://www.cbsnews.com/stories/2008/11/21/paidcontent/main4623706.shtml

[6] http://www.latimes.com/business/la-fi-ct-warner14-2009aug14,0,1452104.story

[7] http://www.latimes.com/business/la-fi-ct-warner14-2009aug14,0,1452104.story

[8] ibid

[9] Ibid

[10] http://en.wikipedia.org/wiki/Revenue_sharing

[11] http://www.crainsnewyork.com/article/20090817/FREE/908179995

[12] http://www.shareholder.com/visitors/dynamicdoc/document.cfm?documentid=2609&companyid=NFLX&page=1&pin=&language=EN&resizethree=yes&scale=1

[13] Redbox and Lionsgate Sign Multi-Year Distribution Agreement." *PR Newswire* (August 12, 2009): NA. *Communications and Mass Media Collection*. Gale. PACIFIC UNIV. 30 Aug. 2009 http://find.galegroup.com.proxy.lib.pacificu.edu:2048/gtx/start.do?prodId=PPCM.

[14] http://www.latimes.com/business/la-fi-ct-redbox26-2009aug26,0,6310965.story

Security

What Would You Give to Never Get Another Viagra Ad in Your E-mail?

View online at: http://bcis.pacificu.edu/journal/2009/07/article.php?id=104

By Pat McGregor

> *Editor's note: Many readers might well ignore Pat's notes; this would be a mistake as they carry a great deal of information for the security conscious among us....*

Unless you're in the market for male enhancement nostrums (in which case it would be better to consult your doctor), you know that getting rid of all the unwanted pharmaceutical advertisements, phishing attempts [1], and other email annoyances is almost impossible without a lot of hassle [2]. Some of this email comes to you (and everyone else) on a random attempt by a spammer to find valid addresses (which is why you *never* answer the things). Some comes because a spammer bought a random list of email addresses that includes yours. But a significant number are sent from marketers who have gotten your email from another agency, a business that has used your activities on the web to profile you. They then sell your email to marketers who want to *target* their advertising to people in your *demographic*.

A *demographic* is a set of characteristics you have in common with many other people. For example, I am female, in the 50-60 age range, have no children under 18, have cats, own one car, am self-employed, own a house, graduated from college, and am a registered voter in a strongly Republican county in Northern California. Because of those characteristics, which matched the kind of voter predicted in the 2008 elections to vote for Mr. McCain, I got a lot of mail, email, and phone calls from his campaign soliciting my vote, or asking my opinion on a number of issues critical to the election.

I also get a lot of mail tempting me with life insurance plans, Medicare Part B plans, annuities, retirement condominium communities, over-the-counter estrogen replacement drugs (as chances are good I am pre-, post-, or menopausal), and equity loans. I seldom get junior and teen style clothing catalogues, baby food samples, daycare, or rock climbing facility ads.

I get a certain kind of ad because I am in those marketers' *target market*.[3] Those who figure I will buy what they sell contact me; those who are looking for a different audience neither send me much email nor kill trees by sending me paper mail.

Targeting is at the heart of the current debate over behavioral tracking. Some people see it as the most evil of the current privacy invasion threats, while others see it as a way to tailor what you see so that marketers don't waste their money showing you ads, sending you email, or (even more expensive), sending you paper mail.

Take a simple example. You are on Google, looking up "women's shelters." Perhaps you are like me, and want to contribute business wear so that those women who have nothing will have interview clothes to look for a new job. [4] Bingo! Up pops The Women's Resource Center, here in San Diego [5].

Hang on a minute! Didn't I just say that I am a registered voter up in Northern California? Why are they showing me shelters in San Diego (the opposite end of the state)?

Because Google thinks I am in San Diego. Why? It's not hard: First of all, I am using an Internet IP address is owned by a provider in the San Diego area. Although I might have a secure tunnel from another location into a connection in San Diego, the adds are good that I am sitting in front of my laptop somewhere in San Diego county. This is the easiest way for any interactive service to make a guess about where you are physically located.

Next, in previous sessions on Google, I have looked up the US Postal service to forward my mail here (sets a cookie), looked for a restaurant in Carlsbad to meet a friend for dinner (sets a cookie), and looked on the AMC theaters website for movies in the Petco Park area (sets a cookie). (No slam on any of those three services. But as I typed in the zip code in a box on an unencrypted page for the last two, those zip codes are stored in the history of my browser.)

By checking those three cookies on my machine, combined with my IP address, Google's software takes an educated guess that I am in San Diego, and based on their experience with billions of searches, gives me results that are most likely to match what I am looking for. If I happen to have a *gmail* account in which my temporary physical address is stored, that improves the likelihood that their guess is correct.

I have been *profiled* using *behavioral tracking.* As I said above, opinions are not only mixed on this issue, but generally at the far ends of the spectrum. In the US Government, the Federal Trade Commission (FTC) strongly opposes it and the Office of Management and Budget (OMB) wants to use it on Federal web sites.

Recent testimony before Congress by Jeff Chester, Executive Director for the Center for Digital Democracy (CDD) outlines what they see as the process of tracking. [6] He defines it this way:

> **Powerful techniques of data collection, analysis, consumer profiling** and tracking, interactive ad creation and targeting have emerged across the online venues Americans increasingly rely on for news, information, entertainment, health, and financial services. Whether using a search engine, watching an online video, creating content on a social network, receiving an email, or playing an interactive video game, we are being digitally shadowed online. Our travels through the digital media are being monitored, and digital dossiers on us are being created and even bought and sold.

Mr. Chester goes on to outline in his testimony all the ways that he and his organization believe behavioral tracking hurts the privacy of individuals.

Should I care?

That is the issue: is this collection of information, by parties known or unknown to us, a risk to our right to privacy? Taken as a whole -- all the data collected by all the websites who do tracking, and accumulated ... somewhere -- is that enough information to identify us and link our web wanderings to us as individuals? Will it be used to help us or hurt us? Will the government get control of this information and use it to weed out terrorists -- possibly catching good guys by mistake?

Do we have control over this information? Do we need to?□□These are the core questions in the ongoing controversy.

Let's examine the various points of view on this issue -- and there are not just two sides. For various reasons, different organizations and types of people line up for the battle, and those reasons generally divide them into three camps: those who think it's a great thing in all its aspects, those who see it as an active threat to consumers; and those who see the value, if controlled.

With apologies to Sergio Leone [7], let's examine these viewpoints in roughly three groups: Good, Bad, and Maybe Not Ugly.

The Good

Marketers are in the business to sell goods or services and make a profit. Marketing dollars wasted on people who don't want the product just lower the profitability of the company. If I have a self-published book, I want to produce it at the lowest possible cost for the right quality paper, printing, and binding for my audience. I want to distribute it into regions where people will want to empty the shelves buying it, and I want that distribution to be as inexpensive as possible while still being effective. And I want every dime I spend on advertising and marketing to go to someone who is more likely to by my book than not. To do that, I need to hire someone who can scope out the target market for my material, where they live, what their demographics are, and deliver the advertising right in front of them in a way that makes them want to go and buy my book.

Advertising and on-line marketing companies think that behavioral tracking lets them target my ads more effectively, allowing me to spend my money on ads displayed to people who will really be interested. I'm happier, because I'm making money, thus I'm likely to spend more to sell more, and use the company that's helped me so much. Then *they* are happy because their profit margins go up.

The Interactive Advertising Bureau (IAB) [8] is a trade organization for media and technology companies. Their approximately 400 members are accountable for selling 86% of online advertising in the United States. Like other business associations, the IAB's goals are to promote the growth of the interactive advertising marketplace, to move a larger amount of marketing dollars to interactive advertising, and correspondingly increase the share of marketing dollars their members receive.

According to the *Economic Value of the Advertising-Supported Internet Ecosystem*, a study issued by the IAB in June 2009:

> Interactive advertising is responsible for $300 billion of economic activity in the U.S. <... The advertising-supported Internet represents 2.1% of the total U.S. gross domestic product (GDP). It directly employs more than 1.2 million Americans with above-average wages in jobs that did not exist two decades ago, and another 1.9 million people work to support those with directly Internet-related jobs. A total of 3.1 million Americans are employed thanks to the interactive ecosystem. These are the key findings of the first-ever research to analyze the economic importance, as well as the social benefits, of the Internet. [9]

Since interactive marketing is such a large part of the business of the Internet, according to these associations, anything that prevents advertisers from delivering their content advantageously will have a serious impact on the economy as a whole.

And, since the Federal and States governments are busy working on laws to restrict methodology used to target ads, interactive marketers have built a self-regulatory framework of seven Principles. [10] Those who sign up to abide by this framework will be protecting consumers, and, they propose, no strict regulation governing this technology will be necessary.

(This is a very common practice in the United States. Since our founding, our business community has claimed to operate under "laissez-faire," an economic doctrine that opposes government regulation. [11] This doctrine holds that government regulation of any sort (minimum wage, duties, tariffs, and other trade restrictions) is interference in commerce beyond the minimum necessary for a free-enterprise system to work. When legislative pressure begins the process of creating government regulation, related industries will band together to create rules for "self-regulation." The next step in the process, usually, is for interested parties and legislators to hammer out legislation that is tight enough to satisfy the constituents and yet not tight enough to strangle business. As in many compromise positions, no-one gets exactly what they want.)

The Seven Principles document [12] describes its scope tightly:

> The Principles [13] apply to online behavioral advertising, defined as the collection of data online from a particular computer or device regarding Web viewing behaviors over time and across non-affiliate Web sites for the purpose of using such data to predict user preferences or interests to deliver advertising to that computer or device based on the preferences or interests inferred from such Web viewing behaviors. The Principles do not apply to a Web site's collection of viewing behavior solely for its own uses. Contextual advertising also is not covered by the Principles as it delivers advertisements based on the content of a Web page, a search query, or a user's contemporaneous behavior on the Web site.

The principles do not cover, for instance, any data the web site captures for its own analysis, any ads triggered by keywords in searches or content of the web site, or anything the user might do at the website. It only applies to data the tracking software can collect from the user's machine, (or PDA, or iPhone, etc.) such as cookies and other information that can be used to analyze the user's web usage patterns.

One developer [14] in the industry describes current technology for tracking this way:

Some of behavioral marketing is demographically based. Some of the newest on the Internet is based upon actual behaviors - they don't know WHO you are, really: but they know your DNS server is in St Louis, you read The New York Times and the Manchester Guardian online, and you clicked through on an ad for a sports car. Best, next time you visit NYT and MG, that they show you ads for Fords or Sports Cars, and not hot tubs and digital cameras.

From this information, such as the history of the user stored in the browser, the tracking and profiling software can see that the user has been going from, say, one camping supply store to another, and has been searching for camping cots. If one of the marketing clients sells camping cots, closed cell foam camping pads, or really effective bug repellant, the marketing company will supply an ad on the page the consumer is looking at for that retailer.

This is good, because the interactive marketing company isn't showing ads to our adventurous camper for luxurious spa services or flat screen plasma HDTV. The marketing company is making the best use of advertising dollars by aiming ads at the right target.

Two important factors, say the marketing community, is that they only collect anonymous, non-identifying information, notify every consumer using the sites and give them a chance to opt out of receiving ads, and that they actively monitor the content on pages where their ads appear, to help protect against associating branded advertising with inappropriate content.

The Bad

That claim, that marketers only collect anonymous, non-identifying information, is what the opponents are worried about. Or, rather, that they collect information about us and we don't know what they have or how it is being used: "Following me online, with behavioral tracking, seems a little "stalkerazi" to me. I don't care for it, and never have. This is especially true when, even if it is done well, it is done surreptitiously. Put your cards on the table, darnit." (Anonymous) [14]

Some adversaries object both to the fact that the collection of data is invisible, and also that the legal controls on the use of the collected data are inadequate. The Electronic Frontier Foundation (EFF) [15], long an activist organization protecting rights guaranteed by the constitution, describes the problems:

New technologies are radically advancing our freedoms, but they are also enabling unparalleled invasions of privacy.

> Your cell phone helps you keep in touch with friends and families, but it also makes it easier for the feds to track your location.
>
> Your Web searches about sensitive medical information might seem secret, known only to you and search engines like Google. But by logging your online activities, these companies are creating a honeypot [16] of personal information, potentially available to any party wielding a subpoena. EFF, 2009 [17]

The FTC, as we mentioned earlier, has gone on record strongly opposing the use of tracking unless consumers have transparency into and have actively given permission for the collection and collation of data to occur. In addition, that active consent must cover not only personal information but that privacy protections [18] should cover any "data that reasonably can be associated with a particular consumer or computer or other device."

One of the biggest problems with behavioral tracking is not just that an advertising agency sees and collates the data, but that ISPs (the service provider that Internet connections come through) may also be collecting the data on their customers and not just using it for their own benefit. When an ISP take statistics on web hits and click-throughs, as well as peak usage periods and other items, they can improve service for all subscribers. If they sell that data to *anyone* without direct consumer consent, according to opponents of tracking, they are threatening the privacy and security of those subscribers.

If, for example, "Big Cable Network," sells its database on customer behavior and movement to "Big Grocery Chain," and the grocery chain can combine the data on what consumers are looking at with their own loyalty card database, the grocery chain could potentially use that data to modify the specials they run in certain geographic areas. If they do filtering on the data from the cable company they might discover that a 50-60 year old female registered voter in Northern California who owns a home, one car, and has no children under 18 is watching a lot of shows on the SyFy channel between 6 and 10 PM every evening. Because the information can be obtained from the Cable company, they might find that the SyFy channel is advertising a lot of ads for "Crunchy Fiber Wheat Squares" and "Absolutely NoChol Margarine" during that time period. If they similarly filter their grocery loyalty card database and find they have a customer who matches that profile and eats a lot of high-fiber, low cholesterol foods, "Big Grocery" could sell coupon space to either the same products or a competitor.

The next time that woman (does she sound familiar? [19]) goes shopping, the little coupon printer that comes with the cash register tape will spit out some coupons for those foods to her. (Granted, they could do the same thing simply from her shopping record alone. But if her record shows she's been buying a competitor's brand, the grocery chain can use this tracking info, possibly combined with a lot of other data on customers who also watch SyFy and eat those foods, to convince the brands to buy coupon space from them, as a reinforcement for the commercials on the TV.

Perhaps the best way to sum up the threats that the various consumer advocacy groups see is to list the controls they have asked the US Congress to enforce via legislation:

- Sensitive information should not be collected or used for behavioral tracking or targeting.
- No behavioral data should be collected or used from anyone under age 18 to the extent that age can be inferred.
- Web sites and ad networks shouldn't be able to collect or use behavioral data for more than 24 hours without getting the individual's affirmative consent.
- Behavioral data shouldn't be used to unfairly discriminate against people or in any way that would affect an individual's credit, education, employment, insurance, or access to government benefits.

Business Week, [20] Tech Week, 1 Sept 2009

Wondering if your ISPs actually have that kind of info? That's grist for a much longer article, but as of August there have been bills introduced in the US Congress that would allow the President to declare a "Cyber-emergency" and either disconnect certain computers from the net or track every keystroke from certain individuals.

Watch These Spaces...

Internet companies and civil liberties groups were alarmed this spring when a U.S. Senate bill proposed handing the White House the power to disconnect private-sector computers from the Internet. Declan McCullagh, CNET.com News. [21]

Huntington, WV: Civil liberty questions have emerged surrounding the drafting of a bill by aides of West Virginia Senator Jay Rockefeller that would allow Presidential power to disconnect private sector computers from the internet. On one hand, the legislation has been compared to President Bush shutting down private air traffic on September 11, 2001, but other see such vagueness that privacy and constitutional rights come into the spin. [22]

The Not So Ugly

You probably figured out by now where the path I'm going leads: by shaping the message I see to match what I really want, advertisers are more likely to sell me things. And how do they shape that message? By knowing more about me, my preferences, and where I've been paying attention.

Marketing guru Seth Godin spelled this out in 1999, before any of this technology was available:

> [B]usinesses can no longer rely solely on traditional forms of "interruption advertising" in magazines, mailings, or radio and television commercials. He writes that today consumers are bombarded by marketing messages almost everywhere they go. If you want to grab someone's attention, you first need to get his or her permission with some kind of bait--a free sample, a big discount, a contest, an 800 number, or even just an opinion survey. Once a customer volunteers his or her time, you're on your way to establishing a long-term relationship and making a sale. "By talking only to volunteers, Permission Marketing guarantees that consumers pay more attention to the marketing message," he writes. "It serves both customers and marketers in a symbiotic exchange." Amazon review [23]

Godin stood alone for a long time, but his successes, first with the company he started, Internet marketer Yoyodyne, and then with Yahoo!, have pointed out that people will buy something from you if you offer them something free to go along with it. Today, to keep those customers, you have to keep their trust. Loyalty - brand loyalty and product loyalty - both have a base in trust. These days, for a big part of your customers, that trust has to do not only with how you treat them during the transaction, but what you do with the information you give them. Respect their intellect and their preferences. The old adage about the best outline for a speech could be modified to be a paradigm for privacy disclosure: Tell them what your going to do with their data. Do what you said you'd do. And then tell them what you've done.

Will it matter to most customers? Back in 1999, then-CEO Scott McNealy of Sun Microsystems said that consumer privacy issues were a 'red herring.' [24] "You have zero privacy anyway. Get over it." Interestingly, while most privacy experts were incensed that he said it, very few people were able to discredit it. It's very true that people will give away their name, address, and phone number easily on a slip of paper for a prize drawing at the grocery store, or on a web form for a survey. Name and address are two key pieces of Personal Information, if you consider that many regulations define PI as data that will allow another person to locate you. But these people are giving this info away for something -- a chance at a free cart full of groceries, or a walk-on part on a favorite TV Show. Godin's maxim still holds true. But, more and more I observe that if the reason for collecting the data isn't disclosed, people are more leery of giving it away. At a locally-owned linens and soft goods store, when the cashier asked for a zip code, people balked. But when there was a huge map at the front showing where all the customers were coming from, indicated by zip code, folks were less likely to complain. And when the manager explained that they were trying to see if their coupons were in the right local papers, people were even more willing to give their zip codes, and sometimes even which local paper they subscribed to. They got something for their data.

As a persnickety consumer, and as the former owner of a music production company, I have similar goals. I want offerings directed to me that match what I want. If the store loyalty card ensures I continue to get coupons for my choice of shampoo, it's worth it. I don't want to get coupons for shampoo that smells like bubble gum.

As a business owner, I want to get the best info I can on my customers, so I can match the kinds of CDs I'm selling to the kinds of people who want it. Folks who like Heavy Metal aren't going to want our acoustic Celtic music, and so sending them flyers for our concerts is a waste.

I think McNealy knew what he was talking about. There really is no personal privacy, in terms of true anonymity, any more; too much of our data is out there for collection and use, and has been for a long time. But the law is catching up and we are shedding our collective naïveté. We can get a leash on our data, and make sure it's being used for our advantage. I want to be sure my financial info is correct, and properly protected, because I don't want to turn up owing a mortgage for a house I don't own because someone stole my financial identity. I *do* want to keep seeing ads on web pages that are for products, services, and causes that I am likely to be interested in. And so companies that use profiling to give me what I want will keep me as a customer. Like Godin said we could be, back in 1999, we're happy symbiotes, cruising along.

Endnotes

[1] Phishing: a scam by which an e-mail user is duped into revealing personal or confidential information which the scammer can use illicitly. Merriam-Webster Online Dictionary, http://www.merriam-webster.com/dictionary/phishing/. Retrieved 26 Aug 2009. □□Also sometimes called spoofing, a typical phishing email will pretend to be from your bank, or eBay, or some other site you may have an account with, asking you to click on a link and fix something with your account. The link may look like the nominal sender, but will actually be the phisher's site, where they can record your account and password. If you get one of these messages, use a new window on your browser to type in the website URL for the sender (DO **not** click on the link!), and find out if they really sent the message. If is isn't for real, send the whole message, including all the headers, to the security email address given by the site you really have an account with. (Usually directions are available from the real site.) Do NOT include identifying info in the reporting message, or in any other email you send to anyone.

[2] There is excellent advice on reducing spam on the Federal Trade Commission (FTC) website. See http://www.ftc.gov/spam/

[3] Target market: Group of persons for whom a firm creates and maintains a product mix that specifically fits the needs and preferences of that group. For example, the furniture market can be divided into segments described as Early American, contemporary, or traditional. A marketer may choose to target the entire furniture market with the generalized product, promotion, distribution, and pricing strategy meant to appeal to everyone, or may go after one segment of the furniture market with a customized strategy or several segments of the furniture market with more than one strategy. □Market segments can be defined in several other ways besides product types-for example, consumer types, channels of distribution, or price levels. Consumer market segments are defined in terms of geographic (place of purchase or use), demographic (age, income, occupation of consumer), and psychographic (buying motives, product usage level, lifestyle) criteria.

Imber, Jane, and Betsy-Ann Toffler, Dictionary of Marketing Terms, 5th Ed. Copyright 2000, 2008. Barron's Educational Series, Inc. Retrieved from Answers.com, http://www.answers.com/topic/target-market , 26 March 2009.

[4] One of my favorite causes, by the way. All shelters can also use sample size bottles of shampoo, deodorant, soap, toothpaste, and other personal care items, to give to people who come in with nothing. (OK, this is an unsolicited ad, and it's over now.)

[5] The Women's Resource Center

[6]5] Chester, Jeff, Executive Director, Center for Digital Democracy. Testimony on Behavioral Advertising: Industry Practices and Consumers' Expectations. Testimony before the House Committee on Energy and Commerce, Subcommittee on Commerce, Trade, and Consumer Protection, and the Subcommittee on Communications, Technology, and the Internet For the hearing on Behavioral Advertising: Industry Practices And Consumers' Expectations, 18 June 2009. http://www.democraticmedia.org/doc/cdd-testimony-20090618. Retrieved 26 Aug 2009.

[7] from The Man with No Name Rides Again

[8] The Interactive Advertising Bureau

[9] Economic Value of the Advertising-Supported Internet Ecosystem

[10] Self-Regulatory Principles for Online Behavioral Advertising

[11] Downes, John and Jordan Elliot Goodman, eds. Dictionary of Finance and Investment Terms, 7th edition. As compiled on Answers.com's Financial and Investment Dictionary, http://www.answers.com/topic/laissez-faire, accessed 26 June 2009.

Doctrine that interference of government in business and economic affairs should be minimal. Adam Smith's The Wealth of Nations (1776) described laissez-faire economics in terms of an "invisible hand" that would provide for the maximum good for all, if businessmen were free to pursue profitable opportunities as they saw them. The growth of industry in England in the early 19th century and American industrial growth in the late 19th century both occurred in a laissez-faire capitalist environment. The laissez-faire period ended by the beginning of the 20th century, when large monopolies were broken up and government regulation of business became the norm. The Great Depression of the 1930s saw the birth of Keynesian Economics an influential approach advocating government intervention in economic affairs. The movement toward deregulation of business in the United States that began in the 1970s and 80s is to some extent a return to the laissez-faire philosophy. Laissez-faire is French for "allow to do."

[12] Self-Regulatory Principles for Online Behavioral Advertising

[13] Released in July 2009. The cross-industry Self-Regulatory Program for Online Behavioral Advertising was developed by leading industry associations to apply consumer-friendly standards to online behavioral advertising across the Internet. Online behavioral advertising increasingly supports the convenient access to content, services, and applications over the Internet that consumers have come to expect at no cost to them.

The Self-Regulatory Program consists of seven Principles. These Principles, described in the PDF, correspond with the "Self-Regulatory Principles for Online

Behavioral Advertising" proposed by the Federal Trade Commission in February 2009, and also address public education and industry accountability issues raised by the Commission.

Participating organizations were: Interactive Advertising Bureau (IAB), American Association of Advertising Agencies (AAAA), Association of National Advertisers (ANA), Direct Marketing Association (DMA), and Council of Better Business Bureaus (CBBB).

[14] Anonymous, LiveJournal, retrieved Aug. 27th, 2009. Because of his position and role in creating these technologies, this source has asked for anonymity at this time.

[15] Electronic Frontier Foundation: http://www.eff.org

[16] A **honey pot** is a computer system on the Internet that is expressly set up to attract and "trap" people who attempt to penetrate other people's computer systems. (This includes the hacker, cracker, and script kiddy.) To set up a honey pot, it is recommended that you:

- Install the operating system without patches installed and using typical defaults and options
- Make sure that there is no data on the system that cannot safely be destroyed
- Add the application that is designed to record the activities of the invader

Maintaining a honey pot is said to require a considerable amount of attention and may offer as its highest value nothing more than a learning experience (that is, you may not catch any hackers). SearchSecurity.com Definitions, http://searchsecurity.techtarget.com/sDefinition/0,,sid14_gci551721,00.html, 29 May 2007. Retrieved 2 Sept 2009. For the most recent updates on the Honeypot Security research, view this video: WASC Web Honeypot Project enters next phase (Jul. 30, 2009)

[17] Staff writers, *Privacy*, Electronic Frontier Foundation, http://www.eff.org/issues/privacy, last updated Sept 2009. Retrieved 3 Sept 2009.

[18] Privacy Protections (both processes for getting consent from the consumer plus safeguards to protect the masses of data collected from all users)

[19] Wondering how the ISP has that data on me? Remember in the first section of this article, where I described how a lot of data goes over my connection in clear in answer to questions on some web sites? If any of that data stays in cookies on my computer, and the cookies are collected as part of behavioral tracking, all the info here can be tagged as belonging to my computer. Now, remember that I am not my computer, and I may not be the only user. My profile indicates, however, that I am the only user -- I have no young children and seem to live alone.

[20] Hof, Rob. "Consumer Groups Call for Online Privacy Guarantees," Business Week Tech Beat, 1 Sept 2009. http://www.businessweek.com/the_thread/techbeat/archives/2009/09/consumer_groups.html Retrieved 1 Sept 2009.

[21] Declan McCullagh, CNET.com News, http://news.cnet.com/8301-13578_3-10320096-38.html?tag=rtcol;pop, 28 Aug 2009. Retrieved 31 Aug 2009.

[22] 29 August 2009. http://www.huntingtonnews.net/political/090829-rutherford-politicalrockefeller.html

[23] Godin, Seth. *Permission Marketing: Turning Strangers Into Friends And Friends Into Customers,* 1999. As quoted by Amazon Editors, http://www.amazoncom/Permission-Marketing-Turning-Strangers-Customers/dp/0684856360/ref=dp_return_1?ie=UTF8&n=283155&s=books. Retrieved 31 August 2009.

[24] Sprenger, Polly. "Sun on Privacy: 'Get Over It,'" *Wired Magazine.*26 Jan 1999. http://www.wired.com/politics/law/news/1999/01/17538 retrieved 1 Sept 2009.

Social Media: Man's New Best Friend

View online at: http://bcis.pacificu.edu/journal/2009/07/article.php?id=95

By Jenn Hernandez
Berglund Student Fellow

When you get home after a long day of school, work, or whatever, what's the first thing you do? Perhaps you turn on your computer and immediately forget the drag of your day, get lost in colorful pages and animated ads (obnoxious, but nearly inevitable to the online experience). Here's another scenario: walking between classes, you see a group of students on the path together. However, instead of laughing and chatting with each other, they are each on a different device, engrossed in a different world, and hardly acknowledging each other for their colorful backlit LCD screens as they communicate themselves away from one another. Social interaction is gaining momentum in just as monumental a way as the technology itself is changing and adapting to the demands we place on it as users.

As users of any communications technology, we expect to keep connected to our digital worlds, and in turn, to events and happenings which go beyond our screens. Friendships can be a part of this cycle, whether they are built upon, or excluded from it. Our Facebooks [1] and MySpaces [2], Twitters [3] and Google calendars [4] can be extensions of our daily lives, a virtual water cooler or digital notification and RSVP system.

In addition, as we grow more used to the instantaneous nature of our communication via faster networks and cables, we expect faster and easier communication. Now, coffee shops and university buildings (for example) without Wi-Fi are passé and get passed over for wireless hotspots elsewhere, no matter how good the coffee.

I've been called the quintessential geek (thanks, Jeffrey -__-), but I'm not sure that I am. I can definitely attest to being introverted, however. A study (summarized in the NY Times) conducted by the Carnegie Mellon University found that, "'Extroverts, who like making new friends, are using new technology to express that,' Dr. Kraut said. 'When introverts are using the Internet,' he said, 'it seems to hurt their social well-being, their social connectedness.'"[5].

I do think that, for me, spending a lot of time using the Internet, while more comfortable in some cases, or necessary, bites into the time that I could be spending actually hanging out with friends. It's a lame excuse sometimes, because I can "Facebook" (yes, I use it as a verb. I place it in the same category as "to Google" something—made up out of its utility and ease) someone instead of call them to tell them something or ask a question. It becomes a comfortable habit, or perhaps just laziness. I prefer to think of it as a habit!

The habit extends year 'round: sometimes, when I'm out of school much earlier than my state university friends (Pacific University, a private school which I attend, ends the school year at least a few weeks before the public universities do), I feel lonely and disconnected, so I turn to the Internet, where they are still in school-Facebook mode, like I was a few weeks ago as well. I log on to Facebook and see that little red box in the bottom right hand corner announcing that I have any number of new notifications: photo comments, wall posts, replies to links I've posted. I don't know why it's so exciting, and maybe it's also a little bit sad that I find it so. It means people are paying attention and "interacting" with me, though indirectly, and sometimes, very distantly. This isn't a new thing to me.

Back when I posted faithfully to xanga [6] in my early high school years, I experienced the same satisfaction in checking for comments each day to my silly teenage ramblings. It meant someone was, in effect, listening to what I had to say. My "journal" became a visual link between the world and me.

Why keep all this in my head? It actually started with a physical shared journal between my friend---also a Jennifer---and I. Our journals were probably the most intimate and meaningful connection I had with anyone via the written word. I wasn't merely writing a paper and submitting it to a teacher, but recording and reacting to everything throughout the day, "commenting" all over entries Jennifer had written. Our own personal notification system was in each other's scrawly and unique handwriting in a myriad of multi-colored inks.

So, while we had a more intimate conversation, there was still a sort of screen between us at most times, though this one was of paper. I can see the argument that even communication such as this could diminish real contacts (we were communicating solely with one another, therefore leaving everyone else out; time spent writing was taking away from time spent doing; etc). The difference with journals is that we had to get together to trade them, while with the computer, the contact and conversation are one in the same, whether instantaneous or delayed.

Along the same lines of intimacy: I began talking to my now fiancé through Facebook, and then AOL Instant Messenger [7] after formally meeting him at my martial arts school. I found it much easier to talk to him that way at first, rather than face-to-face, especially since he kept calling me cute and I had to threaten to punch him in the face, which I didn't actually have to follow up on, thankfully. The most I could do to let him know my great discomfort was to use my time-honored set of emoticons, which he didn't understand anyway, and plenty of action-words enclosed in asterisks. *sigh* -__- Silly boy.

Now, my fiancé has an iPhone [8], and when there's nothing to do, or we're just relaxing, he'll occasionally pull it out either in response to a little chime that means he got a text or to check anything from e-mail to movie times. Sometimes he checks his Twitter. I don't really get Twitter. I'm amazed by the ability of one little device to bring the world of the computer out a step farther into the real world. He's not bound to a desk, or even to a laptop. Thinking about this article, I thought about how tied we can be to technology, even when we're spending time with loved ones.

Being engaged led to a curiosity on my part about a website called The Knot [9]. I didn't know anything about it besides that you can put your name in the URL, which is pretty cool to me. So, now I'm getting e-mails about wedding related services and events in Portland. I'm not too sure where I'd look for these kind of things besides the Internet. The same goes with ring shopping. I can't show you the ring I found in case my fiancé reads this, but I definitely wouldn't have been able to find something so perfect at a local jewelry store---jewelry stores are very intimidating, by the way.

Anecdotes aside, in a poll on "Generation Next" by the Pew Research Center for the People and the Press, 65% of those surveyed responded positively to the question of technology making people more isolated. 30% responded negatively; they do not think that technology isolates us. [10] Findings such as these begin to point to a growing concern that we have about technology replacing real social connections with digital ones.

Surely, it can be argued that it's not necessarily the friendships and connections that are changing, but the way we view and use them, respectively. The way we communicate is changing, and so should our realization that it's not always a change for the better if we can't keep up with it.

Analyst and writer Stowe Boyd [11] comments on the changing nature and definition of friendship: "It's not about metrics, because my yardstick has changed along with everything else. It's really about an enriched self-identity, meaning, and purpose: and those -- for me, at least -- have changed irrevocably through the web, through my connections: and all for the better." [12]

Just as definitions in dictionaries change over time—reflecting the change of social meanings, if not necessarily intellectual meanings—then so should it be expected that, given the factor of pop culture and social changes in general, views and attitudes towards just what constitutes a "friend" are shifting. The Internet can be a useful tool for staying in contact with others—friends from high school, family in faraway places, college roommates, when away for the summer. There is no replacement for face-to-face conversation, however.

In the future—in our futures—it will be interesting to see what kind of new and improved technologies come up to further enhance our communications and aide in our burgeoning social lives; that is, if we keep in touch.

Endnotes

[1] http://www.facebook.com

[2] http://www.myspace.com

[3] http://twitter.com

[4] www.google.com/calendar

[5] http://www.nytimes.com/2001/07/26/technology/cyberspace-isn-t-so-lonely-after-all.html?sec=technology&spon=&pagewanted=2

[6] http://www.xanga.com

[7] http://dashboard.aim.com/aim

[8] http://www.apple.com/iphone/

[9] www.theknot.com

[10] http://people-press.org/questions/?qid=1674270&pid=51&ccid=51#top

[11] http://www.stoweboyd.com/about.html

[12] http://www.stoweboyd.com/message/2007/08/anne-truitt-zel.html

Book Review

A Review of Michael Connelly's *The Scarecrow* and Jeffery Deaver's *The Broken Window: A Lincoln Rhyme Novel*

View online at: http://bcis.pacificu.edu/journal/2009/07/article.php?id=96Michael

Connelly, *The Scarecrow.* Little, Brown, 2009.

Jeffery Deaver, *The Broken Window: A Lincoln Rhyme Novel.* Pocket Star Paperback, 2009.

Review by Jeffrey Barlow

One of the perennial conundrums of the mystery or crime fiction writer is how to concoct a story in such a way that the reader can solve it along with, if not slightly ahead of, the sleuth. While some stories may turn on character development or the horrors of great puddles of gore, it is generally the reader's desire to solve the crime that attracts.

Stories conventionally then, though not always, must turn on the discovery of clues or data. Solving the case sometimes depends on the protagonist stumbling over data, as in the many iterations of the "clueless sleuth" who somehow muddles through, or upon the protagonist seeing meaning in data that appeared unconnected to those who are not Sherlock Holmes, Miss Jane Marple, or Nero Wolfe. Most readers have not responded well to clues from heaven—data unexpectedly introduced from some previously unknown source. [1]

At some point after traditional crime novels appeared--no authority seems to agree exactly when [2]--the criminal's own voice or point of view was also introduced into the novel. This gave the author new flexibility, and the sleuth new problems as the reader inevitably begins wondering how the detective can possibly catch up with the perp.

The Internet has introduced new problems. One is how the writer is to keep the sleuth in the dark while building suspense. If the sleuth seems not to know information that we ourselves know, our first reaction may well be a heartfelt "Duh! —So why didn't you Google that, dummy?"

In the spring of 2009, two crime novels by very successful writers [3] came out in paperback within weeks of each other. Each involved a killer with access to all the data in the "Hidden Internet," the information stored everywhere in massive data farms and searchable via data mining. The two works were Michael Connelly's *The Scarecrow* [4] and Jeffrey Deaver's *The Broken Window*. [5] Both play upon current widespread fears about the Dark Side of the Internet.

In each case, the criminal is not only a mastermind in that he or she has arcane computer skills most of us lack (Including the sleuth in both cases), but also has access to all the information there is, while the sleuth labors along with a very limited view. In the case of Deaver's detective, Lincoln Rhyme, he has the additional handicap of being a paraplegic, pretty much confined to his admittedly very tricked-out apartment.

Each of these novels is also to an unusual degree cautionary or exhortative. Both writers feel that important cultural values are being lost with the rapid expansion of data storage and the Internet. In Connelly's case, it is newspapers that are being lost, and investigative journalism is going with them. In Deaver's case, it is privacy.

Deaver's concerns about the loss of privacy are reflected throughout the book. At one point, Deaver's detective, Lincoln Rhymes, has a skilled programmer do data mining on the personal information of Emilia Sachs, his partner and lover. The result is a 500+ page file of personal information. [6] Another data mining of Sach's telephone and credit card usage gave a complete record of her activities and movements in real time and for the past 24 hours. [7]

All of this information on any real person is, of course, available to those with sufficient access, which is Deaver's point.

Deaver's plot hinges on an individual with a murderous psychosis and the skills and access which permits him/her to data-mine information. This permits the criminal to orchestrate complex crimes beyond anything dreamed of by Poe or Conan Doyle.

Deaver has sold a great many books, and his fertile mind continues to play with the "what ifs" of popular culture. He clearly feels that culture is at a critical point in its history, if not in risk of outright endangerment. He concludes the book with a list of web sites where others with similar concerns can research the current state of privacy, and perhaps join efforts to preserve it. [8]

Michael Connelly's work, *The Scarecrow* introduces quite a different protagonist, Jack McEvoy, and another psychotic perpetrator. Jack, a journalist of the old school (and also a character with a series of works of his own, like Deaver's Rhymes) is losing his job at the Los Angeles Times to a "mojo."

> "—a mobile journalist nimbly able to file from the field via any electronic means. She could file text and photos for the website or paper, or video and audio for television and radio partners. She was trained to do it all but in practice she was still as green as can be. She was probably being paid $500 a week less than me, and in today's newspaper economy that made her a greater value to the company. Never mind the stories that would be missed because she had no sources." [9]

It is not irrelevant that the author was formerly a journalist, associated with a number of newspapers which have since ceased to exist. Just as Deaver warns us of the loss of privacy, Connelly, a bit less obviously, continuously tells us what we are losing with the demise of major daily newspapers such as *The Rocky Mountain Times*, where, coincidentally, his protagonist worked in a previous work, *The Poet.*

Jack muses about the future:

> Think of all the great journalism we've seen in our lifetimes. The corruption exposed, the public benefit. Where's that going to come from now with every paper in the country getting shredded? Our government? No way. TV, the blogs? Forget it. [10]

While Jack is not completely without Internet savvy, the search to uncover the criminal is largely a struggle between Jack's unaided mind using traditional investigative techniques, such as personal interviews and library research, vs. the perpetrator's command of data mining. At one point the perp electronically stalks a potential victim:

> "It was always amazing to X how trusting or naive young people were. They didn't believe that anybody could connect the dots. They believed that they could bare their souls on the Internet, post photos and information at will, and not expect any consequences. From her blog X was able to glean all the information X needed about Angela Cook…X was circling her and she didn't even know it."

This protagonist, like Deaver's, is seriously warped and raises in our minds the insane criminal, something like Poe's narrator in "The Tell-Tale Heart," or Dostoyevsky's in *Crime and Punishment*. A critical distinction between these classic killers and the Internet killers is that they may be stalking us on the Internet but we cannot see them. If they babble and drool, they do it in their cubicles, and we cannot know to cross the street to avoid them.

Clearly, each of these two works in their own way takes our fears about the impact of the Internet in general, and the evil possibilities of mining data collected by gigantic corporations or huge government bureaucracies, to a new level. Some readers may take the authors' concerns as overly exaggerated. To do so would be to ignore the truly massive extent to which data has been collected and aggregated and is, in fact, available to the determined hacker. [11]

There is now so much data that at present the question as to even roughly how much is stored is unanswerable. It was announced in the summer of 2008, for example, that a number of major universities and corporations were creating a research consortium to answer that question. [12] It is very likely, however, that whatever techniques the group designs to estimate or measure stored data, the reality will continue to outstrip our imaginations. [13]

Each author is imminently readable, though I sometimes find Deaver's characters a bit too superhuman, whether good or evil, and they can be hard to identify with, unlike Connolly's cynical, but ultimately accessible, Jack McEvoy. The audiences for these books are, of course, extensive. Each has a cult following and determined publishers who keep all of their works before us at our every trip to the supermarket.

Crime or mystery writing is a very venerable form. It began, some argue, with the *Tales of Scherazade*, elements of which may date back to the 9th century. With the almost simultaneous release of these two works, it is clear that each new major development on the Internet will inevitably become a setting for crime writers and may well be a new sub-genre of writing.

To see Internet-mystery writing move forward, occupying a creative space somewhere between the locked room mysteries solved by John Dickson Carr's venerable Doctor Gideon Fell [14] and the escapades of science fiction sleuths such as Philip K. Dick's Rick Deckhard of *Blade Runner* [15], would be a welcome and entertaining development. It will be hard, of course, for fiction to keep pace with reality. We have already had real world Internet-related killings. [16]

Those of us who insist on both entertainment and realistic descriptions of such critical factors as technology and those personalities who choose to immerse themselves in it in our leisure reading should be satisfied with Michael Connelly's *The Scarecrow* and Jeffery Deaver's, *The Broken Window*. And we can learn a great deal about popular perceptions of the Internet as we read.

Endnotes

[1] And in my own case, I respond even less well to the author who feeds the reader misleading data---information that later turns out to be incorrect, as in the case of my personal least favorite but nonetheless highly popular writer, Stephen King. At the same time, I also find King's *Hearts in Atlantis* one of my favorite works, because of what it has to say about the addictive pleasures of gaming in college communities, whether those games are "Tour of Duty" played on an X-Box or "Hearts" played with greasy decks of cards. See book site at: http://www.stephenking.com/library/story_collection/hearts_in_atlantis.html

[2] In English language fiction at least, I personally think it likely to be In Poe's "The Tell-Tale Heart". See http://www.literature.org/authors/poe-edgar-allan/tell-tale-heart.html

[3] That is, each has written many bestsellers and has established well-known series characters, some of whom have featured in several films.

[4] See book site at: http://www.michaelconnelly.com/Book_Collection/Scarecrow/scarecrow.html

[5] http://www.jefferydeaver.com/Novels_/Broken/broken.html

[6] Deaver, Loc. 6606-6832 (This is a citation to the Kindle file location in which I read this work.) The data report, formatted as in the text, reads: *"Welcome, NGHF235, please enter (1) the Subject's 16-digit SSD code; or (2) country and number of Subject's passport, or (3) Subject's name, current residence, Social Security number and one telephone number. "Type in the information for the person you're interested in." Rhyme dictated the details about Sachs. On the screen appeared: Confirm access to 3E Compliance Dossier? Yes No. Cooper clicked on the former and a box appeared, asking for yet another passcode. With another glance at the ceiling, Whitcomb asked, "You ready?" As if something significant was about to happen. "Ready." Whitcomb gave them another sixteen-digit passcode, which Cooper typed in. He hit ENTER. As the text began filling the computer screen, the criminalist whispered an astonished, "Oh, my God." And it took a lot to astonish Lincoln Rhyme. RESTRICTED POSSESSION OF THIS DOSSIER BY ANY PERSON NOT HOLDING AN A-18 CLEARANCE OR HIGHER IS A VIOLATION OF FEDERAL LAW Dossier 3E—Compliance SSD Subject Number: 7303–4490–7831–3478 Name: Amelia H. Sachs Pages: 478 TABLE OF CONTENTS Click on topic to view Note: Archived material may take up to five minutes to access PROFILE Name/Aliases/Nics/Nyms/A.K.A.s Social Security Number Present address Satellite view of present address Prior addresses Citizenship Race Ancestral history National origin Physical description/distinguishing characteristics Biometric details Photographs Video Fingerprints Footprints Retinal scan Iris scan Gait profile Facial scan Voice pattern Tissue samples Medical history Political party affiliations Professional organizations Fraternal organizations Religious affiliations Military Service/discharge DOD evaluation National Guard evaluation Weapons systems training Donations Political Religious Medical Philanthropic Public Broadcasting System/National Public Radio Other Psychological/psychiatric history Myers-Briggs personality profile Sexual preference profile Hobbies/interests Clubs/fraternal organizations INDIVIDUALS TETHERED TO SUBJECT Spouses Intimate relationships Offspring Parents Siblings Grandparents (paternal) Grandparents (maternal) Other blood relatives, living Other blood relatives, deceased Relatives related by marriage or tethering Neighbors Present Past five years (archived, may be*

delay in accessing) Co-workers, clients, etc. Present Past five years (archived, may be delay in accessing) Acquaintances In person Online Persons of Interest (PEOI) FINANCIAL Employment—present Category Salary history Days absent/reasons for absence Discharge/unemployment claims Citations/reprimands Title 7 discrimination incidents OSHA incidents Other actions Employment—past (archived, may be delay in accessing) Category Salary history Days absent/reasons for absence Discharge/unemployment claims Citations/reprimands Title 7 discrimination incidents OSHA incidents Other actions Income—present IRS reported Nonreported Foreign Income—past IRS reported Nonreported Foreign Assets currently held Real property Vehicles and boats Bank accounts/securities Insurance policies Other Assets, past twelve months, unusual disposition or acquisition of Real property Vehicles and boats Bank accounts/securities Insurance policies Other Assets, past five years, unusual disposition or acquisition of (archived, may be delay in accessing) Real property Vehicles and boats Bank accounts/securities Insurance policies Other Credit report/rating Financial transactions, U.S.-based institutions Today Past seven days Past thirty days Past year Past five years (archived, may be delay in accessing) Financial transactions, foreign-based institutions Today Past seven days Past thirty days Past year Past five years (archived, may be delay in accessing) Financial transactions, Hawala and other cash transactions, U.S. and foreign Today Past seven days Past thirty days Past year Past five years (archived, may be delay in accessing) COMMUNICATIONS Present phone numbers Mobile Landline Satellite Prior phone numbers past twelve months Mobile Landline Satellite Prior phone numbers past five years (archived, may be delay in accessing) Mobile Landline Satellite Fax numbers Pager numbers Incoming/outgoing phone/pager calls—mobile/PDA Past thirty days Past year (archived, may be delay in accessing) Incoming/outgoing phone/pager/fax calls—landline Past thirty days Past year (archived, may be delay in accessing) Incoming/outgoing phone/pager/fax calls—satellite Past thirty days Past year (archived, may be delay in accessing) Wiretaps/intercepts Foreign Intelligence Surveillance Act (FISA) Pen registers Title 3 Other, warrants Other, collateral Web-based telephone activities Internet service providers, present Internet service providers, past 12 months Internet service providers, past five years (archived, may be delay in accessing) Favorite place/bookmarked Web sites E-mail addresses Present Past E-mail activity, past year TC/PIP history Outgoing addresses Incoming addresses Content (warrant may be required to view) E-mail activity, past five years (archived, may be delay in accessing) TC/PIP history Outgoing addresses Incoming addresses Content (warrant may be required to view) Web sites, present Personal Professional Web sites, past five years (archived, may be delay in accessing) Personal Professional Blogs, lifelogs, Web sites (See appendices for text of Passages of Interest (POI)) Social Web site memberships (mySpace, Facebook, OurWorld, others) (See appendices for text of Passages of Interest (POI)) Avatars/other personas online Mailing lists "Buddies" on e-mail accounts Internet Relay Chat participation Web browsing and search engine requests/results Keyboarding technique profile Search engine grammar, syntax and punctuation profile Package delivery service history Postal boxes Express Mail/Registered/Certified USPS activity LIFESTYLE ACTIVITIES Purchases today Threat-oriented items or commodities Clothing Vehicles and vehicle related Food Liquor Household items Appliances Other Purchases in past 7 days Threat-oriented items or commodities Clothing Vehicles and vehicle related Food Liquor Household items Appliances Other Purchases in past thirty days Threat-oriented items or commodities Clothing Vehicles and vehicle related Food Liquor Household items Appliances Other Purchases in past year (archived, may be delay in accessing) Threat-oriented items or commodities Clothing Vehicles and vehicle related Food Liquor Household items Appliances Other Books/magazines purchased online Suspicious/subversive Others of interest Books/magazines purchased in retail stores Suspicious/subversive Others of interest Books/magazines checked out from libraries Suspicious/subversive Others of interest Books/magazines observed by airport/airline personnel Suspicious/subversive Others of interest Other library activities Bridal/shower/anniversary gift registries Theatrical films Cable television programs/pay-per-view watched past thirty days Cable television programs/pay-per-view watched, past year (archived, may be delay in accessing) Subscription radio stations Travel Automotive Owned vehicles Rental Public transportation Taxis/limos Bus Trains Airplanes, commercial Domestic International Airplanes, private Domestic International TSA security screens Appearance on no-fly lists Presence in Locations of Interest (LOI) Local Mosques Other locations—U.S. Mosques Other locations—international Presence in or transit through Red Flag Locations (RFL): Cuba, Uganda, Libya, South Yemen, Liberia, Ghana, Sudan, Democratic Republic of Congo, Indonesia, Palestinian Territories, Syria, Iraq, Iran, Egypt, Saudi Arabia, Jordan, Pakistan, Eritrea, Afghanistan, Chechnya, Somalia, Sudan, Nigeria, Philippines, North Korea, Azerbaijan, Chile. GEOGRAPHIC POSITIONING OF SUBJECT GPS devices (all positions today) Vehicular Handheld Mobile phones GPS devices (all positions past seven days) Vehicular Handheld Mobile phones GPS devices (all positions past thirty days) Vehicular Handheld Mobile phones GPS devices (all positions past year) (archived, may be delay in accessing) Vehicular Handheld Mobile phones Biometric observations Today Past seven days Past thirty days Past year (archived, may be delay in accessing) RFID reports, other than highway toll readers Today Past seven days Past thirty days Past year (archived, may be delay in accessing) RFID reports, highway toll readers Today Past seven days Past thirty days Past year (archived, may be delay in accessing) Traffic violation photos/video CCTV photos/video Warranted surveillance photos/video Collateral surveillance photos/video In-person financial transaction hits Today Past seven days Past thirty days Past year (archived, may be delay in accessing) Mobile phone/PDA/telecommunications hits Today Past seven days Past thirty days Past year (archived, may be delay in accessing) Incidents of proximity to security targets Today Past seven days Past thirty days Past year (archived, may be delay in accessing) LEGAL Criminal history—U.S. Detention/questioning Arrests Convictions Criminal history—foreign Detention/questioning Arrests Convictions Watch lists Surveillance Civil litigation Restraining orders Whistleblower history ADDITIONAL DOSSIERS Federal Bureau of Investigation Central Intelligence Agency National Security Agency National Reconnaissance Organization NPIA U.S. Military Intelligence Agencies Army Navy Air Force Marines State and local police intelligence departments THREAT ASSESSMENT Assessment as security risk Private sector Public sector And this was just the table of contents. Amelia Sachs's dossier itself was close to five hundred pages long."

[7] Deaver Loc. 6860-75 That report reads: " GEOGRAPHIC POSITIONING PROFILE SUBJECT 7303–4490–7831–3478 Time parameters: Past four hours. 1632 hours. Phone call. From subject's mobile phone to landline of Subject 5732-4887-3360-4759 (Lincoln Henry Rhyme) (tethered individual). 52 seconds. Subject was in her Brooklyn, NY, residence. 1723 hours. Biometric hit. CCTV, NYPD 84th Precinct, Brooklyn, NY. 95% probability match. 1723 hours. Biometric hit. Subject 3865-6453-9902-7221 (Pamela D. Willoughby) (tethered individual). CCTV, NYPD 84th Precinct, Brooklyn, NY. 92.4% probability match. 1740 hours. Phone call. From subject's mobile phone to landline of Subject 5732-4887-3360-4759 (Lincoln Henry

Rhyme) (tethered Individual). 12 seconds. 1827 hours. RFID scan. Manhattan Style Boutique credit card, 9 West Eighth Street. No purchases. 1841 hours. Biometric hit. CCTV, Presco Discount Gas and Oil, 546 W. 14th Street, Pump 7, 2001 Honda Civic, NY License Number MDH459, registered to 3865-6453-9902-7221 (Pamela D. Willoughby) (tethered individual). 1846 hours. Credit card purchase. Presco Discount Gas and Oil, 546 W. 14th Street. Pump 7. Purchase of 14.6 gallons, regular grade. $43.86 US. 1901 hours. License plate scan. CCTV, Avenue of the Americas and 23rd Street, Honda Civic MDH459 northbound. 1903 hours. Phone call. From subject's mobile phone to landline of Subject 5732-4887-3360-4759 (Lincoln Henry Rhyme) (tethered individual). Subject was at Avenue of the Americas and 28th Street. 14 seconds. 1907 hours. RFID scan, Associated Credit Union credit card, Avenue of the Americas and 34th Street. 4 seconds. No purchase."

[8] Deaver Loc. 7715-22 "Readers wishing to know more about the issue of privacy might want to peruse some of the following organizations' Web sites: Electronic Privacy Information Center (EPIC.org); Global Internet Liberty Campaign (www.gilc.org); In Defense of Freedom (www.indefenseoffreedom.org); Internet Free Expression Alliance (http://ifea.net); The Privacy Coalition (http://privacycoalition.org); Privacy International (www.privacyinternational.org); Privacy.org (www.privacy.org); and the Electronic Frontier Foundation (www.eff.org). I think you'll also enjoy—and be unnerved by—the excellent book from which I borrowed several quotations to use as epigrams, No Place to Hide, by Robert O'Harrow, Jr."

[9] Connelly, Loc. 281-85.

[10] Connelly Loc. 467-70

[11] A useful recent article is TOM VANDERBILT, "Data Center Overload" *The New York Times* found at: http://www.nytimes.com/2009/06/14/magazine/14search-t.html?pagewanted=all

[12] Barry Jagoda "Groundbreaking University of California, San Diego Research Study to Measure "How Much Information?" is in the World" Multi-Year Study With Sponsorship From AT&T, Cisco Systems, IBM, LSI, Oracle, Seagate Technology and PARC to Examine the Quantity and Quality of Global Information. June 3, 2008. Found at: http://ucsdnews.ucsd.edu/newsrel/international/06-08InfoInTheWorld.asp

[13] See, for example, Michael Lesk "How Much Information Is There In the World?" (1997) http://www.lesk.com/mlesk/ksg97/ksg.html

[14] See http://en.wikipedia.org/wiki/Gideon_Fell

[15] See http://www.wsu.edu/~brians/science_fiction/bladerunner.html

[16] See Marshall Kirkpatrick "Facebook Murder Reflects Cultural Shifts" June 8, 2009 *Read Write Web* at: http://www.readwriteweb.com/archives/facebook_murder_reflects_drama.php

Editorial

Peaceful Evolution in China and the World Wide Web: Part I, Two Democracies?

View online at: http://bcis.pacificu.edu/journal/2009/07/article.php?id=98

Editorial by Jeffrey Barlow

Introduction

Clearly, there are relationships between globalism, the rise of the World Wide Web, and what we might loosely call democracy. Unfortunately, none of these relationships are really *clear*. [1] Having studied both China and the World Wide Web for some years, I try to clarify those relationships here.

We might usefully begin at the question, what do we mean by democracy? Many would be surprised to hear that, in fact, Asian communists think of their systems as democratic. Many Asians, including many who are not communist, also think of the American system as only qualifiedly democratic or actually undemocratic. [2]

The Chinese argument is a simple one. They view the role of the Communist Party in China as to focus the inchoate sentiments and hopes of the broader population and then to put into policy what that population truly wants and needs. Lacking a leading party then, there would be no democracy.

The American view of democracy thinks that a multiparty system is necessary to true democracy. In this perspective then, the Chinese system cannot be democratic.

The American Case Against Chinese Democracy:

For most Americans, the notion of "Chinese Democracy" almost inevitably and necessarily implies opposition to the Chinese government. [3] The underlying reasoning is, I think, quite simple: Chinese Communists are *Communists* first and *Chinese* second. The Party, in this view, represents a totalitarian monolith, which speaks and acts in a united voice, guided not by the needs and desires of the people, but by "Communism."

Recently, there is another American view which holds that China is no longer capital "C" Communist, but rather that the Chinese Communist Party has simply become a corrupt elite which uses ideological appeals to hang onto power. Many are balanced rather uneasily between these two views.

The hope of many Chinese and some foreigners and certainly my own position, is that as Chinese gain a broader international perspective and China achieves the economic base which creates a larger middle class and reduces the potential costs of economic failures, then it will peacefully evolve.

But for many Americans, the notion of peaceful evolution in the Chinese system is an illusory hope. For these individuals the only realistic policy is "Regime Change"---

here we capitalize the term to identify it as an external policy of outsiders rather than as an internal process. [4]

Surely it is necessary for any reasonable person to be suspicious of the motives of many who support Regime Change in the governments of others. Regime Change in Iraq, for the Bush administration, clearly implied dragging Iraqi natural resources, especially, of course, oil, into American-dominated economic relationships.

Many interests which support Regime Change are demonstrably less concerned about democracy than about market access, control, and a stable climate for their own investments. The evidence for this is all around us, in every totalitarian regime supported by those interests from the Mid-east to Latin America. In those regimes, citizens may have less freedom than any Chinese, but their totalitarian leaders nonetheless enjoy American state and corporate support.

China has been a frustration to supporters of extreme free market capitalism because the Chinese insist on controlling foreign ownership and investment right down to the local level, but especially banking and insurance, the financial centers of market capitalism. Until China undergoes thorough Regime Change, there will be no place for the sort of predatory offshore capitalism that many global firms prefer to practice.

This distinction between peaceful evolution and "Regime Change" is, of course, sometimes very artificial. It is possible to have what we might call "Regime Change Light" by giving external support or stimulus to internal groups and processes. [5] This is what foreign regimes, like China, often see as the sole meaning of "Peaceful Evolution," which is, in their view, a forced process amounting to external intervention in their internal affairs. We mean something quite different here, and hence do not capitalize the term when using it in our own more limited sense.

Many of us, while in general opposing the notion of imposing our views on others, can be brought into support of Regime Change Light no matter our reluctance for interventionism if <u>our</u> issues are believed to be at stake: the freedom for our religion to proselytize, gender equality, animal rights, the environment, global warming, full Internet access, the rights of selected minorities—peaceful Buddhists but not polygamists—and so on.

For those who support the peaceful evolution of foreign states, China included, uninfluenced by external self-interested forces, the issues remain complex. Obviously, all bureaucracies respond most satisfactorily when there is at least some pressure for reform, and a relatively open market for ideas that might generate peaceful and positive changes.

From this perspective then, some change or continual evolution is necessary in all states, and particularly in those that are in some way markedly deficient by accepted international standards. Lacking such change the argument for Regime Change comes to seem more palatable, a matter of balancing potential goods against potential bads.

This makes the central question in assessing the pace of change a stark one: how much change is enough, and how fast must such changes occur? This is a daily question for many of us, and hard to assess even with regard to the policies of our own government, let alone within such very different systems as the People's Republic of China.

However, despite its complexities, I find the "peaceful evolutionary" position much the more realistic and satisfactory one. This is because I think that "Regime Change" necessarily implies violence and chaos. In China, with its limited food resources and its huge populations, anything remotely resembling systemic chaos inevitably results in death and suffering on a scale simply unthinkable to most Westerners.

I also support peaceful evolution, because I think that changes growing out of indigenous historical and cultural roots are much more likely to prove successful and enduring than forced or externally generated "Regime Change." Surely events in Iraq, to name only the most recent example, are a case in point.

I think it best then, that Chinese notions of democracy evolve along with their governmental practices at their own measured pace without direct foreign pressures. And there is much reason to believe that the World Wide Web will be highly influential in engendering such changes. But first, let me return to the Chinese case against American democracy, because I think we can learn much from it, about both their system and ours.

The Chinese Case Against American Democracy.

Many Chinese have a perspective toward the American system that we might find puzzling. To us, the very essence of democracy is a multiparty system. In practice, this means a two party system, and for the foreseeable future, one divided between Democrats and Republicans--- (fair disclosure: I am a life-long registered Republican).

This multiparty system is one that has evolved in the American system. It is not written into the constitution, and many founders saw such partisanship or "factionalism" as an evil to be feared and avoided. [6] Nonetheless, it remains in the minds of most, the critical difference between the American and the Chinese systems.

The Chinese, however, see no real difference between Republicans and Democrats. To the Chinese, the two major American parties are basically participants in a Beijing opera in which variously painted characters whirl across the stage, distracting the audience with loud noises and colorful costumes, while basic policies remain the same.

The Chinese believe that the American democracy is so corrupted by market capitalism that policy is, in fact, for sale. American citizens, they would say, have clearly expressed their desires for such policies as universal health care, universal access to education, full employment, women and minorities' rights and many other issues which the great majority of us consistently support. A true democracy, the Chinese think, surely would realize those goals, the central job of the government in the Chinese system.

American special interests, the Chinese believe, simply buy political influence via a highly corrupt process for financing elections. These interests first oppose change, but if necessary, simply shape any changes which might occur as to be less reforms than new ways to expand their own huge share of the wealth and power of the United States.

An intelligent and well-read Chinese worker, with whom I had quite a long discussion in Beijing the day after the last presidential election, had a very elaborate perspective. He believed that since the problems of the U.S. were clearly intractable, the elites had chosen to allow the election of Obama in order to discredit both minorities and reform. To him, Obama is just an especially colorful character in the ongoing opera.

We might tell my Chinese discussant that at least our system lets minority parties emerge and have a chance at becoming majority ones. He might well reply, truthfully, that the Chinese system has minority parties as well, and unlike our system, their minorities are guaranteed minimal representation in the key governmental bodies. And as an Oregonian, while arguing that point, I would be aware of an element of hypocrisy in my position---Oregon's electoral laws, like those of most states, make it all but impossible for minority parties to emerge, the one point upon which Democrats and Republicans can be counted to agree.

The Chinese perspective on the American two party system clearly has some merit. There is considerable disaffection with the system as shown by the increasingly high percentage of Americans who register as independents or having lost faith in the American electoral system, refuse to vote at all. [7] And reportedly, the election of Obama has stimulated the growth of right-wing militia groups that believe in the necessity of violently overthrowing an American political system gone very wrong. [8]

The Chinese would argue, or at least many have to me, that their system in fact works rather like ours in many regards; it is just that the candidates in their elections must be of the same party. In our case, the candidates, regardless of party, must represent the same interests in order to achieve the financing necessary to win election, and even if the are elected for their maverick reputation or earlier record, they soon find that in Congress, in Sam Rayburn's immortal words, "If you want to get along, go along." [9]

Conclusion

We must, of course, recognize many of our own views in these Chinese perspectives. What many of us might ruefully say is that such problems do exist, but Americans are making progress anyway. Certainly, Obama supporters see his election as the dawn of a hopeful new era in which real progress will be made on such of the above issues as we might recognize to be real ones.

One of the reasons, it is believed, that Obama was elected was his group's very skillful use of the Internet. [10] Many have felt that the Internet is permitting Americans to more fully realize the promises of democracy. In the next segment of this editorial, I will argue that the Internet is also doing so for the Chinese democracy, as different as it is from the American one. This is because the two share one common element, inevitable in any politicized process that permits transitions within elite groups: factions.

Endnotes

[1] Walter Pincus discussed this issue in an editorial, "Peaceful Evolution Angst" in the May 25 2009 *The New York Times* at: http://www.nytimes.com/2009/05/25/opinion/25iht-edcohen.html

[2] See for example the review of Indrajit Banerjee (ed.). Rhetoric and Reality. The Internet Challenge for Democracy in Asia. Singapore: Eastern Universities Press, 2003, found at: http://bcis.pacificu.edu/journal/2005/03/banerjee.php. While Banerjee thinks of the American system as a democracy, it is in his mind only one possible type thereof, and in many ways an inferior example.

[3] As evidence of this see the many articles found on Google Search (Chinese Democracy NOT Guns N Roses):

http://www.google.com/search?hl=en&client=firefox-a&rls=org.https://mail.google.com/a/pacificu.edu/ - search/label%3Aberglund-center+print+version/123dd9b5c062d6edmozilla%3Aen-US%3Aofficial&hs=4mH&as_q=chinese+democracy+&as_epq=&as_oq=&as_eq=Guns+N+rose&num=10&lr=&as_filetype=&ft=i&as_sitesearch=&as_qdr=all&as_rights=&as_occt=any&cr=&as_nlo=&as_nhi=&safe=images

[4] For a useful perspective see Minxin Pei, "Will the Chinese Communist Party Survive the Crisis?" How Beijing's Shrinking Economy May Threaten One-Party Rule. *Foreign Affairs*, March 12, 2009 at: http://www.foreignaffairs.com/articles/64862/minxin-pei/will-the-chinese-communist-party-survive-the-crisis

[5] I wrote about the perils and costs of supporting internal dissidence in disequillibrated states in "Attila to Soltan: Media Savvy and Democracy" found at: http://bcis.pacificu.edu/journal/2009/06/article.php?id=88

[6] See, of course, James Madison, *The Federalist* No. 10, "The Utility of the Union as a Safeguard Against Domestic Faction and Insurrection." http://www.constitution.org/fed/federa10.htm For a different position which suggests that Madison in fact encouraged factionalism, see: "Partisanship: The glue that holds the union together," *The Roanoke Times*, April 12, 2009, http://www.roanoke.com/editorials/commentary/wb/200701

[7] I am aware that there are many reasons other than loss of faith in the system for not voting, and that claim is often a cover for sheer sloth.

[8] See, for example, The Southern Poverty Law Center at: http://www.splcenter.org/ I have had some doubts about these reports as the Left is often as willing to demonize the Right in America as vice-versa. However, I recently found in discussions with what I can only call a right wing extremist that there is indeed a nexus of agreement between the so-called "birthers" (See a birthers site at: http://www.thebirthers.org/) who argue that Obama is an usurper because not American born, and the militia movement. This individual believes that an armed uprising, led by militias, would be joined by regular military forces and overthrow the Obama regime.

[9] http://thinkexist.com/quotation/if_you_want_to_get_along-go_along/218894.html

[10] See, for example, Sarah Lai Stirland, "Propelled by Internet, Barack Obama Wins Presidency" Wired, at http://www.wired.com/threatlevel/2008/11/propelled-by-in/

October 2009 - Volume 9, Issue 8

Articles

Book and Site Reviews

Editorial

Feature

When Online Lives Create Offline Problems: Internet Addiction Disorder

View online at: http://bcis.pacificu.edu/journal/article.php?id=111

Shawn Davis
Ph.D. Pacific University – School of Professional Psychology

> "Why is it drug addicts and computer aficionados are both called users?" - Clifford Stoll [1]

Introduction

Let me begin with a confession. The first thing I do in the morning (and often the last thing I do before sleep) is check my e-mail. Rarely does a day go by without a visit to my favorite websites and a little more-than-reasonable amount of time is spent pouring over updated player statistics that will undoubtedly give me a competitive edge in my fantasy football league. I find that I am spending an increasing amount of time online and often include in my daily activities a frustrating search for the ever-elusive hotspot. Do I have a problem?

It's true that more of our daily life is becoming progressively Internet-centered. In fact, in the United States the amount of time spent online daily rose 117% from 2004 to 2009 with an average of 12 hours per week being reported [2]. But how much time online is too much? This has become a topic of much debate in the mental health community. Professionals deliberate not only the impact of increasing levels of time spent on the Internet, but also the likelihood of a formal diagnosis that has found life in the popular media: Internet Addiction Disorder.

What is Internet Addiction Disorder?

Internet Addiction Disorder (IAD) is the term commonly applied to an ongoing pattern of excessive computer use that interferes with daily life [3]. The term Internet Addiction was first put forth in 1995 by Ivan Goldberg, M.D. in a satirical description of addictive Internet behavior which he based on diagnostic criteria for pathological gambling [4]. From the time when Dr. Goldberg first made his farcical diagnosis, a number of mental health practitioners have begun to seriously consider the concept of Internet addiction and how to best provide treatment.

According to the Center for Internet Addiction Recovery, Internet addiction is defined is:

> ...any online-related, compulsive behavior which interferes with normal living and causes severe stress on family, friends, loved ones, and one's work environment. Internet addiction has been called Internet dependency and Internet compulsivity. By any name, it is a compulsive behavior that

completely dominates the addict's life. Internet addicts make the Internet a priority more important than family, friends, and work. The Internet becomes the organizing principle of addicts' lives. They are willing to sacrifice what they cherish most in order to preserve and continue their unhealthy behavior. [5].

While this definition of Internet addiction provides a starting point for researchers and an initial framework for establishing appropriate treatment, no diagnostic criteria has been agreed upon. Furthermore, debate still remains over the existence of this disorder and whether it should be recognized as a problematic behavior worthy of unique definition.

Diagnostic Issues

The American Psychological Association (APA) does not recognize a specific definition for addiction, but views this as an umbrella term for a variety of problematic behaviors. However, n the current 4th edition of The Diagnostic and Statistical Manual of Mental Disorders (DSM-IV), the APA does provide clear criteria for substance dependence [6]. To be diagnosed as having such an addiction, an individual needs to have at least three of the following criteria within the same year:

1. Tolerance, as defined by either of the following:
    a. A need for markedly increased amounts of the substance to achieve intoxication or desired effect.
    b. Markedly diminished effect with continued use of the same amount of the substance.
2. Withdrawal, as manifested by either of the following:
    a. The characteristic withdrawal syndrome for the substance.
    b. The same (or a closely related) substance is taken to relieve or avoid withdrawal symptoms.
3. The substance is often taken in larger amounts or over a longer period than was intended.
4. There is a persistent desire or unsuccessful efforts to cut down or control substance use.
5. A great deal of time is spent in activities necessary to obtain the substance (such as visiting multiple doctors or driving long distances), use the substance (such as chain smoking) or recover from its effects.
6. Important social, occupational, or recreational activities are given up or reduced because of substance use.
7. The substance use is continued despite knowledge of having a persistent or recurrent physical or psychological problem that is likely to have been caused or exacerbated by the substance.

While the first two criteria are directly related to physiological dependence, it is important to note that an individual can be appropriately diagnosed with substance dependence even in the absence of such physiological dependence. By allowing for a diagnosis of dependence in the absence of physiological markers, many feel that the door is open for appropriate identification of a host of problematic behaviors such as computer games, television viewing, and even cartoon watching [7].

Some view Internet Addiction as a disorder common enough to merit its inclusion in the upcoming 5th revision of the Diagnostic and Statistical Manual of Mental Disorders (DSM-V). Jerald Block, M.D., a psychiatrist practicing in Portland, Oregon believes a diagnosis for Internet Addiction to be conceptually similar to that of a compulsive-impulsive spectrum disorder that consists of (at least) three subtypes including e-mail and test messaging, excessive gambling, and sexual preoccupation [8][9]. According to Dr. Block each of these shares similar components including withdrawal, excessive use, tolerance, and negative repercussions. Dr. Block does acknowledge that a diagnosis of Internet Addiction is problematic; however, 86% of study subjects presenting symptoms of Internet Addiction also exhibit other diagnosable mental health disorders.

While many within the field don't disagree that pathological Internet use is problematic, it's inclusion in the upcoming DSM remains uncertain. Part of the hesitation stems from a lack of clear definition of what Internet Addiction truly is. Researchers from the United States and South Korea performed a meta-analysis of empirical studies centered on Internet Addiction that has been published in peer-reviewed academic journals from 1996 to 2006. According to the authors, there is a need for researchers to "work to develop a standard definition of Internet addiction with supporting justification" [10]. Without such definitional clarity, research on the issue will likely remain inconsistent and appropriate (and agreed-upon) diagnostic criteria will fail to be established.

Furthermore, according to Vaughan Bell, a research fellow within the Department of Clinical Neuroscience at King's College London, the Internet is a medium for communication rather than a true activity and therefore Internet Addiction is a fundamentally flawed idea [11]. Dr. Bell believes that excessive computer and Internet use results from the individual dealing with more underlying problems such as social anxiety or depression. He contends that these underlying problems already have well-established treatments and the creation of new addictions will result in confusion for both the individual and the mental health field.

Treatment

Regardless of the ultimate outcome of the "Internet-Addiction-in-DMS-revision controversy", a number of mental health practitioners have begun treating it as they would other forms of addictive behavior. Recently, the first residential treatment center for Internet Addiction within the United States opened (ironically) near the Redmond, Washington headquarters of Microsoft [12]. The center, named ReStart, is similar to those currently operating in China, South Korea, and Taiwan and is able to provide intensive and personalized treatment for individuals who, until now, have had to rely on traditional outpatient services including content-control software, cognitive behavioral therapy, and counseling.

Such intensive treatment, however, is not inexpensive. The 45-day program will run around $14,000 and is generally not covered by insurance because Internet Addiction is not a formally recognized diagnosis. The program is designed to help the individual deal with issues including, "obsessive use of video games, texting, Facebook, eBay, Twitter and any other time-killers brought courtesy of technology." [13]. The ultimate success of such a program, however, remains to be seen as there is currently only a single resident at the treatment center designed to handle up to six patients at a given time.

Conclusion

While it is unlikely that the debate over the existence of Internet Addiction Disorder (and the complexities of appropriate treatment if it indeed does exist) will not be settled in the short term, this area promises to be one rich in research opportunity. Given the current increase in time spent on social networking sites such as Facebook and Twitter, it is likely that the average user will spend more time online than ever before. Reports that Twitter saw a 752% increase in 2008 (to a total of 4.43 million unique users) and that Facebook holds a user base that is nearly as large as the entire population of the United States speaks to the increasing importance of the online world in our daily lives [14][15].

Regardless of whether the influence of our time spent online proves to be positive or negative, it is safe to say that the Internet will remain a presence in every individual's daily life. To conclude, I thought I should provide a response to Dr. Stoll's question that was presented at the onset of this article...and I promise I will, but first I need to check my e-mail.

Endnotes

[1] http://thinkexist.com/quotes/clifford_stoll/

[2] http://news.cnet.com/8301-1023_3-10297935-93.html

[3] http://en.wikipedia.org/wiki/Internet_addiction_disorder

[4] http://web.urz.uni-heidelberg.de/Netzdienste/ anleitung/wwwtips/8/addict.html

[5] http://www.netaddiction.com/faq.htm

[6] American Psychiatric Association (2000). Diagnostic and statistical manual of mental disorders (Revised 4th ed.). Washington DC: Author.

[7] http://www.articlesbase.com/alternative-medicine-articles/tv-addiction-as-serious-as-drug-addiction-382100.html

[8] Dr. Jerald Block, M.D. is a fellow member of the Berglund Center Advisory Board and a frequent contributor to Interface.

[9] http://ajp.psychiatryonline.org/cgi/content/full/165/3/306

[10] Byun, S., Ruffini, C., Mills, J.E., Douglas, A.C., Niang, M., et al. (2009). Internet addiction: Metasynthesis of 1996-2006 quantitative research. Cyberpsychology and Behavior, 12 (2), 203-207.

[11] Bell, V. (2007). Online information, extreme communities, and Internet therapy: Is the Internet good for our mental health? Journal of Mental Health, 16(4), 445-457.

[12] http://www.breitbart.com/article.php?id=D9AG15703&show_article=1

[13] ibid.

[14] http://mashable.com/2009/01/09/twitter-growth-2008/

[15] http://www.cnn.com/2009/TECH/09/16/facebook.profit/index.html

Gaming

The Realities of Game Development

View online at: http://bcis.pacificu.edu/journal/2009/08/article.php?id=112

By Chris Pruett

An advertisement for an educational institution—Westwood College Online—made the rounds on the Internet a few years ago and it suggests that, by attending the college's online training course, you can get a job in game development, which, if we are to believe the commercial, consists mostly of sitting around playing games all day [1]. The video is humorous in its obliviousness; it was clearly made by people who have no understanding of video games nor of the people that play them (nor, apparently, of contemporary fashion trends). It was popular enough to spawn an Internet meme based on its script, and a key phrase from the ad—"tighten up the graphics,"—now means "to attempt a feat without knowledge of how it can be done" [2].

As out-of-touch as the Westwood College commercial is, it is representative of many casual misunderstandings about the game industry. "Wow, it must be fun to play games all day!" is a refrain that I often hear when I tell people that I work in video games. It's not just people unfamiliar with games that make this kind of mistake. At game development conferences I've often had conversations with folks from academia who, while experts in a field related to game technology, have absolutely no understanding of the logistics of game creation and are therefore unable to apply their knowledge concretely. Modern game development is an extremely problematic exercise. Though it can be a lot of fun, most games require blood, sweat, and tears to move into production.

Let's take a look at the mechanics of the industry from an outside perspective. The three major types of participants are publishers, hardware manufacturers, and game development studios. Studios make games to run on machines made by the hardware manufacturers (such as Sony, Microsoft, and Nintendo). The work studios do is funded by the publishers (like EA, Activision, and Ubisoft) who, in turn, manage marketing and physical distribution of video games. There are exceptions to this structure but, generally, games are made when publishers pay studios to develop games for specific hardware platforms [3].

Game development teams employed by studios can typically be broken down into five separate disciplines: testing, art, programming, management, and design. The testers are the people who actually do play games all day, but not for fun. People in this role must play the same game over and over again for months, looking for and reporting any problems that they find. They are usually the largest group on a game team, but also the lowest-paid.

Artists, who are responsible for textures, 3D models, animation, buttons, fonts, and any other visual data required by the game, normally make up the second-largest group. The programmers build the game but they are also often responsible for the tools the artists need to transfer completed art into the game. Most of their work nowadays is infrastructural: the biggest problems that must be solved pertain to getting data from the art and design teams into a format that is efficient on a specific hardware platform.

Managers of game teams, as in other industries, are tasked with the difficult job of navigating the rest of the team towards a timely and high-quality product while dealing with changing requirements from higher-ups and unpredictable schedule failures. There are a few other miscellaneous roles that some game teams fill such as sound designers and script writers. Game designers, however, are a ubiquitous and unique group.

With a couple of exceptions, most universities do not offer degrees in game design. There is no one set of skills that all game designers employ, and most come to the role from other disciplines in the industry. Game design can involve creating 3D architectural designs, writing dialog for characters to speak, defining variables that influence a game's physics, programming in a scripting language, or writing technical specs for the programmers and artists to follow. Game designers are tasked with designing the content in the game, specifying how it will all be glued together, and then orchestrating the actual moment-to-moment experiences that exposes that content to the player. Imagine if the same role existed in film; that person would be responsible for directing, set construction, script writing, editing, and cinematography. It's an all-encompassing creative role. On top of that, a good designer is one who can deal with the constant push and pull from other disciplines to make sure the game is made so that their vision is actually attainable. Despite the difficulty of this role, game designers do not command high salaries unless they have a proven track record of making hit games. Everybody wants to be a game designer, and the surplus of supply relative to demand drives wages down (even though good designers are few and far between).

Here's how a typical game development cycle plays out. The first part of the project is often spent on prototyping—building quick tests to see if the ideas that the designers have actually translate into something fun to play. At some point a high-level design is decided upon, and the team enters a phase called pre-production. During pre-production the team attempts to create the infrastructure it will need to produce the game: guidelines, methodologies, and software. The goal is to move into the next stage—called production—with the team set up to be a well-oiled game-making machine. During production the primary goal is to generate all of the game content so the team often grows in size during this period. This phase usually takes up the majority of the development schedule. At the end of the process, games go through a few finalization phases to stamp out bugs before being cleared for sale. This cycle can take anywhere from a few months for a simple handheld game to several years for a PC or console opus.

At least, that's how it is supposed to work. In reality, game development almost never goes that smoothly. The problems seem to be similar across studios and publishers. The pages of Game Developer Magazine are consistently filled with the same laments about "what went wrong" during development. Perhaps the prototype phase ended too soon, or the production phase was started prematurely. Or maybe the publisher changed their mind about a core component of the game and the well-oiled machine had to stop and change course. Very often the initial plan is simply too complicated and requires morc work than can be completed in the time allotted. Many games suffer from the inability to cut content back early enough to save the team from unnecessary work. All of these problems boil down to a basic challenge that is intrinsic to modern game development: scheduling the amount of work it will take to turn an idea into a fun experience is close to impossible.

Many games today get mediocre or bad reviews from game journalists despite being built out of reasonably high-quality components. There are a huge number of games that, despite excelling in art or graphics, technology or story, fail to "gel" and are consequently boring or frustrating to play. This generally means that the game was not given "enough time to bake," before it was released. In other words, not enough time was spent polishing the core systems that make up the moment-to-moment experience. This is a common issue because it is very hard to predict how much polish a game will require before it "clicks." Should Mario jump ten pixels in the air or eighteen? Should the player have reduced control over his lateral velocity while in the air? Until the results can be tested and compared within the context of other game systems (which requires much of a game's core production to be complete), it's impossible to judge. And by the time these things can be decided upon, the team is probably already working overtime to meet their pre-determined end date and is barely going to be able to get all the content in, let alone go back through and polish it.

Some companies in the game industry are experimenting with non-traditional development methods in an attempt to avoid this time crunch. One of these methods is called "SCRUM" and it involves working furiously in short bursts (called "sprints") on short-term goals. The idea is to remove the traditional "waterfall" method's need for a "big design up front" and instead deal with a list of feature requirements that are expected to change dramatically throughout the development process. The jury is still out on whether or not this method is applicable to game design; many companies have had success with it but it often does not fit the traditional publisher milestone schedule and some managers find the change difficult to make.

Whatever the methodology, game development is frequently hectic and chaotic. It's a large-scale, multi-disciplinary endeavor set to a schedule that often cannot sustain any sort of major revision or setback. The highest quality games are usually built by companies that have enough financial or political clout to set their own schedules, but for the rest of the industry, development can be a Sisyphean task. Though the phrase "tighten up the graphics" is funny because it betrays a serious lack of understanding about how games are made, as an Internet meme it has come to describe exactly how games are made: they are attempted without complete understanding of what will be required to finish the job.

Endnotes

[1] The commercial can be viewed at GameSpot (http://www.gamespot.com/users/Jeff/video_player?id=IiMzwjGt5bsF), as well as YouTube and similar video sites.

[2] See the Urban Dictionary's entry on the phrase: http://www.urbandictionary.com/define.php?term=tighten+up+the+graphics

[3] It is worth noting that alternative game platforms like the iPhone may challenge the traditional mechanics of this market.

Media

Everything You Need is in Your Shirt Pocket

View online at: http://bcis.pacificu.edu/journal/2009/08/article.php?id=118

By Lynda R. Irons

Remember Dick Tracy? And his watch? How futuristic was it to even imagine that you could talk to your wrist watch, let alone watch television or movies on it? Well, it's not so futuristic now. There are gadgets available today that make that science-fiction watch look no more sophisticated than a stick as DVDs have become blase and video streaming itself is becoming the way to see movies. With Warner Brothers and Turner Broadcasting signing agreements with YouTube to video stream their content, it seems it is only a matter of time until this capability will reach mobile devices [1].

Mobile entertainment is a growing industry estimated to make $47.5 billion in global business in the next few years [2]. Leading devices in this mobile-entertainment wave are Apple's second generation iPhone Touch and Nokia's smart phones. In a recent Business Traveller article, Mike Prigg vouches for Nokia and Archos saying that these companies have excellent devices that match the iPhone for end-user experience and quality [3]. Nokia is pushing to transform itself into an entertainment industry by introducing its technologies to Hollywood studios. In August 2007, Nokia announced an Internet service called "Ovi" to compete with Apple for the social networking functions of photo and video sharing on cell phones, but it only recently came online [4].

With the plethora of downloadable "apps" (or applications) newly available for popular cell phones, end users have a lot of options with how to fully enjoy and use their mobile entertainment and make their device a "media-center" instead of a plain old cell phone. One those apps is Flixster which is now offering "movie apps for the Palm Pre, the Blackberry , and Android-based devices" [5]. Between the movie reviews, show times, and ticket purchases the user has access to everything they need to catch a show on the fly. Flixster began in 2006 and its popular "Movies" application is the "leading mobile movie application on the iPhone, with an estimated 20 percent market share of all United States iPhone users [6]. Capitalizing on the social networking phenomenon, Flixster offers subscribers the opportunity to share their views, rate movies, answer quizzes, and watch movies for free regardless of the users' physical location or device. Other similar applications are provided by Rotten Tomatoes and Movie Genic [7].

Even if the user has the latest gadget available, it is still up to the studios to make their content accessible and by which method. To that end, Paramount Pictures and NBC University recently announced that, even though their films will be available via video streaming on iPhones, Blackberries, and other devices, users will not be using apps from iPhones but rather a new service called mSpot [8]. mSpot Mobile Movies hopes to expand its motion picture library by negotiating deals with other studios and content providers [9].

The mobile entertainment business is a rapidly increasing industry with over 1 billion cell phones sold in 2007 [10] and that is a lot of potential customers for applications and content.

Endnotes

[1] http://find.galegroup.com.proxy.lib.pacificu.edu:2048/gtx/retrieve.do?contentSet =IAC-Documents& resultListType=RESULT_LIST&qrySerId=Locale(en%2C%2C)%3AFQE%3D(ke%2CNone%2C15)video+streaming%24& sgHitCountType=None&inPS=true&sort=DateDescend&searchType=AdvancedSearchForm&tabID=T00

[2] http://www.lexisnexis.com.proxy.lib.pacificu.edu:2048/us/lnacademic/ results/docview/docview.do ?docLinkInd=true&risb=21_T7484808988&format=GNBFI&sort=RELEVANCE&startDocNo=1&resultsUrlKey= 29_T7484808991&cisb=22_T7484808990&treeMax=true&treeWidth=0&csi=235906&docNo=2

[3] http://find.galegroup.com.proxy.lib.pacificu.edu:2048/gtx/retrieve.do?contentSet =IAC-Documents& resultListType=RESULT_LIST&qrySerId=Locale(en%2C%2C)%3AFQE%3D(ke%2CNone%2C11)Mark+Prigg+%3AAnd% 3AFQE%3D(TX%2CNone%2C5)nokia%24&sgHitCountType=None&inPS=true&sort=DateDescend&searchType= AdvancedSearchForm&tabID=T002&prodId=AONE&searchId=R7&currentPosition =3&userGroupName=s8865459& docId=A176904341&docType=IAC

[4] http://vnweb.hwwilsonweb.com/hww/jumpstart.jhtml?recid= 0bc05f7a67b1790e25785094fd403b907304e22681747b 9dfa40c8a21d15ed87c2997f1a71b4aa0b&fmt=C Holson, L. M. An Unlikely Promoter Drives Nokia's Push in Hollywood. New York Times (Late New York Edition) (June 23 2008) p. C1, C5

[5] http://www.lexisnexis.com.proxy.lib.pacificu.edu:2048/us/lnacademic/ results/docview/docview .do?docLinkInd=true&risb=21_T7484716105&format=GNBFI&sort=RELEVANCE &startDocNo=1&resultsUrlKey= 29_T7484716108&cisb=22_T7484716107&treeMax=true&treeWidth=0&csi=246798&docNo=1

[6] Ibid

[7] http://blog.buttermouth.com/2009/09/best-iphone-movie-apps.html

[8] http://www.lexisnexis.com.proxy.lib.pacificu.edu:2048/us/lnacademic/ results/docview/docview .do?docLinkInd=true&risb=21_T7484817530&format=GNBFI&sort=BOOLEAN&startDocNo=1&resultsUrlKey= 29_T7484808991&cisb=22_T7484808990&treeMax=true&treeWidth=0&csi=140595&docNo=6

[9] Ibid

[10] http://news.cnet.com/8301-10784_3-9881022-7.html

Education

Google Goggles: The Dawn of Distributed Cognition for Educators Part 2

View online at: http://bcis.pacificu.edu/journal/2009/08/article.php?id=113

By Mark Szymanski

Google Docs. Think Microsoft Office. There are many reviews available to read about Google Docs. The ReadWriteLab [1] has a nice article comparing the features of Google Docs to Microsoft Office Live. The conclusion is familiar. Most products that are created in response to a Google product fall short in their technical elegance. But one way in which Google Docs surpasses the competition is in its simple built-in features to facilitate collaborative work. From a cognitive science perspective, and a learning perspective, Google Docs facilitates distributed cognition. It's thinking and working in a Web 2.0 world, a world that K12 educators have generally been slow to embrace.

Steve Downs, of the National Research Council of Canada, states that Web 2.0 "is not a technological revolution; it is a social revolution...It's about enabling and encouraging participation through open applications and services...with rights granted to use the content in new and exciting contexts...It enables the Web to shift from being a platform in which content is created, shared, remixed, repurposed, and passed along" (Downs, 2006) [2] .

K12 educators have struggled to integrate the rapidly evolving Web 2.0 technology into their daily practice precisely because they have tried to integrate the new tools into their daily practice-which hasn't changed much. It isn't every educator's struggle. Many educators, schools, and districts have embraced the Web 2.0 world and have told stories about paradigm shifts in their own thinking and practice. But, that's the point, K12 educators, like any other person integrating Web 2.0 tools into their practice, have to rethink their practice. This can be difficult for educators who work in systems and schools that insist on Web 1.0 thinking and practice

Google has perhaps compounded this problem. Historically, they have been a leader with web-based work, and I would argue, until recently, have been a bit too far ahead of educators in their applications.

Over the years, the Google Educators' site [3] has evolved into a very useful one for K12 educators. There are a wide range of applications and now, even a way to become a Google certified teacher. The effective change is that Google has slowly developed products and tools for educators that more precisely reflect the current needs of teachers. This is where Google Docs lands on the continuum. During the early days, Google educator tools naturally had a clear focus on being web-based. This worked fine for Google, but not for educators who have been slow to adopt web-based tools and were just getting used to a Web 1.0 world.

There are a number of variables that contributed to this. First, a reliable Internet connection and computers in students' hands was the problem. Over time, this has changed and we can now safely assume most students have access somewhere in their world. Second, there was a culture of Microsoft Office that was cemented in schools. Some educators were very skeptical of leaving a safe world, even though that world was laden with software bloat and the inevitable upgrade. Finally, as I referred to in the beginning, educators, like all professionals have had to reconsider their work in a Web 2.0 world. In this case the physical and temporal nature of schools has not changed. So, to ask educators to consider using a Web 2.0 world in their practice created a cognitive dissonance that proved debilitating to most.

In the Web 1.0 world, most students and teachers continued to operate in ways that reflected a back and forth one-to-one way of working. This practice was based on a competency model of learning that was not distributed in nature. Meaning that people learn about a body of knowledge, and create a product that reflects their understanding that will be assessed. This also meant that to get a clean assessment, there was no collaboration allowed. Well, as collaboration has become common practice, educators have begun to discover that collaboration, formerly called "cheating," was a more accurate reflection of how work is done in the real world. This helped to nudge things forward.

So, it seemed to make sense for educators to begin with the familiar, an Office Suite. It's the baby step forward that Google now provides educators. The next challenge for educators is to consider how to use the Web 2.0 features of Google Docs. They have done so in a wide variety of ways that are not technically complex, but in practice spread cognition across a community. For example, in the past, I had my students submit papers after they received feedback from students. I had no way of reading the comments, but with Google Docs, the writer can identify the people who are allowed to comment on the writing online. The same is true for the spreadsheet, and slide show tools.

In addition to the collaborative production features, there are the collaborative sharing features when products are complete. Slide shows can now be posted online and of course can be commented on after the fact. Consequently teachers can set up shows for other students to critique. Of course, Google also allows these documents to be linked to their Google calendars and many other tools. The point is that the simple act of moving to a Web 2.0 environment with familiar tools is an effective way to involve anyone in the collaborative process. It's a simple solution that may be an elegant solution as well.

As the sun rises on a new day for educators, it's much different than the 1.0 sunrise. In the new day of the Web 2.0 world, Google has taken a step back and extended a hand to K12 educators who might have felt like they were running after an accelerating train. And did I mention it was free???

Endnotes

[1]http://www.readwriteweb.com/archives/office_live_workspace_vs_google_docs_feature_by_feature.php
[2] E-learning 2.0. National Research Council of Canada Elearn Magazine. http://www.elearnmag.org/subpage.cfm?section=articles&article=29-1
[3] http://www.google.com/educators/index.html

Site Review

Website for Transforming Education through Information Technology

View online at: http://bcis.pacificu.edu/journal/2009/08/article.php?id=114

Review by Jeffrey Barlow

Occasionally we choose to review a site rather than a book, thinking each to be very useful tools in understanding the impact of the World Wide Web. This month we introduce Educause.edu. In its own words, "EDUCAUSE is a nonprofit association whose mission is to advance higher education by promoting the intelligent use of information technology." The site, although generally oriented toward higher education, is also broadly useful because of its focus on higher technology. The tone of its lead publications, though academic in that its authors are usually drawn from colleges and universities, is open and intended for a general audience. For example, most articles use a limited number of notes, and usually the sources are web accessible and do not require immediate access to a research library,

In addition to serving as a non-profit lobby for higher education, the organization is also a link between institutions and the corporations that serve the I. T. industry. More than 250 corporations are registered as partners and this wide corporate support has enabled an extensive program of research, conferences, and publications. The Educause Center for Applied Research, for example, both funds and reports on major issues of concern to institutions. At present more than four hundred reports and additional presentations are available [1].

Educause also publishes a number of regular periodicals, including a monthly review as well as a quarterly. Presentations, Blogs, and Podcasts fill out a broad range of available media [2]. We have chosen to take monthly hard-copy delivery of the Educause Review (free with registration) because we find that we are more likely to read it thoroughly if it lies around on our desk top until we do so, rather than joining the dozens, if not hundreds, of electronic sources that we fully intend to get to regularly, starting any minute.

Our attentions were recently drawn by a particular article, Brian Alexander's "Apprehending the Future: Emerging Technologies, from Science Fiction to Campus Reality" [3]. It is typical of a certain Educause encyclopedic look at current topics, drawing on a wide variety of materials, and frequently involving multiple authors. Brian's article surveys a broad range of means of "apprehending the Future," from reading science fiction to elaborate operations such as the Delphi Project which regularly has assembled experts since 2002 and consulted them on where higher technology seems to be going. He also discusses prediction markets, role-playing scenarios, and a number of other approaches and applications. While his conclusions are appropriately hedged, (he ends with N. Taleb's "Black Swan," which simply holds that history periodically sends us unforeseeable and improbable events which require that we cast all of our assumptions aside [4]) his sources are very rich and his introductions to them make for a wonderful beginning. The article, like much of Educause materials, was thorough, accessible, and enlightening.

Our survey of Educause resources has done little more than skim the surface of a very extensive site. It is, so far as we are aware, entirely free and publically accessible. Anyone interested in learning technologies or education in general should find it quite useful.

Endnotes:

[1] http://www.educause.edu/ECAR/ECARHome/ResearchPublications/172
[2] Because the site is not completely user friendly, I will post anchors to specific sections which I mention here. The publications can be found at: http://www.educause.edu/resources/browse/pub
[3] Found at: http://www.educause.edu/EDUCAUSE+Review/EDUCAUSEReviewMagazineVolume44/ ApprehendingtheFutureEmergingT/171774
[4] Nassim Nicholas Taleb, The Black Swan: The Impact of the Highly Improbable (New York: Random House, 2007), pp. 11, 149. Cited in Alexander at: http://www.educause.edu/EDUCAUSE+Review/EDUCAUSEReviewMagazineVolume44/ ApprehendingtheFutureEmergingT/171774

Book Review

Community, Space and Online Censorship. Regulating Pornotopia.

View online at: http://bcis.pacificu.edu/journal/2009/08/article.php?id=109

Beattie, Scott. *Community, Space and Online Censorship. Regulating Pornotopia.*, Franham, Surrey, England: Ashgate Publishing, 2009.

Review by Jeffrey Barlow

Dr. Scott Beattie' s work, *Community, Space and Online Censorship. Regulating Pornotopia.*, almost defies categorization[1]. It is meant to be a close analysis of the Australian Internet regulation regime, particularly the controversial Broadcasting Services Amendment (Online Services) Act of 1999. This act gave Australia what many have felt to be the most oppressive Internet control mechanism around, at least in the so-called Western world.

This focus might make Beattie's work of intense interest to Australians and comparative legal analysts, and perhaps to those interested in an understanding of Internet control regimes in general. But the fact that the subject of the Act was on-line pornography immediately makes it interesting to a far broader audience, as the issue of digital pornography is a vexing one to almost the entire English-speaking world.

However, this is not, unfortunately, a book for the entire English speaking world. It is written in the dense vocabulary of cultural studies, a post-modernist discipline which is both elusive and intellectually demanding, in part, of course, because of its relative unfamiliarity. The author does have persuasive reasons for adopting this analytical approach. In his words:

> As the pornography debate has developed over time, the critical terrain has shifted from primarily social science oriented approaches, focussing on issues of causation and harm, to critical perspectives informed by cultural studies, exploring issues of representation and reception....In part, this trend has been generated by the deadlock in the debate and the failure of social science to provide convincing empirical evidence one way or another regarding causation. Studies informed by critical theory have promoted an understanding of the multiplicity of meanings in pornography and the relationship with social space that is shared with other discourses, including regulatory and cyberspace discourses [2].

The intellectual rationality of the choice of approach aside, however, it is inherently distancing. Many of those interested in the topics, even in the approach itself, are going to find the book a very heavy read. This is unfortunate because it has a great deal to offer a variety of audiences.

Dr. Beattie is broadly trained, both in censorship law and media regulation and has authored a number of books and reports. He is also highly versed in cultural studies. His quick surveys of the relevant literature in a number of difficult areas important to the debates over law and censorship are extremely impressive. In some parts of the book he introduces and succinctly summarizes the works of as many as ten authorities in one or two paragraphs [3]. This awareness of the broad areas of the many fields alone makes the work useful to anyone wishing to better understand Internet censorship and the regulatory frameworks, as well as the intellectual underpinnings of such regimes.

And, as elusive as the book's central focus—the Australian Broadcasting Services Amendment (Online Services) Act—might occasionally seem to the reader, the Act is an important one. It attempts to bring together approaches from Australia's two major cultural influences, England and the United States, and weld them together around a supposed Australian definition of community. This means that as Beattie analyzes the Act, he simultaneously analyzes both American and English culture and law.

The Act also combines government regulation with privatized enforcement. Anybody can bring offensive Internet content to the attention of what must be called a censorship board—though the Board prefers to think of itself as classificatory. By issuing classifications for such content, it then puts Internet Provider firms in the position of enforcing the law by refusing certain classifications or unclassified content audience access. The IPs must also make available to their users commercial filtering programs keyed to the government's categories. Most citizens, as might be expected, simply ignore these, although their incorporation into the regime has made filtering software a major Australian industry. Perhaps the major virtue of such an approach is its apparent simplicity and its claim to embody local community values.

Beattie, however, brings out the failure of the Australian law to deal with a wide variety of controversies familiar to any attempt to rationalize legal efforts at regulating adult materials, whether called erotica or pornography. These include a close analysis of the various parties involved in the debate. For example, feminist critics of such material who attempt to approach it in the language of the oppression of women as opposed to the suppression of speech, producers and distributors of adult materials who apparently are quite happy with the law and wish only to understand the rules so as to expand their businesses, and legal scholars who hope to determine the best ways of regulating cyberspace—assuming it's possible. In particular, the works of the influential American legal scholar Lawrence Lessig come in for frequent close analysis by Beattie.

Beattie also pays due and fascinating attention to various genres of pornography, while wheeling quickly through the history of various social movements attempting to regulate it. A recurring theme is the "moral panic," in which various historical societiesm‐Victorian England is particularly scrutinized—cry wolf not about the content itself, with which they are more than familiar, but about its spread to rising middle or lower classes with their unfortunate pedestrian tastes. As L. O'Toole (a scholar quoted by Beattie and the author of a very influential work) puts it: "Art is not porn because it sublimates desire. Erotica is not porn 'because they drink wine and the women have smaller breasts'" [4].

The book is also, unfortunately, extremely expensive [5]. However, because of its wide coverage, it should certainly be in every institutional academic library, as well as in the hands of the audiences noted above.

Endnotes

[1] See the author's faculty page at the Victoria University, Au, at: http://www.businessandlaw.vu.edu.au/About_Faculty/profile/Display_Staff_Profile.asp?person=253&dept=6

[2] Beattie, p. 175.

[3] The bibliography runs thirty-three pages long and includes legal cases as well as written materials and useful web sites.

[4] L. O'Toole, Pornocopia: Porn, Sex, Technology, and Desire. London: Serpent's Tail, 1998., p. 17

[5] $114.00 at Amazon: http://www.amazoncom/Community-Space-Online-Censorship-Beattie/dp/0754673081

Editorial

Peaceful Evolution in China and the World Wide Web: Part II, Factionalism and Democracy

View online at: http://bcis.pacificu.edu/journal/2009/08/article.php?id=108

Editorial by Jeffrey Barlow

Introduction.

In the first part of this editorial [1], we examined the notion of democracy within the Chinese and American political cultures. Here we argue that because the Chinese system contains an element also common to the American one, factionalism, it will inevitably evolve under the impact of the Internet to become more democratic in practice. However, it will not necessarily become more similar to the American system.

Factionalism in the Two Systems:

In the preceding editorial I stated that the Chinese believe the American multi-party system camouflages the control of economic elites and that, through the system of financing elections, these economic elites ensure candidates who support their perspectives are far more likely to be elected.

However, the Chinese perspective overlooks one virtue of the two-party system and a major defect in one-party politics: the dominant party, if lacking an opponent to call them on their mistakes and outright peculations, easily and, possibly inevitably, becomes arrogant and corrupt [2].

In the Chinese case, the ties of family, locale, and dialect often produce political groups similar to "machines" in American politics. These local elite groups often make it impossible for Chinese national policy to be implemented at local levels. At present, for example, the national government of China has clearly decided that the country must stop relying on an export-driven economy, and is providing funding to ease the transition to alternative domestic markets. However, elite groups tied to export-oriented industries often dominate local and provincial governments. These groups have misused such funding in an attempt to strengthen local export industries in direct opposition to national policies [3].

This problem of the political influence of local elites is not new in the Chinese system. Prior to the modern era the imperial government had one inviolable practice in the elaborate Confucian civil service system: "The Rule of Avoidance." The Rule absolutely prohibited posting a bureaucrat such as a local Magistrate or even a Provincial Governor-General to his home province, where he would invariably be corrupted or hamstrung by the local ties mentioned above.

It is true that the old society could become incredibly corrupt, but this was much more likely at the Imperial Court than in the Civil Service system itself. The Confucians usually avoided conspicuous spending and displays of wealth and emphasized an almost puritanical simplicity. What they wanted was power, and corruption was a hindrance to gaining and holding power.

Additionally, Confucians genuinely believed that good government flowed from basic Confucian principles and that factionalism—such as the interference of local elites—was not only an evil, but also a fatal flaw in policy [4]. The Confucian bureaucracy, then, was intended to be a unitary one, not one torn by differing interpretations of basic values or policies. To be charged with factionalism at the Imperial Court would result in banishment, physical punishment, or execution.

In this regard, the Confucians had a very different perspective than did the American Founding Fathers, though Americans too, initially saw factionalism as an evil. This classic American sentiment comes from James Madison's *The Federalist* No. 10, "The Utility of the Union as a Safeguard Against Domestic Faction and Insurrection" [5].

Madison believed factionalism evil, but inevitable [6]. It could be prevented—in his words—only by removing its causes, which lay in human nature: *There are again two methods of removing the causes of faction: the one, by destroying the liberty which is essential to its existence; the other, by giving to every citizen the same opinions, the same passions, and the same interests.*

The Communist Party agrees with Madison in that it also thinks factionalism is inevitable, at least at the initial stage in the policy-making process. Democracy, in the sense of a multiplicity of opinions and outright factionalizing, is permissible only while the Party is forming policy. This involves a period of closed-door Party discussions, replicated at lower levels of the system as various alternatives are examined [7]. However, once policy is announced from the top, factional disagreements can be met much as the Confucians would; that is, with violence, if gentler methods of suppression fail [8]. The Party, in short, attempts in Madisonian terms to quell factionalism by giving *"...to every citizen the same opinions, the same passions, and the same interests."*

This analysis may seem both antiquarian and overly theoretical. However, it is clear that Communism was able to supplant Confucianism in China because, in many regards, the two are very similar. This should not surprise us. Both systems had to be appropriate to the Chinese historical and cultural context in order to survive and become dominant. Confucianism itself repeatedly evolved to meet new historical circumstances; so has Communism.

The Confucians, like the Party, believed that good policy comes fundamentally from moral and ethical agreement. To disagree with the dominant policy was literally immoral. The most common basis for political attacks then, was to charge that the opposition was corrupt or dishonest or, in some manner, violating the Confucian value system. This avoided the charge of factionalism because it cloaked itself as a defense of core Confucian values. Because shared values remain critically important within the current system, this political tactic will remain necessary and useful [9].

This means that changing the basic political line or orientation in either the traditional or contemporary Chinese system was and is very difficult. Creating the pressure to do so implies or requires factionalism. The safest way to remove powerful political opponents is still to catch them in corrupt behavior.

How the Internet Facilitates Chinese Democracy

This game of charging corruption, however, has always been a closed process. Officials, Confucians or Communists, could play it. The people could not—they lacked both information and influence upon policy. These discussions were closed ones, dominated by totalitarian forces, whether the Emperor or the Party Central Committee. These kept the discussions and factionalism safely within bounds. The people did, at various times, violently force new policies upon their leaders in a desperate attempt to force the government to deal with unbearable suffering at local levels.

To argue that the present Chinese system functions exactly or largely like the imperial system is, of course, naïve. There are countless new factors at play which the Confucians had never faced. It was their failure to find solutions to new problems, after all, which resulted in decades of turmoil and ultimately, the founding of the People's Republic in 1949.

Now that government also faces new challenges. Looming large among these are the forces of globalization, including the Internet. The Chinese people, like all of us, now live amidst complex production chains, global markets, interdependent fiscal systems, and instantaneous digital communications systems.

There are many examples of the political use of the Internet in China. Here we will ignore the international aspect, wherein internal Chinese issues quickly become noted globally, and focus upon local internal ones. It is noteworthy that many of these are, as we would expect, related to moral or ethical issues, particularly those facing children and family—these are the issues to which Chinese leadership is particularly sensitive [10]. And in a country with 100 million blogs and 290 million Internet users, these issues immediately become nationally known [11].

Other issues which quickly go viral on the Internet in China deal with local groups who are not using the Internet so much to condemn national government or party officials, but instead to call attention to local incidents which violate national policies. These frequently include collusion between local elites and industries resulting in local harm to the environment or health, or misuses of political power to quell local labor disturbances. Sometimes these incidents seem relatively minor, but determined participants—outraged relatives of alleged victims, for example—can quickly make them a regional or national issue [12].

Some Internet issues, of course, amount to attacks on national policy, or are driven by local ethnic issues. These, if seen to be driven by foreigners, have frequently resulted in nationalist outbursts by Chinese both at home and abroad condemning foreign reports which are often felt to be politically motivated or outright incorrect, whether deliberately so or not. This reaction to foreign interference has produced a new and strident Internet-enabled nationalism among some so-called "Angry Youth" [13].

The Chinese government has tried, of course, both to stifle the spread of such information and to manipulate it to their advantage. However, the critical issue is not that there are attempts at suppression, but the fact that such suppression is now necessary. In even the recent past, local issues had to grow to a sometimes staggering scale or local abuses of power had to become truly outrageous before authorities were forced to focus on them at all.

The Chinese government has few good choices in such situations. Local and national officials can and often do try to suppress news of the events, but if these do leak—and if they are of any scale or importance, they will, thanks to the Internet—then the government looks worse than it would have if it had dealt with such issues properly at the outset.

We do not have direct insight into internal Party discussions over such local questions, but it is easily inferred from the almost inevitable punishment of local authorities that bad policy is seen as just that, and condemned [14]. These events are certainly producing factional reactions in inner governmental circles, and the trend is clearly for the government to be more and more transparent and open. This is inevitable; a failure to deal with issues quickly becomes a factional issue. It could also result in being condemned as neglecting corruption at the local level, hinting at personal corruption. The government is still far, of course, from meeting the more extreme demands of idealists both at home and abroad for transparency and the rule of law. But the momentum is for becoming more open, and this trend is irreversible. The very fact that issues which could earlier be safely ignored now must be discussed internally creates a system that functions increasingly like a democracy, in the sense that various factions are heard, and conflicts are compromised.

This is not to say that China will necessarily evolve into a two-party system, or that it should. As Thomas Friedman recently pointed out in *The New York Times*, the centralized nature of one-party control, autocratic or not, gives the Communist Party the power necessary to "...impose the politically difficult but critically important policies needed to move a society forward in the 21st century" [15]. We must necessarily wonder, given the disarray of the American system and the stultifying partisanship of entrenched interests, if the American two-party system has the equivalent will and power to do the same.

We also think that it is ultimately in the interest of democracies in general and the idea of "democracy" in particular for there to be a wide variety of differing types of democracies in various stages of evolution. The recent crises in free-market capitalism have shown not only weaknesses in Western democracies (which are finding it difficult to act against entrenched interests) but the strengths in Eastern ones (which can do so because of a more unitary heritage).

Conclusion

Political systems, to be stable, must reflect history and culture in both their forms and functions. The American and the Chinese systems differ markedly, especially in form, but it is difficult to claim that the multiparty system is superior to a one-party system in which factions may be so prominent as to be recognizably consistent in membership and policy inclinations. Chinese history and culture is capable of producing a system democratic in function, is doing so at the present, and will inevitably continue do so under the impact of the Internet.

Endnotes

[1]See "Peaceful Evolution in China and the World Wide Web: Part I, Two Democracies?" Found at: http://bcis.pacificu.edu/journal/2009/07/article.php?id=98

[2]It may be of course, that the minority party also becomes corrupt.

[3]For examples of this process see my *Chinatripper* Blog entry for November 10, 2008, found at:
http://bcis.pacificu.edu/blogs/chinatripper/chinatripper_archives.php?id= A2008115

[4]For an academic discourse on this issue, see James T.C. Liu's "Some Classifications of Bureaucrats In Chinese Historiography" at:
http://books.google.com/books?id=zy-sAAAAIAAJ&pg=PA167&lpg=PA167&dq=confucian+factionalism&source=bl&ots=rVhpXjyxrK&sig=dFFfir2RETkisGRakcEJDY9NoYs&hl=en&ei=9miESuSOA6KxmAeo68DgBg&sa=X&oi=book_result&ct=result&resnum=2#v=onepage&q=confucian%20factionalism&f=false
See also: Benjamin A. Elman, "Imperial Politics and Confucian Societies in Late Imperial China: The Hanlin and Donglin Academies" *Modern China*," Vol. 15, No. 4. (Oct., 1989), pp. 379-418. Downloadable PDF for those with JStor access at:
http://links.jstor.org/sici?sici=0097-7004%28198910%2915%3A4%3C379%3AIPACSI%3E2.0.CO%3B2-E

[5]http://www.constitution.org/fed/federa10.htm

[6]For a contemporary conservative statement which disagrees that factionalism is evil, or that Madison truly believed that it was, see: "Partisanship: The glue that holds the union together", *The Roanoke Times*, Sunday, April 12, 2009:
http://www.roanoke.com/editorials/commentary/wb/200701

[7]Often policies which are truly departures from the status quo are allowed to be instituted in local areas which particularly favor them; if successful, they are then put into effect on a wider scale. In doing so, the architects of such changes are then usually promoted to more important responsibilities as well, and have often constituted a recognizable faction.

[8]The incredible turmoil of the Great Proletarian Cultural Revolution (1968-78) was a prolonged period of just such factionalism. I believe the Tian An Men violence of 1989 to have been so pronounced precisely because it grew out of a serious factional

split within the party when reformers attempted to rally around Zhao Ziyang and position him to succeed Deng Xiaoping. Zhao, I believe, attempted to utilize student and worker unrest and the conservatives met what they regarded as escalation (going outside the Party to pressure policy making internal to the Party) with escalation—armed violence.

[9]For a recent example from the Confucian cultural sphere, in this case Taiwan, see: Edward Wong, "Life Sentence for Taiwan Ex-President," *The New York Times*, 9/11/2009. Found at: http://www.nytimes.com/2009/09/12/world/asia/12taiwan.html?hpw

[10]See, for example, Ariana Eunjung Cha, "China Food Fears Go from Pets to People" *Washington Post Foreign Service*, April 25, 2007 at: http://www.washingtonpost.com/wp-dyn/content/article/2007/04/24/AR2007042402539.html

[11]See *"China blogger population exceeds 50 mln: report"* January 7, 2009. The Age.com: http://news.theage.com.au/technology/china-blogger- population-exceeds-50-mln-report-20090107-7btm.html

[12]See, for example, Kathrin Hille "How China polices the internet,"FT.Com, July 17 2009: http://www.ft.com/cms/s/2/e716cfc6-71a1-11de-a821-00144feabdc0.html

[13]View an article and a transcript of a Brookings Center Presentation Event "Understanding China's "Angry Youth": What Does the Future Hold?" at: http://www.brookings.edu/events/2009/0429_china_youth.aspx

[14]It could be argued that they are being punished for failing to suppress information, not for implementing bad policy. I would argue that in practice the distinction is unimportant; the result is still pressure to mediate problems before they create bad publicity.

[15]Thomas L. Friedman, "Our One-Party Democracy" *The New York Times*, September 8, 2009 http://www.nytimes.com/2009/09/09/opinion/09friedman.html?_r=2&em

November 2009 - Volume 9, Issue 9

Articles

Book and Site Reviews

Editorial

Feature

Email Traps and Troubles

View online at: http://bcis.pacificu.edu/journal/2009/09/article.php?id=123

By Leonard D. DuBoff and Christy O. King

Email communications are extraordinarily efficient, whether you are corresponding across town, across the country, or around the world, but, unfortunately, they open the door to many pitfalls. Email users must, therefore, be careful to avoid the problems that can arise from using electronic correspondence.

It is quite common, for example, for people to "carbon copy" (or "cc") others on emails. If your email cc's someone and the primary recipient of the email uses "reply to all," that response will be transmitted to the person you cc'd, even if you were not planning for that person to receive it. To avoid this kind of problem, you should, when appropriate, blind copy (or "bcc") parties instead of cc'ing them.

Conversely, you should remember not to inadvertently *reply to all* when responding to email communications because that reply will then not go only to the party for whom it is intended, but will also wind up being transmitted to all the parties who received the initial communication.

Email users should check to be sure that an email does not contain the stream of communications between the sender and any others that led to that communication, unless, of course, you want the ultimate receiver to see that email stream.

Many organizations have some form of standard disclaimer at the end of their emails. Frequently, this is automatically inserted by the organization's email program. When emails are exchanged within the sender's office so that a colleague can assist in refining the communication, the program may automatically add an additional disclaimer. When this communication is ultimately sent out, it may have two or more disclaimers stacked up at its end. This will alert an astute recipient to the fact that this communication has been wordsmithed by several people. To avoid this problem, if your organization's email inserts such a disclaimer at the end of outgoing emails, you should delete any disclaimers that have accumulated at the end of the email language.

It is also important to carefully review emails for spelling and grammar before they are sent. In many email programs, spellcheck does not catch misspellings in the subject lines of emails. Also, it corrects only spelling errors; that is, it does not determine whether the word is properly used (for instance, "you" is often typed for "your"). Thus, you may find that words in your email are all correctly spelled, but they may not be used in the proper context or even make sense.

Email users are frequently careless with the subject line of their communication, which typically refers to the first communication. It is rare for recipients who respond to that communication to revise the subject line to reflect the response, even if the actual subject of the correspondence changes. As the stream of emails continue, the original subject line may become less and less relevant to the ultimate communication's content, so it is a good idea to revise the subject accordingly.

When someone receives an acrimonious email or one from someone with whom there is a strained relationship, it is quite common to prepare a vitriolic response, which may ultimately prove embarrassing. It is for this reason that prudent email users will delay sending a response until they have either had time to cool off or can obtain input from colleagues who are more removed from the situation.

While it is important to pay attention to the content of your email and make sure that it effectively communicates just what you want to communicate, you should also pay attention to whom the communication is directed. When, for example, the communication deals with subjects that should be restricted to certain individuals in an organization, care should be taken not to send the email to a general email box. Nor should you send emails to individuals at their work addresses without their express consent, since many companies have policies providing that email in their systems is not private and can be read by supervisors and others in the company. Similarly, sending an email to a family's email address when it is intended for just one of the family members could be problematic.

Autofill, the feature of some email programs that automatically places a full email address in the "To" or "cc" position once a few letters of that address/name are typed in, can also create difficulties. If you are not careful to confirm that the email is actually directed to the right person, then the communication could easily go astray. For instance, you may have read about the lawyer for Eli Lilly & Co. who was trying to email co-counsel Bradford Berenson with confidential information on settlement talks with the government but, instead, sent the communication to the New York Times reporter Alex Berenson [1].

Metadata is another area of concern. Such information, which is invisible but retrievable, is often found in word processing documents and may include details such as editing time, comments, authors and even the edits themselves. If the metadata is something you would not want your recipient to review, be sure to either convert the document to PDF or to use a metadata scrubbing program before sending an email attachment.

Organizations should have email policies in their handbooks covering a host of issues. These would include, among other things, the fact that the organization's computer system belongs to it and emails received on it belong to that organization. Policies should also prohibit the use of profanity and other offensive, embarrassing or derogatory language, as well as all forms of harassment and discrimination. Other issues to cover include a prohibition on sending emails with viruses, worms or the like, or with content that infringes intellectual property or other rights.

Finally, you should remember that merely deleting an email does not expunge it from the system; rather, it remains on the hard drive until a special electronic scrubbing program is used to cleanse the hard drive or until the email is overwritten by other data. Thus, you should be judicious when deciding whether to communicate via email or through another less permanent form of communication.

You should be diligent when using your email system, and it cannot be overemphasized how important it is to carefully read the final version of a co mmunication before hitting send.

Leonard DuBoff is author of more than 20 books on business and intellectual property law. He was a law professor for almost a quarter of a century, teaching at the Stanford and Lewis & Clark law schools. He is the managing principal of The DuBoff Law Group, LLC, which focuses on complex business and intellectual property. Christy King is a member of the DuBoff Law Group, LLC, and editor-in-chief of the firm's newsletter *Critical Issues*, and coauthor with DuBoff of the *Deskbook of Art Law, Art Law in a Nutshell, The Law (In Plain English) for Restaurants and The Law (In Plain English) for Doctors, Dentists, and Other Health Care Professionals*. Her practice areas include intellectual property, business and corporate law. For more information and to obtain a copy of the firm's newsletter, see www.dubofflaw.com.

Endnotes

[1] "Did Lawyer's E-Mail Goof Land $1B Settlement on NYT's Front Page?" at www.abajournal.com/news/lawyers_e_mail_goof_lands_on_nyts_fgront_page, 2/6/08; and "Lilly's $1 Billion E-Mailstrom" at www.portfolio.com/news-markets/top-5/2008/02/05/Eli-Lilly-E-Mail-to-New- York-Times?, 2/5/08.

Technology

Surf's Up: HTML Five-oh! (Part 1)

first of a two part series

View online at: http://bcis.pacificu.edu/journal/2009/09/article.php?id=124

By Michael Geraci

HTML, the markup language used to create Web pages is getting close to an evolutionary threshold. If that sounds like an intentionally ambiguous way of saying "it's about to be upgraded to a new version" then please bear with me, for not only is HTML slowly shedding its old skin and adding to its genetic profile, it's going to be doing so for the next 13 years. That's right; HTML 5 is coming to a Web browser near you in 2022 [1].

While the above statement is technically true, it fails to point out the fact that certain elements that are in the HTML 5 language can be implemented *right now*, assuming you've done your homework and are willing to accept some level of minor disappointment. The fact is that this upgrade can't happen overnight, but we don't have to wait until it's "done" to begin using the parts of it that have begun to find their way onto the Web.

You see, upgrading HTML from its current version 4 status to the next iteration is a big deal and is nothing at all like installing the newest version of your tried and true software applications or operating system and here's why:

A new version of HTML is going to bring with it all sorts of new page elements (tags) and APIs (functionality) that will have to be supported by all the major Web browsers to insure consistent user experiences with all Web content. There are five "major" Web browsers and according to Wikipedia about 65 others in circulation [2]. These will all have to be rewritten to render the new markup *while being 100% backward compatible* with every Web page in existence that is written in a previous version of HTML.

Older Web browsers, like Internet Explorer 6 and 7 that are still in use by 27% of Web surfing public (Yes, Mom, I'm talking to you!), need to be able to read and make sense out of pages written in the newest form of the language even if they don't understand all the markup, otherwise the disincentive to adopt HTML is 5 is far greater than any advantages it may bring.□

Every Web creation or Web savvy application, from site builders and content management systems to screen readers and other assistive technologies are going to have to be upgraded to understand all the new vocabulary in the language in order to be useful.

Another reason that upgrading HTML is infinitely tricky is a little harder to grasp. Unlike desktop software applications, no one industry or organization owns or has responsibility for the development of HTML. Nowhere was this more evident than during the first "browser war" [3] where Netscape and Microsoft fought for browser dominance by implementing their own versions of HTML that only worked in their products. An outcome from this dark period in Web history is the rise to prominence of the World Wide Web Consortium (W3C) which brought the myriad stakeholders together and pushed hard, along with the Web developer community, for a common set of standards by which sites could adhere to in order to render predictably on as many platforms as possible. The W3C does not create *specifications* as these are considered to be akin to "laws" in the software world, and the W3C does not pretend to have this authority over markup languages. Instead they make *recommendations* for markup languages and other associated technologies and, in the absence of real specifications, these hold a lot of weight in the Web development community.

It is the W3Cs involvement in the HTML 5 development that contributes to its pending availability as *the* standard for Web page markup, but not before almost leading to its demise.

When HTML 5 was proposed by a few of the major browser companies back in 2004 the W3C had no intention of working on it as they were focused on upgrading the current version of XHTML 1 that was quickly overshadowing the ten year-old HTML 4 standard as a more reliable and future-proof markup language. I realize that XHTML sounds *a lot* like HTML, but the addition of that X makes a world of difference. The languages are based on a different set of rules and are interpreted differently by browsers. In effect, we went from a very public browser war ten years ago to a somewhat low-key, and probably quite polite, *language* war in the more recent past. The good news: in 2007, the W3C joined with the WHATWG, the consortium developing the HTML 5 specification, and put XHTML 2 on the back burner, possibly forever [4]. With two very dedicated organizations carrying it forward, HTML 5 is quickly progressing to the point where Web developers can start to use it and end users may start to reap the benefits of the new language.

This newfound commitment to developing HTML 5 has yielded the following timeline [5]:

October 2007: First W3C working draft. *Translation*: The W3C is saying "we're on board, let's develop an agreed upon draft version of the language and open it up to the community for comments and proposals.

October 2009: Final call for the working draft *Translation*: no more comments or proposals will be accepted; it's time to start finalizing the recommendation.

2011: call for contributions to the test suite. *Translation*: the W3C doesn't make anything, but browsers and the like have to be tested to insure they are fully compatible with the new markup. The testing services that will be made available to Web applications developers will essentially be in development until 2011 by various third party organizations working through the W3C development protocols.

2012: Candidate recommendation. *Translation*: HTML 5 is available for implementation.

2012 – 2019: Test suite development. *Translation*: Continue to create and test HTML 5 aware applications and testing services for them.

2020: Last Call Working Draft. *Translation*: Test suites for Web applications need to be finalized.

2022 (after two years of testing): Proposed recommendation. *Translation*: HTML5 is the official language of the Web and comes with some level of guarantee as to its interoperability and stability.

Despite how official all that sounds, the fact remains that enough has already been developed in HTML 5 that some of the major browsers have already started to support the more significant enhancements made possible in the new version: most notably, support for audio and video on Web pages without the need for third-party plug-ins. I realize that to most, this doesn't appear like an enhancement to our daily Web lives, but remember that we access audio and video through the graces, and on-going maintenance of proprietary software from Adobe (Flash), Apple (QuickTime), and Microsoft (Window's Media, Silverlight), to name a few. HTML 5 treats audio and video like it does text or images, it just works out of the box and Web page creators will be able to add their own user interface elements (playback controls, for example) without the need for authoring tools like Dreamweaver or Flash (some basic JavaScript will be required to create custom controls).

As of this writing, Google Chrome and Apple's Safari browsers have the most support for HTML 5 with Mozilla Firefox and Opera running just slightly behind. To be clear, these browsers are only supporting a few of the dozens of enhancements promised under HTML 5, but each new update brings further refinements and additions to the level of HTML 5 that's possible.

Still wondering exactly why you should even care about HTML 5? Come back to this space in the next edition of Interface and I'll break it down for you, or if you can't wait, check out the WHATWG's site.

References:

[1] http://wiki.whatwg.org/wiki/FAQ#When_will_HTML5_be_finished.3 F

[2] http://en.wikipedia.org/wiki/List_of_web_browsers

[3] http://en.wikipedia.org/wiki/Browser_wars#The_first_browser_war

[4] http://www.w3.org/News/2009#item119

[5] http://wiki.whatwg.org/wiki/FAQ#When_will_HTML5_be_finished.3 F

Further reading on the development of HTML 5:

W3C's ongoing documentation site: http://dev.w3.org/html5/spec/Overview.html

Preview of HTML 5 at A List Apart:
http://www.alistapart.com/articles/previewofhtml5/

Browser compatibility with HTML 5 at Wikipedia:
http://en.wikipedia.org/wiki/Comparison_of_layout_engines_(HTML_5)

Security

Snips, Snails, Truffles, Malware Warnings, and other Tidbits to Chew On

View online at: http://bcis.pacificu.edu/journal/2009/09/article.php?id=125

By Pat McGregor

Danger! Have your "Fans" been Checking you out on Facebook?

Your friends on Facebook may have been urging you to remove the increasingly popular "Fancheck," which does the numbers and gives you some info about the totality of your friends, such as "most common name" and "average age". But the malware is actually the interesting Facebook app "Removal Kits," which many people have been buying and consequently giving fraudsters their personal info and credit card info.

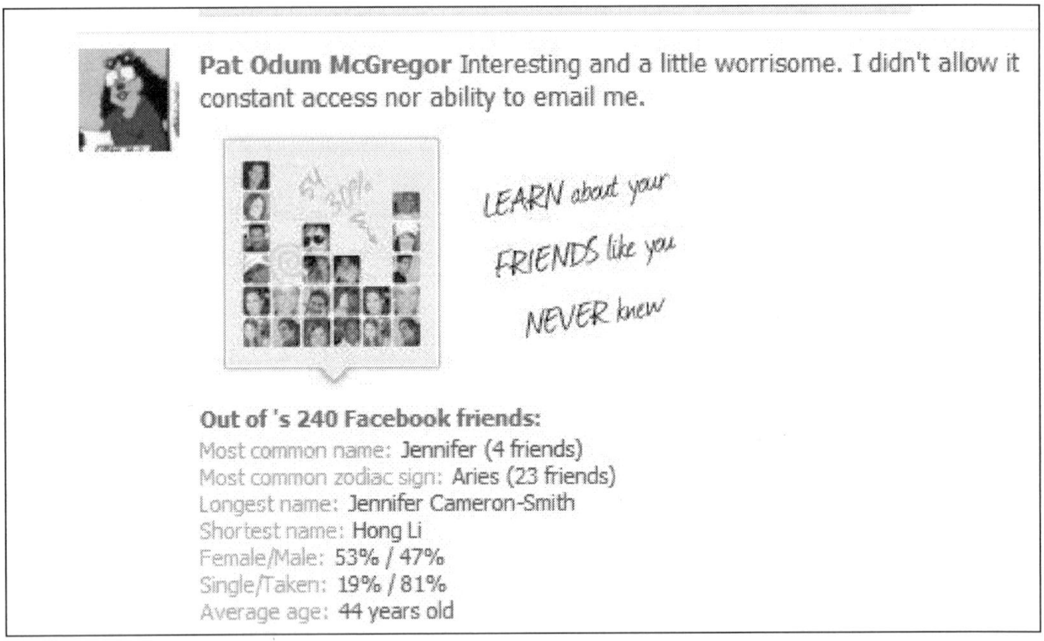

Sophos Software Online expert Graham Cluley warns,

> ...hackers have set up websites pretending to be about the "Facebook Fan Check Virus", but which really host fake anti-virus software which display bogus warnings about the security of your computer in an attempt to get you to install fraudulent software and cough-up your credit card details [1].

But, Facebook isn't the only site plagued by this. Even the venerable New York Times had malware ads injected in the middle of September 2009.

Even worse, the Times says that the advertiser, posing as Internet phone company Vonage, sold the ads directly to them rather than through an ad vendor:

> The creator of the malicious ads posed as Vonage, the Internet telephone company, and persuaded NYTimes.com to run ads that initially appeared as real ads for Vonage. At some point, possibly late Friday, the campaign switched to displaying the virus warnings.
>
> Because The Times thought the campaign came straight from Vonage, which has advertised on the site before, it allowed the advertiser to use an outside vendor that it had not vetted to actually deliver the ads, Ms. McNulty said. That allowed the switch to take place. "In the future, we will not allow any advertiser to use unfamiliar third-party vendors," she said. Mr. Frons said it was unclear how many people saw the ads [2].

This was a huge surprise to those of us who track these sorts of events. You're more likely to see this on websites without such a scrupulous reputation, and generally with those using ad networks to manage what ads show up on their sites. (See my article last month on Behavioral Tracking for more info on how online ads work [3].

In August, US Healthcare Debate Topped the Inbox Chart, But Then, Most Email Is Now SPAM

According to Austin Modine in the online website The Register,

> Health-care spam held a solid lead with 68.8 per cent of unsolicited emails. Miscellaneous offers accounted for 12.3 per cent, education 4.4 per cent, gambling 1.3 per cent, and foreign language spam only 1.1 per cent [4].

But, as you probably noticed, most of the email sent (and received) is now spam. Although your personal filters or your email provider may filter it out, spam now accounts for nearly 95% of the email whizzing around the Internet [5].

Let's do the Numbers

CSO Magazine always has an interesting column on "numbers" with InfoSec factoids or Trivia. This month's:

$704,610: Amount of money attackers siphoned out of bank accounts belonging to the Western Beaver County School District.

11: Number of vulnerabilities fixed in Firefox 3.0 in late July.

10: Number of Firefox flaws that were considered *critical.*

4: Approximate number of months remaining until Mozilla kills of Firefox 3.0 and forces users onto Firefox Version 3.5.

9: Number of security patches Microsoft released in August.

300: Number of companies attacked by the same malware that enabled the data security breach at Heartland Payment Systems (according to Heartland CEO Robert Carr) [6]

Antimalware: Not just about Viruses Anymore...

A great many people figure that the Norton or Symantec suites that come on their pre-loaded machines will do the stuff -- not realizing that it's no longer just virus software. Information Security Magazine polled their readers for the best business-grade desktop and server antivirus and antispyware products. You won't be surprised to find that many security-savvy home users use these products (or their single-user products) instead of the more familiar ones. But what may surprise you is the variety of apps you get rolled into one. Natalie Lambert, an analyst at Forrester Research, says:

> Generally speaking, antimalware is antimalware; what you get from one vendor is not much different than what you get from another. Where the market is changing is that there are lots of components required to have a comprehensive strategy. Antimalware alone is not going to cut it. It's hard to buy antimalware alone; vendors are almost forcing you to buy a client suite [7].

You may be surprised to find that the big players you may be most familiar with are not in the top three. Instead, we find:

(GOLD) Kaspersky Open Space Security, Kaspersky Labs

"Kaspersky Open Space Security is the company's suite of antimalware protection for the gateway and endpoint. It includes: Work Space, which keeps workstations secure; Business Space, which adds file server protection; Enterprise Space, which adds mail server security; and Total Space, which adds gateway protection to the previous offerings. It received high marks for detecting, blocking and cleaning malware, and in the speed and frequency of signature updates" [8].

I recommend you look at their home protection suites as well (Internet Security 2010, Anti-Virus 2010, Security for Ultra Portables, Mobile Security), as they have gotten high marks from fellow security geeks.

(SILVER) Sophos Endpoint Security and Data Protection, Sophos

"Sophos' Endpoint Security and Data Protection wraps antivirus, firewall, network access control and encryption into a neat package that voters liked for its quick signature updates, and reporting and alerting capabilities. You can also centrally manage the security status of your endpoints from one console; the product supports Windows, Unix and Linux" [8].

Sophos is not only hot software, but they maintain a terrific online source of threats, mitigations, and top-notch white papers and expert discussions.

(BRONZE) ESET NOD32 Antivirus, ESET

"ESET NOD32 Antivirus offers not only antivirus and antispyware protection, but a personal firewall and antispam capabilities. Voters were keen on the product's ease of installation, configuration and administration. NOD32 requires 44MB of memory, less than other similar products. Voters also said they were able to get a significant ROI from this product" [8].

ESET also received the CNET Editor's Choice in April, 2009. I have just been learning more about them, myself, but these two selections make me advise that you take a look, too.

And, finally....

Even the President gets caught by the Law of Unintended Consequences...

President Obama, in an unguarded moment, referred to a recent spat between two music stars at MTV's Video Music Awards, and said he thought one of the people was "a jackass." Now, the unintended consequence wasn't that someone heard him say it, or even that someone twittered away immediately with "Pres. Obama just called Kanye West a 'jackass' for his outburst at VMAs when Taylor Swift won. Now THAT'S presidential." [9]

Nope, it was this small event that toppled big dominoes and caused a fuss:

> Harwood [from CNBC. Ed.] had sat down with the president to tape an interview following his appearance on Wall Street on Monday. Although they are competitors, CNBC and ABC share a fiber optic line to save money, and this enabled some ABC employees to listen in on the interview as it was being taped for later use [10].

I am certain that CNBC and ABC never thought when they made the deal that in sharing dark fiber (unused bandwidth) they would enable a competitor to listen in, and use a social media tool no-one had invented to immediately share an off-the-record remark in the warm-up to an interview. At some point later we can debate whether

Twitter is going to be the final spike in the process that kills the ability to control one's personal information.

Endnotes

[1] Cluley, Graham. "Facebook Fan Check Virus scare leads to malware",*Sophos company Blogs,* 7 Sept 2009. http://www.sophos.com/blogs/gc/g/2009/09/07/facebook-fan-check-virus-scare-leads-malware/ Retrieved 8 Sept 2009.

[2] Vance, Ashlee. "Times Web Ads Show Security Breach," *The New York Times,* 14 Sept 2009. http://www.nytimes.com/2009/09/15/technology/internet/15adco.html . Retrieved 15 Sept 2009.

[3] McGregor, Pat. "What Would You Give to Never Get Another Viagra Ad in Your E-mail?", *Interface.* Sept 2009. http://bcis.pacificu.edu/journal/2009/07/article.php?id=104 . Retrieved 15 Sept 2009

[4] Modine, Austin. "US health-care debate clogged world's inboxes, Pharma-spam cashes in," Register, 31 Aug 2009. http://www.theregister.co.uk/2009/08/31/mx_logic_august_spam_report/ Retrieved 15 Sept 2009.

[5] MDX Logic Threat Forecast, August 2009. http://www.mxlogic.com/pdf/forecast/threatforecast0909.pdf Retrieved 15 Sept 2009.

[6] "By the Numbers," CSO Magazine, Sept 2009. page 10. www.csoonline.com. (Sorry, you'll have to read this one in hardcopy!

[7] Lambert, Natalie. "Trends," *Readers' Choice Awards, 2009: Antimalware*, Information Security Online. http://media.techtarget.com/searchSecurity/downloads/0909_ISM_eM_v3.pdf , retrieved 13 Sept 2009.

[8] Eds. *Readers' Choice Awards, 2009: Antimalware*, Information Security Online. Sept 2009. http://searchsecurity.techtarget.com/magazineFeature/0,296894,sid14_gci1365969_mem1,00.html, Retrieved 14 Sept 2009

[9] Bauder, David. "President's opinion of Kanye West sparks debate," Yahoo News, 15 Sept 2009. http://news.yahoo.com/s/ap/20090915/ap_en_ot/us_tv_obama_tweet . Retrieved 16 Sept 2009.

[10] Ibid.

Social Networking

"My dad and Me are Asian. My mom's not": Multiracial Identity and Disassociation Before and After the Internet Age

View online at: http://bcis.pacificu.edu/journal/2009/09/article.php?id=126

By Jenn Hernandez
Berglund Student Fellow

Growing up, I'd tell people that "my dad and me are Mexican, my mom's not". (I suppose my future kids could say something similar: "my dad and me are Asian, my mom's not".) Surely, many kids growing up these days could say something like this because, of the total American population, as taken from a 2005 internet-only publication of a population profile by the U.S. Census Bureau, 13.9% identified themselves as being of "two or more races"[1].

I didn't necessarily know what this all meant when I was a kid. Later, I learned that my mom is a mix of European heritages, and my dad is of a line that I'm only guessing comes from Mexico a few generations back. We've talked about using Ancestry.com [2] or something similar to find out where we really come from, but we've never actually followed up on the idea. (I don't want to pay for a membership, and my dad is too busy anyways. I considered trying out Ancestry.com for this article, but I'm sure I'd forget to cancel after the 14-day free trial and end up having to pay the subscription fee for something I'd probably never use again).

I wondered how others deal with this issue, so I took my query to the Internet, where I can be part of a bigger group that transcends traditional demographics and borders. Out of curiosity, I searched within popular social networking sites--general ones, as well as ones specifically geared towards ethnic groups, such as Asian Avenue, MySpace Latino (which is the regular MySpace in Spanish), and Black Planet--a small survey of what's out there. All had at least a few groups pertaining to multiracial people and issues [3][4][5].

In my search, I found an array of groups and forums for multiracial people in specific categories: raising multiracial children, giving multiracial teens a voice, etc. (Teen Ink [6], Project Race [7], Fusion Program [8], Melting Pot Moms [9], and Blur Digital [10].)

I also came across one particularly interesting line of products geared towards multiracial people. Different racial combinations mix different types of hair, right? Yes, multiracial (in a small part) means having different types of hair--and a need that isn't necessarily noticed in mainstream society. I have a mix of straight hair from my mom's side and thick, black frizzy hair from my dad's side. Then I seem to have everything in between: tight kinks, big wavy curls, and tighter corkscrews. All in all, from a hairdresser's perspective, I'm a mess. The beauty tips in Seventeen [11] and

CosmoGirl [12] never worked for me. So, I come across Blended Beauty [13], which is available primarily online, besides at a handful of specialty boutiques and shops internationally and in the U.S., and is most specifically for the purpose of smoothing and containing the mixed curls of mixed girls.

That said, an issue that has recently come back to the front of my concerns, while discreetly poking at me from the back of my mind all these years, has been that of raising multiracial children. Someday, my children with my husband will be half Vietnamese-American and half Mexican/English/Irish/German. In addition to having an intense dislike of "Paris by Night," which I take to be some kind of popular Vietnamese variety show [14] ("our kids are NOT watching Paris by Night! If we go to anyone's house and they're watching it, we are going right back home!"), my fiance doesn't really identify with the Vietnamese culture. He does, however, know and speak enough to order food at Vietnamese restaurants. (Mmm pho!) I don't know any better, so he sounds okay to me.

I don't blame him, because I'm not very whatever-I-may-be either. I'm not sure if our kids will know, or what they should know. Do we try to get them to learn Vietnamese for family's sake? I would learn Vietnamese. Does that make me weird?

My fiance suggested that Spanish was more useful. But I just can't get away from the fact that my dad never wanted to learn Spanish and that his family is slowly becoming "white-washed" as far as the whole being aware of their heritage and language thing goes. In high school I tried taking Spanish language classes and even forced myself to continue in college, past the minimum foreign language requirements, trying to feign an interest and fool myself into thinking that I'd find a place somewhere when I could speak the language. Trying to do something when not interested is not a good idea. It's probably horrible to say this, but I don't care to learn Spanish at all. I'm much more intrigued by Chinese. Yes, I know it's completely different from anything I've had access to, what with the character system and all, but I'd like to try something new. (Not to mention that a large part of my personal music library consists of Jay Chou [15], which I buy online from overseas. Jay Chou is amazing!)

So, neither my fiance nor I are by far the best examples of a single culture or heritage, me never quite finding my own, and my fiance not entirely embracing his. I don't find fault with any of this, but our children might potentially grow up just as confused as I was, and still am, regarding their racial and cultural identity.

So, can the racially confused citizens growing into the Internet find an outlet? Not that this is a huge social problem, by the way; I think of it as a personal journey, which is more and more likely to be experienced as attitudes change about interracial unions. There are sources out there on the Internet if one takes the time to find their niche, as some have by blogging about their experiences. [16][17] As discovered, the Internet forms a community where discussions can be raised, questions answered, and identities sorted out much more conveniently than before.

Notes

[1] http://www.census.gov/population/www/pop-profile/files/dynamic/RACEHO. pdf

[2] http://www.ancestry.com

[3] http://www.asianave.com/groups/search.html?category_id=13

[4] http://searchservice.myspace.com/index.cfm?fuseaction=sitesearch.results &orig=search_Header&origpfc=Browse&type=AllMySpace&qry=multiracial& submit=Buscar

[5] http://www.blackplanet.com/groups/group.html?group_id=33771

[6] http://www.teenink.com/hot_topics/pride_prejudice/article/14815/ Multiracial-Children/

[7] http://www.projectrace.com/statefederalcensus/

[8] http://www.fusionprogram.org/resources.php

[9] http://meltingpotmoms.org/default.aspx

[10] http://www.blurdigital.com/

[11] http://www.seventeen.com/

[12] http://www.cosmogirl.com/

[13] http://www.blendedbeauty.com/index.html

[14] http://www.thuyngaonline.com/default.aspx?Lg=3&Cat=77

[15] http://www.jay-chou.net/forums/portal.php

[16] http://blogs.myspace.com/index.cfm?fuseaction=blog.view&friendId= 13584300&blogId=452124615

[17] http://blogs.myspace.com/index.cfm?fuseaction=blog.view&friendId= 13584300&blogId=453634448

Site Review

VuNow

http://www.vunow.com/

View online at: http://bcis.pacificu.edu/journal/2009/09/article.php?id=127

Review by Jeffrey Barlow

This site review is a bit of a deception in that it is really about a piece of technology and we usually leave such reviews to those who truly understand the technology in question. The virtue of this review is that if I can use this technology, then rest assured that you can too.

The technology, Verisimo's "Vunow," looks like a conventional modem and truly does nothing new; it just does it far more conveniently than the geekier alternatives. Essentially, it brings a variety of programs available for free on the Internet into one convenient menu via its box. You don't even need a computer; its modem box serves as a computer as well as your channel selector. You get Internet TV with little fuss and do not have to tie up a computer.

I first saw the Vunow operating in Pacific University's dazzling new "CLIC" facility (The Center for Language and International Collaboration) where it brings in international Internet TV channels for the use of our World Languages Department. These channels, seen on a huge, wall-mounted, high-definition display, were truly impressive and I checked it out and found it affordable.

Programming includes a dazzling variety of satellite channels delivered to Vunow's servers and thence to your box, which is controlled with the familiar hand-held remote. These include eighty to one hundred news channels from all over the world, some in multiple languages. We watch two Chinese channels regularly, one in crisp English and one in Chinese, when we want the news before it is digested for foreign audiences. BBC is there, of course, also Al-Jazeera (out of Washington D.C. to my surprise) and many more. Christian broadcasting is well-represented, as are specialized channels, some fairly...unusual, including a Yogi who broadcasts from the former Soviet Bloc in English to crowds of rapt Eastern European twenty-somethings in huge theaters. Each continent, all of the world's major languages and a surprising number of minor ones are represented.

In addition to the satellite news you get a variety of movie channels, mostly oldies but goodies; also Youtube, Internet Radio, Hulu, and Netflix in streaming downloads. You can also browse the Internet at will, though using a cursor to type URLS and to search will probably send you back to your computer for that.

Installing the device is a cinch. You simply take an Internet line out of your Internet connect ion—a router connected via a cable modem in my case—plug it into the Vunow box, then plug the usual array of cables into your set. It is much easier, I think, than setting up a DVD player.

A possible alternative to a direct link is operating wirelessly. The Vunow box does so with its simple menu, but our wireless, at least, is just too slow, even at supposed "N speeds". The small delays as programming buffers (brief pauses while incoming signals in effect build up before resuming a natural flow) were annoying so I opted for a direct connection.

In my case, the simple connection from router to Vunow was not very simple because my "media room" is as far away from my computers as is possible in our home. I had to run a hundred-foot long Internet cable through the study floor into the basement, drill through the foundation, crawl under the porch and then take the cable up the outside of the house to the second floor; hopefully most readers have built their computer system more thoughtfully than I have. And in fairness, I learned a great deal about opossum nests while doing this, though I could have gotten a more comfortable view from the wildlife channel.

Even with a direct link, some of the channels will periodically experience brief buffering, but most do not: English language Chinese TV buffers (CCTV 9) for example, but Chinese language programming rarely does. Films, in our experience, do not.

Our usual evening finds me working on the computer and Christine prowling world news in English, French, or Chinese or searching out documentaries for her classes on the Vunow Internet, and watching more than a few films. While Christine is not actually proud of her very limited ability with computers, she does tell with some relish the story of sitting down in the school lab beside a fellow teacher whose unattended machine crashed the moment Chris sat down. She has become very proficient with the Vunow menu and finds it intuitive and easy to program.

Rarely, while we are each in our separate digital worlds, I experience some brief issues in using the Internet, but these seem not to affect the Vunow programming. I may have set my system up a good deal less than optimally, and someone who really knows what they are doing may not have similar experiences.

The Vunow is available in three versions from 129.00 to 179.00—depending on the definitions and speeds desired. This is a one-time charge, though, at least for now, there are no monthly access charges whatsoever. The variety of cables and devices included with the kit make it seem like a good deal; the HDMI cable (for connecting to a High-def display) alone was close to fifty dollars in discount stores when I checked. The on-line ordering process was simple and delivery took less than a week.

You do not, of course, have access to regular broadcast channels, cable TV or pay-per-view. Another limitation is your bandwidth. Dial up modems are not going to work and you will want cable modem speeds. See their web site for particulars, all carefully delineated.

We killed our cable TV some time ago, but missed the news and films. Vunow has us back in the broadcast media consumption game, but with much more choice than earlier, and at much less cost.

Book Review

Teaching Writing Online. How & Why.

View online at: http://bcis.pacificu.edu/journal/2009/09/article.php?id=128

Review by Jeffrey Barlow

Warnock, Scott. *Teaching Writing Online. How & Why*. Council of Teachers of English: 2009.

Scott Warnock's *Teaching Writing Online* is simply an excellent book and should be read by anyone who teaches writing, whether face-to-face or online. It will be particularly useful to those who are contemplating teaching writing online, whether within a fully electronic environment or in a hybrid or blended classroom incorporating both face-to-face and synchronous or asynchronous environments.

Many teachers might believe that the pedagogical mysteries of learning to write well, and to teach others to write well, simply cannot be performed in an impersonal electronic environment. Warnock argues persuasively that not only is this incorrect, but that writing often can be taught better online than in conventional teaching environments.

The book, while intended for an audience of writing teachers, is also very useful for anyone who works with written materials at all. While a historian, I myself remain a teacher and inescapably work with student writing. While the book is not really intended to improve everybody's writing, it certainly could improve writing in the unfamiliar environment of the World Wide Web.

Warnock is very well qualified to make these arguments. He has directed Drexel University's Freshman Writing Program for several years. Drexel has long had one of the most extensive distance learning programs, including degree programs, of any university [1]. Warnock was responsible for taking the residential freshman writing course online and has rich experience in working with a variety of teachers and teaching styles.

This is a very dense book for its size (235 pages) and not meant to be read sequentially, but rather for the reader to select those chapters of particular interest to him or her. There are, of course, some key points, which are repeated throughout. Probably the central one is that the online instructor must deliberately create an online personality, which should be founded in one's native personality, but should be shaped for the electronic environment. As odd as this advice might seem, Warnock repeatedly makes its importance relevant to the teaching tasks he discusses.

The work also embodies the author's key beliefs in that it is written very much as though the audience is one of the teachers with whom he has worked in the past. For those actually desiring interaction with Warnock, he has had an extensive blog on the subject of online writing available since fall, 2005 [2].

In addition to hundreds of very practical tips, Warnock also shows a very strong understanding of the literature of the field of teaching writing, and especially of teaching it online. The bibliography of nearly two hundred entries has familiar canonical works in it such as the very well received *Writing With Power* of Peter Elbow and, in addition, the writings of those who, like Warnock, are heavily engaged in the practice and the theory of teaching electronically. It is hard to imagine the teacher who might find this work inadequately stimulating or too general, but the references could lead such committed souls down any number of highly specialized paths.

The work is also adapted to any conceivable electronic environment. Whether an institution provides (or requires) a full Coursework Management System (CMS) such as "Blackboard", or the instructor is largely on his or her own with off-the shelf or on-the-web applications, Warnock has useful advice. His preference seems to be for a relatively lean electronic environment comprised of email and a bulletin board/message board. He believes in using a blended or hybrid classroom when possible. He also provides, however, useful introductions to a variety of CMS and even to emerging technologies such as on-line interactive video.

Many current teachers naturally want to know what all the fuss is about; why should I change my approach, particularly change it so dramatically as to move from my familiar classroom to the unfamiliar, somewhat challenging if not downright eerie electronic environment? How will I keep my students from cheating? How often should I respond to them? Am I going to wind up working 24-7 like many of those who send me email at 2 a.m. seem to? Must I be their "buddy"? I don't know how to do all that! Or why I should, either!

There are, fortunately, a wide variety of appropriate responses to such questions—one of the reasons why Warnock continually cautions us to purposively adapt our personalities to an on-line teaching environment—and they are all covered in this work.

There has always been something of a false dichotomy between reading and writing in the classic sense—which for centuries has meant that the essential medium would be some form of paper—and in digital environments. The move to digital materials has caused a great deal of anxiety because of that assumed dichotomy: paper or bytes? The reality is, however, that there is much more in common to reading and writing on paper and online than many choose to believe.

This is not to minimize real issues: there is a digital divide; there are issues of authority and legitimacy in online materials, etc., etc. But at the last, readers and writers have switched media many times over the millennia, and the essential acts of inscribing one's words—writing—before an audience of readers remains essentially the same. Scott Warnock's *Teaching Writing Online* is a wonderful introduction to new possibilities and new environments.

Endnotes

[1] See the online catalogue at: http://www.drexel.com/online-degrees/degrees.aspx

[2] http://onlinewritingteacher.blogspot.com/

Editorial

An Educator Reconsiders the Kindle

View online at: http://bcis.pacificu.edu/journal/2009/09/article.php?id=129

Editorial by Jeffrey Barlow

We have written several times on Amazon's electronic reader, the Kindle [1]. We have found it an exciting reading technology and feel that most criticisms of it have been launched by those insufficiently familiar with it. We think that the more you use the Kindle, the more transparent you will find it and soon reading is simply reading. We did have some doubts, particularly about economic and political issues, which we expressed as well. We now have been using the Kindle for an additional several months since we last wrote, and are comfortable with it and look forward to packing it for our next trip to China in December-January, rather than a heavy box of books. However, as an educator, we have discovered some new causes for concern.

We have noted in the last several months a definite price creep, at least in the works we wish to read. It seems to us that the statement from the Kindle site reading: "Low Book Prices: New York Times Best Sellers and New Releases are $9.99, unless marked otherwise [2] is no longer true, or perhaps "...unless marked otherwise." was more significant an exception than we, in our geeky enthusiasm, had hoped.

We would welcome evidence either for or against this suspicion, but cannot find any on the web at present, either way [3]. There is a wonderful site, ebookprice.info. that will let you check prices of various versions of e-books, but this is not enough to validate or disprove our sense that prices are rising [4].

The last several works we purchased, e-versions of hardbacks not yet released in paperback, were within five dollars of the store cost at Amazon. At this price differential, we have some serious concerns and have resolved to check discount prices at big-box bookstores such as Barnes & Noble, which have often significant discounts for new books, for educators or members, and periodic on-line coupons.

It is not that we are solely motivated by price differentials. We still find the Kindle a more convenient way of reading than a heavy hardback with fixed fonts. But we will only pay so much for an electronic text that we do not own, at least in Amazon's view. When we buy a Kindle, we in effect sign a contract not to move that text to another Kindle, nor to pass it on electronically or in any other form [5]. This is a particularly damaging limitation for educators.

Here are the relevant portions of the contract:

Use of Digital Content. Upon your payment of the applicable fees set by Amazon, Amazon grants you the non-exclusive right to keep a permanent copy of the applicable Digital Content and to view, use, and display such Digital Content an unlimited number of times, solely on the Device or as authorized by Amazon as part of the Service and solely for your personal, non-commercial use. Digital Content will be deemed licensed to you by Amazon under this Agreement unless otherwise expressly provided by Amazon.

Restrictions. Unless specifically indicated otherwise, you may not sell, rent, lease, distribute, broadcast, sublicense or otherwise assign any rights to the Digital Content or any portion of it to any third party, and you may not remove any proprietary notices or labels on the Digital Content. In addition, you may not, and you will not encourage, assist or authorize any other person to, bypass, modify, defeat or circumvent security features that protect the Digital Content [6].

Teachers have long had protection against copyright violations with regard to printed content when used solely for educational purposes, under the doctrine of "Fair Use." We have often placed such digitized scans on line for our students. "Fair Use" has some important limitations: scans were to be placed on sites available only to our students, the use was not to be repeated, and in practice, most of us believe that "limited amounts" means a chapter or less.

But the Amazon contract reproduced above, which one accepts by purchasing a Kindle and Kindle texts, is quite different than "Fair Use." It is so limiting that the librarian at Pacific University Oregon does not feel it is safe, legally speaking, for me to download even a very small portion of a Kindle text to my computer, format it in HTML, and post it in my course materials. This is a peculiar situation. I could buy the same book in paper form, scan and post limited portions, all quite legally.

The Kindle contract also attempts to draw a line between "use" rights and ownership rights in order to enforce still other restrictions. If I buy a paper text, it is not only physically but legally mine. I can give it to you, even sell it to you, or donate it to the library for its permanent collection—which I have recently done with hundreds of volumes collected over forty years of teaching. Even the IRS recognizes that I have ownership rights and can be compensated for donating those rights to a library. But with the Kindle what I have purchased is the right to use, not own, content. As the license reads:

No Illegal Use and Reservation of Rights. You may not use the Device, the Service or the Digital Content for any illegal purpose. You acknowledge that the sale of the Device to you does not transfer to you title to or ownership of any intellectual property rights of Amazon or its suppliers. All of the Software is licensed, not sold, and such license is non-exclusive.

It is not only readers who have cause to be concerned about the all-embracing nature of the Kindle contract. Writers have also complained publicly that their rights to their works are being much limited by Kindle content contracts and can be transferred under Amazon's conditions, not under their own [7].

These limited rights I get with a Kindle and its content need to be viewed against opportunity costs: what am I really paying to use a Kindle and its digital text? What additional opportunities am I giving up by doing so? Many Kindle readers have been concerned about price for some time [8]. The comfortable assumption has been that as new producers enter the market, prices of both reading appliances and e-texts will be under price pressure and should, by our usual free-market assumptions, if anything, decline. However, the market is at present awarding the gold-filled palm to Amazon. Other producers such as Sony and the most recent entrant, Barnes & Noble with its new "Nook," would not make the first page if the competition were a google search.

Largely on the basis of Kindle sales, Amazon has just reported record profits and seen its share prices rocket [9]. Given this record, Amazon might be forgiven if it is now thinking of testing the limits of the concept of monopoly, rather than of competition.

"Fair Use" has long been regarded as an important exception to copyright rules, and for Amazon to so clearly attempt to negate it is a very unwelcome development. I do not dispute Amazon's legal or moral right to profit from its investments in the Kindle. It is clear that the development of the device has been a cost sink for several years, and that the device is a wonderful product, fully worthy of its success.

But for me as a teacher, in many cases it is going to be back to those heavy, smelly, limited-format paper books. At least I can share them, one of the basic pleasures of reading, and one of the important elements of teaching.

Endnotes

[1]See the first of these articles, "To George Orwell: It's the Kindle Baby, it's the Kindle!"

[2]See http://www.amazoncom/Wireless-Reading-Display-International-Generation/dp/B0015T963C/ref=amb_link_85650291_1?pf_rd_m=ATVPDKIKX0DER&pf_rd_s=left-1&pf_rd_r=0K1F7HSY7ZC9N3K1AM4Z&pf_rd_t=101&pf_rd_p=496327371&pf_rd_i=1286228011

[3]Prices have definitely been hiked in the U.K. See MacUser, 10/12/09 "Amazon hikes UK eBook price by 40%" at: http://www.macuser.co.uk/news/270142/amazon-hikes-uk-ebook-price-by-40.html This may have more to do with fluctuating currency values than with actual price increases, of course.

[4]http://www.ebookprice.info/

[5]See one writer's copy of the contract with comments at: http://www.stoweboyd.com/message/2009/07/kindle-license-agreement-annotated.html

[6]From: http://www.amazoncom/gp/help/customer/display.html?nodeId=200144530

[7]See noted Sci-Fi author Cory Doctorow's statement at: http://boingboing.net/2009/07/09/amazon-kindle-contra.html

[8]See: http://www.google.com/search?q=e-book+prices&ie=utf-8&oe=utf-8&aq=t&rls=org.mozilla:en-US:official&client=firefox-a

[9]See: George Stahl and Geoffrey A. Fowler, "Amazon Shares Hit Record as Profit Triggers Frenzy" *The Wall Street Journal*, 10/24/2009 at: http://online.wsj.com/article/SB10001424052748704754804574491684134407204.html?mod=googlenews_wsj

December 2009 - Volume 9, Issue 10

Articles

- **Feature: Michael Geraci** - Surf's Up: HTML Five-Oh! (Part 2)
- **Social Networking: Jeff Cain** - The Trouble with Friends
- **Media: Lynda Irons** - Can you afford a movie tonight? Or rather, will there be one for you to see?
- **Media: Valerie Horres** - Boobs or Bitches: The Way the Internet Portrays Women

Book and Site Reviews

- **Jon Walter Williams's** This is Not a Game. A Novel.
  Review by Jeffrey Barlow
- **Graeme Kirkpatrick's** Critical Technology. A Social Theory of Personal Computing.
  Review by IProfess

Editorial

- Digital Evidence and Scholarly Practices

Feature

Surf's Up: HTML Five-Oh! (Part 2)

second of a two part series

View online at: http://bcis.pacificu.edu/journal/2009/10/article.php?id=618

By Michael Geraci

If you've been watching the development of HTML 5, the next version of HTML, or you caught my last article in *Interface*, then you know that it's a long and complicated process that has been creeping along for over five years and will continue to find its way onto our collective screens for years to come. This article will give you a glimpse of some of the new features and application programming interfaces (APIs) that HTML 5 will bring, and in many cases, are already available to you if you're using the latest versions of the major browsers.

Native support for audio and video

Currently, when audio and video is displayed in a browser window, it's being decoded via proprietary plug-ins that have to be downloaded, installed, and upgraded on a regular basis. QuickTime, Flash, and the Window's Media Player are all software additions that have to be in place for rich media to work in our Web browsing experiences. While free and generally easy to obtain, these third-party plug-ins can interfere with the user experience when incompatibilities occur. Over time, users spend an inordinate amount of time gathering and maintaining these plug-ins simply because audio and video file formats have always been the domain of software companies and not browsers.

HTML 5 addresses this by decoding "open" a/v formats at the browser level. The open-source Ogg format developed by Xiph.org has struggled to keep up with the quality and low file sizes made possible by today's commercial formats, but recent efforts to enhance the free Ogg Theora video format and Ogg Vorbis audio format have gained enough ground that Firefox has included the decoding engine for them in version 3.5[1], making native audio and video possible. HTML 5 will include new <audio> and <video> tags that are designed to replace the current, and aging <embed> tag, which, simply put, cuts a hole in the Web content where externally decoded media appears — or doesn't if you haven't been keeping your plug-ins up to date.

The addition of specific HTML elements for audio and video means that other enhancements are possible. For example, content creators can host multiple versions of media files that are best suited to particular platforms and even connection speeds and then the browser can determine which format is best for the user. For example users of handheld devices, such as smartphones, might automatically get a version of a video that was created for the small screen and lower-bandwidth environments associated with these devices.

Of course, the major players in the digital video world have something to say about the idea of open-source video taking over the Web instead of their well-established formats, so adoption of the native video frameworks might take a bit longer while the major browser makers decide when and how to implement the feature. For now, Firefox has adopted the standard and is not looking back.

More descriptive page elements

The Web design community has been relying on the very generic <div> tag as a means for establishing layout areas in the page for over a decade now. Div simply refers to a division, or box, in the document that can have certain properties associated with it via CSS such as width, height, and background color. While <div> is a useful way to structure a page, it does little to describe what is in the area it defines nor is it very useful for assistive devices that have to sort the page content from other items like navigation. This very page that you are reading in Interface contains approximately 20 divs that block out areas of the page.

Web page creators will like the new ways in which a page can be laid out with new elements in HTML 5 that actually describe the content. The new page elements currently included in the specification are:

1. <header> for introductory information typically found at the top of a page.
2. <footer> for bottom of page content.
3. <nav> for page and site navigational controls.
4. <article> for self-contained compositions, like blog posts or this content you are now reading.
5. <section> for sub-units, like chapters, of a larger piece of content.
6. <aside> for tangential information that is related to a larger piece of content, like a pullquote or sidebar.
7. <address> for the contact information for the author or publishing body for a piece of content or for the page as a whole.

These new elements won't make much of a difference to users, but computer-to-computer applications, like RSS, and search technology will likely find these highly semantic page elements to be a real boon, and they will cut down on some of the complexity of writing CSS style rules.

Drag and drop

HTML 5 will allow for elements on a page to be dragged around the screen and deposited elsewhere, which should open up some interesting new opportunities for user interfaces. E-commerce experiences will likely employ this technology to re-order items in a page, add or subtract items to a shopping cart or list, and customize the overall presentation. Just as items will be draggable, other elements will then have target-like functionality thereby knowing when something has been moved into its boundaries, which could trigger other functions.

Drag and drop will almost certainly lead to more application-like behavior on many Web sites without the computing overhead of script libraries and Flash running in the background.

Local storage

HTML 5 will allow for more data to be stored on your computer while you surf. This will reduce the amount of time that is spent waiting to post information to a server for storage and processing. The current stateless model of the Web means that data gets handed back and forth between your browser and the server from which you are receiving content. With local storage, information that needs to span your entire session can be stored locally — even after you end the session — and then sent to the server for processing in one fell swoop. A basic example might be the typical multi-page forms used for online survey instruments, like Survey Monkey. Under the current model, you answer some questions, send those answers to the server for storage while you continue answering successive questions. With HTML 5, all your answers can be stored in a standard database format on your system, allowing you to go back and review or edit them and save them for later. When you're ready to submit, the sum of the stored data gets posted.

The above list of enhancements made possible in HTML 5 are just the biggies, there are numerous other changes that will slowly find their way into our Web experiences, but it really depends on how quickly the different improvements are refined by the standards bodies that are developing them and how well the features get implemented in the browsers. For a checklist of which browsers are keeping up with HTML 5 functionality, please see the somewhat complex, but highly detailed compatibility chart at the Wikipedia.

References:

[1] http://www.webmonkey.com/blog/
How_Firefox_Is_Pushing_Open_Video_Onto_the_Web

For more information on HTML 5 features:

- http://en.wikipedia.org/wiki/ HTML5
- http://www. w3schools.com/html5/html5_reference.asp
- http:// www.alistapart.com/articles/get-ready-for-html-5/
- http://html5tutorial.net/
- http:// orderedlist.com/articles/structural-tags-in-html5
- http://www.webmonkey.com/blog/ How_HTML_5_Is_Already_Changing_the_Web

Social Networking

The Trouble with Friends

View online at: http://bcis.pacificu.edu/journal/2009/10/article.php?id=619

By Jeff Cain, EdD, MS
University of Kentucky
College of Pharmacy

The popularity of social media has created a new social communication paradigm. Within this new paradigm, the definition of "friend," [1] as many have known it, has now expanded. This is due primarily to Facebook's (the most popular online social networking application) [2] use of the term "friend" as the mutually agreed upon connection between two users. The term has underlying meaning as it represents the major element of this application. For example, when I discovered that my cousin was on Facebook, I sent her a friend request that she accepted. My profile now displays her as one of my Facebook friends and vice versa. Among other things, this friend connection allows us to access each other's profile information (photos, personal information, etc.), as well as receive real-time updates on what each of us posts on Facebook. Becoming someone's Facebook friend is almost imperative if one wants to take full advantage of the features offered for connecting with that user.

During my frequent lectures and talks with students, faculty, and civic organizations regarding all aspects of social networking, this issue is usually raised. Because of its immense popularity among those populations, Facebook tends to become a focal application for discussion. When speaking to audiences with members older than 35, inevitably someone will comment or ask a question pertaining to the Facebook "friending" nature of younger generations. It has recently become apparent to me that a generational divide exists with regard to this simple term and what it means in online social networking. In this paper, I discuss the reasons for this divide and why this seemingly innocuous term has created angst among many in the older generations.

How Older Audiences View Friends

Older adults with whom I speak often express incredulity over the volume of "friends" that younger generations have. "How can anyone really have that many friends?" they ask when they realize that typical college-aged Facebook users list hundreds to thousands of friends. Their perception is that this large volume of friends is the result of nothing more than vanity or ill-advised connections with unknown people. Over time, I have come to realize why this question comes from older generations and never from the younger generations. The two generations are operating under different paradigms of social communication and therefore view the term "friend" differently.

Older generations define a "friend" as someone with whom a close personal relationship has been formed. This relationship has typically involved substantial face-to-face communication and implies more than just a casual acquaintance from school, work, or other social event. The word "friend" holds deep meaning and is not a label doled out freely to everyone encountered. To them, friendships do not occur at the click of a mouse, but are developed over time. They reserve friendship for the select few with whom intense bonding has occurred and in whom they have placed substantial trust. When asked how many friends (of the traditional sense, not Facebook) they have, the answer ranges from 3 to 50, indicating the exclusivity of the term. Friend is not a title to be bestowed upon others without some form of personal connection. The word is so deep-rooted among some over the age of 35 that they are reluctant to accept friend requests from former real life friends due simply to a disconnect over the years. That they have not seen or spoken with someone for twenty years places some sort of mental barrier to calling them a friend.

Why are there Generational Differences?

I attribute part of the generational differences in the definition of a Facebook friend to the evolution of social networking and its use by the different age groups. When Facebook was first developed, college students were the only users. Similar to other rites of passage, Facebook became another method of conveying one's personality and interests to the rest of the world. Making and strengthening friendships is an important element of young people's lives and Facebook provided a perfect medium to facilitate this. The desire to learn more about someone met in history class is a perfectly valid reason for sending a Facebook friend request. Friending someone on Facebook and allowing access to personal profiles became the new equivalent of face-to-face conversations with regard to the personal backgrounds of new acquaintances. Because people in this age group are frequently in situations with new acquaintances, their Facebook "friends" lists grow rapidly.

Now, contrast this with older generations of users who adopted social networking long after it became popular with younger audiences and you will find different reasons for adoption and, therefore, different perspectives of use. Those 35 and older joined Facebook primarily to renew old friendships and connect with family members [3]. Of course, there are some who also joined to monitor their children! Establishing and facilitating new relationships is typically not of major importance for their decision to adopt Facebook. To these users, a Facebook friend is typically a real-life offline friend of many years. In other words, their Facebook friends are customarily friends in the traditional sense of the term. The word friend still holds significance in how it is elaborated online, and therefore most users of older generations have not quickly amassed hundreds of Facebook friends.

Who are Friends in the New Paradigm?

Facebook friending behaviors vary among individuals, and what I have stated thus far are generalized observations. Each person has his or her own philosophy on Facebook friending. Whether my philosophy is typical or not with others in older generations can be debated, but it is worth exploring in order to examine this new definition of online friends. My personal philosophy is that I usually do not send friend requests to others unless they are someone with whom I have had a traditional friendship. However, I do accept all friend requests from others unless I have never met or communicated with the person in some other format.

My Facebook friends list tends to be quite diverse. I of course have friends who are my real life, offline friends. I have friends from my hometown, friends from elementary school, friends from high school and friends from college. Co-workers, neighbors, fraternity brothers, relatives, and in-laws also compose a large percentage of my friends. Former students, education and pharmacy colleagues across the country, and friends of my wife are also represented. Some of them I know intimately and have close, real-life connections with; others though, I have only had passing relationships with over time. From the perspective of someone a little older than the majority of Facebook users, do I consider all of those people "friends"? No, I do not. If I were to ask a college student if she considered all of her 984 Facebook friends as friends, I suspect she would answer the same. Younger audiences can easily separate their "true" friends from their Facebook-only friends; therefore, the angst over the term is unfounded. This becomes clear when one relinquishes his/her grasp on the traditional use of the term friend, and realizes that it is just a term indicating an acquaintance (regardless of how strong the relationship is).

Conclusions

Within this new Facebook world, the term friend does not really mean "friend" as many of us define it. "Connections", "links", "relationships", or many other terms may be more accurate descriptors, but Facebook has established the term "friend" and therefore we must recognize it. It is interesting to think that one software application initially developed for a small group of college students has begun to revolutionize what the term "friend" connotes to many. While younger generations never question the semantics of Facebook friends, many older users tend to be concerned with the use of this moniker. Some become overly concerned to the point that they cannot understand the many benefits of online social networking. If they begin to understand the paradigm differences in the definition, maybe they could become more comfortable with how others use these applications for building and maintaining relationships. Just because we view and use social networking applications differently does not mean that one generation has it right and the others have it wrong. It simply means that each person uses it for his/her own unique purposes and will determine for him or herself how to react to the word 'friend".

Endnotes

[1] Definition of friend. Available at: http://dictionary.reference.com/browse/friend Accessed October 23, 2009.

[2] comscore: Facebook passed MySpace in the US for the First Time in May. Available at: http://www.insidefacebook.com/2009/06/15/comscore-facebook-passed- myspace-in-the-us-for-the-first-time-in-may/ Accessed October 23, 2009.

[3] New study shows how different generations use Facebook. Available at: http://www.insidefacebook.com/2009/07/30/new-study-shows-how-different- generations-use-facebook/ Accessed October 23, 2009.

Media

Can you afford a movie tonight? Or rather, will there be one for you to see?

View online at: http://bcis.pacificu.edu/journal/2009/10/article.php?id=620

By Lynda Irons

The numbers are not looking good. September unemployment is at 9.8 percent, up from 8.9 percent in April 2009 [1]. The Consumer Price Index for all items except food and energy increased 0.2 percent in September after increasing 0.1 percent in August [2]. And according to the National Association of Theatre Owners, average ticket prices in the United States have increased from $5.65 in 2001 to $7.18 in 2008 [3], representing nearly a 25 percent increase. While it appeared for a while that consumer spending was on the uptake, recent reports indicate that consumers are becoming a bit more hesitant about opening their wallets as indicated by a 0.5 percent decline in September 2009. The Commerce Department said this was the largest decline since December 2008 [4]. As a result of these continuing economic factors, including the impact of the Internet, the motion picture industry has significantly changed the way they do business.

The numbers in Figure 1 reflect overall gross of the tracked films released by the major studios that year [5]. With only 2 months remaining in 2009, the movie picture industry is so far experiencing a 12 percent decrease in overall gross receipts from 2008. While the box office grosses did hold relatively steady from 2007 to 2008, attendance dropped 4.8 percent during that time. It can be speculated that the higher grosses can be explained by the higher ticket prices [6].

Figure 1

2009	2008	2007	2006	2005	2004
8.461 billion	9.630 billion	9.664 billion	9.210 billion	8.842 billion	9.380 billion
136 films	160 films	182 films	196 films	175 films	174 films

Warner Brothers has consistently garnered the lion's share of the market place, ranging from 12.9 percent market share in 2004 to the number one position so far in 2009 with 20 percent [7]. However, according to the March 19, 2009, Industry Survey Reports, Warner Brothers (part of Time Warner Inc.) revealed that they plan to reduce their global workforce by nearly 10 percent. This represents nearly 800 jobs [8]. The report continues by noting they plan to release 15 fewer films, citing "a changing entertainment business landscape, shifting consumer demand, and the overall state of the economy." [9]

Warner Brothers is far from being alone as the economic situation wreaks havoc with all the studios' business models. Actions ranging from downsizing, closing independent film labels, restructuring, and consolidating operations are all part of this new industry landscape. Standard and Poor's reports that the industry's stock index performance indicators has decreased dramatically, including a 42.3 percent decline in 2008 versus a 38.5 percent decrease in the S&P 500 Index [10].

As part of the shifting environments, the industry has been casting its collective eye toward other outlets for distributing their content as the motion picture industry represents a relatively small portion of the total entertainment dollar spent. Other forms include home video sales (which declined in 2008 5.5 percent), pay-per-view, and video-on-demand, premium movie channels, and Internet downloads. Consumers spent nearly 50 billion in 2008 to be entertained [11]. The Internet and the rapidly increasing focus on mobile devices are forcing the industry to "refocus" its traditional models. Developments such as iTunes, Hulu.com, MSN Video, and Amazon Digital on Demand service are allowing the studios to distribute their content in the digital mediums [9]. While the industry continues to make films, it is no longer relying strictly on the box office for its revenue streams as the traditional gap between box office release and DVD release has "shrunk to 30-45 days (from 60 to 90 days) [12].

Industry Survey Reports notes that DVDs costing the lower end of the price range (<= $20) tend to be purchased by consumers while the higher end (>=$25) are rented. Still, even with the lower prices, consumers are not purchasing or renting DVDs as they used to. Sales and rentals climaxed in with $24.1 billion in 2006, dropping to $21.6 billion in 2008 [13].

Additionally, the average cost of making a movie has risen from $105.8 million in 2003 to over $106.6 million in 2007. While only a .75 percent increase, it is still higher than the Consumer Price Index. Those costs are passed to the consumer in higher ticket prices as it costs the distributors more to rent them as rental fees typically average 50 percent of ticket sales [14].

The challenges for the movie industry are complex and multi-faceted. New forms of content distribution are coming to the forefront as the traditional movie-going experience is undergoing changes. Movies are not staying in the theaters as long; production costs are increasing; the rise of other viewing opportunities; consumer whimsy and fickleness; and the fact that the consumer doesn't have the disposable income to afford the experience are all leading toward a gradual turmoil in the industry.

Endnotes

[1] http://www.bls.gov/eag/eag.us.htm

[2] http://www.bls.gov/cpi/

[3] http://www.natoonline.org/statisticstickets.htm

[4] http://www.lexisnexis.com.proxy.lib.pacificu.edu:2048/us/lnacademic/results/docview/docview.do?docLinkInd=true&risb=21_T7767585921&format=GNBFI&sort=RELEVANCE&startDocNo=1&resultsUrlKey=29_T7767585924&cisb=22_T7767585923&treeMax=true&treeWidth=0&selRCNodeID=59&nodeStateId=411en_US,1&docsInCategory=841&csi=6742&docNo=5

[5] Figure 1.

[6] http://www.boxofficemojo.com/studio/?view=company&view2=yearly&yr=2009&p=.htm

[7] Bossong-Martines, Eileen N., ed. **Standard & Poor's Industry Surveys**. Vol. 1. New York: Standard and Poor's, April 2009. p.2.

[8]
http://www.boxofficemojo.com/studio/?view=company&view2=yearly&yr=2009&p=.htm

[9] Survey Industry Reports, p. 1.

[10] Ibid, p. 1.

[11] Ibid, p. 7.

[12] Ibid, p. 11.

[13] Ibid, p. 13.

[14] Ibid, p. 20.

[15] Ibid. p. 19.

Media

Boobs or Bitches: The Way the Internet Portrays Women

View online at: http://bcis.pacificu.edu/journal/2009/10/article.php?id=621

By Valerie Horres, Berglund Student Intern

As an increasingly integral and influential part of international culture, it is only natural that the Internet affects the portrayal of men and women. While the general trend of global mores appears to be toward gender equity, in many ways Internet content proves to characterize women as one of two things: boobs or bitches.

Part of this negative portrayal of women occurs because of how the different sexes utilize the Internet. Traditional gender roles influence the use of the web by men and women. For example, females are more likely than males to utilize the net to research health information [1]. Customarily, as mothers put themselves in charge of the well-being of household members, this makes sense.

Women are also more likely than men to search for spiritual and religious information, and to participate in support groups [2]. There are hundreds of support groups online aimed singly at women. Some sites, such as http://www.dmoz.org/ [3], can be utilized to locate many of these online support groups. These groups specialize in topics like health, divorce, religion, pregnancy, motherhood, menopause, and many others [4].

Males, on the other hand, employ the Internet to read news, add content to the web, deal in finances, and find entertainment at a higher rate than females [5]. Instead of the stereotypic patriarch reading the newspaper at the breakfast table, or trading stocks and bonds from his study, men are now doing these acts online.

However, it is the area of online entertainment that tends to propagate the degradation of women. Some activities, such as making travel plans and participating in online auctions, do not portray women in a negative light. Nevertheless, other modes of amusement affect society by promoting demeaning interpretations of women. These activities extend from checking sports scores and viewing games, listening to and downloading music, and streaming television shows, to viewing online pornography.

The media sources listed above lean toward depicting women as bitches or sexual objects. For example, business women on streamed television shows are often characterized with a Hilary Clinton-esque stigma of trying to do a manis job or being emotionless bitches [6].

Media sources also show scantily clad cheerleaders—such as those found on http://twitter.com/ twiCheerleaders [7]—dancers, singers, actors, and contain offensive characterizations and lyrics. A prime example of a song degrading women is iBitches Ainit Shiti by Dr. Dre [8].

Another sort of entertainment that more male online users engage in than females is video games. Analysis of these games reveals there are ino female characters in 41% of the games with characters. In 28% of these, women were portrayed as sex objects and 21% depicted violence directed at womeni [9]. The virtual gaming world contains few female characters, often depicts females as sex toys, and/or females as a target for abuse. One such game over 2.5 million people play is Castle Age, a role playing game on Facebook, where many of the characters are nearly naked females [10].

One additional online activity that men entertain themselves with more than women do is the viewing of online pornography [11]. Whether videos, pictures, cartoons, or text, a great deal of pornography presents females negatively. Women often appear as mere sex toys, normally willing to engage in any act and suffer many abuses for the purpose of arousing the viewer. Furthermore, if the pornography depicts a female refusing to participate in a sexual act, she is called names, or even forced into participating against her will, which again, the viewer is supposed to get off on and enjoy.

Online pornography is more widespread than some might think. Wordtracker.com supplies reports on the top 200 long-term search phrases—those that reappear through the weeks, months, and years—and the top 200 short-term search phrases—phrases that appear within a one day period—that are put into its database. 42% of both long and short-term search phrases are direct searches on porn sites, searches for women celebrities known for their sexual appeal, phrases whose top hits are pornography, such as "girls showering," and phrases that relate to women in a sexual fashion, such as "boobs" [12].

An article in the *Psychology of Women Quarterly* reported that in the 1980s all "X-rated materials in the U.S. represented '... an estimated $8 billion industry of misogyny per year' (Cowan, Lee, Levy, & Synder, 1988, pp. 309-310) and the U.S. Attorney Generalis Commission reported that violent pornography was '[...] the most prevalent form' of sexually explicit material" [13]. 30 years later the numbers have risen. In 2006, the Internet pornography industry made over $2.84 billion, and total the porn industry made $13.33 billion [14]. More Internet pornography increases the amount of online materials which debase females.

Not only are women depicted in a poor light on the Internet, but when women protest against these negative portrayals, they are often ridiculed and picked on. A woman online who "speaks out steadfastly and strongly against [...] pornography, prostitution, who writes as a feminist or as a human rights advocate, can expect to be harassed and attacked [...] not only for her specific views and perspective, but in ways that are distinctly sexist" [15]. It is not the ideas that are assaulted, but rather an attack on the female writeris appearance. iShe will be described as a man-hater, her writings, activism and life's work will be dismissed and trivialized, she will be called shrill and strident, or she will be threatened in ways that are sexuali [16].

The Internet affords anyone the opportunity to metaphorically stand on a soapbox and express opinions in any way they desire. In the United States, these reactions, even if they are violent ad homonym harassments toward a writer, the responses (remember men are the ones most likely to add content to the web [5]) are "understood to be matters of someone's 'freedom of speech,' while [female writers'] objections and our outcries [against the debasement of women], are called 'censorship' by some. And yet it is this efreedom of speechi of some that ultimately silences us and robs us of our own freedom of speech" [17].

It ultimately does not appear to be the Internet itself that degrades women, rather the content of the various media associated with it. The Internet simply is a convenient source to access a large amount of the degrading material, and provide it to the large audiences that access the Internet.

In the United States, 93% of children are online [18]. The culture of the upcoming era is set by the youth. As the adage goes: children are the future. They are blogging, instant messaging, social networking, streaming and downloading music and television, and playing online games [19]. Teenagers and young adults are the majority who are bombarded with the Internet content which sometimes degrades women. Because this new generation is influenced to regard females in such a manner and also sets the tone for the future, the general trend towards gender equity could be reversed.

Endnotes

[1] "Different People Use the Internet in Different Ways," Infoplease, accessed 28 Oct. 2009, http://www.infoplease .com/ipa/A0931238.html.

[2] Ibid.

[3] "Open Directory Project," dmoz, accessed 28 Nov. 2009, http://www.dmoz.org/Health/Women's_Health/Support_Groups/.

[4] Online women support groups, Google search, accessed 28 Nov.2009, http://www.google.com/search?hl=en&source=hp&q=online+women+support+groups&aq=0&oq=online+women+sup&aqi=g1.

[5] "Different People Use the Internet in Different Ways," Infoplease, accessed 28 Oct. 2009, http://www.infoplease .com/ipa/A0931238.html.

[6] Joanne Lipman, "The Mismeasure of Woman," *The New York Times*, accessed 25 Oct. 2009, http://www.nytimes.com/2009/10/24/opinion/24lipman.html?pagewanted=1&_r=1&em.

[7] "TwiCheerleaders," Twitter, accessed 28 Nov, 2009, http://twitter.com/ twiCheerleaders.

[8] Dr. Dre, "Bitches Aini't Shit," The Chronic, 1992.

[9] Tracy L. Dietz, "An Examination of Violence and Gender Role Portrayals in Video Games: Implications for Gender Socialization and Aggressive Behavior," *Women and Language* 23.2 (2000): 64,UeAcademic OneFile, accessed 4 Nov. 2009, http://find.galegroup.com.

[10] Castle Age, Facebook, accessed 28 Nov. 2009, http://www.facebook.com/apps/application.php?id=46755028429&ref=search&sid=1595268849.2015195435..1.

[11] William A. Fisher and Azy Barak, "Internet Pornography: A Social Psychological Perspective on Internet Sexuality," *Journal of Sex Research* 38, no. 4 (2001): 315, accessed 4 Nov. 2009, http://web.ebscohost.com.

[12] "Top 1000 Search Phrases," Wordtracker.com, accessed 28 Oct. 2009, http://www.wordtracker.com/ database.

[13] William A. Fisher and Azy Barak, "Internet Pornography: A Social Psychological Perspective on Internet Sexuality," *Journal of Sex Research* 38, no. 4 (2001): 313, accessed 4 Nov. 2009, http://web.ebscohost.com.

[14] Jerry Ropelato, "Internet Pornography Statistics," TopTenReviews, accessed 28 Nov. 2009, http://internet-filter-review.toptenreviews .com/internet-pornography-statistics.html.

[15] Cheryl Lindsey Seelhoff, "A Chilling Effect: The Oppression and Silencing of Women Journalists and Bloggers Worldwide," *Off Our Backs* 37, no 1 (2007) 18, accessed 4 Nov. 2009, http://web.ebscohost.com.

[16] Ibid.

[17] Ibid, 20.

[18] "Generational Differences in Online Activities," Pew Internet, PEW Internet & American Life Project, http://www.pewinternet.org.

[19] Ibid.

Book Review

This is Not a Game. A Novel.

View online at: http://bcis.pacificu.edu/journal/2009/10/article.php?id=622

Review by Jeffrey Barlow

Jon Walter Williams. *This is Not a Game. A Novel.* Orbit, 24 March 2009.

Jon Walter Williams is one of the most prolific writers in the Sci-Fi Fantasy genres; in fact, he is several of them, having also published successfully and repeatedly an "alternate history" series as Jon Williams [1]. His works have been nominated for an astonishing number of the key honors in these genres, including Nebula, Hugo, and Philip K. Dick awards. In addition to novels, short stories and teleplays, he has written games, including related fiction and rulebooks. He is sometimes said to have a cyberpunk flavor to his work [2].

The work under review here, *This is Not A Game*, can be said to combine cyberpunk with gaming, and is presented as an "alternate reality" in effect, though usually this genre branches off a specific real event by answering questions such as "What if Lee had won at Gettysburg?" The book is narrated in a just-around-the-corner setting which is easily recognizable from today's events and technology, with a bit of extrapolation.

This novel is worth consideration by anyone interested in the impact of the web because the game presented, while not digital as such, is computer enabled. It is a live-action role-playing game presented on a global scale with hundreds of characters, a few of whom we get to know. It also deals with the impact of digitally enabled currency arbitrage.

Here is an excerpt from the book, which introduces the central character as well as the game that features prominently in the book. It provides a strong flavor of the work's tone:

> Dagmar's job was to create online games for a worldwide audience. Not games for the PC or the Xbox that gamers played at home, and not the kind of games where online players entered a fantasy world in order to have adventures, then left that world and went about their lives. Dagmar's games weren't entertainments from which the players could so easily walk away. The games pursued you. If you joined one of Dagmar's games, you'd start getting urgent phone calls from fictional characters. Coded messages would appear in your in-box. Criminals or aliens or members of the Resistance might ask you to conceal a package. Sometimes you'd be sent away from your computer to carry out a mission in the world of reality, to meet with other gamers and solve puzzles that would alter the fate of the world.

The types of games previously described, Alternate Reality Games or ARGS, are, in truth, quite popular and just as intricate as the game that drives the plot in this work [3]. The author, as might be expected, has considerable experience with them.

The title of the work comes from a frequent statement made in such games: "This is not a game," sometimes abbreviated TINAG. The work begins with the protagonist, Dagmar, caught in a chaotic social breakdown in Indonesia, and as she seeks help, her worldwide audience assumes that this is, in fact, a new game; hence, TINAG.

As the plot develops, perhaps predictably the boundary between real world events and in-game events begins to blur and real deaths begin to occur, which the protagonist brilliantly works into an on-going game in order to put the gaming world to the task of solving the crimes.

One of the attractions of science fiction or fantasy is seeing a well-prepared and technically knowledgeable author playing with reality. One of the central issues of *This is Not a Game* is the nature of fluctuations in the world economy, all too real-world an issue over the past several years. In this work the fluctuations result from an attempt to use artificial intelligence to improve currency trading. Software— "Forlorn Hope"—was set up on a net of illicitly hacked computers, which housed "bots," or computer programs which function almost autonomously as agents—a common enough occurrence on today's World Wide Web. Here is the flow of the resultant developments in the words of Charlie, another central character:

> "I checked the Forlorn Hope account every hour, then every day. ...And then I looked at the Forlorn Hope account for the first time in a couple of weeks, and there the money was, just sitting there." He looked at Dagmar. A loose-lipped grin spread across his face. "Eleven point two million dollars. All grown from that twenty-thousand-dollar seed...
>
> "And then, back in June"— face turning blank— "the bots leveled." Leveled. A term from gaming, where a character cashed in experience points and gained a host of new magical abilities. "The agents started crashing whole countries," Charlie said. "The day that Indonesia started to go down...I saw all this cash sitting in the offshore account, and I knew that something bad had to have happened somewhere, on the other side of the date line, where it was already Monday." He looked up at Dagmar. "I would have warned you if I'd known you would head for Jakarta that day. ....He looked at her. "Back in 'ninety-two, George Soros crashed the English pound with ten billion in positions. The bots now have twice as much money as Soros did." "More than twelve billion?" "More than twenty now. Now that Chile's burned."

It would be a plot spoiler to reveal much more than this, but the work is a worthy addition to the literature that gives us insight into the many impacts of the World Wide Web. This plot, of course, turns on extrapolations from present conditions, but they are believable possibilities considering the rapid pace of technological development and the close ties to current political and economic trends.

The work should be a good read for anyone willing to suspend critical judgments and, as the characters say, "break the glass wall" between the real and the virtual. And any gamer or sci-fi fan will very much enjoy the combination of the two as created by a highly accomplished author.

Endnotes

[1] See his home page at: http://www.walterjonwilliams.net/

[2] See the useful Wikipedia entry on him at: http://en.wikipedia.org/wiki/Walter_Jon_Williams

[3] For a thorough explanation with many examples of the genre as well as a general introduction to gaming in general, see: http://en.wikipedia.org/wiki/Alternate_reality_game

Book Review

Critical Technology: A Social Theory of Personal Computing.

View online at: http://bcis.pacificu.edu/journal/2009/10/article.php?id=623

Editorial Review by IProfess
Elvin Druid of Zuljin, Azeroth

> ***Editor's Note:*** *This piece is written by IProfess, self-proclaimed avatar from the on-line game World of Warcraft. With our commenting function, readers can now leave appropriate remarks following the piece. IProfess states that he will respond in the comments to interested readers and would love to hear from other 'Toons. Please note, that as always in Interface, the author's opinions are his, hers, or its own and do not represent those of Interface nor those of the Berglund Center at Pacific University Oregon.*

Graeme Kirkpatrick. *Critical Technology: A Social Theory of Personal Computing.* Ashgate Publishing, 30 November 2004.

IProfess begins: Most readers are probably familiar with World of Warcraft (WoW), if only through the cautionary tales told and retold via flickering television sets in TRW (The Real World). I myself am an avatar, in the popular parlance, a "'toon," who crosses over from time to time from WoW to TRW, principally to write for this journal [1].

For 'toons, the most elusive knowledge is self-knowledge. I have much to criticize in the work under consideration here (Graeme Kirkpatrick's *Critical Technology. A Social Theory of Personal Computing*); but I also aver that I have acquired considerable self-knowledge as a result of the reading of it. I therefore conclude that any intelligent, determined, and well educated 'toon or gamer could find it profitable if also, alas, frequently painful. However, as a noted troll sage said, "Pain is the beginning of knowledge, mon."

As 'toons we lack self-knowledge simply because we are born as adults, seemingly out of nothing. We awake to find ourselves "Level 1" in some city of Azeroth, the World of Warcraft. The minute we learn to stumble around and get outside, some crazed monstrous being attacks us. Of course, we lose these combats because we are utterly unfamiliar with our own resources, tools, weapons, or for that matter anything at all.

So, created *ex nihilo* as we are, we are denied childhood training, real education, parental advice, everything but the occasional tip from other players who have been in similar circumstances. How could we possibly have self-knowledge?

If one levels to the point where one can crossover into TRW, one gets some additional perspective, but does not learn much more about truly critical questions such as: Where did I come from? What is with this whole good and evil dichotomy? What's up with being and non-being? The denizens of TRW are even more confused and divided than are those of us from Azeroth.

Graeme Kirkpatrick, however, offers us some shards of self-knowledge by presenting, as the sub-title has it, "A Social Theory of Personal Computing". He is a Senior Lecturer in the School of Social Sciences at Manchester University in England. He is a sociologist but he's also trained in philosophy and deeply interested in the relationship between computing and societies—both in TRW and in game worlds such as my own.

We know from his estimable position that he doubtless speaks English with great clarity and precision, upon selected occasions. Unfortunately, not every page of this work was written upon such occasions. His prose, while not impenetrable, requires considerable grinding—enough to produce a substantial reward if the equivalent time had been spent, say, collecting herbs in Azeroth rather than reading.

The problem is that the author writes in a sub-dialect of post-modern academic English—Critical Theory. One wishes that Mr. Kirkpatrick had defined Critical Theory, but the work is written primarily for those who already care passionately about the field, and are familiar with the jargon.

A general knowledge of the theory does eventually emerge from the work [2]. It is important to be aware that Critical Theory is deliberately meant to move individuals to political action. It is a kind of ideology of liberation, though opposed to mainstream Marxism. It sees Communist and Socialist states, so far as technology is concerned, as playing the same game as Capitalist ones. That is, using technology to dominate their populaces.

Once the reader acquires, largely by osmosis, the vocabulary necessary to understand *Critical Technology*, some important arguments emerge. Following Andrew Feenberg, one of his key influences, the author posits the following:

1. In the past, social critics like Karl Marx have incorrectly believed technology to be essentially free of values; tools are tools.
2. However, in analyzing television, Frankfurt School theorists--the founders of one wing of Critical Theory (the other focuses upon literary theory)--realized that both the use of technology and the manner of its deployment have very real and often undesirable social consequences [3].
3. Feenberg built upon these basics to argue the "Design Critique." Technology is part of an overall social system and hence reflects the goals of the dominant class within that society. It is literally designed to do so.

In the case of computing, those goals are to create a technology that serves the purposes of industrial society in its latest phase, "informationalism" [4]. Computers were once usable only by highly trained specialists. But it became evident that moving them to the desktops of many more workers would increase productivity and facilitate greater accumulations of wealth by those directing the technology. One of the many results of this deployment has been globalization and the rapid spread of informationalism.

As the reader may already have decided, the above is not everybody's cup of thistle tea. The arguments bulleted above emerge from a very specific ideology, and the author does not bother to establish every step in the chain, nor could he possibly do so, the book would be very lengthy indeed. Rather, he cites other authorities in the same school as his own, Critical Theory. The highly motivated reader could trace down the argument step by step using the work's copious notes, but most of us must accept the argument, reject it out of hand, or as I have done, suspend either disbelief or belief to review the work. Kirkpatrick's argument continues....

The rapid dissemination of computers through the work place produced several problems: they were difficult to use and when mastered, they empowered the users.

These users communicated freely, necessarily acquired authority, but questioned the necessity of hierarchies.

According to Critical Theorists, the managerial class quickly found it desirable to keep most of those employing computers more or less ignorant of the finer points of computing—what actually goes on in the mysterious box itself. According to the Design Critique, computers were made easier and easier to use, to the point where employees could work very efficiently without having any real idea of what was happening behind the interface. These new office drones had to work more cheaply than the earlier highly trained experts. Operators were further alienated from the technology that they ran and which increasingly conditioned their lives, both at work and at home.

However, two groups have subverted this paradigm, Kirkpatrick believes: hackers and gamers. Hackers began as enthusiasts in the relatively early days of computing— this work gives very good brief histories of both hacking and gaming—who wanted to learn to do things for themselves. In so doing, many of them created new technologies and made major contributions to computing. Many aligned themselves with other enthusiasts, supporting various collective and oppositional forms of computing such as the Open Source movement.

Out of this group branched others who were actively political: "hacktivists." This group began to employ technology to facilitate computer-based social movements such as the anti-globalization movement and the Zapatistas. Hactivists are essentially the knights-errant of Critical Theory. Other hackers evolved, alas, to be "crackers," criminal in their intent, lending their talents to every conceivable form of computer crime.

This brings us, at long last, to 'toons and gamers. Because the author cannot conceive of autonomous 'toons such as myself, we will combine these two distinct groups here.

In one of his chapters, "The Cynicism of the Computer Gamer," the author treats us all very roughly indeed. I found my own virtual heart repeatedly pierced by his prose, after I puzzled out the meaning. It is his contention that most gamers have become slaves to their machines, engaged in repetitive actions that have lost all semblance of fun, but are engaged in purely for distraction—grinding in the worst sense of the word.

While most gamers, like office workers, rarely have any real technical knowledge, the very enthusiastic learn better ways to manipulate the interface and to modify the game in what are often subversive ways. Avatars intended to represent servants of the repressive state are modified ("modded") to rather represent liberation fighters. Scenarios originally set in decayed urban areas which paramilitary forces attempt to take back from terrorists are modded to occur in high schools—often the very high school of the modders—producing Columbine-like games. Sex grows out of control as secret levels are programmed. Gaming companies respond by creating games in which participants can play forces earlier described as "the enemy," automobile thieves, Nazis, Viet Cong, Soviet armies. The kids are no longer "all right."

This subversion only goes so far. Aware of the growing loss of their sense of purpose, gamers cloak their failure by showing an awareness of that loss not with the "resignation" of the office interface drone, but with a cynical awareness and the "well-timed cheeky gesture". The author finds gamers bright, witty, and socially aware rather than dreary and mechanical, but only in a cynical fashion which essentially denies the possibility of progress, at least insofar as they might contribute to it.

Ironically, this active disengagement via gaming continues, nonetheless, to serve the purposes of the managing class, because it "...produces a kind of relaxation of tensions in the public sphere" [4]. Kirkpatrick believes, paradoxically, that violent gaming reduces the rage that should appropriately be manifested by those enslaved by computing.

Gamers, then, are no less failures than office drones because they are not working toward liberation from the social alienation that drives them to the game. The repetitive action of gaming distracts them from the unpleasant alternatives, but it nonetheless is, in the mind of the author, a political failure.

As a 'toon, I can claim some authority in this area, and it seems to me that none of these categories are as clear cut as Critical Theorists might believe. I find that many 'toons with whom I play are, in their disguises in TRW, hackers, hacktivists, programmers, crackers, drones, and game players, sometimes in bewildering combinations.

And were he aware of us, it surely would follow to Kirkpatrick that 'toons like myself are little better than convicts doing data entry for points toward cigarette purchases. I, for example, write, cheekily, about my world of Azeroth and compare it favorably to the insanity of TRW; but cynicism remains my dominant motif. I stop far short of calling upon all 'toons to break through the glass wall, to seize the mouse, and to end this nonsense! To do so would interfere with my leveling, and if too many 'toons listened, there would be nobody to duel in the battlegrounds of Azeroth! Like gamers, to use a metaphor derived from *The Matrix*, a popular film at about the time the book was researched, 'toons have swallowed both the red pill of awareness and the blue pill of resignation.

But, Kirkpatrick thinks, even enslaved gamers and 'toons might well serve a higher social purpose. Together with hacktivists and others opposed to the dominant paradigm of computing—the impenetrable interface—they may be creating a new form of mass culture that greatly facilitates communication and offers at least the promise of a new "cultural platform" and a new "public sphere" [5]. (My argument above that Kirkpatrick's categories are really not that distinctive, could be, I suppose, indications that this sphere is already emerging.) This would, he believes, be potentially much more open and democratic than the status quo. In so doing, he follows many other e-democracy hopefuls.

To sum up, this work is not for everybody. It requires the reader to level quickly in puzzling out its jargon. It is intensely if almost opaquely political. It is extremely critical of the individual, the society, and the economy of TRW. It ultimately condemns gaming worlds as delusional obstacles to true knowledge and to progress. But Kirkpatrick also hopes that the changes resulting from hacking and gaming are creating dynamic new social forces. To move this virtual democracy forward requires that we all achieve self-awareness of our relationship to our computers, the purpose of the book itself.

Endnotes

[1] See; "The Tales of Azeroth" and "Toons and Terrorism" and most recently, "Protecting Human Children in the World of Warcraft." See too my book reviews, the

first of R. V. Kelly 2's *Massively Multiplayer Online Role-Playing Games*, and Edward Castronova's work, Synthetic Worlds, The Business and Culture of Online Games, and most recently: Hilde G. Corneliussen and Jill Walker Rettberg, (editors,) Digital Culture, Play, and Identity: A World of Warcraft Reader

[2] Here we will define it from the source of all human electronic wisdom, Wikipedia, as: "The initial meaning of the term *critical theory* was that defined by Max Horkheimer of the Frankfurt School of sociology in his 1937 essay *Traditional and Critical Theory*: Critical theory is a social theory oriented toward critiquing and changing society as a whole, in contrast to traditional theory oriented only to understanding or explaining it. Horkheimer wanted to distinguish critical theory as a radical, emancipatory form of Marxian theory, critiquing both the model of science put forward by logical positivism and what he and his colleagues saw as the covert positivism and authoritarianism of orthodox Marxism and Communism." http://en.wikipedia.org/wiki/Critical_theory

[3] Kirkpatrick 114

[4] Kirkpatrick 83

[5] Kirkpatrick 85-87

[6] Kirkpatrick 126-131

Editorial

Digital Evidence and Scholarly Practices

View online at: http://bcis.pacificu.edu/journal/2009/10/article.php?id=624

Editorial by Jeffrey Barlow

Introduction:

"Evidence" is a very broad category in human affairs. It can mean everything from traces of pre-hominid skeletal remains to the "smoking gun" beloved of conspiracy theorists. Even in the highly formalized world of academia it means different things to physicists, historians, and sociologists, for example. Here I discuss two issues relating to the digitization of materials and the use of the World Wide Web to disseminate them. The first deals with how we evaluate our own production of digital materials; the second with how we take account of student use of digital evidence in our classes.

The Problems:

For centuries evidence was assumed to be necessarily tangible and capable of being exhibited in some physical form, ideally widely accessible and capable of being reproduced or copied for the evaluation of peers. Juries want to see the evidence, and so do college professors when guiding student research.

The unprecedented transfer of analogue data to the digital realm has had many unforeseen consequences. Photographic evidence, for example, has been very nearly entirely devalued as "photoshopping" has become ever more widespread and easily accomplished even by relatively unsophisticated computer users [1].

For historians—and I write here primarily as an historian—evidence has been the keystone in our intellectual practices. For us, documentary evidence is the *sine qua non* for truly complex historical arguments. Even eyewitness accounts are now often dismissed as "memory"—of value but also fraught with potential qualifications (subjectivity, cultural biases, conflicting views of others, etc., etc.) which keep it from having the status of documents, the older and more yellowed the better.

Now we face the unprecedented transfer of existing evidence, safely preserved in "real" forms—primarily books—into digital forms, primarily electronic documents, most often displayed in HTML on the World Wide Web. We do not know quite what to do with these. These are not merely, particularly to historians, "academic questions." They are key to how we prove our claims to knowledge.

Digital Scholarship and Academic Evaluation:

Evidence is also key in how we evaluate each other's performances as professional members of the academy. Again the question of digitization is problematic. For most of us, evaluation for "promotion and tenure" invariably means publication; even in performance-oriented fields like Music, Art, or Theater, "evidence of intellectual activity" often requires publication.

Publication has long been defined as occurring in one form: paper. We sometimes now use the term "hard copy" to show at least a primitive awareness that there are actually other forms of publication, but these are too problematic for us to evaluate, in most cases. This is because publication in paper usually proceeds only after passing a number of gates: these include peer review, selection by university presses, citation by others, inclusion in bibliographies, being reviewed in paper journals, all the labyrinthine paraphernalia and practices of centuries of academic traditions [2].

This practice is slowly changing, driven as is usual in the academic world, by realities beyond our control from the Ivory Tower, particularly by the increasing cost of publication in hard copy format. But practice and preference makes us slow to change our beloved traditional usages. At Pacific University Oregon we have recently been charged, department-by-department, with revising our own standards for promotion and tenure. After evaluating the standards of other departments in our own institution, and those of other institutions, followed by hours of face-to-face and megabytes of email discussions, we came up with the statement reproduced below at Appendix 1.

As this document—still not officially accepted by the University—suggests, my home department is blessedly able to distinguish between forms of publication and principles of evaluation—in part because of my colleagues' amazing tolerance for my own tiresome ranting over our tenure together. Other institutions, however, stubbornly resist even trying to discuss issues of the quality of digital data in evaluation processes [3].

Student Use of Digital Materials:

If we are slowly making progress in adapting our own self-evaluation in academia, there remains one area where we just don't quite know what to do and have failed to establish best practices: how should our students use digital data as evidence? The problem here is a stubborn one. We want our students to read widely and to cite evidence for their positions in their assigned writing. This is, again, particularly critical for historians because we can only really know the past from evidentiary traces. But how are our students to judge the relative authority of particular bits of information?

From long practice at the college level we discourage students, if not outright forbid them, from using dictionaries or encyclopedias, which we see as "high school." But what of *Wikipedia*? Here we are using Wikipedia not only as the most common source to which students now immediately resort, but also as a scapegoat for every other digital document found on the WWW [4].

Judging from discussions with students and colleagues, a common practice is to tell the students that they may well begin with a Wikipedia entry, but they should not rely upon it as sole source, nor cite it. This might be described as the liberal or permissive practice. Other instructors prohibit their students from using digital sources at all, though this requires in my experience, continual explanation and draconian enforcement, such as a genteel professorial tantrum while sheltering behind the podium. This is not so much an educational experience for the students, as an "oh whatever" moment, once again being told to follow dimly understood rules which seem totally irrelevant in the real world.

Students tell me that their own response to either the permissive or prohibitive professorial position is that often they follow up on the sources cited in the Wikipedia entry, and then cite those. This is probably indeed somewhat more reliable in that the evidence at least exists independently of Wikipedia, but it really simply puts the issue at one remove—we still often do not know why the second level information was considered reliable or even by whom it was so considered.

The prohibitive position can ultimately be logically consistent only if the instructor disallows all digital sources. This can, of course, be done, often by specifying those sources which can be used, or defining certain categories of resources—those found in our library, or only university press books, etc.—but this position is eroding steadily as librarians much prefer to buy access to bundled digital materials to buying a book which may well sit on shelves unread. One librarians' rule of thumb is that about 10% of their collection will get 90% of reader traffic, while the other 90% gets 10%. The problem, of course, is identifying the critical 10% before ordering the 90%.

Strict prohibition, then, begins to erode under new collections policies. Some bundled collections will lead only to digital copies of once hard-copy publications,[5] but increasingly the distinction is being lost as digital journals too are bundled, and in some cases, web sites captured to such collections.

It seems to me that neither the permissive nor the prohibitive position with regard to digital evidence is even now fully satisfactory, and given the accelerating digitalization of content, the situation can only deteriorate. What are we to do, for example, with the student who cannily finds on Amazon a partially digitized volume, does a search on digitized pages and cites some nugget relative to his or her topic never seeing nor handling the book? What happens if Google succeeds in digitizing everything despite the opposition of half the world's publishers and writers?

Conclusion:

These two problems really have a common solution: Academics must better understand the nature of digital evidence. At present many of us have, sadly, reversed the classic Chaucerian description of a good teacher to rather read: "...and reluctantly would he learn."—at least so far as digital materials are concerned.

Having ourselves better understood the nature and rapid development of digital evidence, we must then teach students how to evaluate the relative authority of digital sources and require them to do so. At present, I myself am requiring every student paper to include an annotated bibliography, requiring that they evaluate the relative authority of web pages based upon the five-point scale we have long used at the Berglund Center [6].

Teaching the evaluation of digital materials should really begin in primary school; perhaps including teaching an understanding of plagiarism and intellectual property and the reasons why hacking in the black-hat bad guy sense is not a clever thing, but actually a criminal act. But for the present, at the college level we must begin to create best practices, which can ultimately become standard ones, akin to rules for proper citations and other stylized academic usages.

Endnotes

[1] See the article "Photo manipulation" at Wikipedia: http://en.wikipedia.org/wiki/Photo_manipulation See also "Photoshop" at: http://en.wiktionary.org/wiki/photoshop

[2] We continually reinforce this preference by a number of well established emotional arguments, my favorite of which might be called the "Argument from Olfactory Appeal," usually stated as, "Ah, nothing smells like a book!" I earnestly hope that one day this statement might be known as *Booksniffian*, derived, of course,

from the term "Pecksniffian," beloved of Dickensians. See: http://en.wiktionary.org/wiki/pecksniffian

[3] See the work of my colleague at *The Journal of the Association for History and Computing*, Deborah Lines Andersen, Digital Scholarship in the Tenure, Promotion, and Review Process. See, in a more accessible format, her many articles in the JAHC beginning at: http://mcel. pacificu.edu/jahc/indexes/?index=author

[4] The alert reader is aware that, to this point in this piece I have cited Wikipedia or one of its derivative sources three times...yet none of those citations can be attributed to a known author. Anyone could have written any section of those pieces; in fact, we do not even know how many different people contributed, let alone what their authority or expertise might be. How do I justify this? The short answer is that I have a Ph.D. The long answer would be that to get that Ph.D. I had to learn to judge all sorts of evidence in a wide variety of fields, and have done so here. Too, the evidentiary requirements for an editorial such as this one are fortunately lower than those for peer-reviewed journals.

[5] Jstor is one such collection: http://www.jstor.org/

[6] See Appendix 1 on page 339 of volume.

Appendix 1

Here are the draft scholarship standards for Tenure and Promotion as accepted by the History Department at Pacific University Oregon. They have not yet been adopted nor approved by either the College of Arts & Sciences or by the University as a whole, but they reflect our professional judgments as to appropriate standards.

Scholarship Standards for Tenure and Promotion
Pacific University Department of History
(DRAFT OF November 2009)

The Department of History recognizes that standards of Teaching and Service should be consistent across the College of Arts & Sciences, and, as such, should reflect policy articulated by the college faculty as a whole. However, in recognition that standards of scholarship, particularly in terms of what forms this may take, vary according to discipline, the Department of History has outlined its scholarship standards below.

These standards are premised on an amalgam of both amount and quality of scholarship. In History, unlike many disciplines, the ultimate form of scholarly production remains the book. As such, publishing a monograph has priority over other forms of scholarly work. Built into this set of standards is the importance of professional peer review and a recognition, from Very Significant to Significant to Less Significant, of the rigor and prestige of peer review attributed to publishers, journals, grants, conferences, and so on. That said, it is the job of the applicant for tenure or promotion to demonstrate the quality of scholarly production in regard to the rigor of peer review. Ideally, this should be done in conjunction of (with) the departmental Chair who can direct the Personnel Committee on the validity of such claims. We recognize that all levels from Very Significant to Less Significant work might be produced and disseminated within a digital environment as opposed to hard copy. Providing that it undergoes the same level of professional peer review as do equivalent hard copy publications, it will be given the equivalent significance in any review process.

It is important to note that the bar for Professor is substantially higher than it is for tenure and promotion to Associate Professor. The former requires a record of sustained high quality publication. Sustained implies clear consistency over time, and high quality refers to the kind of achievements listed below. In the case of tenure and promotion to Associate Professor, strong promise must be shown through sustained activity with some record of publication.

Department of History Tenure and Promotion Standards: Scholarship

Very Significant

1. Book in field (monograph, survey, or textbook)
2. article in top-tier journal (AHR, JAH, etc.)
3. large external grant (NEH, ACLS, Fulbright, Guggenheim, etc.)

Significant

- article in peer-reviewed journal
- article/chapter in edited collection
- article published in conference proceedings
- small external grant
- presentation of research (conference paper, invited talk, keynote)
- Editor in Chief of Journal
- Edited collection

Less Significant

- encyclopedia entry
- book review
- historical writing published in other media (editorials, blogs, web, etc.)
- applying for external grant
- getting internal grant
- article submitted to peer-review journal
- attending conference, serving as chair or commentator
- solicited reader for article and book manuscripts

Minimum Requirements for Tenure and Promotion to Associate Professor:

- Any Very Significant
  OR
- one published peer-reviewed work
- one other Significant while at Pacific
- three Less Significant

Minimum Requirements for Promotion to Full Professor:

Cumulative in career:

- One Very Significant
- Since Tenure:
  - five Significant OR one other Very Significant
  - three Less Significant

Appendix 2: Authority System

Evaluating Trust and Authority in Electronic Materials

By Jeffrey Barlow
Editor, *Interface*

At the Berglund Center for Internet Studies and the Matsushita Center for Electronic Learning at Pacific University we have long searched for a means to indicate the level of authority of the electronic materials we post. We are well-established centers with well over five million hits per year into our servers. We publish several journals of significance and influence, such as the *Journal of the Association for History and Computing* (JAHC), *Interface on the Internet*, and *E-AsPac*. However, we also publish many projects done by graduate and undergraduate students. Between these two poles we publish conference papers and occasional papers done by members of our audiences. These materials, then, are created for different purposes and to different review standards.□□We know that our audience often selects these materials indiscriminately, based more on their immediate research needs than on the reliability or authority of the materials. In an effort to further educate our audiences, and out of our desire to help establish standards and practices for electronic materials, we have decided to begin "stamping" our materials posted from fall of 2004 with seals indicating their Authority Level.□□By Authority Level we do not mean to indicate "good" and "bad" but rather authoritative and non-authoritative or those with higher levels of trust and those with lower levels. Many important works have been created by writers who did not undergo peer-review, did not possess a terminal degree in the field, and who wrote badly with scant attention to scholarly niceties. However, such materials should best be judged by other scholars, or by the test of proving useful or provocative over time. They cannot be trusted at the first reading; they do not speak with great authority.□□By applying a seal attesting to Authority Level, we are stating that insofar as we can determine, the reader can "trust" the conclusions of the pieces posted with the indicated level of confidence. In short, pieces at lower levels may be excellent, but we can't determine that they are, and the reader should have a lower initial level of confidence in them.□□These levels are explained below, but it should be noted that invariably some materials are in grey areas between categories.□□

Authority Level 5 materials have to pass a number of tests and represent the highest possible level of trust or authority. They are equivalent to materials published in paper form by scholarly journals or presses. They could be placed in a library and should prove useful for some length of time. □□They have the following characteristics, but no piece, of course, will necessarily have all of them:

- Materials certified as Authority Level 5 have been reviewed by scholars in the appropriate field following practices long utilized in scholarly journals and other refereed publications. That is, they have been read closely by one or more established professionals comfortable with the topic area of the piece. The review process was "double-blind." That is, neither the authors nor the reviewers were aware of each other's identities.
- In the judgments of these readers, the piece makes a contribution to the topic being discussed; that is, they are not merely a restatement of existing scholarly opinions.
- The materials have both citations and bibliographies sufficient to permit readers to retrace the author's research steps so as to form their own opinion as to the strength and

weaknesses of the pieces when measured against the set of evidence on which they were constructed.

- The author should discuss methodology as well as evidence: how do they know what they know?
- The articles show an awareness of the current state of the topic by referencing or discussing recent scholarship in both important books and articles. The author should probably indicate areas where there are differences of opinion among authorities.
- The author of the piece is known, can be contacted to discuss or defend his or her positions, and themselves have some specialized education, training, or experience relative to their topic.
- The piece is well written and organized and has a minimum of spelling, grammatical or formatting errors, showing the qualities of mind necessary to good research, thought, and writing.
- Such publications would usually include research done in the language(s) of the subject field as appropriate.
- Limitations of Level 5 materials: Despite these strict standards, even the best research and writing has areas of relative weakness, and scholars in the field will often disagree about each others' positions. The more "cutting edge" a piece, the more likely it is to be controversial. For the average reader, however, these controversies are likely to be unimportant ones.

Authority Level 4 materials are not different so much in quality as in degree from Level 5 materials. They might have the following characteristics:

- The level of authority of the writer may not be the highest possible in the field of study and the process of review may be less thorough.
- The pieces have been read by somebody with some expertise in the field and in effect are certified as free from egregious errors of fact or important omissions.
- The authors are known, can be contacted, and have some relative level of expertise in the field about which they are writing.
- The materials used in the research are obvious if not always strictly cited. A reader should be able, then, to roughly reconstruct the author's research paths.
- The author's methodology should be at least strongly implied if not obvious.
- The pieces should be based on at least some original materials (those written by eyewitnesses or participants with direct knowledge of the events or issues discussed) rather than entirely in secondary materials (those written from analyses of original materials).
- There should be a bibliography.
- The author should demonstrate some expertise in dealing with scholarly controversies and materials.
- Limitations of Level 4 materials: These materials can be used with confidence, but it may well be that there are better materials to be found on these same topics.

Authority Level 3 materials are often the result of research projects done by inexperienced authors, but guided by experienced ones. These might include extensive undergraduate research projects. They have the following characteristics:

- Level 3 materials should be free from errors of fact. If some of their conclusions are controversial ones, these should be held by at least some authorities in the field of study.

- Level 3 materials should depend to a considerable extent upon published and easily available materials so that readers can themselves explore the topic further with some confidence.
- The basis of conclusions drawn in level 3 materials should be clear and rooted in research, not in mere opinion or prejudice.
- Level 3 authors should be known, and can be contacted to discuss their works.
- The works are dated as to time of origin and any updates that occurred,
- Limitations of level 3 materials: Level 3 materials may provide an adequate beginning for serious research, but should not be the sole foundation of such research. They might well provide a good orientation to the topic and suggest additional research paths, but this is their major strength.

Authority Level 2 materials have serious limitations and it is our intention not to publish such materials. For our purposes, however, they might be known by the following characteristics:

- Writing is poorly organized, there are spelling and grammatical errors, all indicators of superficial thinking and research.
- Materials are inadequately cited and there is no useful bibliography so that it is impossible to retrace the author's steps.
- The nature of the evidence relied upon is not clear.
- The author in no way relies upon any obvious authoritative sources or materials.
- The author is not known or cannot be contacted.
- The materials are not dated.

Utility of Level 2 materials: It may be that serious scholars or researchers could utilize such materials, but most often as the raw material of their own studies. For example, scholars studying popular culture might find blog entries on current films or music or politics useful but would be unlikely to cite them to support their own positions.

Authority Level 1 materials: Again, we will never post such materials, but for analytical purposes we would define them as having the following characteristics:

- A hypothetical "reasonable reader" would find them indicative of non-logical thought processes.
- Writing would be confusing or ambiguous.
- Organization would be so poor as to leave the reader lost and confused; we do not know why paragraphs are arranged as they are.
- There would be no indication of author and no attempt to establish authority.
- Utility of Level 1 materials: Like Level 2 materials, they might be useful for some scholarly projects, but not to convey information or analysis.
- Please note that the standards for Level of Trust for posted pieces vary from those appropriate to electronic sites or clusters per se. For a discussion of the qualities of "good" sites see: http://mcel.pacificu.edu/jahc/features/epeef.html

Made in the USA
Monee, IL
08 November 2026

67971947R00197